Seancing Shaking Spirits

Embodying Spirit Powers in Conjuring Abodes

Jay Miller, PhD, ed

© 2020

Contents

edits

Edits update these texts and simplify punctuations, such as placing "quotes" inside periods to allow for outside footnote numbers. Tribal ethnonyms have replaced older alien terms or use preferred spellings, such as the final E on Assiniboine and divinatory instead of 'diviniatory'. This rite predominates among central (Ojiway~Chippewa, Cree, Menomini) and western (Blackfoot, Cheyenne) Algics, along with some Siouians (Assiniboine, Lakota *Yuwipi*) of the Plains and Salishans of the Plateau, with whom Ktunaxa share ancestry. Farther afield versions occur among Alabama Mvskogi Creeks, Arctic Inuit, and Native Siberians.

The Conjuror

The theory and practice of the Wisconsin Chippewa is essentially the same as described in detail by Hallowell for the Berens River Saulteaux in his excellent monograph "Conjuring in Saulteaux Society." One variation is that the Wisconsin tent is not the extreme barrel-shape, but instead, cylindrical, with the framework open at the top (Fig. 8), or the poles joining to form a dome (Fig. 9). It is to be expected that such variations will occur inasmuch as each conjuror must have his tent built according to instructions received in his fasting dream as to shape, number of poles, kind of wood, etc.

The procedure of the conjuror is to call the assisting supernatural spirits into the tent (their entrance causing it to shake) and consulting with them on problems demanding a clairvoyant or prophetic solution. The doctor is thus equipped to determine the cause of illness whether it be natural or any of the five supernatural reasons: sorcery, spirit intrusion, disease-object intrusion, breach of taboo, or soul loss. With this intelligence at his command the doctor is then able to prescribe a cure. It is interesting to note that the conjuror who himself may kill or cause sickness by the technique of soul-stealing sometimes gets involved in shamanistic duels over a patient.

The number of such doctors extant at the present time is meagre. I know of only four Wisconsin Chippewa who have practiced in recent times, and there are none left at the Lac Court Oreilles Reservation. This is very different from the situation at Berens River, Canada, where nearly 10 per cent of the people were known to have practiced tent-shaking in recent times (Hallowell, p. 27). The decrease in numbers in Wisconsin seems to be due not so much to the decrease in demand as to the disappearance of the custom of fasting. The power to conjure was obtained through the fasting dream, and there is only a small group of people at present who are equipped with such an experience. The phrase they use, i.e., "He has no dream," applies to not only nearly all the middle-aged group, but also to nearly all of the old people. The few conjurors that are left seem to be in considerable demand and circulate their services over a wide area. There are records of a conjuror being imported from Lac du Flambeau, a distance [202] of eighty miles, or, where the patient could be moved he was taken to Flambeau. A Potawatomi, well known for his conjuring abilities, makes the rounds of the Chippewa Reservations exercising his skill in the role of "guest artist." In one case which I had the opportunity to observe, a woman offered to pay all traveling expenses if I would drive her and her ailing son to a doctor of the St. Croix band some sixty miles away. She had already made one trip there to arrange for the ceremony. The time and expense involved in such procedures is often considerable, and serves to demonstrate their faith in the practice, but the art seems fated to die in the hands of the present practitioners. The following is a description of the ceremony I witnessed in 1942:

"Laurence Butler, about 25 years old, was working in a defense plant in Detroit for a year and a half, until he was called into the army. His examination showed incipient tuberculosis. He went to the Municipal Sanitorium in Chicago and stayed there for six weeks. His mother, Mrs. John Butler, wrote him a letter and asked him to come home and to go to this Indian doctor, John King at Sand Lake, a *jiziki'wini'ni*. Laurence came home Sunday, and Tuesday we were asked to drive them down to Sand Lake.

"We got there about 2 P.M. Wednesday, and sat around waiting for dusk. Mrs. Butler told John King what she wanted him to do. Talking to Laurence, we learned that he had never seen a *ji'zikən* shake and did not know much about it. He didn't believe much in the efficacy of the *jiziki'winini* and was apparently going through the whole thing mostly to please his mother, although he said he had heard of people being cured by these doctors, and he admitted that he had nothing to lose by it.

"We were told, at first, that we wouldn't be allowed to watch the curing, that they never allow any white people around. John King said he couldn't work with people of another race around (*gawe•sa'* – I can't do it). Mrs. Butler talked to him, and told him that we had brought them down, so he changed his mind and consented to our watching, providing we gave tobacco and didn't take any pictures or tell any other white people about it.

"At dusk, about 8 P.M, Charley Littlepipe, the *škabe'wis* or runner, went out to fix up the *ji'zikən*. Charley Littiepipe had been invited to come up by Mrs. Butler, who had gone down to his house about seven o'clock, and had given him a package of standard tobacco, and told him what was going to happen. The framework was already built and had been used previously. It consisted of six ironwood saplings set into the ground and six smaller pieces going around. The ironwood stakes were set about a foot and a half into tile ground, bent over the top and tied to the opposite stake about half way down. They were 1½ inches thick at the base. Six ironwood branches, three-fourths inch in diameter, were bound onto these, starting about a foot and a half up from the ground. They were about four inches apart and left a gap of about 2 feet at the top.

"The structure was just about 6 feet high and 2½ to 3 feet in diameter at the base. It was tied together with *wi'gop* – basswood twine, and shook rather easily, John said no dogs were allowed near it; they were all shut in the house.

"Charley shook the framework to test it and replaced some of the *wi'gop*, binding it at various places on the framework. Then he bound bands of sleigh bells on four of the uprights near the top. He tied them tightly with *wi'gop* and tied one big leather band with some larger bells across the top (on the two remaining uprights). [203]

"He went into the house and brought out six blankets and a small pail of wooden skewers. He said these blankets were used for the *ji'zikən*. He laid one blanket on the floor inside on some hay that had been placed there. Then he wrapped four of the blankets around the sides, one at a time. He fastened them to the framework and to each other with the wooden skewers which were about 4 to 5 inches long with one end pointed. The other blanket was thrown over the top and fastened down to the others. There was no entrance left.

"Charley worked in a very efficient and business-like way, as though he had done it many times before. He knew just what to do and how to do it, and the whole process only took about 15 minutes. When he had finished, he picked up the can of wooden skewers and went into the house and told them it was ready. He came out and laid out a blanket next to the *ji'zikən* and put a bowl of tobacco on it and a pipe in that, and then he went over and sat down with the Chief Drum he had brought.

"Shortly after that John King came out followed by the three women who help him on such occasions; his wife, Maggie Little-pipe, and her daughter, each of whom carried a rattle made of a wooden stick about 2 feet long and 2 inches wide with numerous tin *cones* nailed on which jingled when shaken. John pushed up the blankets in one place and crawled into the *ji'zikən*. The women filed around the *ji'zikən*, grabbing it several times on the way and shaking it. Then they sat down on a bench.

"When everyone was seated, the wigwam began shaking very slowly. This seemed to be a signal for Charley to start drumming rapidly on the Chief Drum and women to begin shaking their rattles. Soon the *ji'zikən* began shaking rather violently, and then slowed up again, and shook hard again. This went on for about five minutes (this is when the spirits come into the *ji'zikən*). Then a disguised voice was heard and the drumming and rattling stopped.

"The voice (supposedly the spirit *bebo'kowe*) said, *'atai'ya'* (holy smoke, or goodness gracious), what's been going on here. Look at my *nošišse* (grandson, referring to John King, who had been drinking rather heavily). That's the work of *akiwe'si* (Pat Kasabin). At this all the people watching started to laugh. Then the spirit went on and said, 'What's that white man doing here?' and the people laughed again. John Kasabin said that the white man was only there to watch and had paid well for it (referring to the tobacco we had given).

"Then the spirit asked, 'Why did you call me here?' Mrs. Butler answered (after being prompted by Mrs. King) and said she had brought her boy here and wanted him, the spirit, to find out what was wrong with him and if he had any medicine he could tell her about. Then Charley filled the pipe on the blanket and lighted it for Mrs. King and passed it to all the others. They each took a few puffs and then he handed it in to John King.

"The spirit said, 'All right, I'll try. I've helped a lot of Indians and I'll see what I can do for this one.' The spirit spoke to Laurence and told him to come closer. Laurence moved to 1 seat about 2 feet from the *ji'zikən*. The spirit asked Laurence if he could understand Chippewa and Laurence was slightly confused. Mrs. Butler told him to answer the spirit, so Laurence said that he could speak Chippewa (all the talking was, of course, in Chippewa).

"The spirit then said, 'If you believe in me, I will tell you the truth, but if you don't, I will tell you lies. Come closer and I will look at you.' Laurence leaned a little closer, and the spirit said, 'That isn't bad. That sickness will leave you.' Mrs. King then told Mrs. Butler to ask the spirit to work on him, so Mrs. Butler spoke to the spirit and said, 'I would like to have you doctor him and *boda'nzik* (blow on him) and tell me if there is any medicine that you know will help him.'

"The spirit said, 'Drum for me and I'll see what I can do.' So Charley started drumming and the women shook the stick rattles, (these are used in the Chief Dance) [204] and the wigwam began to shake hard and every once in a while the sound of blowing was heard. (Whoo', unvoiced. The sickness is supposed to be blown away from the person like this.)

"The wigwam shook for a few minutes and then quieted down, the drumming stopped, and the voice of the spirit was heard again. It said, 'That isn't a bad sickness and you can get over it by taking medicine.' Every so often a spirit would talk in an unintelligible growl, and John King would say *ani'wgwənə*) (all right then), as a sign that he understood what the spirit was saying in that special spirit language.

"Mrs. Butler then asked what kind of medicine she should get and who should make it. The spirit answered, 'Anyone' who knows good medicine could make it.' (Usually the spirit will name a certain medicine and name the person who should make it). Mrs. Butler told the spirit that she had been using some of her own that's all.' Then he told Laurence to take good care of himself and use the medicine.

"Then the spirit said, 'Now then, in regard to that preacher (*gagikwe'winini*) medicine on him, and the spirit said that was good. Then the spirit said *'miyu'* – out there, the one who is checking up on the Indians. Have him come up close here and I'll tell him all about the Indians in a short time.' He meant me", but Mrs. Butler interrupted and told him, 'No, don't be concerned about him. He is only here because he brought my boy here. He is only watching!' The spirit said, 'All right then, we'll go home.'

"The wigwam began shaking, and when it shakes hard it means that a spirit is leaving. There must have been at least two spirits there, one who talked clear Chippewa and one who talked Chippewa in a growl that no one could understand except the doctor. No drumming went on while the spirits left, and the wigwam shook hard a few times, then slowed down and stopped. The people got up and started home and Charley took all the blankets off the *ji'zikən*. John King stayed inside the wigwam in a kneeling position until all the blankets were off, then he crawled out and came over to me. "Can you do that?' he said, in Chippewa, and I said *'gawi'n* – no!' And he laughed.

"Mrs. Butler went into the house for a few minutes and then we took them home. She had brought a pint of whiskey for the doctor. They usually pass the bottle during a curing like this, but John King had been drinking wine. Mrs. Butler had gone down to Sand Lake to see him about two weeks before this, and had given him tobacco, a blanket, and two half-pints of whiskey. She had told him she wanted him to work on her son. He had said that he would and told her to bring her son down, but not to bring any more blankets or anything except a pint. There was no date set.

"The spirit that spoke was *bebo'kowe*. He's only about 4 ft. tall, with hair all over his body. He's a *manido*, some people have him for their guardian spirit. There is a special song that goes with him, they sing it at the Chief Dance and for the *ji'zikən*." (Field notes 1942.)

BULLETIN
OF THE
PUBLIC MUSEUM OF THE CITY OF MILWAUKEE

Vol. 19, No. 4, Pp. 175-258, Figs. 1-13, December, 1953

Chippewa Preoccupation With Health;
Change in a Traditional Attitude Resulting From Modem Health Problems

A thesis submitted in partial fulfillment of the requirements for the degree of
Doctor of Philosophy, in the Faculty of Anthropology^ Columbia University^

By Robert E. Ritzenthaler

MILWAUKEE, WIS., U.S.A.
Published by Order of the Board of Trustees

VISION PREROGATIVES

David G Mandlebaum

In [175] addition to {Plains Cree} curing and bundle-owning capabilities, other rights could be granted in a vision. The power of divining might be bestowed upon a visioner. It was usually given as the ability to foresee the enemy. This was an important qualification since the leader of a war party was expected to know where the hostile camps were located and plan the attack accordingly. This knowledge came to the leader as he sang his power songs while on the warpath.

The ability to operate a conjuring booth was another type of divining power which could be obtained from a spirit helper. The *koca•pahtcikan,* the booth, was constructed inside a tipi. Stout logs, four or five inches in diameter and about six feet long, were implanted in the ground to a depth of two feet and reinforced by two hoops made of willow withes. Robes and hides were bound around this frame which was so firmly built that a strong man could hardly shake it. The finished booth was about four feet in diameter and four to five feet high.

When the divining performance was to take place, the shaman stripped to his breechclout. The procedure always took place during the night. A pipe offering was made and two men bound the diviner with thongs. They placed his hands behind his back, palms out, and tied together the similar fingers of the opposing hands. Then the shaman knelt and bowed his head to the ground. A thong was fastened around his neck and tied about his ankles. Many turns were taken around his body until he was very tightly trussed. A rattle was stuck in the thongs on his back and he was placed against the booth. Some diviners entered the booth without human help, according to tales. Jefferson, however, states that the shaman "was inserted through the top as gently as might be."[9]

Then the fire was stamped out and a man with a drum began to beat. The tipi was always packed with onlookers, who helped sing one of the diviners' power songs. Soon the thongs which bound him came flying out of the top of the booth, each loop in turn still in place as though the shaman had slipped right out of them. The structure began to shake more and more violently, ringing bells which were attached to the top of the poles. Voices which identified themselves as various spirit powers were heard, sounding as though they had hurried to come in response to a summons. An old man put questions to the spirit powers and they answered. They [176] might be asked to diagnose an illness, to tell whether it was auspicious to start on a particular journey, to report the welfare of distant relatives. When all the questions had been asked and answered, the fire was rekindled. The posts which had been driven deep were now loosened. One was extracted and the shaman came out of the booth.

Only a few shamans among the Plains Cree could manipulate the conjuring booth. They were not affiliated in any order or society although Skinner[10] implies that they were.

Baptiste Pooyak, a well-read Indian and a devout Christian, told of a conjuring booth performance he had witnessed in 1903. The shaman, Owl-thunder, had made it to ascertain why a patient of his had fallen ill.

Two men tied Owl-thunder outside the tipi. After they tied him, they ran back into the tipi, a distance of about ten yards, but Owl-thunder was in the booth before they entered." Soon the ropes were thrown out at the top. I saw that the knots had not been untied. It was as if he had slipped right out of the bonds. The booth shook. There were bells on it somewhere and they rang. We could hear all kinds of animals and birds – and also Old Woman spirit power. Then Thunder spirit power was asked, "Why is this man sick, Thunder?" [The reply was], "He had many horses. He refused to lend one to *kumustusumit,* Cattle Owner, and that man sent a *pitcitcihtcikan* (an intrusive object) into him."

Many other questions were asked. White-calf had lost two horses. He asked where they were. "Directly south of your house there is a small slough with willows all around it. They are feeding there now. In the morning they will be a little west of there." The next morning I myself went there to look. There were the two horses that had been lost for a week. White-calf later promised to give a cloth to Owl-thunder [as an offering to Owl-thunder's spirit helpers].

Another man had married a young girl and he asked if the child she bore were his. The answer was, "Yes [you are right] that is not your child; it is the child of your testes." We laughed.

Then we saw sparks fly upward. It was the spirit powers leaving. Owl-thunder came out and the fire was built up.

Certain methods of divining did not require vision sanctions. One might see his future state by peering into the coagulated blood of a badger which had been left in the card over-night. Coming-day furnished this account of badger blood divining.

If you kill a badger, lay it on its back. Take the entrails out, but leave the blood in, and you can tell something the next morning. If a man looks into it he can see himself there. I knew of four young men who did it. One saw a black faced man, just [176] skin and bones. He died after a long sickness. Another saw a very old man with many wrinkles and hair white as snow. He lived to an old age. One saw a man who had been scalped. He was killed in battle shortly afterward. The last saw a young man with his eyes closed. He died at an early age.

These men were all young. The old men told them not to do it, for it is the one certain way of knowing how you would die. The old people thought it would worry the young men and disturb them. This badger blood looking was discovered accidentally once when a man was out hunting.

Information on scapulimancy and water scrying was given by Fine-day. He was not certain as to whether these were learned or vision-revealed techniques.

I knew an old Saulteaux who could foretell the future by heating the shoulder blade of an animal and reading the cracks. I never saw any Cree do this.

The Plains Cree did tell the future by looking into water. On the warpath each man would carry a cup [for drinking]. On one trip the leader filled his cup half full of water- Then he talked to Manito. The men built a big fire. The leader kneeled, pulled a robe over his head, grasped it on both sides so as to shade his eyes. He peered at the water intently – gazing from different angles continually. He asked, "Does the fire shine brightly on the water?" The men answered, "Yes." When the fire died down he told them to build it up again. Finally he said, "Tomorrow, the enemy will discover you while you are hunting buffalo." What he said came true. I never saw this done except in war but it may have been done for the hunt, too. It was called *wapi•munipi*, Mirror Water. It sometimes didn't turn out as the seer had predicted, but pretty often it did."

A vision prerogative which carried with it considerable prestige was the privilege of constructing a buffalo pound. A man had to have supernatural guarantees that he would be able to entice buffalo into a pound before he could build one, for its success depended on the aid of the shaman's super-naturals. It is noteworthy that the making of a fish weir did not require vision authorization.

Not all of the capabilities obtained through vision contacts could be transferred. We have already noted that a bundle could be passed on and would protect the new owner as it did the visioner. The knowledge of various herbal medicines was considered to have been originally given through visions, but was almost always acquired through purchase. The ability to doctor, however, was not entirely transferable. Shamanistic curing tricks and procedures were certainly taught by one shaman to another, but the right to undertake a cure had to be sanctioned in a dream. [178]

One [220] of Skinner's {sources} informants indicated as much[21] and Fine-day made this statement: –

I remember that, long ago, I saw an old man kill a bear in his den. He spread the bear out with its head toward the sun (to the south). He smoked a pipe, talked to the powers, offered the pipe to the bear. But in my day this was not done. We had no special way of hunting bears. I myself caught many with steel traps. But I have heard that they used to sing and make medicine before they went out to hunt for bears.

Coming-day said that when a bear was being butchered, a person who was suffering from an ailment would cut out a piece of the flesh. A man who had a pain in his shoulder would cut a piece from the shoulder of the carcass, saying, "I have a pain in my shoulder and now I cut it out." Another bear custom was described by Coming-day: –

I have not seen this, but I have heard of it many times. When a bear was killed, a bit of the breast fat, some meat from the ribs, and the large intestine were boiled together. Then the people were called in. One man took the intestine, held it to his ear saying, "What is it? I don't understand you. He tells me that I shall have good luck on the warpath." He bit off a piece of the intestine and passed it on. He didn't really hear anything, it was only a wish. They passed the intestine all around, even to the women. They wished for all kinds of things until it was all eaten. Then they served the rest of the food.

While Bear was one of the most venerated and feared of the spirit powers – perhaps because he was so venerated – tales were told of men who had foiled him. The following story, related by Fine-day, illustrates the type of narrative in which the most sacred characters or objects are flouted by the *dramatis personnae*. The stories concerning *wı•'sahketca•hk*, the mythological trickster, were considered as fabulous and imaginary tales by my informants. But incidents such as the following, in which the principal character was placed in a kinship relation to the narrator or to someone known to the narrator, were given somewhat greater credence.

I knew one man who beat out a spirit power. It was my grandfather's *osima,* his parallel cousin, whose name was *pı•hpa•hkwat,* Pot-belly. When he was young he was afraid of nothing and he used to laugh at everything. He had many dreams, but nobody knew it for he would never tell anyone.

When the frost was on in the fall, an old man got into a conjuring booth. A lot of people were there to listen and Pot-belly was also there. One spirit power came and the rattle on [221] the tipi shook to announce his presence. "You know who I am. I am *ukimaw okusisa•n,* 'Chiefs-son'." That is a name for Bear.

Then Pot-belly called out, "The one that's afraid of you calls you Chiefs-son. But I call you *Kispa•tıkitcisk,* 'Shaggy-rump'."

The spirit power answered, "I know you very well. You are Pot-belly. When the berries are ripe, I will watch for you and change you." The spirit got mad and stopped shaking the booth. It went on saying, "You are too young to know of all the people whom I have twisted and whose looks I have changed." Pot-belly answered, "Yes, but I am not a bit afraid of you. I will change your appearance."

When Pot-belly got home his father scolded him, but he was laughing all the same; it was so funny. Pot-belly bought a good gun, cut the barrel down, and cut the stock just long enough to hold. He bought a knife of the kind called flat knife, which was sharpened on both sides.

Now when the young men went out hunting they saw the berries ripening one at a time. It was close to the time when they should meet each other. Pot-belly oiled his little gun. The criers went around telling the people to move to where there were more berries. Pot-belly loaded his gun and sharpened his knife. His time was getting close. He went where there weren't many people. He started picking berries and before he had a handful the bear was out. It came out of a bush.

Pot-belly had his gun ready. As the bear jumped he aimed and fired, but the gun didn't go off, the cap missed fire. The bear struck the gun out of his hand. Pot-belly grabbed his knife and at the same time stuck his hand down the bear's throat and held it fast there. The bear kicked the knife out of his hand but he couldn't bite. They wrestled. Pot-belly tried to drag the bear over to where the knife was lying, saying, "Come on, we are going to fix each other." The bear gasped, "Let me go." Potbelly said, "I am going to cut the hide from around your eyes and your ears." The bear was scared and tried to settle with him, "If you let me go, I will be there when you want to save a person from dying." Pot-belly answered, "No, you'll fool me. If I let you go you'll forget everything. I am going to drag you to where my knife is." "If you let me go, Pot-belly, I will give you power in battle. As many hairs as I have on me, so many shots will miss you." "No, we've got to fix each other." "Potbelly, you have me. I'll give you my claws so that you can even cure those who have consumption." "No, I'll fix you when we get to my knife." "You've beaten me, Pot-belly, I promise to listen to you all the time. Wherever you are, I will be there also, under the ground. I will give you power to cure all the people that send for you to save them because I'll always be with you." "You promise a lot. People believe in you and then you fix them up and change their appearance." "You have beaten me and I promise you that I will give you all I say. There are two things you must not do. Never point at me with a gun or knife and never taste of me. But I will even give you something to save yourself with if you do eat of me." "If you promise me [222] that truly I will let you go." "I do." He let him go. The bear went back into the bush, his mouth full of blood.

He told Pot-belly that there was a young fellow who had been hurt in the back. "They will try to get you to cure him. I will help you do it and that is how you will be sure that I am keeping my promise." The bear gave his middle claw to Potbelly with which to remove the sickness. Pretty soon a man leading a good horse and carrying a gun, came up to Pot-belly. Sure enough, he wanted him to cure the boy. Pot-belly sang a bear song, put his finger on the boy's back, and drew the matter out. Before he started doctoring he told his story. "If Bear is here, listening under the ground, he will cure this boy." He did.

My grandfather went along to help Pot-belly sing. He told me this story many times. *pɪ•hpa•hkwat* used the bearclaw many times. But he would always suck the last of the matter out with his mouth. He was one who had won out over a spirit power.

EAGLE CEREMONIALISM

Eagle feathers adorned most objects in ritualistic use and lent them additional potency. Eagle wings were carried as badges of prestige by important men in ceremonies. They were used as fans in hot weather and also utilized as fire fans. A man who needed eagle feathers for any purpose would make a pipe offering to Eagle spirit power. He would ask Eagle to allow itself to be taken. If he did manage to secure an eagle, a feast would be given in which pipe offerings were made and berries consecrated and eaten. The feathers were plucked out and the eagle carcass was abandoned in a secluded place. When the feathers were to be used on a war bonnet or on other martial regalia, the eagle was eaten.

The use of the pit ambush method of trapping eagles was not known. Eagles were shot or obtained by strewing bait about and allowing the birds to gorge themselves until they were unable to fly.

FIRST EVENT CEREMONIALISM

The first berries of the season were not eaten until a feast had been given. The feast was not a communal affair; each family group conducted its own ritual. The berries were cooked and an old man invited to consecrate them. After the usual pipe offering, he held up a bowl of berries. First Great *Manito* was invoked and thanked for allowing men to eat berries again. Then the bowl was held toward the sun. Sun was asked to do his work faithfully – to ripen the berries – since he had been put there for that purpose. ...

THE PLAINS CREE
AN ETHNOGRAPHIC, HISTORICAL, AND COMPARATIVE STUDY

DAVID G. MANDELBAUM

CANADIAN PLAINS STUDIES 9
J. ARCHER, GENERAL EDITOR of OCCASIONAL PUBLICATIONS
CANADIAN PLAINS RESEARCH CENTER
UNIVERSITY OF REGINA
1979

The Role of Conjuring in Saulteaux Ojibway Society

by

ALFRED IRVING HALLOWELL

Jay Miller, PhD, ed

Publications of the
Philadelphia Anthropological Society
Brinton Memorial Series
Volume II
1942 / 2020

FOREWORD

WITH this publication the PHILADELPHIA ANTHROPOLOGICAL SOCIETY inaugurates a series of monographs of varying length, uniform in format with Twenty-fifth Anniversary Studies, Volume I of the Society's Publications, which appeared in 1937; the volumes of the present series will appear at irregular intervals.

The early volumes of this series will constitute a "Brinton Memorial Series," dedicated to the memory of the great local anthropologist Daniel Garrison Brinton. These publications are largely made possible through two contributions from the heirs of Dr. Brinton, the nucleus having been given by Mrs. Emilia Garrison Brinton Grant to the Delaware County Institute of Science, at whose quarters in Media, Pennsylvania, a meeting was held on May 13, 1937 to commemorate the hundredth anniversary of his birth. These funds, graciously transferred by the Institute to this Society, were later augmented by the proceeds from the sale of certain Brinton publications, received through Dr. Christian Brinton.

The first volume, *The Role of Conjuring in Saulteaux Society*, by Dr. A. Irving Hallowell, has been further aided by a grant from the Ella Pancoast Widener Fund of the Committee on the Publication of Research, University of Pennsylvania. To all the above, and to all others who have aided in the inauguration of the present series, the PHILADELPHIA ANTHROPOLOGICAL SOCIETY and the undersigned express their great appreciation.

PUBLICATION COMMITTEE, 1942
J. Alden Mason
W. Norman Brown
A. Irving Hallowell

To CHIEF WILLIAM BERENS
whose genial companionship in camp and canoe,
in fair weather and foul, never failed to enliven my task.

PREFACE

REFERENCES to conjuring by means of the "shaking tent" are scattered through the literature on Algonkian tribes of the Eastern Woodlands over a span of more than three centuries. Yet descriptions of actual performances by eyewitnesses are few and often meager in detail. Strange as it may seem, only two professional ethnologists have reported first-hand observations of such performances. However, to understand a conjuring seance requires more than external observation of it. It necessitates a knowledge of the world view of the people among whom it occurs and the role conjuring plays in their lives.

The present study, based on an intimate knowledge of one branch of the Ojibwa-speaking peoples – the Saulteaux of the Berens River in Manitoba, Canada – combines two objectives. On the one hand, it is an account of how conjuring functions in Saulteaux society and, on the other, the details of every aspect of conjuring are compared with what is known of conjuring practices in other Algonkian groups. While this comparative documentation is not exhaustive, I believe that it is sufficiently representative to indicate the range of variation manifested by most of the items found in the conjuring complex.

The information on which this account of Saulteaux conjuring is based was collected in a series of periodic summer trips to the Lake Winnipeg country beginning in 1930. During my entire investigation I was fortunate in having the services of Chief William Berens, now in his middle seventies, as interpreter, guide and, sometimes, cook. His mother was a white woman and he has been bilingual since childhood. In addition, Chief Berens' great-grandfather was a conjurer of note. What amounted to probing into some of the more esoteric aspects of a familiar institution interested him as much as it did me. Constant discussion between ourselves as well as [x] the inquiries we instituted together among contemporary conjurers, usually reluctant to divulge information on such matters, made him a virtual collaborator in my task. Whatever their defects, the data collected would be far less complete had I not had his assistance.

So far as I am aware, the photographs showing a conjuring lodge in the course of construction are unique. These structures are usually erected at dusk, so that it is almost impossible to obtain good photographs. On the occasion when these pictures were taken, preparations were started earlier than usual and, happening to live close by, I managed to take them before darkness fell.

I am very grateful to Dr. John M. Cooper, Dr. Frank G. Speck, Mr. Leonard Mason and Mr. Allan Nelson for allowing me to incorporate comparative material on the Gros Ventre, Blackfoot, Montagnais-Naskapi, Oxford House Cree, and Saulteaux from their unpublished field notes.

Although my investigation of conjuring among the Berens River Saulteaux was carried on simultaneously with many other lines of inquiry, all the results of which have not yet been published, I wish to take this opportunity to acknowledge my appreciation for the financial assistance derived from a number of sources which has enabled me to pursue work in the field over the past decade.

In addition to a number of very substantial grants from the Faculty Research Committee of the University of Pennsylvania, the Social Science Research Council enabled me to make my first trip to Lake Winnipeg in 1930 and in 1940 made possible another visit during the course of which I checked my manuscript and obtained some new details of importance. It was during the summer of 1930 that I witnessed my first conjuring performance and my interest in conjuring was first aroused. Two years later, Dr. Ruth Benedict was instrumental in obtaining a generous grant from funds at the disposal of the Department of Anthropology, Columbia University, which made it possible for me to make my first trip two hundred and fifty miles up the Berens River to Lake Pekangikum. It was during this season that I first observed [xi] conjuring among the inland Saulteaux at Little Grand Rapids. Finally, I am indebted to the John Simon Guggenheim Memorial Foundation for the opportunity to devote a portion of the time during which I was a Fellow in 1941 to the final preparation of the manuscript for the press.

A.I.H.

CONTENTS

ILLUSTRATIONS

I

INTRODUCTION

No one is more aware than the ethnologist that human beings always live in a meaningful universe, not in a world of bare physical objects and events. But the individual does not invent or discover these meanings for himself. They are communicated to him and he introcepts them in the course of a socialization process. They are derived from the amazingly variable belief systems of mankind which, however different in content and pattern, arc part of the cultural heritage of our species. The world in which human beings think, feel and act is always a culturally constituted world. It is a world seen not only from a human but from a culturally circumscribed point of view. This is as true of occidental man as of the savage. The world is always perceived and derives its meaning and significance from the beliefs and presuppositions of a particular culture. Or, to put it figuratively, it is viewed through the spectacles with which our culture has provided us.

Science has provided us with one such set of spectacles, and educated men of the modern era view the world through them. Our provincialism, our characteristic bias, is derived from the viewpoint engendered by the results of scientific investigation of the nature of things. Whether it more nearly approaches Truth in an absolute sense is not an issue here. I merely wish to emphasize the fact that as individuals we have acquired it in much the same way that any primitive has acquired his outlook.

In a recent paper Kohler[1] has expressed the opinion that the reputed difficulties which have arisen in understanding and explaining the mentality of primitives is probably quite as much the result of the bias created in our world outlook by scientifically oriented thinking as it is due to any intrinsic [2] peculiarities of primitive mentality itself, "In a way," he says, "scientifically trained people of our time may be particularly unfit for the understanding of less intellectual cultures." Certain it is that a convinced spiritualist would more readily find himself in rapport with a Saulteaux conjuring performance than most scientists. In fact, references to some of the data I shall present have long been cited in spiritualistic literature.[2] Kohler goes on

---

[1] See Bibliography.

[2] e.g., Howitt (1863) devotes a chapter (XVII) to the supernatural among the American Indians and draws liberally upon Kohl's account of Ojibwa conjuring (pp. 402 ff.) and clairvoyance; Hardinge (1870) quotes Henry's account in full, cites a letter from Judge Larrabee of Wisconsin (a spiritualist) to Governor Taltmadge in which the former quotes the observations of John Du Bay, an agent of the American Fur Company, who had spent many years among the Indiana, and quotes a newspaper article by W.M. Johnson in which he recounts his conversation with a converted conjurer. Mrs. Hardinge (p. 487) then comments:

Such are some of the phases in which spirit communion exhibits itself amongst a people whom we call "savage," and whom, in comparison to our more advanced civilization, we may justly call so; and yet, does our knowledge of the occult and invisible forces in nature furnish us with any clue to the mystery of these astounding manifestations or the power by which the unlettered "savage" can avail himself of a knowledge which all our control over the elements fails to compete with? In a word, the red Indian can do what we can neither explain nor imitate. The few quotations, from most reliable authorities, which our space has

to say that it might be an advantage therefore, if [3] ... in studying the appearance which the world has for primitives, we could overcome the tendency to use our own view as a norm. Anthropologists have generally been at pains to follow this principle. More might be done, however, if even in the application of psychological thought to primitive perception the white man's customary outlook were recognized as a disturbing factor.

Anyone who has attempted to study the magico-religious beliefs and practices of a primitive people soon becomes painfully aware of this difficulty. This area of thought, feeling, and action, more than any other, is so intrinsically bound up with native metaphysical notions that are not clearly denned or articulated that it is sometimes difficult to be absolutely certain of our grasp of it. Yet we know that their conduct proceeds on the basis of such assumptions. But even at best our comprehension of the belief system of a primitive people remains on the intellectual level. We never learn to feel and act as they do. Consequently we never fully penetrate their behavioral world. We never *wear* their culturally tinted spectacles; the best we can do is to try them on. [no 4]

---

allowed us to make, are but a tithe of the evidence which travellers amongst those people furnish us with, and which the author's own experience no less than that of many of her personal friends, amply corroborates. The medicine and Ches-a-kee men here mentioned, are neither rare nor phenomenal characters, but simply representative men amongst their tribes and nation. And where lies the clue to these mysteries? It is not the results nor the value of the power here displayed which arrest our attention; but the subject of deepest interest is its existence at all, connected, as it would seem, with a realm of being of which even the modern Spiritualist, in orderly communion with the souls of his ancestors, can give no explanation; furnish no analogous testimony.

(P. 489.) The clairvoyant faculties, prescient powers, and general results obtained through their (i.e., American Indian) Spiritualism, correspond closely with that of their civilized neighbors, but the modes of invocation differ essentially, and the characteristics which seem to mark the communicating intelligences are equally repulsive and incomprehensible to the American Spiritualist. Whether the red man succeeds in evoking and controlling to his service a race of beings hovering on the precincts of a sub-mundane sphere, or his exercises predispose him to those ecstatic conditions in which the spiritual vision is broken and refracted, and he actually communicates with undeveloped human spirits, but amidst the fumes of tobacco with which his system is poisoned he mistakes them for animals, birds, etc., we do not pretend to decide. Every Spiritualist, in the new dispensation, stands at the threshold only, of that vast and wonderful temple of science which conceals the mighty laws that govern and hold in their embrace, the universe of mind, and all the invisible forces kindred with it.

Cf. C. de Vesme (1931) Chap. VII, who reprints some of the material collected by Hardinge, E. Lawrence (1921), H. Carrington (1927), and E. Bozzano (1927).

II
THE BEHAVIORAL WORLD OF THE SAULTEAUX

IN this monograph I shall attempt to communicate the lineaments of a strange behavioral world – the universe of a group of some nine hundred Indians who live scattered along two hundred miles of a river which empties into the eastern side of Lake Winnipeg. In particular I wish to make intelligible the operation of their system of magico-religious beliefs by describing the role of conjuring in Saulteaux society, an institution which, more than any other, reflects the kind of world in which they actually live. The fact that the geographical locale of these Indians is on the Berens River in a subarctic physical environment, that they hunt, trap and fish for a living and have little contact with any white people except traders, missionaries and prospectors, is of less moment from the standpoint of our present discussion than the content of their beliefs about the nature of the surrounding world. Their native belief system, in short, defines the psychological or behavioral environment in which they live, and no purely objective account of their geographical locale, its topography, its fauna and flora would be sufficient to account completely for their behavior in relation to this physical environment.

One example must suffice at this point. During the spring and summer months thunder is heard with increasing frequency and often there are severe storms. Sometimes an Indian will be seen turning his pipe in a characteristic manner when a severe clap is heard and he may even murmur a few words. Someone else may say, "Ah! *pinésīwak* (ah! Thunder Birds)," and look upward. This behavior is derived from a belief in the Thunder Birds who live in the South during the winter and spend the spring and summer in the North. When you hear them they are pursuing monster snakes that live on [6] the earth – other mythical creatures from our point of view, but none the less real from the standpoint of the Saulteaux. They are water monsters living in the lakes and swamps and some of the Indians have seen them. Thunder Birds and monster snakes, then, are important items in the behavioral environment of these Indians. Since from our point of view thunder is part of their physical environment and monster snakes are not, we might be inclined to make a distinction between them. But if we do this we are making our categories a point of departure. We are assuming them as a universal norm. I prefer to consider both the Thunder Birds and the monster snakes as part of the behavioral environment of these Indians and to ignore any such distinction. Both are "real" in the sense that they have actual effects upon behavior.

From this point of view the essential items of the behavioral world of the Saulteaux may be briefly described as follows:[3]

(a) COSMOGRAPHY, The earth itself is not only thought to be flat, it is believed to be a great island. Under it is another world, inhabited by other groups of human beings. In this lower world it is day when it is night on the earth and vice versa, for the sun travels above the earth during the day and under it during the night. At the ends of the earth in the four cardinal directions live the "masters" of the winds, anthropomorphic beings whose birth is described in a myth. To the south is the land of the dead.

---

[3] See also Hallowell (1).

(b) SPIRITUAL BEINGS. The ultimate controlling power in the universe is *kadabɛndjigɛt* (Owner), the Supreme Being. His name is seldom uttered, "he" remains unsexed and extremely remote from any direct participation in human affairs. The proximate dynamic agencies in the universe and hence the beings with whom man is compelled to deal may be grouped into three classes: (1) Explicitly anthropomorphic beings like *wísakedjak*, the culture hero, and *tcakábɛc* (great little man). These beings are prominent characters in Saulteaux mythology. Although they exist somewhere on the earth they are [7] no longer seen except in dreams. But semi-human beings called *memɛŋgwecīwak*, who live in the rocks, are sometimes met by human beings. (2) The "masters" or "owners" of what we term natural phenomena. In the case of animal and plant species there is in theory a "master" for each group, for bears as well as for birch trees. But in practice certain masters have assumed greater prominence than others, e.g., *mikīnák*, the master of the great turtles whom we shall meet in the conjuring lodge. (3) Human institutions like certain dance ceremonies, curing procedures and conjuring have their supernatural patrons. In some cases, like conjuring, the spiritual owner is an autonomous being distinct from any of those mentioned, so that this class of beings must be added to the others.

(c) MAN'S RELATIONS WITH THE DYNAMIC ENTITIES OF THE UNIVERSE. The major medium of communication between man and supernatural beings is through dream experiences. Hence one generic term for a spiritual being is *pawágan* (dream visitor). Another term is "grandfather," which conveys an attitude of respect in addition to any connotation of relationship. The characters in mythology are called *átsokan*, as are the myths themselves. This term can be used synonymously with *pawágan*, since mythological characters may be dream visitors as well. In the old days all males went through a puberty fast which was the means for securing spiritual helpers or guardian spirits. In Saulteaux belief, life could not be lived successfully without such helpers. Women might obtain guardian spirits, too, but not in a puberty fast. No one ever dreams of the High God – so the Supreme Being can never become a guardian spirit. Leadership and the exercise of professional services of all kinds originate in dream blessings from *pawáganak*. No one is supposed to undertake such activities without divine license. However, certain kinds of magic are purchasable.

(d) METAPHYSICAL NOTIONS. Neither animism in its classical formulation nor animatism is the unequivocal foundation of Saulteaux belief. An analysis of this problem would require [8] extended discussion, but it may be categorically stated that animal-human metamorphosis, transmigration, reincarnation, action at a distance, the separation of soul and body during life, as well as after death, are all conceivable in terms of Saulteaux belief. [9]

III
CHARACTERIZATION AND DISTRIBUTION OF THE
SAULTEAUX TYPE OF CONJURING

CONJURING, in Saulteaux society, is an institutionalized means for obtaining the help of different classes of spiritual entities by invoking their presence and communicating human desires to them. The conjurer is a specialist in invocation. The most characteristic function which he exercises through the aid of his spiritual helpers is seership or clairvoyance. Whatever the occasion upon which his services are demanded or whatever the problem to be solved, it is the clairvoyant powers which he uses that differentiate him from other types of shamans.[4] This fact is reflected in the terminology of conjuring.

For the act of conjuring, the Saulteaux usually speak of *kosábandamowin*, which corresponds to a widespread, but not universal, Ojibwa term.[5] The meaning of this word is connected [10] with an act of visualization as in *nindosábadan* (I am able to see something from a distance).[6] The other Ojibwa term, *djisákīwin*, likewise is known but not used on the upper reaches of the Berens River,[7] although it seems to have been employed by the band at the mouth

---

[4] Rev. S.G. Belcourt, one of the earliest Catholic missionaries among the Ojibwa-Saulteaux-speaking people in the West, wrote this excellent characterization of conjuring in the middle of the nineteenth century.

It consists of certain formalities, songs, invocation of spirits, and bodily agitations, which are so energetic that you are carried back to the times of the ancient Sybils: they seem to say to you Deus, ecce, Deus, and then submitting to the questions of the spectators, they always have a reply, whether it be to tell what passes at a distance, or reveal the place where objects which have been lost may be found. As the skill of the prophet consists in replying in ambiguous terms upon all subjects of which he has not been able to procure information in advance, he is always sure of success, cither more or less striking. Cf. Hoffman (1) p. 157.

The *Jessakid* is a seer and prophet ... the Indians define him as a "revealer of hidden truths." He is said to possess the power to look into futurity; to become acquainted with the affairs and intentions of men; to prognosticate the success or misfortune of hunters and warriors, as well as other affairs of various individuals, and to call from any living human being the soul, or, more strictly speaking, the shadow, thus depriving the victim of reason, and even life. Cf. Schoolcraft (1) I, p. 359; V, p. 405; W. Jones; Ruth Landes (1) p. 121; Skinner (3) p. 192.

[5] Cf. Cooper, p. 9, and Baraga. The latter defines this term as "Indian divination and jugglery in order to know the future, in regard to sicknesses and their remedies." The Plains Cree (Mandelbaum, p. 261) and likewise the Rupert's House Montagnais employ a cognate term (Flannery, p. 15).

[6] See Baraga, p. 223. There are cognates in other Algonkian languages; to my personal knowledge in Abenaki.

[7] This term is likewise given by Baraga. Cf. Belcourt, Hoffman, Densmore (1) (2), Jenness, Coleman, et al. It will be unnecessary to go into the further vagaries of terminology here, but attention may be drawn to a third term, *onotcikeivinini* (foretelling man), applied to a conjurer at Rainy Lake (see Cooper, p. 25). This term is not used with this connotation by

of the river.

When a conjurer undertakes to divine, a small structure is built and, upon entering it, he summons his spiritual helpers. They manifest themselves vocally, the voices issuing from the conjuring lodge being distinguishable from the voice of the conjurer who kneels within. Each *pawágan* upon entering the tent usually sings a song and sometimes he names himself. If it is the master of the moose, for instance, the spirit may say, "*mozezizīnikázwīän* (moose I am called)."[8] Another manifestation of their presence is the movement of the lodge itself. From the time the conjurer enters it is seldom still.[9] It oscillates and sways from side to side, behaving in a most animate fashion.[10] The masters of the winds are responsible for these [11] movements.[11] I

---

    the Berens River Saulteaux, although it may be applied, generically, to anyone who prophesies. My interpreter called it a "church word." For whatever it may be worth, I quote the statement of Schoolcraft [(1) I, p. 389] that "to *jeesuka*, in the language of the Ojibwas, is to mutter or peep. The word is taken from the utterance of sounds of the human voice, low on the ground. This is the position in which the response is made by the seer or prophet, who is called *jossakeed*."

[8] Leonard Mason notes for the Oxford House Cree that "the spirits could be heard continually, speaking to the audience, as in one instance, 'I am the Raven, Caw, Caw,' sounding off as the bird would in the flesh."

[9] Unless the dogs start barking. Mason obtained the same statement from the Oxford House Cree. Anyone who has lived in an Indian camp does not soon forget the wolf-like howling of the dogs. Since there are dozens of these northern canines within earshot of one another the antiphonal effects produced sometimes seem interminable. My own inference is that the conjuring tent stops shaking because dogs are unclean animals and objectionable to the pawáganak. I have never heard of any "master of the dogs" functioning as a *pawágan*. One reliable informant said this was possible. Yet dogs always arc ejected from dance or ceremonial grounds.

[10] Everyone who has seen a conjuring performance is impressed with this characteristic feature. Le Jeune describes it as vividly as any observer since. At first, he says (Vol. 6, p. 165), the conjurer shook this edifice gently; but, as he continued to become more animated, he fell into so violent an ecstacy {ecstasy}, that I thought he would break everything to [11] so much strength; for, after he had once begun to shake it, he did not stop until the consultation was over, which lasted about three hours.

    Indians have frequently made extreme statements about the movements of the conjuring lodge. One of Densmore's Ojibwa informants, for instance [(1) p. 124], "stated that he had seen the lodge bend like a sapling, so that the top almost touched the ground and the cloth covering was torn to fragments" – yet afterwards three men found it impossible to sway the structure at all. I have been told the same thing by the Saulteaux, and equivalent statements were made to Le Jeune in the seventeenth century (Vol. 12, pp. 17, 19). It is true that the movements of the lodge are sufficiently impressive. Kohl's informant (p. 279), a white man married to an Indian woman, remarked, "I could not understand how these movements could be produced by a man inside, as we could not have caused them from the exterior." But it is obvious that perceptual impressions received during the course of a seance are not only influenced by the nature of the occasion, but by the mental set of the observer as molded by tradition. For example, the tradition from Le Jeune's day up to the present that the top of the

was told by one conjurer that the winds blow with greater force inside the lodge than outdoors.

Thus a Saulteaux conjurer, in the tangible exercise of his powers, brings into the midst of a group of human beings seated around a barrel-like structure[12] a large selection of pieces, shaking his house with so much force and violence, that I was astonished at a man having [12] spiritual beings.[13] The single exception is *kadabinjiget*, the High God or Supreme Being.[14] With

---

lodge almost touches the ground leads to positive assertions that it has been sun to do what is a physical impossibility. But such testimony is to be expected as a support to the native theory. Flannery (p. 12) states that during its most violent oscillations the "top of the tent sometimes described an arc of about three feet," and my own observations support her testimony.

[11] Cf. Le Jeune (Vol. 12, p. 10). Wa-chus-co, the converted conjurer interviewed by Schoolcraft [(2) p. 2103, is reported to have attributed "the agitation of the lodge to be due to the currents of air, having the irregular and gyrating power of a whirlwind."

[12] Cf. Landes (1) p. 122. The form of the conjuring lodge has been variously characterized. Oldmixon referred to it as a "small tower"; Carver describes it as a "chest or coffin ... of an oblong shape"; Schoolcraft likens it to "an acute pyramid with the apex open" [(2) p. 210]; Me Kenney (p. 329) says it "resembles in figure a shot tower"; Kohl's informant (p. 278) refers to it as a "basket-work chimney," and Godsell as "an elongated bee hive." We have so few structural details in most cases that it is impossible to discuss local differences with certainty, but the poles, in most cases, seem to have been placed in the ground in a circle so that the resulting structure could not have been oblong in such instances. However, Hoffman [(2) p. 147] refers to a four-poled lodge and illustrates one surrounded with birch bark, and for the Ojibwa he declares [(1) p. 252] that "four or more" poles were used, but he says that the lodge may be described as "cylindrical." Skinner [(1) p. 14] is unique in describing the structure as "dome-shaped" and constructed in the same manner as dwellings of this form. He is in error here; such a structure would be unshakable. Densmore [(3) plate 20, c] has published a photograph of a conjurer's lodge that is of a distinctly different type from those I have seen among the Cree and Saulteaux. Skinner (3) p. 193, published the same photograph. Schoolcraft C (1) V) plate 32, fig. 1, opp. p. 428] illustrates the conjuring lodge by a sketch but I cannot find any reference to the artist.

[13] I once asked a man about seventy years of age to name all the *pawáganak* that he remembered having heard in the conjuring tent. He gave me the following list (the classification is my own): (a) Anthropomorphic beings that also appear as characters in mythology: *wisakedjak, tcakábec, mätcikwis, aásī, wematīgózī*; (b) semi-human entities: *memkɛŋwecī, págak, misábe, wíndŋgo*; (c) masters of animal species: moose, caribou, elk, deer, lynx, otter, fisher, martin, beaver, porcupine, skunk, racoon, ground hog, wolverine, wolf, badger, turtle (*mikīnak* and *miskwadesi*), frog, trout, perch, sucker, sturgeon, jackfish. Cf. Jenness, p. 66, who refers to "souls or spirits of animals like the bear and the serpent, who have assembled together with the spirit of thunder, their chief, and of snapping turtle, longest lived of all the creatures, their interpreter." One of Densmore's Menominee informants [(3) p. 104] said "he had heard voices of crows and many sorts of animals."

[14] So far as the Berens River Saulteaux are concerned, Schoolcraft's statement [(1) I, p. 357] that "the *Jossakeed* addresses himself exclusively to the Great Spirit" is false (italics ours). I doubt whether this is literally true anywhere, but at least we need some evidence, Flannery

the aid of his spiritual tutelaries a conjurer is able to secure news about people who are hundreds of miles away, or learn of events that are taking place in another part of the country.[15] He can discover what is going to happen in the future and he can find out a great deal about the past lives of his fellows. As occasion demands he may recover lost or stolen articles for their owners or discover the hidden cause of some puzzling malady. On the other hand, with malevolent ends in view, he can abduct the souls of human beings, causing sickness, mental disorder or even death, if this vital animating agency is not returned to them.

While the powers attributed by the Saulteaux to their conjurers are not unfamiliar to students of shamanism, there is a typological distinction which is based upon native concepts. In the terminology of E.M. Loeb the Saulteaux conjurer, as is usually the case in American Indian shamanism, belongs to the "non-inspired" type in which the spirits speak to or in the [13] presence of the shaman, rather than enter his body and speak through him. This latter type is called "inspirational shamanism" by Loeb. It is well typified by Siberian shamanistic practice, although in certain other regions of the Old World Loeb finds evidence of the non-inspired type. He claims that this is older than the inspired type.

How far possession as a theory of shamanism is connected with actual psychic phenomena, such as dissociation, I do not know. Shirokogoroff says that the Tungus shaman "falls into a state of ecstasy."[16] So far as I know, nothing of this sort is believed to happen to Saulteaux conjurers, nor do I think that trance actually takes place. Bogoras[17] characterized the Chukchee shamans whom he knew as "extremely excitable, almost hysterical" and a few as "half crazy." "Their cunning," he says, "in the use of deceit in their art, closely resembled the cunning of a lunatic. It is certainly a fact that the expression of a shaman is peculiar – a combination of cunning and shyness; and by this it is often possible to pick him out from among many others."

My impressions of Saulteaux conjurers were quite the reverse. Nothing seems to distinguish them, as a group, from other Indians in respect to psychological type or psychic peculiarities of major significance. But the Rorschach protocols which I recently obtained include those of nine individuals who at one time or another have conjured. The personality of these conjurers will be discussed in connection with the general results of my Rorschach investigation.[18] [14]

---

however has statements of informants who have heard the voice of the High God issuing from the conjuring lodge (correspondence, July, 1940). For the Minnesota Ojibwa, Coleman (p. 57) says, "The conjuring and Supreme Being rites seemed to be very closely related, since Mikenak, the chief spirit of the shaking tent, was directly responsible to the Great Spirit."

[15] This clairvoyance is reflected in the words of the songs heard in the lodge. One of my informants once heard the master of the moose sing, "I'm listening in every valley of the earth." The greater the variety and number of *pawáganak* a conjurer has the more he can find out.

[16] Shirokogoroff (1) p. 276. Cf. the more detailed discussion in his monumental work *Psychomental Complex of the Tungus*.

[17] W. Bogoras, pp. 415-416.

[18] References in the literature to conjuring as an institution or to particular conjuring performances do not as a rule include even impressionistic observations on the personal appearance, personality traits or peculiarities of the conjurers themselves, so that we know

Saulteaux conjuring, in addition to lacking the ideology of possession,[19] is inextricably associated with the conjuring lodge which offers complete concealment of the conjurer from his audience during the entire course of the séance. In the New World, conjuring,[20] associated with the type of lodge described, appears to have been confined to the Algonkian peoples of the Woodland area, or tribes in contact with them.[21] Champlain makes reference to it in the early

---

little or nothing about these men as individuals. An Ojibwa conjurer of the late nineteenth century called "Little Jake" is so colorfully portrayed by Haupt (Winchell, p. 611) that it seems worth while to give the full quotation here:

He is a short Indian, a little over 5 feet with a well-knit frame and it is said he is as strong as a lion, that he can lift and carry a heavier weight than any Indian in the camp. His face is the most hideous mask we ever beheld on an animated creature. His smile was the grin of a wolf. The corners of his mouth receded with an upward curve, and the skin of the cheeks broke into concentric wrinkles, exhibiting a set of irregular green teeth. His ear was small and close to his head and the very small gray eyes, arched over with heavy overhanging eyebrows, were quick like the eyes of a snake, and when we add to all these features the coat of pigment daubed upon his sallow skin the result was a picture not to be forgotten. In the dance no Indian was more animated or graceful in his contortions than Jake, and he watched every movement of the other dancers with keen intent.

[19] The belief that a spirit may enter the body of a human being and control his behavior is as foreign to most New World cultures as it is conspicuous in many Old World ones. Cf. Boas, p. 27, and Oesterreich, pp. 292-93.

[20] Striking analogies to the conjuring performance of the eastern Indians are found among the Semang of the Malay Peninsula. Evans summarizes the observations of Schebesta along with his own. The *pano* hut of the Semang is similar in *form* to that of the Saulteaux and other Algonkian peoples (see Evans, p. 184 and Schebesta, pp. 216, 241, for photographs), but it is built by women. The performance takes place at night with the conjurer inside the hut and others outside. Evans writes (p. 194), "The antics of the *halak* [shaman or conjurer], while hidden from sight within the *panoh* [hut], are worth alluding to. Sounds of grunting, whistling, growling, shouting, singing, chest-beating and slapping with the hands on the walling proceeded from the inside before he began his chants under the inspiration of the *chinoi* [supernaturals used by the shaman]." In conformity with the prevalence of the idea of possession in the Old World, these spirits as a rule speak *through* the shaman rather than to him, although some may sit on his knees and shoulders. The Semang *halak* gets his powers in a dream (p. 201, cf. p. 220), and he exercises curative (p. 204) as well as clairvoyant functions (p. 205n.). As among the Saulteaux, sometimes there is jesting between the supernaturals and the humans present. I am not citing these analogies in order to raise the question of any possible historical connection, but they do seem interesting because, so far as I know, similar parallels do not occur in the Boreal regions of Asia. If they did, it would be difficult to dismiss the possibility of historical connections with North America.

[21] [11] Cf. Flannery (1) p. 14. One striking lacuna is particularly noticeable in the documentary sources. This is the absence of any description of conjuring among the New England Algonkians. It is true that Maurault refers to it and that Champlain's account might concern some New England people. But if conjuring of the type described was as typical in this

seventeenth century, as do Sagard and Le Caron,[22] while Le Jeune gives a much more [15] detailed account. At the present day conjuring survives among the Cree.[23] Montagnais-Naskapi and the Ojibwa-Saulteaux.

Outside the Woodland area, the shaking tent is reported for the Plains Cree by Mandelbaum and for the Cheyenne by Grinnell and Hoebel.[24] Inquiry among the Athabascans

---

region as elsewhere, it is strange that we do not have other accounts.

[22] Le Caron is the source of Hennepin's reference to conjuring. This is quite plain from the internal evidence. Cf. the remark of the editor (Introduction, p. xxxix) on Hennepin's borrowings from Le Clercq.

[23] Despite this persistence of conjuring among the northern Algonkians most of the references to it in the literature yield extremely meager data. While I have not attempted to exhaust all possible documentary sources I think that the annotated bibliography appended includes the major sources of information. I have starred the names of those individuals who have given us first-hand observations of conjuring performances and have indicated by a dagger those items which contain valuable data obtained at second hand from Indian or white informants. Double-daggered titles are chiefly primary sources that simply mention conjuring without contributing details of importance. Since page references are given in the bibliography these will not be repeated in the footnotes, except where necessary.

[24] Dr. E.A. Hoebel obtained a much more detailed account than that given by Grinnell (personal information). Cf. Flannery (1) p. 14n. Dr. John M. Cooper has been kind enough to provide me with excerpts from his field notes on the Gros Ventre and the Blackfoot (Montana). The conjuring lodge of the Woodland Algonkians is not utilized by these people but a rite in which ghosts act as spiritual helpers has definite analogies to the conjuring procedures described in this monograph. There also are analogies in social function. Among the Gros Ventre a deceased relative may visit a survivor from time to time and finally offer ritualistic instructions and aid in performing clairvoyant, prophetic and curative services. The survivor has to accept this role, although few individuals in the past generation have had ghost helpers. The ritual is carried out in a darkened tipi. The performer is trussed up in a blanket tied with ropes and deposited behind a curtain. A whistling sound is heard as the ghost approaches; 'it imitates an owl's cry on arrival and the tipi shakes violently as with a big wind. The ghost uses either a natural voice or a whistling language when answering questions. Among the Blackfoot the performer or medium is a woman who summons spirits of the dead to answer questions. Only the medium understands their language and can converse with them. The performance is carried out in darkness and the medium sits behind a curtain while the other people present disperse themselves in the main part of the tipi. During the rite noises are heard and "everything moves, including the tent itself." Recently Verne F. Ray has drawn attention to the striking parallelism between eastern Woodland conjuring and conjuring rituals of the Colville of eastern Washington and the Kutenai of British Columbia. The Gros Ventre and Blackfoot data cited above appear to be variants of this same complex. Ray believes that the sporadic distribution of the conjuring complex in the Plains and Plateau areas is a consequence of Algonkian migrations. The diffusion has been from east to west and he infers that the "Plains-Cree emerge as donors of the northwestern [conjuring] complex." But in the process the shaking tent feature which is so characteristic and stable a feature everywhere in the East, was dropped.

appears to have led to negative results. Flannery states that "it is not Chippewayan" and that it "has been reported only for [16] those Beaver who have undoubtedly been strongly influenced by the Cree.[25]

So far as eyewitness accounts of conjuring by ethnologists are concerned, Flannery and Densmore offer the only published data. The former observed a seance among the Montagnais of Rupert's House in August, 1938. Densmore's observations pertain to the Ojibwa. She witnessed a performance in July, 1930, at Grand Portage, Minnesota.[26]

The first conjuring performance that I saw was at Cross Lake, Manitoba, in 1930. The conjurer was a Cree, a picturesque old-timer by the name of papamotewiglmau (walking boss), said to be ninety years of age.[27] Among the Berens [17] River Saulteaux I have seen three

---

[25] Flannery (1) p. 14. A mid-nineteenth century observer referred to by Osgood (p. 48) describes a type of conjuring seen at Great Bear Lake which closely resembles that found among Algonkian people, but Osgood states that "no information concerning conjuring lodges was gained from sources ~ informants."

[26] The conjurer, Sun-Climbing-the-Sky, was known to her, but she came upon the seance by accident and first viewed it from a distance of about three hundred feet. Referring to the same occasion (3) and speaking in the third person, Densmore says (p. 103), "Standing still, she watched it for about 15 minutes, then approached near enough to hear the singing and drumming and, without being noticed, remained at least half an hour." Under these circumstances, of course, no intimate details of the seance were obtained.

[27] I found out later that he was known by reputation to the Saulteaux of the Berens River. His father, *tepastänam* [radiates light (an allusion to the sun)] was also a conjurer and one of the most famous shamans of the Lake Winnipeg region. The conjuring lodge built for the seance consisted of seven poles and two hoops, with bells attached at the top. It was covered with canvas and in form was identical with those seen later on the Berens River, The seance itself was very short, less than an hour, and only a few *pawáganak* were present. The master of the bears played a considerable part and Jack Fish was there but not *mikīnák*. There was a small flap left open in the canvas at the "front" of the tent. The audience sat opposite to this at a distance of some five or six feet. During the performance this flap was periodically thrown open and the conjurer could be seen dimly within. I asked what kind of a journey I would have, as I expected to leave in a couple of days. The conjurer said that I would arrive at my destination safely, but that I would have a little trouble on the water. (On the way back the canoe was flooded in lining a rapid and I almost lost my notes, photographs and some of my belongings.) I also inquired about the health of members of my family. The answer to this was that they were well. When I inquired what certain individuals were doing at that moment, there was no answer. The old man likewise predicted that I would be successful in my work during the next few years, more so, he said, than in the past. He added that I would know what he had said to be true because on my journey back to Norway House I would run across a certain animal – not he said, a duck (which were plentiful at that season). On our return journey we did have a novel experience. As we approached a point extending out into a lake, far from any camp or settlement, we sighted a dog. The Indians with me [17] speculated how it could have got there. When we rounded the point we found some Indians encamped who had been windbound for two and a half days; the dog belonged to them. My friend J. Wynne Meginnes was my companion on

performances by two different men,[28] both of them under fifty years of age.

What I wish to do in this monograph is to give an account of how conjuring functions in Saulteaux society.[29] First, I shall explain how a man becomes a conjurer, followed by a discussion of the incidence of conjurers in the population today as compared with the past. Then I shall give a description of one of the séances I witnessed, followed by the presentation of some illustrative material indicating the occasions on which conjuring is practiced, and some observations upon the way in which native thought reacts to skepticism in regard to the validity of conjuring. Finally, I shall conclude with a discussion of some less ostensible but extremely important social functions which conjuring as an institution performs in Saulteaux society. [no 18]

---

 this trip.

[28] The first in 1932 and the others in the summer of 1934. My colleague Dr. Dorothy Spencer was present at these latter séances.

[29] [13] With comparative notes to details that have been recorded for other Algonkian peoples, especially the closely related Ojibwa.

IV

THE MAKING OF A CONJURER

ACCORDING to native dogma the ability to conjure is acquired as a "dream blessing" during the puberty fast.[30] It is a supernatural revelation to a human being. There is no other traditionally recognized means of acquiring conjuring powers. A dream gift of this kind cannot be purchased; consequently it is positively denied that one individual teaches another how to conjure. This seems doubtful, but I have no evidence that such is not the case.[31] Conceivably an individual may learn the rudiments of the art for himself by close observation of public performances. But children are not allowed to make a conjuring lodge in play. One of the old men at Little Grand Rapids, not a conjurer himself, but whose father was a famous one, said, "Once when I was a boy I made a lodge and shook it myself. But I did not understand what I was doing. I was trying to do what I had seen done. My father stopped me immediately. He said something bad would happen to me if I played with things like that."

In terms of native theory, a woman can never become a conjurer. This is in harmony with the corollary that men in this society are looked upon as the "natural" intermediaries [20] between the supernatural and man so that women are categorically debarred from the exercise of professional services that require supernatural license. There is one loophole in native theory, however, that makes it possible for women to exercise such functions in exceptional cases. They may do so after menopause when they are considered to be much more like men. Despite this possibility, inquiry yielded knowledge of only two women who had conjured. Both of them lived several generations ago.[32]

---

[30] Cf. Hoffman (1) p. 157; Jenness, p.65; Flannery (2) p. 16. For a general discussion of the nature of this fast see Blumensohn. It is worth emphasizing the fact that formerly all men undertook a fast and except under unusual circumstances received guardian spirits. Consequently, there is nothing distinctive about the procedure through which the conjurer receives his blessing. J.G. Frazer noted this and concluded that "in some communities shamans or medicine-men differed originally rather in degree than in kind from their fellows; they did not form a separate class or profession, but merely claimed to possess in a fuller measure than others that spiritual power to which every adult fancied himself capable of attaining." If it is recognized that the powers of the conjurer are also qualitatively different in some degree, Frazer's statement may be applied to the Saulteaux.

[31] Landes (1) p. 125, says, "... there is circumstantial evidence showing that the *tcisaki* learns his technique in quite lay fashion from several localities" and goes on to give several instances.

[32] Landes (2) p. 177, at the end of her chapter on the occupations of women writes: "Curiously enough, the shamanistic technique of *tcisaki* divining is never attempted by women. Maggie said that years ago there was one woman foolish enough to attempt it, but she soon realized her error and abandoned it. This consistent observance of this one taboo emphasizes the fact that all other masculine techniques – though formally taboo to women as is the *tcisaki* – are adopted by numerous individual women." Evidence that there sometimes were outstanding exceptions to the rule that only men achieve status as conjurers is on record in the form of an abbreviated autobiography of a successful woman conjurer. Her name was Blue-Robed-Cloud-Woman and she came from the Lake Superior country (*Chegoimegon*). Schoolcraft [(2) pp. 169-74] obtained her personal narrative after she was converted. This woman

Raw Hide was well past menopause when she decided to find out what made the conjuring lodge move. She made a sweat bath and invited an old conjurer to it. When they were alone inside she said to him, "Do those *pawáganak* look like human beings?" "No, not exactly," he replied. Again she fixed a sweat bath and when the old man came she asked him how she could find out what the *pawáganak* looked like. "I don't know," he said, "I never look up, I just listen to the voices when I am in the lodge." Raw Hide was determined to find out so she made a sweat bath for the third and fourth time. The last time she gave him a kettle and a pan. "Why are you laying these things before me?" the old conjurer asked, "Do you want to try and manage to do this thing with my help?" "Yes," she said, and gave him more. "All right. I'll let you have half of my *pawáganak* and you can try it," he [21] said.[33] "There is a child who is sick and I'll be in the lodge soon again asking for Life. Notice the kind of sticks out of which the lodge is built. Use the same kind as I do." Later Raw Hide dreamed that she was sitting beside the old man in the conjuring lodge.[34]

When her grandchild was taken ill, she decided that she would try to do what she could. So she had a conjuring lodge made, put on clean clothes and went into it. As soon as she had her hand on the pole the old man had told her to grasp the lodge began to move. She heard voices and she knew which one to ask for Life for her grandchild. The next day this child got better and after that she helped many people. But there are always foolish young men about. One of these thought he would play a trick on Raw Hide when she was conjuring. He shoved his hand in the lodge when it was "rolling." He touched her anus. The *pawáganak* knew what had happened and the lodge stopped shaking. But the woman took no notice of what had happened and the *pawáganak* told her not to quit, so she went on conjuring.

The other woman conjurer about whom I was told lived about four generations back and no one recalls her name although I have one of her sons recorded in my genealogies. No details were given about how she became a conjurer but what is remembered is an episode comparable to that mentioned in the case of Raw Hide. In this instance it was stated that the woman must have been standing on one of the hoops of the lodge with her legs stretched apart, because the man's hand came in contact with her genitals. The tent stopped shaking at once and she never conjured again. The conjurer (B)[35] who told me the story and my interpreter both expressed [22] the view that this woman must have been a faker. It was also stated that she had not reached

---

obtained supernatural validation for her powers in a puberty fast but under exceptional circumstances. Her mother was a widow and furthermore had no grown sons; so she suggested to Blue-Robed-Cloud-Woman that she blacken her face and really fast so that someone in the family would be prepared to meet the hazards of life in their little family group. Le Jeune (Vol. 9, pp. 113-14) refers to a conjuring performance by a woman at Three Rivers, although her tribal identity is not clear.

[33] It is worth noting that the woman was not using spiritual helpers she held acquired for herself; a man who was attempting conjuring for the first time would be assumed to do this.

[34] This fits the pattern of dream validation for conjuring despite the fact that this woman did not obtain her supernatural aides independently.

[35] In the text I have symbolized information obtained from some of these men, or about them, by using capital letters: A, B, etc. My most intimate talks about conjuring were with J. Important checks were obtained from B and L. The performances witnessed were those of J and C.

menopause.

These cases suggest that while women might conjure it was extremely difficult for them to achieve the same recognized status as the men who offered the same kind of service.

In the last generation, since the practice of puberty fasting has declined, native dogma has been elastic enough to sanction dream revelation at *any* time as being equally valid with revelations at adolescence itself. With this exception the old dogma persists, and it is likewise under a disease sanction. Anyone who attempts conjuring without such a blessing is sure to bring some kind of illness upon himself or members of his family. One man (G) of the Berens River Band who developed a phobia which prevented him from going into the woods alone, even as far as two hundred yards, confessed that he had been conjuring without divine license. His mental illness was considered a retribution for this transgression.[36] Unsuccessful conjurers are likewise under suspicion.

As I have pointed out elsewhere[37] I think we can assume that

> in this culture, dream validation of conjuring is not merely a theory, it actually involves real dream experiences of the required pattern interpreted as divine revelation. The mechanical means employed to shake the tent may then be looked upon as a sort of necessary materialistic "evil." Since everyone accepts the supernatural origin of significant dreams, the sincere conjurer is supported by this common tenet of belief, as well as by his private experience. Within such a cultural context, surely this must be convincing enough to make most individuals feel that their efforts are supernaturally inspired, The native charlatan then is a man who has not experienced the stereotyped dreams demanded by the culture pattern, yet, motivated by a desire for prestige or the material compensation involved, undertakes to conjure.

The pattern of the conjurer's dream revelation involves certain nuclear elements which can be definitely specified. Since conjuring, like certain other professional services, is under the [23] patronage of a supernatural entity, the latter is the one who specifically confers a conjurer's powers upon a human being in a dream revelation, whether at puberty or at some other time. The man (J) with whom I talked most intimately about these matters said that he had his first dream about conjuring at two years of age, although at the time he did not understand what it was all about. This man, moreover, did not fast at puberty, but dream experiences in infancy are a sure sign of future greatness.

The "master" of conjuring always appears in the dream. There is no proper name for this entity.[38] He is simply *kádabɛndaŋg* (master) but he is also referred to as *ozagɪzɪɪ ɪwe* (the one

---

[36] Cf. the discussion of this case in Hallowell (2) pp. 1299-1301.

[37] *Ibid.*, p. 1300.

[38] Hoffman, referring to the Ojibwa (p. 157), says conjuring is a gift of the "thunder god." Cf. p. 252 where native pictographs of the conjuring lodge are reproduced. Jenness was also told that thunder was the patron of conjuring (p. 65 and 66n). Berens River informants denied this but they said that the *pawáganak* call the conjuring tent "Thunder Birds' house" (*pinesiwīgamik*) so that it is possible that my information is not complete. On the other hand, the possibility of local and tribal variation must be taken into account. In Flannery's account, for example, *mistabeo* "is the chief spirit of the rite, a sort of master of ceremonies,

who takes them out) – of the conjuring lodge. Every conjurer dreams of the master. In one of my interviews with the man mentioned above, he said, "the one that gave me the tent is not far away. He is listening to all I say." I could not obtain a description of the appearance of the master of conjuring, however. All my informant said was, "There is one *ätsokan*[39] who is great and looks great. Some of them look like men but not this one."

I was told that the individual dreams that he is in the conjuring tent which is shaking. This is due to the presence of the winds which are thus inextricably linked with conjuring.[40] So is *mikīnák*, the Great Turtle, who acts as an intermediary and as a messenger in all performances.[41] Together with the [24] master, these are the nuclear group of *pawáganak* which are traditionally associated with conjuring on the Berens River. Other *pawáganak* may become associated with them in the dream of a particular individual and thus become interwoven in the pattern. The dream pattern of conjuring for the individual is a gestalt; the different *pawáganak* associated are not dreamed of separately, but together. It is believed, however, that other familiars of the conjurer can be called to the tent in a particular performance. This is what makes some conjurers stronger than others. Consequently, outside of the nuclear group, the spirits which appear in the tent of one conjurer are not necessarily those which appear in that of another. This individuation is also reflected in the structural details of the tent, the number of poles used and the kind of wood from which they are made. These vary from conjurer to conjurer.[42] All these details are part of the dream revelation. Furthermore, it is necessary that this dream occur four times. And it is illegitimate to attempt to conjure after the first or second revelation. If a man tries to do so, he will fail; none of the *pawáganak* will come to his lodge. The man (J) who told me this said that a couple of years before, a young man came to him and, after laying some presents before him, said he wished to ask something. He said that he had dreamed of conjuring and that later he tried to do it and failed. "How many times did you have this dream?" my informant asked. "Twice," the young man replied. "That is the trouble; you did not wait long enough." It was useless for the young man to make any further attempts. His chances were spoiled. He never could become a conjurer.

The home of the master of conjuring is located in the West, but it is not conceived to be

---

    an interpreter for the other spirits." But *mikīnák* (*mistce-naku*) is extremely important, being one of the three spirits who *have* to be there.

[39] One of the synonyms for *pawágan*.

[40] This may be too categorical a statement since J said that the boss of the west wind does not come except when he is specially needed.

[41] *Mikīnák* was the messenger on the occasion described by Henry in the eighteenth century. The same function is ascribed to this spirit by Coleman (p. 53) and Densmore (2) p. 46. Hoffman (1) pp. 158, 252, refers to the role of *Mikīnák* as that of an intermediary. Cooper found the Great Turtle connected with conjuring among the Lake of the Woods and Rainy Lake Ojibwa.

[42] Schoolcraft says [(l) I, p. 389], "The number of poles is prescribed by the *jossakeed*, and the kind of wood." Henry says the poles of the conjuring lodge he saw were "of 5 different species of timber." Cf. Densmore (3) p. 102. Speck (MS) remarks that the Montagnais lodge may be of different kinds of wood, indicating that the conjurer is going "to control the various trees to further his work." The use of different kinds of trees must be an old and integral part of the rite.

on the earth. In the first three dreams which an individual experiences he finds himself in this western region. In the fourth dream the master brings [25] the neophyte to this earth and instructs him in the selection of the materials to be used in making the conjuring lodge and the construction of it. The master also tells him when to conjure for the first time. He specifically designates the moon in which he is to do it, and it is important that it take place during this period without fail. If a conjurer fails to follow any instruction given him his *pawáganak* may not come when he summons them and he may run the risk of being overcome by another conjurer.

Conjuring must not be done too frequently, or just for fun, or to show off. There must be a real need for it. The master of conjuring knows the situations which demand it. You cannot expect him to work for fun.[43] It has been said that conjurer J at Little Grand Rapids conjurers too much. There is the implication that he might have been more successful on certain occasions if he had conjured less frequently.

An examination of the family connections of conjurers living at present and those of earlier generations that appear in my genealogies did not reveal any striking facts. It is true that there are several cases in both present and past generations where a father and one or more sons have been conjurers; but there are just as many cases where this is not so. Consequently, it may be concluded that there has been no regular transmission of conjuring technique in paternal lines[44] that might suggest the existence of an unformalized pattern of transmitting information. This point is worth mentioning since the reverse is true with respect to leadership in the midewiwin, where the purchase of knowledge is conventional, and, although patrilineal succession is not formally recognized, there is positive evidence that such is the case, especially in the Sturgeon sib. [no 26]

---

[43] Jenness, pp. 65-66, assigns somewhat different reasons for the limitations upon conjuring. "The ordeal was too exhausting, or, as the Indians say, the helping spirits disturbed too greatly the medicine-man's soul." Speck (MS) says, "The operation of the conjurer's cabin is so exacting upon the performer that when he has finished his rite, he is left in a very weak physical state. No wonder! Yet this condition is attributed by his followers to the exhaustion of the *mantu*, 'power,' through being drawn upon by his soul-spirit. He recuperates his strength slowly thereafter."

[44] Cf. Schoolcraft (1) V, p. 423, who states that "there is no succession of the office."

V
HOW NUMEROUS ARE CONJURERS?

IN 1934 there were at least seventeen men living on the Berens River who had been known to conjure at one time or another. Despite the fact that it is impossible to know what proportion of the adult male population were conjurers under aboriginal conditions, there is no reason to suppose that the number of conjurers should have increased under modern conditions. Considering the opposition of the missionaries to the practice and the fact that, according to the Dominion Census of 1934, only 130 Indians on this river are listed as adherents of "Aboriginal Beliefs" (a very conservative figure), I was surprised to find the number of conjurers as high as it was; but perhaps it is not so strange in view of the vitality of native beliefs among these Indians; and the functions of conjuring.

A comparison of the number of adult men (i.e. those over 21 years of age in the census) with the number of men who, according to informants, have conjured at some time or other, not only measures the incidence of conjurers in the contemporary population but affords an illuminating clue to past conditions.

BAND	ADULT MEN	CONJURERS	%
Berens River	71	2	2.8
Little Grand Rapids	59	13	22.0
Pekangikum	53	2	3.8
	183	17	9.2

If under contemporary conditions almost 10% of the adult males are known to have practiced conjuring, it seems reasonable to suppose that under aboriginal conditions the proportion must have been considerably higher. My guess would be that [28] in a population equivalent in size there would have been at least twice as many conjurers.[45]

The basis for this estimate is suggested by the vital role which conjuring has always played in Saulteaux life considered in relation to the seasonal groupings and movements of the population. During the season of open water in the spring and summer there is a centripetal movement of the population. Families congregate at the fishing settlements. In the fall and winter there is a centrifugal movement. The entire population splits up into winter hunting groups that live m relative isolation from each other during the months when the waters of the

---

[45] Until recently there were eight or ten conjurers at Poplar River. This is a lakeside band to the north of the Berens River Band. According to the 1934 census there were 41 adult males over 21 years of age in this band so that the proportion of conjurers is comparable with that found in the Little Grand Rapids Band.

lakes and rivers are frozen and when the pursuit of the fur-bearing animals and large game is the major economic activity.

The Indians of Little Grand Rapids and *Pekangikum* still follow this seasonal pattern. They split up into thirty winter hunting groups averaging sixteen persons each. Each group is composed of blood kindred and affinal relatives; they are seldom composed of a single biological family. Although I cannot go into the evidence here, there is reason to believe that the size of these hunting groups was even larger in the past than at present and that there were fewer of them. However that may be, in aboriginal days at least one conjurer must have been found in every winter hunting group.[46] For it is precisely during the long winter months that the hazards of life are greatest and the need for the help and guidance of the supernaturals most urgent. Even today this hypothesis is borne out to some extent by conditions in the Little Grand Rapids Band. These people break up into nineteen winter hunting groups and practically all of the thirteen men who have been known to conjure in recent years belong at present [29] to – or in the immediate past were associated with – different hunting groups. For the Pekangikum Indians still farther up the river I have less detailed information. At the mouth of the river acculturation has proceeded so rapidly in the Berens River Band that while the men still go off to their hunting grounds in the winter they usually leave their wives and children behind in a settlement which is occupied all the year around. In this latter band, then, we find the fewest conjurers, the breakdown of the old seasonal movements of families and, as part of the acculturation process, the most complete conversion to Christianity.

It should be further emphasized that under contemporary conditions the incidence of conjurers in the population does not measure the incidence of conjuring. Most conjurers, in fact, have given up conjuring. Indeed, all of them except one man of the Pekangikum Band are nominally Christian. Besides this, three of the Little Grand Rapids conjurers are old men in poor health so that it is not likely that they will conjure again under any circumstances.[47] On the other hand, one of the men (C) I saw conjure in 1934 was not much over thirty, so that if the practice soon disappears it will be largely due to a change in beliefs and attitudes under present conditions of life and not the result of the passing of an older generation of conjurers.

---

[46] It is interesting to note that Paul Kane, writing of the latter part of the fur-trading period in the West, says that a conjurer was "generally found in every brigade," i.e., parties of Indians engaged by the fur traders or others in travelling through the West.

[47] On my first trip to Little Grand Rapids (1932) I tried to induce one of these men (B) to conjure, but without success. B said his powers were like a fire, they had burned brightly at first but now that he was old they did not give much light. He went on to say that the last time he had tried to conjure (a year before) he had failed. The *pawáganak* would not come. A young man was sick and he was trying to discover what the cause of the trouble was. Then B's brother, another old man (P), went into the tent but with no success either. From other sources it has been stated to me as a generalization that when a man grows old his *pawáganak* begin to leave him so that he is not able to do what he could when he was younger.

VI
THE ECONOMICS OF CONJURING

AMONG the Saulteaux it would be erroneous to speak of conjuring as if it were a profession, that is to say, the occupation from which a person derives his living. No Saulteaux ever earned a small fraction of his livelihood in this way. But conjuring has a gainful aspect. It is a specialized type of service for which a fee is paid to the conjurer. As in comparable transactions among the Saulteaux this fee is always paid in advance but it is not standardized. Certain goods are laid before the conjurer at the time his services are requested. He may refuse to conjure if he does not consider the fee adequate, or for any other reason. If he picks up the goods laid before him this is an indication that he will go ahead with the seance.

Along with the fee a sacrifice (*pagítcīgan*) is always included. This sacrifice consists of tobacco. The distinguishing feature between the fee and the sacrifice is not one of kind, because some tobacco may be included in the fee. But if so, this tobacco, like the goods, is consumed by the conjurer. The tobacco sacrifice, on the other hand, is distributed among those present at the conjuring performance. The smoking of it in this context is an offering to the *pawáganak* present. This is what makes it a sacrifice. I once engaged a conjurer and gave him a good fee as well as some tobacco. For some reason the seance was delayed a few days. On the afternoon of the scheduled performance he came to me in some embarassment because he had smoked the tobacco. I had to give him more because the seance could not have been held without a smoke offering.

One of the reasons why a conjurer cannot make a living by conjuring is because the fee he receives is relatively small. One informant, for instance, said a conjurer might receive some tea and a shirt for his services, or perhaps a couple of [32] dollars worth of stuff in all. In a case mentioned later, tea and tobacco to the amount of two dollars were said to have been the fee given to a conjurer by a woman who wished to have her lost son located. My informant commented that this was very cheap. In another case a conjurer told me that he received a blanket, belt, a pair of pants, a dress and some print for his wife as his fee, in addition to tobacco. He considered this a relatively high fee. It is obvious that a man would have to conjure very frequently indeed if he were to depend upon such fees for his living.

Furthermore, a man is not supposed to conjure too much, and very young men are not believed to have reached sufficient maturity to be good conjurers. It is better to hold one's powers in reserve. It is such considerations which explain both why it is that there are so many conjurers and why a particular man may only conjure occasionally. This was made possible by the large panel of conjurers that existed under aboriginal conditions. In one case that I know of a man only conjured once. He had the proper dream and in the dream he became aware that he would have power to cure a woman under certain circumstances. When these circumstances arose he conjured and cured the woman. He never conjured after that. In the case of the conjurer B, who was an old man at the time I knew him, I was surprised to learn that he had only conjured four times in all. Under modern conditions, however, which have led to the decline in the number of conjurers and in the incidence of conjuring, one might expect to find that the men who can conjure conjure more. This is the case in the Little Grand Rapids settlement where I think it safe to say that a certain man has conjured several times a year during the last decade. However, it is said that this man conjures too much. Paradoxically enough this fellow is miserably poor. Although he may receive only a pittance when he conjures, undoubtedly he is glad to get it.

In the present as well as in the past, certain individuals specialize in curative services in addition to conjuring. Having several strings to their bow this offers them greater possibilities [33] for material benefits. Landes[48] also comments on the economic aspects of these "multi-skilled practitioners" among the Ojibwa groups she studied.

But so far as conjuring itself is concerned, the major compensation in Saulteaux society was the prestige value that accrued to individuals able to perform this service. The reasons for this will be increasingly clear when the occasions for conjuring are discussed. [no 34]

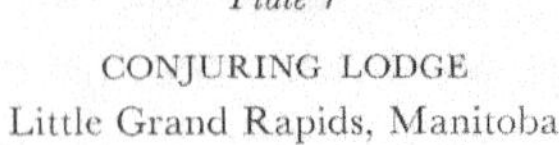

Plate 1

CONJURING LODGE
Little Grand Rapids, Manitoba

Plate 2

SAULTEAUX CONJURERS

---

[48] Landes (1) p. 125.

VII

A CONJURING PERFORMANCE

CONJURING [35] is always done after sunset.[49] The conjuring lodge is put up an hour or so earlier. It is never built by the conjurer himself;[50] he gives instructions to two or more men who build it according to the specifications given them. While the general plan is the same, the details differ somewhat, especially in regard to the number of poles and hoops used[51] and the wood selected. Several of my Berens River informants mentioned lodges of 40 poles; one man said such a lodge was built of a double row of poles. I am not inclined to take this number literally since the Indians are not trained to numerical precision. The significance of their statements is psychological; it reflects their attitude toward conjuring. Conjuring lodges constructed of so many poles would be immobile so far [36] as human strength is concerned, and since they are supposed to have shaken immediately upon the entrance of the conjurer, the inference is that only the "winds" could be responsible. The most extreme instance that I ever heard of was the claim that Chief Fiddler, a Saulteaux of Sandy Lake (north of the Berens River), was known to conjure in a tent sixteen to eighteen feet in height and constructed of sixty poles set close together! A Berens River trader who had been in the employ of the Hudson's Bay Company for fifty years told me that once he bet a conjurer at Little Grand Rapids that he could shake a tent. The agreement was that the trader would build a lodge for the Indian to conjure in and vice versa. The trader said he built one of poles several inches thick which he drove four feet in the ground. He could not budge the tent and neither could the Indian, so that the latter never built one for him.

---

[49] This seems to be without exception so I shall not cite the literature on this point.

[50] Skinner is in error when he says that the Cree "conjurer retires to a secluded spot and builds" a lodge (p. 67). While some of the early accounts, e.g. Champlain and De la Potherie, might lead one to suppose that the conjurer builds his own lodge, this is a point that might easily escape notice without inquiry. LeJeune, at least, makes it clear that the lodge is built by others and scattered observations at later periods make it seem likely that this was the general custom and not a local variation. Cf. Black p. 13, Jenness, p. 66, Coleman, p. 51, Flannery (1) p. 11. Speck (MS) says the conjurer "will often command someone to build him a 'cabin' by using a circumlocution saying 'cut me some sticks,' which is understood to mean 'build me a conjurer's cabin'."

[51] Comparative data on the number of poles used and other structural details are to be found in the following sources: Le Jeune; Le Caron; Oldmixon; Henry; Hoffman (1), (2); Jones; Kane; McDonnell; Cameron; McKenney; Franklin; Densmore (1), (2), (3), (4); Skinner (3); Coleman; Black; Jenness; Godsell; Fannery (1); Winchell; Schoolcraft (1) V; Speck; Nelson; Mandelbaum. The range in the number of poles used is from four to sixteen. The latter figure was given by Coleman's informant who once helped to construct a lodge of this number; six to eight are most frequently mentioned, although it is noteworthy that Le Caron (1618) says; "I have seen a master juggler who raised a cabin with 10 large posts, which he planted deeply in the ground." Landes (1) p. 122, says the framework of the lodge "consists of 16 ploes ...." This cannot be the number ordinarily used.

The conjuring lodge may be either set up in the open, which is usually the case in summer, or it may be erected within a dwelling.[52] In winter the conjuring lodge must of necessity be erected where there is some protection, as it is too cold for people to sit around out in the open. Among the Saulteaux it used to be set up in the *cábandawan,* a multiple family dwelling. In recent years cases are known where a conjuring lodge has been set up in a log cabin by boring holes in the floor for the poles with an auger. It must always be put up in a "clean" place, that is, somewhere free from human or animal excreta. One of the conjuring performances I witnessed did not turn out very well, that is, only a very few *pawágan* could be invoked. Later some human excreta were found on the spot where the tent had been set up and this fact was seized upon as an explanation. [37]

A detailed description of one particular lodge follows.[53] (Compare Plate 1 and Figure I.)

It was constructed of six upright poles driven into the ground to a depth of one and one half feet.[54] These poles were set in a circle whose diameter was four feet.[55] They were not driven

---

[52] This was the case at the seances witnessed by Carver and by Henry. The latter says "the first thing to be done was the building of a large house or wigwam within which was placed a species of tent, for the use of the priest and reception of the spirits." Densmore (4) p. 313, refers to a case in which the conjuring lodge had been set up in the attic of a house. Cf. Mandelbaum who conveys the idea that the Plains Cree conjuring lodge was always set up inside a tipi, and Grinnell who reports it for the Cheyenne.

[53] I was able to make the measurements referred to below by arriving at the spot on the morning after the performance. The conjuring lodge was no longer standing but the poles were there. Later, they were taken back into the bush and left in a "clean" and unmolested place. The sketch is a reconstruction based on the dimensions of these poles. The photographs show the stages in the construction of another conjuring lodge of approximately the same dimensions utilized by the same conjurer on another occasion (1934). The third conjuring tent I observed among these people was constructed of ten poles (eight stout ones and two slimmer ones) and four hoops. I think that it was more than seven feet in height and perhaps four and a half feet in diameter at the ground level. Like the others it was covered with canvas and birch bark. My opportunity to examine it closely came after the performance was over but I was not prepared to take any measurements. It was a more delicately balanced structure than the others and extremely easy to set in motion. It is asserted, however, that the best conjurers can shake a tent that is so stoutly built that it is immovable so far as ordinary human strength is concerned. Densmore (1) p. 124, e.g. reports native testimony to the effect that on one occasion three men entered a lodge after the performance was over. "One stood on the ground; one climbed halfway to the top, and one to the very top. These men tried with all their strength to sway the structure but could not move it in the slightest degree." Yet it was with reference to this lodge that Densmore's informant stated that when his uncle had been inside it bent "like a sapling so that the top almost touched the ground." For the Oxford House Cree Mason reports that the frame of a conjuring lodge sometimes was braced "by ropes in several directions, tied near the top sides and pegged to the ground. The wigwam was very rigid and could not be moved at all."

[54] A Menomini informant {source} told Densmore (3) p. 102, that "a shallow hole was dug for each pole, and this was made deeper by a sharp, heavy pole which was thrust downward into the hole until it was about 10 inches deep." The lodge poles "were blunt at the lower end and

perpendicularly into the ground but inclined downwards toward [39] the center at a slight angle.[56] The poles themselves were nine feet long[57] and two to two and one half inches in diameter. Three were of spruce and three of birch. They were so solidly set that instead of pulling them out after the performance three of them were hacked off at the ground level with an axe. The tops of these poles were attached to a hoop which formed the top of the lodge, the diameter of which was two feet, seven inches. The poles, which were diverging at ground level, were thus bent in a curve, and gave a slightly bulging, barrel-like form to the structure, the maximum diameter being near the middle; I estimated the latter to be about five feet. The lodge was approximately seven feet in height.[58] Three other hoops equidistant from each other were bound to the poles between the ground and the top of the structure. Like the poles, two of these hoops were of birch and two of spruce. They were bound so firmly to the poles that one could stand on them.[59] The bottom of the lodge was covered with freshly cut spruce boughs, such as the summer dwellings of these Indians usually are floored with. To the hoop at the top of the lodge was tied a string of caribou hoof rattlers[60] [40] which sounded at the slightest movement

---

were placed in the holes made in this manner, the earth being firmly packed around them. After a performance the poles were sometimes found to be embedded in the ground a foot and a half." Cf. Densmore, (1) p. 123, where it is said that the poles of the Ojibwa lodge were sunk two to three feet in the ground. P. Jones, p. 151, says they were driven into the ground to a "depth of a cubit." The conjuring lodge described by Henry consisted of "five poles, or rather pillars, about ten feet in height and eight inches (sic) in diameter. The holes to receive them were about two feet deep; and, the pillar being set, the holes were filled again with the dirt which had been dug out." Godsell likewise says two feet, as do Speck and Mandelbaum.

[55] Densmore (3) p. 102, Jenness, p. 66, and Godsell mention the same diameter; Mc Donnell and Kane say three feet. The circular arrangement of the poles is so typical of the lodge among the Saulteaux that the constellation Corona Borealis is called a conjuring lodge.

[56] The only place that I have found this feature mentioned is in the account of an Ojibwa seance narrated by Paul Beaulieu to Hoffman and Garrick Mallery. See Hoffman (1) p. 277.

[57] Longer poles are mentioned by several observers but we are not always told how far they were driven in the ground, or the height of the structure. Densmore (1) says, twelve to fourteen feet (sunk two to four feet in the ground); Coleman, twelve feet; Henry, ten feet; Mandelbaum six feet (sunk two feet); Schoolcraft (1) V, p. 421, is the only one to speak of poles fifteen or twenty feet long; I judge that he heard this but did not see them.

[58] Estimated height in feet as referred to in the literature is: Le Jeune, seven; Henry, eight (deducting two in the ground); Oldmixon, eight; Jones, six; McKenney, twelve; Densmore (1), nine to eleven, (allowing for sinkage of poles); Winchell, eleven; Speck, six to seven; Mandelbaum, four to five. Thus the range is four to twelve feet.

[59] Not all observers refer to these hoops. Godsell mentions them, but does not say how many. Le Jeune, Franklin, Jenness and Henry mention only a hoop at the top. Jones says there are one or more hoops; Black mentions two, Landes three, Nelson three, Flannery (2) four or five (sometimes), Winchell four, Densmore (1) refers to eight, but in (3) says there may be two, four, six, or eight, Speck (MS) has a sketch of a lodge with two hoops, one at the top and the other four feet from the ground. He was told they must be strongly attached.

[60] "' Calkins refers to the noise made by the "rattling of bells and deers hoofs fastened to the

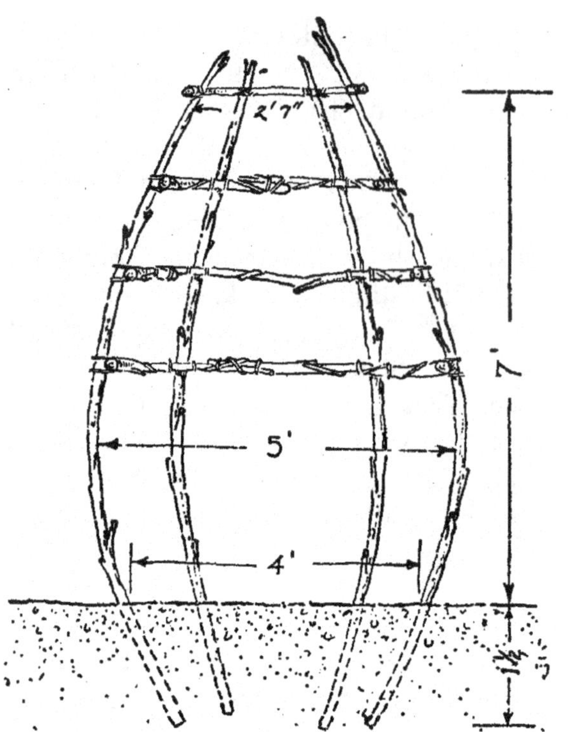

Figure 1 CROSS SECTION OF A SIX-POLE CONJURING LODGE [38]

of the structure. The lower part of the lodge was covered with several rolls of birch bark (*wigwáscxpakwe*), which are the conventional coverings of summer dwellings. Around the top of it was thrown a piece of canvas,[61] the lower edge of which was pulled down below the birch bark covering. In order to hold the birch bark and canvas in place, a carrying strap was tied about the middle of the lodge.[62]

---

poles of the lodge at the top... " Black refers to a can of shot being tied to one of the poles, and Jenness, p. 66, says "four deer dew-claws attached to one of the poles rattled whenever the lodge was shaken...." For the Menomini Densmore mentions bells [(3) p. 104]. Landes (1) p. 122] says: "From the top horizontal [hoop?] suspends a string loaded with bells." Mason also mentions bells used by the Oxford House Cree. Cf. Mandelbaum.

[61] Densmore, (3) p. 102, remarks that for the Menomini "the outer covering was formerly of birch bark, but later was of cloth, on which there was no paint." Hoffman, p. 147, also mentions bark or cloth.   Skinner (3) p. 193, refers to "bark, bulrush or reed mats." Champlain says the structure was covered with the conjurer's robe; LeJeune (Vol. 12, p. 17), that robes or blankets were used. De la Potherie and Oldmixon both mention animal skins, as does Alexander Henry and Franklin (moose). For the Ojibwa-Saulteaux at a later period we find reference to mats, blankets or skins (Winchell), rawhides bound with thongs (McDonnell), bark or skins (Godsell), bark (Kohl, Black, Jones). Jenness (p. 66) says, "... rolls of birch bark, or in recent times cloth," enveloped the framework. Speck says they were bark covered. Beaulieu mentions bark and blankets. Landes [(1) p. 122] says, "... the bottom third of the tent is covered with canvas."

[62] Schoolcraft [(1) p. 421] refers to and illustrates a lodge of eight poles, "one of which is

Thirty or forty people had gathered for this particular seance and they disposed themselves in a circle about the lodge.[63] It [41] was possible to sit as close as one desired, but few

---

terminated by its natural foliage; its summit has several small branches upon which are suspended the offerings to the spirits." The only mention of such a feature anywhere else in the literature is in Landes, (1) p. 122, who says "... the center [*sic*] pole is cedar, stripped naked like the others, but with a tuft of leaves remaining at the top."

[63] Skinner [(1) p. 153] referring to the Saulteaux makes the curious statement, entirely without support anywhere in the literature, that "the bystanders *grovel on their hands and knees* in a circle about the conjurer's lodge" (Italics ours). Skinner, despite his wide contacts with both the Cree and Saulteaux, evidently never witnessed a conjuring performance. This probably accounts for his statement (p. 67) that among the Cree the Indians "gather at least 25 feet away from the spot forming a circle around the lodge through which no one is allowed to pass." At the Cree seance described we sat only a few feet away from the lodge. Black, describing a seance witnessed in 1929 (White Sands Ojibwa) says, "As it darkened and the moon came up, the Indians squatted in a circle around the wigwam at a distance of four or six feet from it."
Schoolcraft's generalized account of a seance [(1) pp. 421 ff.] should be read. It contains a number of unique details that I have not seen mentioned elsewhere nor heard about nor seen among the Saulteaux, e.g., singers who sit on the north side of the lodge, whereas the audience must sit on the south side; details of invocation, etc.
Mr. Allan Nelson, a clerk of the Hudson's Bay Company at Little Grand Rapids, gives an excellent impressionistic account of a conjuring performance among the contemporary Saulteaux (1936). I am indebted to his friend Mr. Leonard Mason for these notes. Nelson writes:

After all preparations had been made a number of Indians squatted in a large circle around the tent and patiently awaited the coming of the conjurer. During the construction of the tent it is customary to give the conjurer a stick or two of nigger-head tobacco, black and vile-smelling stuff it is too.... I took my place in the circle along with A, my interpreter, and sat waiting for things to happen; we sat perhaps ten or fifteen minutes before our magician put in his appearance. There was a campfire burning not far away from us and it cast a red glow over the tent, and on the forms of the hunched Indians and squaws wrapped in quilts to guard against the chill of the evening. It was chilly, as this was taking place early in May. Every time a match was struck and hands cupped to light a pipe, the features of the Indians seemed to stand out remarkably sharp. I was awakened from my thoughts by the appearance of the conjurer.   There was a low hum of conversation as he entered the circle and approached the tent. Immediately he entered the tent, someone was there to close the flap. Almost at once, the tent began a jerky, to-and-fro motion, the bells set up a terrific din and the conjurer began his chant to the spirits.
For some time he kept up his monotonous incantations calling to the various spirits. Wayward spirits they must have been, for it took him some time before the first of them appeared to answer his beck and call. The Indians squatting around the tent must have sensed his difficulty in contacting them, because every so often a few of them would give vent to an enthusiastic "How! How!" As though these exclamations gave him a new burst of

sat nearer than four to six feet. Upon the arrival of the conjurer, his assistant (*skabéwis*)[64] who remains within call during the performance, unloosened the tump line bound around the structure and by shifting the birch bark to one side the conjurer was able to squeeze in.[65] According to native theory the lodge should begin to shake before the conjurer is fairly inside. But it did not do so in this case, which was a matter of slightly unfavorable comment the next day. Instead of entering the lodge at once the conjurer may circle it clockwise. Conjurer D was said to do this. My interpreter's great-grandfather used [42] to do the same. He would grasp a pole here and there and shake the structure. Then he would bend down and enter the lodge. As soon as his head was inside it would start to shake and continue doing so until the end. The conjurer McKenney saw climbed to the top of the lodge and sat there muttering awhile, sang a song and then descended into the enclosure.[66]

The conventional position which the conjurer is supposed to assume in the lodge is one of the common male sitting postures. The knees rest on the ground and the buttocks are against the heels. It is the ordinary posture of a canoeman paddling in the bow; but in the conjuring lodge the upper part of the body is bent forward until the head almost touches the ground.[67] No rattle or drum is ever taken into the lodge by Berens River conjurers as a routine matter.[68] With his right hand the conjurer grasps one of the upright poles not far from the ground. As soon as he does so he "feels something strange," I was told, and the structure begins to vibrate.

---

strength, the tent began rocking at a terrible rate and the conjurer raised his voice in almost religious fervor, to beg his spirits to come.... All this chanting, tent-shaking, and bell-ringing, mingled with "How's" kept up for almost two hours or more ... A told me whenever a spirit was heard and I remember one of them especially. This was the water spirit [*mikīnák?*']. When he, she, or it, spoke, a kind of gurgle seemed to accompany the sound of the voice. There was this faint gurgle in each sentence as though the words were coming through water. I would never have noticed it, had not A drawn my attention to it. ... Before I left, I went over to the tent and gave it a shake. For all its rough usage in the past few hours, it was still firm.

[64] Such assistants function in connection with alt Saulteaux rituals and ceremonies.

[65] The conjurer must put on clean clothes before entering the lodge. This is a symbol that he has purified himself before attempting to get in touch with the supernatural entities, that he is *pékīze*. Boys going on a puberty fast also observe the same rule.

[66] Cf. Densmore (3) p. 105. Jefferson (p. 76) refers to a Cree conjurer who was tied up and then "inserted" through the top of the lodge.

[67] Cf. Schoolcraft (1) I, p. 389. Speck describes the same posture. Mason obtained the same information at Oxford House.

[68] Jenness (p. 65) says the conjurer used neither drum nor rattle in the lodge. Other writers specifically refer to the rattle (Cameron, Kane, Cooper, Jefferson, Mandelbaum) and Schoolcraft [(1) p. 210] refers to both. In W. Johnson's interview with a conjurer (Hardinge, p. 486) the latter himself speaks of the rattle. Nevertheless we cannot be sure whether the Indians believed it was the *conjurer* who used either instrument m the lodge. Among the Berens River Saulteaux I was told that when a drum or rattle was sometimes introduced into the conjuring lodge during the seance, it was the *spirits* who made use of it, particularly the semi-human creatures called *memɛŋgwéciwak.* The conjurer himself is never supposed to use either drum or rattle.

A retired conjurer (A) of the Grand Rapids Band, a man about seventy, told me the following anecdote which happened when he was a boy. His uncle, Flatstone, a conjurer of the previous generation, once took A into the tent when he was going to conjure. Flatstone pointed out a certain pole and told him to hold on tight to it but not to look upward. A did as he was told but found it hard to hold on, the pole was so slippery. Besides he was frightened by the loud voices which came from the top of the tent. Finally he could maintain his hold no longer. He let go and the tent stopped shaking. [43] Flatstone called to the *skabéwis* and he helped A out. A said he had tried to get out himself but the poles were too closely planted together. On this occasion Flatstone was conjuring to find animals for the hunters. He told them where to go and they killed a bear and six caribou.

L, the son of Flatstone, himself a conjurer, said that he too had been taken into the tent by his father on more than one occasion and was also told to hold on to one of the poles. Once he got scared because when he felt around for his father with his free hand the latter had disappeared. He let go the pole and the tent stopped shaking at once. L called to the people outside and asked whether his father was there. The reply was that he was not to be seen. The *skabéwis* removed part of the lower covering of the tent but the narrator remained inside. One of the *pawáganak* spoke. L's mother, who was outside, understood. Then the lodge began shaking again. Then L's mother said, "Listen, someone is shouting." Everyone listened and a sound was heard way off to the east, then another and another, each one closer. Finally there was a fourth overhead and all of a sudden Flatstone was discovered standing in the audience close to the lodge. Then he went in again.

During the course of the performance the conjurer may call the *skabéwis* to the lodge or the *skabéwis* may wish to say something to the conjurer. When he does so he always stoops down and places his head close to the birch bark near the ground where the conversation, sometimes whispered, is carried on. The conjurer's voice, when he spoke in his own character, likewise seemed to proceed from near the level of the ground.[69]

After the conjurer had disappeared within the lodge the *skabéwis* began to distribute the tobacco which is a "sacrifice (*pagítcígan*)" made by the person who requests the conjuring. It is distributed to all present who smoke in honor of the [44] *pawágan* who are potentially present even before they manifest themselves. At intervals during the entire performance the refills the pipes of members of the audient as long as the tobacco lasts.[70]

With the exception of a few brief agitations of the tent from time to time by the masters of the winds, the other spirits were so tardy in making their appearance on this occasion that I thought the séance was going to be a failure. The conjurer engaged in brief bits of conversation with members of the audience during this period. "Nothing is coming (*kanesá*)," he kept mumbling over and over again. But different members of the audience kept encouraging him. "Don't give up," "Wait a little longer," they kept saying. And the conjurer would reply saying

---

[69] In this connection it is interesting to recall what the Indians said to Le Jeune, "Enter thou thyself into the tent, and thou wilt see that thy body will remain below, and thy soul will mount on high." Kohl's informant referred to "two voices speaking inside, one above, the other below. The lower one asked questions which the upper one answered" (p. 279). As he was later informed by the conjurer himself, "the top of the lodge was full of them," i.e., spirits.

[70] For this tobacco fee, see the accounts of Henry and Kane.

that he was doing his best. Among other things he was heard to say, "I'd be glad to hear you for a while." This was addressed to the *pawáganak*. Finally there was a more continuous agitation of the structure and a spirit came in who sang a song. This was *kamändímizawīt*, the master of scapulimancy, although I did not know this at the time. I found out later that it was one of the conjurer's chief guardian spirits, a *pawágan*, which had appeared in his original dream revelation. The song of this spirit might be said to be the theme song of the whole performance.[71] It was sung in a robust vigorous manner and was repeated at intervals during the remainder of the performance. Its mood and well accentuated rhythm made a deep impression upon me. One could imagine a Chaliapin singing it with great effectiveness.

Soon several members of the audience began calling for *mikīnák*, the Great Turtle. "*Mikīnák! Mikīnák!* Whereas *mikīnák?*" the Indians shouted and, as soon as he arrived, a gentle ripple of laughter swept over the audience. *Mikīnák* [45] talks in a throaty nasal voice not unlike that of Donald Duck. It is extremely characteristic and very easily distinguishable from other voices that emanate from the tent.[72] His popularity with the audience was manifested throughout the evening by the almost constant stream of repartee which took place between members of the audience and this *pawágan* when he was present. Anyone may speak directly to *mikīnák* and he always has a witty answer ready. While this custom of direct address also applies to a few other spirits, it is not applicable to most of the spirits which come to the conjuring tent. The character of *mikīnák*, however, which is a semi-comic one in their mythology as well, easily lends itself to this more intimate communication. *Mikīnák* is good natured and easy going. He is quick witted and loves a joke. And to me there was an intrinsic humorousness about the quality of his voice which seemed quite in harmony with his reputed character and the attitude of the Indians toward him. Since *mikīnák* is always present in every conjuring tent, the Indians acquire a familiarity with him which is not vouchsafed them in respect to the other *pawáganak*. And he strikes a note of levity in performances which, after all, are serious enough in purpose.[73] Sometimes *mikīnák*

---

[71] 70a The songs heard in the conjuring lodge are considered to be the songs of different *pawáganak*. My interpreter corrected me more than once when I made reference to a *conjuror*'s songs. A conjuror almost never sings one of the songs of his outside a séance. No one else sings them either. An Indian I know well was much impressed with a song he heard in a séance. It carried the words, Open the sky from the center, i.e. clear away the clouds from directly over head. Once he began to sing this song when traveling with the conjuror's son. The latter made him stop immediately.

[72] Cf. Henry's account in which it is stated that " ... now a voice not heard before seemed to manifest the arrival of a new character in the tent. This was a low and feeble voice resembling the cry of a young puppy. This sound was no sooner distinguished than all the Indians clapped their hands for joy, exclaiming that this was the Chief Spirit, the Turtle, the spirit that never lied!" Among the Menomini it was the small turtle, the mud turtle, that made a whinnying sound. See Densmore (3) p. 104. It may be that Champlain was referring to *mikīnák* when he wrote: "And when they ^the conjurers] speak in a cracked voice, the rest think that the devil is speaking and is telling them what is going to happen in their war and what they must do."

[73] The Little Jack Fish, *kītnozɛs*, is another *pawágan* said to be very amusing in the conjuring tent. He will pick up and repeat phrases or sentences uttered by members of the audience. Sometimes Indians who know a few English words will say these and a great deal of

will wrestle with his brother-in-law (*nīta*) the Lynx and the movements of the lodge will indicate their struggles. Or he has been known even to dance,[74] on which occasions the tent is said to move up and down, following his [46] movements. Often the Indians will pass a plug of tobacco into the tent just for *mikīnák* to enjoy a smoke. When smoking he has the peculiar habit of emitting a long uninterrupted whistle.

The special function of *mikīnák* in the conjuring tent, however, is to act as a sort of intermediary between the other spirits and the conjurer and to serve as a messenger.[75] He it is who is sent on long journeys to distant parts of the country to find out the information requested by members of the audience. When anyone wishes to ask such a question, it is customary to call the *skabéwis* to one's side and state the inquiry to him, at the same time giving him a small quantity of tobacco. The *skabéwis* then goes to the conjuring lodge, repeats the question to the conjurer, and hands him the tobacco. This tobacco is a fee, not a sacrifice. On this occasion I said I wanted to know how my father was, as he had been very ill and I had received no mail. After the conjurer had been told my inquiry he repeated it aloud and someone in the audience called out, "send *mikīnák*!" And in a moment or two *mikīnák* started on his journey to Philadelphia.

The progress of the Great Turtle's various journeys are conventionally symbolized by the decreasing agitation of the lodge as he gets farther and farther away. The caribou hoof rattlers are important here in creating characteristic auditory effects. Members of the audience made various comments as he journeyed on and on.

"I wonder how long it will take him," said one. "He can't travel very fast," said another, a remark which provoked great laughter. "I wonder whether he's stopping somewhere to eat," said a third person, when the tent ceased shaking for a moment but did not remain at rest. "It won't take him long to come back," called out another Indian. [47]

Suddenly the tent gave a jerk and absolute quiet reigned for a minute or so. *Mikīnák* had arrived at his destination. Then a faint swishing sound could be heard and the tent began to shake with increasing violence. Harder and harder it shook and swayed rapidly from side to side, when, with a deep thud,[76] it stopped abruptly. *Mikīnák* had arrived in our midst again.

"What news?" someone called out.

---

amusement is derived from hearing Little Jack Fish trying to pronounce them. Another familiar *pawágan* is *miskwádesi* (the smaller variety of turtle) called younger brother (*niceme*) by *mikīnák*.

[74] Cf. Densmore (3) p. 104.

[75] Schoolcraft [(1) V, p. 421] writes that the turtle "is the babbler, the interpreting spirit, the secretary, the speaker of the assembly of manidos. It is through her that the spirits and the jugglers speak to the people, and she must be addressed to learn something of the juggler and of the spirits." In Schoolcraft's account *mikīnák* is addressed as "old gossip." Cf. Flannery (2) p. 16. "*Miceke* (turtle) is the chief spirit in the tent. He is said to talk just as the Indians do and they can understand him. *Miceke* is responsible for getting the other spirits into the tent ... but while these spirits are heard, the Indiana cannot understand what they say and *Miceke* 'interprets' for them."

[76] For a comparable symbolism announcing the arrival of spirits in the conjuring tent see Schoolcraft (1) V, p. 421; McKenney, p. 329; Hoffman (1) pp. 158, 277; Densmore (2) p. 46; Jenness, p. 66.

"I didn't go," replied *mikīnák*. "I hid behind the poles." This is an old gag of *mikīnák*'s but it brought a laugh. Finally the Great Turtle stated the results of his mission in a sort of recitative style. He said that if he had found the right place my father was no worse. And he added, as if by way of verification, that he had found him living in a stone house, not in a log cabin. He said that I would get further news when I reached the mouth of the river.

Two other persons on the same occasion made inquiries similar to mine. One inquired about his brother who had been sent to jail because he was accused of starting a forest fire. The answer given was that the man was well and would arrive home shortly. We met him coming up the river a week later. The other Indian, who had left a brother sick with double pneumonia at the mouth of the river a few days previously and for whom there seemed no hope of recovery, wanted to know how the sick man was. The answer in this case was that he would recover. When we arrived at the mouth of the river he was up and walking about. And when I arrived home at the end of the summer I found *mikīnák*'s report concerning my father's health was not only judiciously phrased but quite true. He was no worse. Neither had he improved in health.

In the meantime several persons in the audience had called for a spirit called *wematigózi*. While this is a generic term for any white man[77] among the Berens River people it is a specific [48] term for Frenchmen elsewhere and probably one of the earliest terms for white men in Algonkian languages. It is also the specific name for one of their *pawáganak*, who is also a mythological character. In view of the actual source from which these northern natives probably acquired tobacco, it is interesting that *wematigózi*, when he comes into the conjuring tent, usually gives out some tobacco. But although the substance produced by this *pawágan* resembles tobacco in appearance and can be smoked, it is not the commercial variety which is well known and constantly used by the Indians. Just what this *wematigózi* brand is made of is therefore a mystery to the Indians and to me.

The reason why they called for *wematigózi* was to obtain some of this tobacco. Finally he came into the tent and sang his song. Then he told the audience that if any one could repeat his song without making a mistake he would make him a present of some tobacco. He was asked to sing his song again and he did so several times before anyone in the audience ventured to repeat it. Finally one old fellow (L) who was sitting close to the lodge and who had indulged in a lot of repartee all during the evening, tried to sing the song. But he had sung only a couple of

---

[77] Flatstone, a Berens River conjurer of a generation ago, also had this *pawágan* as a helper and used to produce tobacco. Once when everyone was out of tobacco the people asked Flatstone to obtain some from *wematīgózī*. After the conjuring lodge was set up Flatstone took several pieces of paper and folded them. "Put these over there in the bush," he said to a man called Boucher. Then Flatstone entered the conjuring lodge and the *pawaganak* began to come in. W*ematigózi* sang a song as in the performance I have described. After a few trials a member of the audience managed to sing it. At this, *wematīgózi* laughed. "Now you'll get some tobacco," he said. Then the conjurer told Boucher to go into the bush and bring back the papers he had left there. It was moonlight, so it was easy to find them. Boucher brought the papers back and opened them. There was more than a cupful of loose black tobacco in one. In another there were plugs of (twist) tobacco. "Fill your pipes," said Flatstone. So everyone had a good smoke. The twist plug was given to the old men. Flatstone, himself, did not smoke the tobacco. "My father was there" said conjurer B, who told me this story.

phrases of it when he made a mistake and everyone laughed. So *wematigózi* repeated it once more. Another Indian then tried his luck with no better success than the first. Several others did the same, among them a young fellow who started off well enough but who burst out laughing himself as he failed to come entirely through it. *Wematigózi* obligingly sang it over again and said he would give tobacco to the person who would sing half of [49] his song correctly. A young man accomplished this, whereupon the *skabéwis* went to the lodge, obtained the tobacco and delivered the prize to the successful competitor. Immediately there was a rush of some of the younger men to the vicinity of the winner. Matches were struck and someone produced a flashlight so that I was able to catch a glimpse of the tobacco. It was in the form of a round pellet about a half inch in diameter and similar in color to tobacco of the commercial sort. It was passed around and examined with the greatest interest after which it was smoked.[78] I might say that no woman is allowed to touch this tobacco or to attempt to sing *wematigózi*'s song. And no woman took part in any of the repartee, although I do not know whether this is absolutely forbidden.

The audience was not satisfied with such a pittance of tobacco so someone called on *mikīnák* to sing the song of *wematigózi*. The idea was that the Great Turtle, being a spirit, could sing the song perfectly and thus obtain a larger amount of tobacco which he could then be induced to share with the audience. But *mikīnák* refused. He said, "If I sing the song you won't get anything." This caused a laugh and he did not sing the song.

The performance ended soon after this, since one of the hoops of the lodge had broken. This was a matter for amused comment since earlier in the evening *mikīnák* had said that the lodge did not seem very strong. The master of conjuring always dismisses the spirits and, as I said before, he is referred to as "the one who takes them out." He is always the last one to go. But sometimes *mikīnák* cannot be found anywhere. Some other spirit may sometimes be sent to find him. As [50] usual he is discovered lurking behind the poles. But occasionally someone in the audience will warn *mikīnák* that he is being sought and then it may be still harder to find him.

There were a number of other *pawáganak* who had manifested themselves during the performance, but I found that the Indians themselves were not quite sure of their identity in every case and it was impossible to list them contemporaneously under the conditions imposed. The chief difficulty is one that observers from the seventeenth century down to the present have noted: the unintelligibility of the language that issues from the lodge. This feature combined with a certain amount of ventriloquism seems to be an ancient and stable aspect of conjuring.[79]

---

[78] When I was talking privately to the conjurer later about this performance he made some interesting remarks about this tobacco. He said, "You saw that little piece of tobacco? Well, it looked very small, barely a pipeful. But there was more of it than you thought. They told me that quite a few pipes were filled with that little piece," The tobacco, in short, possessed properties of magical increase! This is reminiscent of episodes in Saulteaux mythology of the tiny dish or kettle that automatically replenishes itself after a bit of meat or moss berry is put in it. Nothing could illustrate with more cogency the fact that even today the actual behavioral world of the Saulteaux is not sharply set off from the world as depicted in myth. The same kind of events occur in each. The conjurer also told me on the same occasion that sometimes in the winter when he has run short of tobacco and cannot leave his family to make a trip to the trading post, he has been able to get a little of *wematīgózi*'s tobacco!

[79] Champlain writes that "these rogues ... speak in a language unknown by the savages." Le

     In point of size the spirits in the tent are reputed to be extremely tiny. They sit on the hoops[80] and, when these are [51] full, on the upright poles. To the eye they are said to look like minute sparks or tiny stars. Sometimes an old conjurer will take his grandson into the tent with him for a while and from the reports of such eyewitnesses people know what the *pawáganak* which come to the tent look like. Two men who had been in a conjuring tent when they were boys told me what they saw.[81]

Jeune says the conjurer disguised his voice "so that it seemed to me I heard those puppets which showmen exhibit in France," and that "sometimes he spoke Montagnais, sometimes Algonquian." Henry describes the vocal effects produced as the sounds of numerous voices "some yelling, some barking as dogs, some howling like wolves and in this horrible concert were mingled screams and sobs, as of despair, anguish and the sharpest pain. Articulate speech was also uttered, as if from human lips, but in a tongue unknown to any of the audience. ... During the space of half an hour, a succession of songs were heard, in which a diversity of voices met the ear. From his (the Great Turtle's) first entrance till these songs were finished we heard nothing in the proper voice of the priest." Carver speaks of the "mixed jargon of the Chippeway, Ottawaw and Killistinoe languages" that issued from the tent. Coming down to a more recent period Cameron reports that the conjurer makes "a terrible noise in a language the bystanders cannot understand." Cf. letter from Larrabee to Tallmadge (Hardinge, p. 484) and Densmore (3) p. 104. Wau-chus-co, the conjurer interviewed by Johnson (Hardinge, p. 486) said, "The words of the spirits were audible to the spectators outside, but none could understand them but me." Cf. Landes (1) p. 122 and Skinner (3) p. 194; the latter, referring to the Menomini says that ... "the *je'sako* talks to the gods through the medium of the turtle, *Mikana*, who speaks Ojibway ... the various powers mumble and grumble in a way only intelligible to the turtle and the conjuror. Often the conjuror is unable to follow the discourse and is obliged to fall back on his reptilian interpreter."

[80] Diamond Jenness, p. 66, in referring to the upper hoop, says that its purpose is "partly to hold the frame together, partly to provide a seat for the helping spirits." Speck reports that one of his informants said, "The spirits all come and sit on the hoops according to their power." One of Leonard Mason's Oxford House Cree informants said, "The conjurer sees the spirits as little bits or sparks of fire sitting around the top of the wigwam on the top hoop inside." The same idea was expressed by a second informant. Skinner (3) p. 194, remarks that "It is thought that most of them (i.e., the spirits) seat themselves on the [51] top-most ring of twigs about the lodge frame, but a few always are seated on the floor in a circle."

[81] The man who acted as *skabéwis* in a performance to be described later was a skeptic and asked the conjurer to let him take a look inside the tent. When he stuck in his head and looked upward he said he saw small lights like stars around the top. Jenness, paraphrasing the description of informants, is more specific in regard to the position and appearance of the *pawáganak* in the lodge than any other writer. He says (p. 66); "We cannot see them, but we understand that turtle rests at the bottom of the lodge, feet up, keeping it from sinking into the ground; that thunder is at the top, covering it like a bird; and that the other spirits are perched around the hoop that encircles the frame. They look like human beings about 4 inches tall, but have long ears and squeaking voices like bats." Two other of his informants, however, "maintained that turtle is at the top of the lodge and that thunder never enters, even

The audience quietly dispersed after the performance and the conjurer emerged. He had been in the lodge about three hours[82] and it was close to midnight.

The tent is dismantled the same night or very early the next morning. The poles and hoops are carried to a "clean" place in the bush, stacked against a tree and left there. To disturb them is taboo. They never are used in any other conjuring performance, for firewood or for any other purpose. The attitude of the Saulteaux toward the poles and hoops of a conjuring lodge is vividly illustrated by an experience of Mr. Allan Nelson at Shining Falls, Manitoba in 1936. He says:

It was my first spring among the Indians, and I was still virtually a greenhorn. At that time I had been in the service [of the Hudson's [52] Bay Company] only five months. I had been sent to Shining Falls with a trading outfit for the spring hunt, A coming along as my interpreter. On our arrival we decided to move into an old deserted Indian shack and move into our tent later on. We finally got the store part settled, with a counter being made, and all the goods out on display, we were ready for business. However there was something lacking in our outfits – bunks. There were no bunks to sleep on and I was getting rather disgruntled about having to sleep on a row of wooden cases as I had been doing. A slept on the jumper. We could not sleep on the mud floor as it was soaking wet, even though we had several inches of spruce boughs spread out. I decided one day to make myself a bunk and went out to the bush with intentions of getting some poles to make it with. I had not gone far when I came upon a bunch of dry birch poles leaning against a tree. There, I thought, was just the thing, so wrapping an arm around them I carried them back to the shack. I was busily engaged at hewing them flat on one side when an Indian came up. I went on, hewing all the poles down one side to make them even to lie on when I happened to glance at the Indian's face. I don't think I have ever seen so many emotions registered on a face at one time as I did then. His mouth hung open drooling, his eyes wide with something akin to startled horror depicted in them. Apprehension, above all else, was clearly written on his face. He asked A where I had got the poles. A asked me and I told him. A three-way conversation between the Indian and me took place for a few minutes. Then, with something like a grin, the Indian told A to tell me that these same poles had been used in a conjuring tent once and that if I slept on them spirits would bother me at night. Strange to say I slept on those poles all the time until we moved into the tent and never once did I see or hear anything. They must have been kind spirits because my bunk was quite comfortable – comfortable as far as pole bunks go. [53]

---

[82]   though it is from thunder that most of the conjurors derive their power."
81 It is interesting to note that both Le Jeune (Vol. 6, p. 165) and Calkins refer to this same period of time. Kane estimated the duration of the performance he witnessed as two hours. I have been told, however, that they often continue longer and one might suppose that the time varies widely. One of the other Saulteaux performances I witnessed was cut short; the other was at least three hours. The Cree performance was more in the nature of an exhibition and was shorter than either. Densmore [(3) p. 104] speaks of performances lasting all night.

VIII
THE OCCASIONS FOR CONJURING[83]

IN the performance just described, conjuring was undertaken in order to secure information about the health and welfare of distant persons.[84] However, local persons may be ill and then a conjurer may be consulted about their chances of recovery.[85]

Since a conjurer may exercise curative, as well as clairvoyant, functions, he is at times called upon to treat the sick. Usually this only occurs in cases where both functions operate integrally, that is, in those instances where acute physical or mental symptoms suddenly manifest themselves or where an illness has not responded to other methods of treatment. Under these circumstances the Indians become apprehensive and a conjurer may be asked to discover the hidden, cause of the trouble as well as to cure the patient. This characteristic and specialized function of the conjurer is clearly differentiable in Saulteaux society from other curative services and at the same time it directly reflects certain facets of Saulteaux notions of disease causation. Disease may not only arise from sorcery, [54] in which case its cause must be diagnosed as such in order that proper curative measures may be initiated; it may be due to moral transgressions on the part of the sick person or his parents. It is these hidden causes of disease that call for the services of a conjurer. Until they are known and a confession secured, in the event that they are due to some transgression, no medicine will be of any avail.[86]

An acute situation arose in one of the summer settlements of the Berens River Indians a

---

[83] Cf. Schoolcraft (1) V, pp. 422 ff., where he gives a whole series of questions that may be asked of a conjurer. Informant J said, "Everything that is said in the tent is true. Anyone who wants a true answer gets it. I never knew it to happen otherwise."

[84] This evidently has remained one of the most constant purposes of conjuring. We find it referred to by Henry who writes "... individuals were now permitted to seize the opportunity of inquiring into the condition of their absent friends, and the fate of such as were sick." Cf. Cameron, "... he answers the questions which may be put to him and which generally relate to the return or whereabouts of absent friends for whose safety they may have been uneasy." Kanesays,"... many questions were asked him by the Indians, some inquiring after the health of their families at home, whom they had not seen for many months." Coleman cites a case (p. 52) in which the conjurer informed an Indian that his son, away at boarding school, was ill. The father did not believe it at first, because he had received no word. But finally he went to the school and "found his son at the point of death." See also Calkins.

[85] Cf. Le Jeune, Vol. 6, pp. 167, 169; Calkins and Jenness, pp. 67-68. The séance witnessed by Densmore (4), according to the statement of the conjurer Himself, was undertaken to discover whether his treatment of a sick man would be a success.

[86] Henry (the younger) evidently had this kind of case in mind when, referring to a particular conjuring performance, he writes; "... then he interpreted to the bystanders what his manitow had told him concerning the case – the cause and nature of the sickness, and then some crime committed which prevented the cure." Unfortunately no details are given. Cf. Hallowell (4). Probably there is a similar implication in the statement made to Mason at Oxford House that "if there was a sickness, the spirits could be asked the trouble and the cure."

few years ago when it was thought that a young girl had gone crazy.[87] A conjurer was called in, probably because sorcery was suspected, although this was not openly averred. In this case, the suspicion was not substantiated because the conjurer failed to discover the cause of the trouble.[88] If sorcery is found to be the cause of the illness in such a case as this, then a further step may be taken. If the conjurer succeeds in identifying the sorcerer the soul of the latter may be brought into the conjuring tent for interrogation or even punishment.[89]

In another case, a conjuring performance that I witnessed was precipitated by the fact that a young man lost consciousness on two occasions within a few days. There was no discernible reason for this and his relatives were greatly disturbed. In this instance I was unable to discover whether the boy's father had confessed some transgression privately to the conjurer or not. But gossip had it that years before the old man had conjured illegitimately, that is, without a genuine dream revelation. If this were true, the cause of his son's illness lay in that fact – he suffered because of his father's transgression. [55]

There is a special term (*õdjináduwaso*) for this type of illness, and in this case it would have been brought about by what the Saulteaux term "deceit" (*ewaiejicitiwewin*). Specifically, this means the offering of any kind of professional services under false pretense, that is, without supernatural validation, A person conjures, or uses "dreamed" medicines or attempts to cure by the sucking technique (*nī'bakīwin*) without a genuine dream revelation. He may have been doing any one of these things for years. He may even have enjoyed good health himself. But then one day a child of his falls acutely ill or some sickness persists beyond its usual limits and no medicine seems to cure it. It is such situations that baffle the natives and require the clairvoyance of the conjurer in order to get at the cause of the illness.

Of course there are other transgressions besides "deceit" that may be at the root of the trouble. One large class of these is sexual in nature. How a conjurer arrived at the cause of the illness in one such case is illustrated in the following account.

W could not pass his urine freely. He had been treated by a conjurer but the medicine he had been taking did not help him. When he heard that this Indian was going to conjure, W asked him to try to find out why he did not get better. At the séance W's mother, a woman past sixty years, was sitting at his side. After the performance had been going on for some time and a number of *pawáganak* had manifested themselves, one of these supernatural beings said, "How is the sick Indian feeling tonight?" W replied, "Not very good." Then the *pawágan*, *memɛŋgwecī*, sang a song. After this was finished *memɛŋgwecī* spoke again. "It is some of my medicine that my grandson [i.e., the conjurer] has been giving away. I don't know why it should not do its work. Perhaps some of the old people did something wrong. I'd like to know if I am right about that." At this one of the men in the audience said, "Why don't you speak?" He was sitting near W's mother who asked, "Are you speaking to me?" "Yes," said the other Indian. Then the old woman remained silent for a little while. Finally she spoke: [56]

---

[87] Cf. Flannery (2) p. 17. "Just as on Parry Island the Indians of Manitoulin and the North Shore are terrified lest an enemy bewitch them, and practically every mention of a *djiskid* was in connection with his ability to locate, through the shaking tent, the sorcerer responsible for making someone ill, and the successful removal by him of the 'poison.'" An account of a cure follows.

[88] I have discussed the details of this case elsewhere. See Hallowell (3).

[89] Cf. Jenness, p. 67; Hoffman (2) pp. 148-49, Densmore (3) p. 102.

I don't know. Perhaps it is true. A long while ago there were four of us playing together – two boys and two girls. I was only a little girl then. We had made a little wigwam and we were playing that we were camping like the old folks. Of course I did not know that I was doing anything wrong. I had a little thimble belonging to my mother and I was sewing. One of the little boys was lying down and I was lying down, too. His little penis was standing erect. I took the thimble and shoved it on the end of his penis. Then I told him to go and piss. He said, "I can't. I can't. It's too tight. It hurts." Then he started to cry a little. So I took the thimble off and we told him not to tell.

After this recital the conjurer said, in his own voice, "I thought there was something that stopped the medicine from working."

But what happens in cases where the parents of an individual are dead and yet may be suspected of being the innocent cause of some illness suffered by their children? This contingency is also provided for. If a conjurer be strong enough he can bring the souls of the dead into the conjuring lodge.[90] This is of infrequent occurrence, but an eyewitness of one such performance gave me the following account.[91]

In the early fall [October] of the year[92] when the War started I[93] was camping at Sandy Bar. There were several other families from Berens River and a Poplar River man, William Franklin. We were fishing. One evening when some of us were sitting in his tent, William said, "I'd like to try something. I want to conjure before the snow falls, but the kind of trees I need for the lodge don't grow here."

"What kind of sticks do you want?" I asked. "I'm going to take my fish to Berens River tomorrow." [57]

"I want seven ciŋgubīwatigok [94] and one or two green birch sticks, straight ones," said William. So I agreed to cut the kind of trees he needed and bring them back with me. After I had returned the next day two other men and myself put up the conjuring lodge. We started before dark and it took us an hour or a little more. The same day another man and his family had arrived from the Berens River Reserve. This man, Jacob Berens, was sickly, and when he found that William was going to conjure he went to his tent and asked him to try and find out why the medicine he had taken did him no good.[95]

---

[90] Cf. Hallowell (6) for an extended account of the spirits of the dead. So far as the literature goes I have not been able to discover a single reference to the presence of spirits of the dead in the conjuring lodge. That it is not merely a local development, however, received verification on an occasion when, through Dr. Hoebel, I met an old Cheyenne who said that it occurred. A contemporary Saulteaux conjurer (B) whose father was a much more famous man of the same class, told me that *djibaiyak* sometimes enter the conjuring lodge voluntarily while the seance is in progress.

[91] Note the emotion engendered in this case by the reputed presence of deceased kindred.

[92] 1914.

[93] Arthur Felix who was a close friend of the man who did the conjuring.

[94] The generic term for the evergreens.

[95] The description of the conjuring performance is oriented with respect to this man's request and is thus only a partial account of all that took place.

After sunset William came out of his dwelling. He had his coat on and carried a blanket and pillow. He used the pillow to kneel on while in the conjuring lodge. He went into the lodge and at once it began to shake. All the people were seated around it. Before he went in William called me to him and handed me some tobacco wrapped in a handkerchief.[96] He said, "Give this to the people, give everyone a pipeful." I did as he told me and after he was inside I called to him and said I had some left. At this William replied, "That tobacco does not belong to me. It belongs to 'our grandfathers.' Pass it to anyone that wants a smoke."

By this time the tent was shaking harder and the *pawáganak* had started to come in. They named themselves and sang their songs. All the winds were there and, of course, *mikīnák*. There were also present *memɛŋgwecī, pījīu* (Lynx) and many others. After a couple of hours some one came in singing very, very strongly. I heard William saying to it, "One thing I was asked and I don't know the answer. You are one of those that sees many things. You can look around and tell me what I don't know." Then this *pawágan* sang again, a very long song. It was the boss *djībai*.[97] Then this *pawágan*, spoke, "I saw something a long, long way back. It's the old people's fault this man here is sick."

Then the boss *djībai* talked to the sick man (J.B.):

D: How long have you been sick? '.

J.B.: Quite a long while.

D: Where are you sick?

J.B.: I'm always feeling pain around my waist. It is as if there were something drawing me together there. [58]

D.: Your father has something to do with this. If you like I'll call him and ask him to come in here.

J.B.: (half to himself)[98] I wonder if it can be so?

Then someone whispered to J.B.: It's all right. Go ahead.

So he said: I'd like to hear my father.

The boss *djībai* sang again. All at once, while this was going on, someone else came in the conjuring lodge. The singing stopped and everyone sat very quiet.

Then William spoke: Here is the one you asked for. You can talk to him. (The tent was shaking very gently now.)

J.B.: Is that you, father?

F.: Yes, my son.

J.B.: Who are you with?

F.: I'm with my grandchild. Ever since I left, I've always been happy. I've never been hungry. I've never been thirsty. I've never suffered any pain. It is a beautiful country where I am living. When I was alive I always tried to do what was right. Try to do the same thing, my son; don't do anything wrong to anyone. If there is ever anyone who says something bad to you, don't answer. That's the way I tried to act. If you act this way you will be glad. You'll see me some day, too, I see some people I

---

[96] The narrator was acting as *skabéwis*.

[97] i.e., the master of the spirits of the dead.

[98] The narrator commented here that it seemed as if he did not believe it could be true.

know sitting outside. I see my oldest daughter!

Suddenly another voice, that of a child, came from the conjuring lodge.

C.: I see my mother sitting there. Don't do that, Mother. I don't like to see you do that. (The woman whose father and adopted daughter appeared in the conjuring tent was crying.) You hear my voice here. I'm happy. It is always bright like day where I live. It is never dark. There are pretty flowers where I live, it's like a great garden. And there are lots of us. There are great singers there, too. Don't forget what I am telling you. Live right and some day you'll find me.

Then the father of J.B. spoke again:

F.: Have you taken much medicine for your sickness, my son?

J.B.: Yes, but it has not helped me.

F.: There was one time, my son, that I made a mistake. A man died and I dressed him for burial. I pulled his belt too tight. I pulled as hard as I could. That is what makes you sick now. [59]

That is the reason the medicine you have taken has not helped you. The medicine cannot work itself down into your body.

J.B.: I hope I will get well now.

F.: My son, I hope you will. It's my fault that you have been sick around your waist.

Then William spoke again: I don't know what kind of medicine to give this man tomorrow morning. Is there anyone here inside that has some medicine I can give this man?

At this point *memɛŋgwecī* spoke up: I'll give him a little.

William: You can give it to him tomorrow morning.

M.: No, I'll go and get it now.

So he went out.

J.B.: I wonder how far he has to go.

Pawágan: There is only one place to go.

Someone in the audience: Where is that?

Pawágan*: ɛŋgwecīwak* live at kickábiskan, high rock.

Soon the *memɛŋgwecī* was back in the conjuring lodge and said to William: When morning comes you give that Indian this medicine of mine I have brought you and tell him how to use it.

Conjurers are able not only to detect sorcery and moral transgressions as the cause of illness, they can exercise sorcery themselves. "Soul abduction" is believed to be their characteristic modus operandi. But it is necessary to stress the fact that this power is not always used with malevolent intent. The soul of a man from a distant community, for instance, may be brought into the conjuring tent to find out the latest news about the people there or just for a brief visit. One of my informants once attended a séance in which the conjurer was heard to say, "I'm calling for the man from Lac Seul." Shortly afterwards there was a thump, indicating a new arrival in the tent, followed by a strange voice which said, "I was sleeping, but I heard you calling me." This was the soul of a noted Lac Seul conjurer. People in the audience asked for news and received replies to their questions. Then the soul of the visiting conjurer sang a song and departed for his home some two hundred miles away.[99] [60]

---

[99] 98 Densmore [(l) p. 124] says that an eyewitness of a séance on the Grand Portage Reservation

But a conjurer may also summon the soul of a sleeping individual to his lodge because he wishes to do this person an injury. The latter may have insulted him, or one of the members of his family. This was believed to be the case by a man who told me how his soul was once summoned by a conjurer.[100]

I was just about 16 years old when someone tried to kill me. This is what happened. We boys were playing ball one day and I got one of them mad. I guess it was my fault. He was a "humpy" and his father was a conjurer. The humpy looked so funny when he ran that I ran the same way to tease him. All the boys laughed but he got mad and said to me, "You'll remember this." This happened in the summer and I soon forgot all about it. I was too young to understand what he meant. The next winter, in *migazīwīzis* (eagle moon),[101] we were camped about four miles up the river and all ready to pull out the next day. Everybody was well. That night after I had gone to sleep I saw someone coming from the north directly toward our camp- It was a young man. He came and stood at my feet as I lay sleeping. He spoke to me, "You are wanted over there" (motioning with his lips toward the north).[102] I got up and started off with him. I found that we were traveling through the air, not along the ground. I looked down and saw a river ahead of us and just one *pi'kogan*,[103] I could see the kind of trees growing there. There were lots of very straight jack pine, on the north side of the river. Now we came down to the ground near another kind of tent. I walked into it. There I saw the humpy's father in the center. I could see no end to the tent, it stretched out as far as I could see and it was full of all kinds of people. I knew then that I was inside a conjuring lodge. "I'm going out," I said. But the old man said, "No! You can't go." Then I saw my own head rolling about and the "people" in the lodge were trying to catch it. I thought to myself that if only I could catch my head everything would be all right. So I tried to grab it when it rolled near me and finally I caught it. As soon as I got hold of it I could see my way out and I left. Then I woke up but I could [61] not move my legs or arms. Only my fingers I could move. But finally I managed to speak. I called out to my mother to make a light. I told her I was sick. When morning came I was still sick. I could not even manage to move my head, I told my father about what had happened. He knew at once that someone had done something to me and that I had really been in a conjuring lodge. All that day and the next I lay sick. Then I got better. It was my soul that the conjurer had drawn away while I was asleep. If it had not found its way back to my body, I would have been found dead in the morning.

---

told her that "a friend who lived many miles away was suddenly present in the lodge and that she heard his voice distinctly." Among the Oxford House Cree, Mason was told that "a man could not call the spirit of any dead ancestor, but could of a living one. For instance if a man here wanted to talk to his grandfather at York Factory, the spirit appeared within the tent and talked to his grandson in a natural voice, recognizable to the grandson."

[100] Cf. the case mentioned by Jenness, p. 68.

[101] Corresponding to our month of March.

[102] A typical gesture for indicating directions.

[103] A conical wigwam.

Another Indian had a similar experience. The circumstances leading up to it were as follows: Once he was out hunting with some other young fellows. They came up to the traps of an Indian of another band. The Indian had to defecate. His companions started to tease him by asking him whether he would be bold enough to defecate on one of the traps. (Insulting not only to the owner of the traps, but a certain deterrent to any animal which might come that way.) He did so and sprung the trap so that a piece of dung was left sticking out. Some months later he dreamed that his soul was taken into the conjuring tent of a man of the same band as the Indian whose trap he had defiled. He did not know how to escape. But one of the poles from which the lodge was constructed hid him in the center of it. In this way he escaped death. The inference is that the young man must have had the master of the particular species of tree from which the pole was made as one of his *pawáganak*. It was this familiar which helped him to escape.

In all cases where persons who are apparently in good health when they go to sleep are found dead in the morning the explanation is that some conjurer has abducted their souls during the night. It is believed that not many individuals escape death whose souls are called into a conjuring lodge with malevolent intent. On the other hand it is possible that the conjurer may only desire to cause a temporary illness or insanity. A person who loses his senses or goes out of his mind is spoken of as *kawín otcatcákwsī* (no soul), and it is believed that this condition is caused by a conjurer who has maimed the soul of this individual. [62]

A conjurer may likewise summon to his lodge the soul of a rival conjurer or one whom he believes to have done him injury, for a showdown.[104] Each conjurer then summons all his *pawáganak* in turn and there is a battle royal between the opposing sides. It is a dramatic struggle to the death, right before the eyes of the audience.

I was told a story about a contest between conjurers in which my interpreter's great-grandfather, Yellow Legs (*uzáuwaskogat*), was victorious. There was a conjurer by the name of Lynx Head, *pijīustigwan*, who lived on the Winnipeg River, 150 miles to the south. He was very powerful but he was a bad one, too. During the winter he starved out Yellow Legs by sorcery and one of the latter's children died. This made him very angry. Yet he feared that he was not strong enough to overcome Lynx Head. So he asked another conjurer, *ndábazis*, whom he called *nīta* (cross-cousin or brother-in-law) to help him. *ndábazis* is agreed and so these men ordered two conjuring lodges to be built, each one of them to be made of forty poles. As soon as the sun went down these conjurers went into the lodges. Lynx Head knew already what was going on and very soon after Yellow Legs had entered his lodge Lynx Head could be heard talking to him there.[105]

"You can't manage this," he said. "You are not good enough to defend yourself against me. I'll get the better of you."

And Yellow Legs answered, "You've been after me a long time. I want you to quit."

"No! I won't leave you alone," said Lynx Head.

"All right then, we'll have it out," replied Yellow Legs.

All three conjurers now began to bring their *pawáganak* into the two conjuring tents. Lynx Head divided his between the two. It was not long before Lynx Head said *kawesá* (that's enough) because the conjuring lodge of *ndábazis* was full. But Yellow Legs, who was feeling more powerful all the time, replied, "Bring them all in here," and he

---

[104] Cf. Skinner (3) pp. 195-96.

[105] i.e., the soul (*otcalcákwin*) of Lynx Head was present.

still kept bringing in more of his own. So Lynx Head brought all his helpers [63] into Yellow Legs' tent. Finally Lynx Head said, "That's all I've got." But Yellow Legs did not believe him. "You're lying," he called out, "but I'll find out for myself." So he asked one of his familiars, who was the master of the wolves, to find out if any of Lynx Head's helpers were hiding anywhere about. (If even one were missed, it would be impossible to overcome Lynx Head.) So the wolf started out to look for the *pawáganak* of Lynx Head and he succeeded in finding several of them. One was even hiding in a hollow piece of grass.

"Now, we'll have it out," said Yellow Legs. And all the different *pawáganak* of these two men now began singing. They began to form themselves into two bodies for the final test of strength.

While this was going on, Yellow Legs called out to his *skabéwis*, "Pass me *tago''*." This is what he called a carved representation of *pinésī*, the Thunder Bird. So the *skab'ewis* passed in the carving.

Yellow Legs was getting so strong that even *ndábazis* was scared. He called on four of his strongest *pawáganak* to help him. One of these was *kak* (porcupine), the others have been forgotten. *Ndábazis* said to *kak*, "I remember when I dreamed about you. You looked just like a mountain to me. This is the time I need you for my shelter." So *kak* took the old man away to protect him.

But the fight between Yellow Legs and Lynx Head had only started. Both of them began to sing and to use all the magic power at their command. It was just as if there were only two bodies in the tent now. It was bending and shaking like trees in a storm. Every now and then a thump could be heard. This was when one of the spirits was hit. Yellow Legs was depending on *pinesi* most of all and gradually as Lynx Head began to lose strength the tent shook less and less. Finally Lynx Head was heard moaning and crying as he realized the end was near. Then the tent stopped. This was the last of Lynx Head. He was found dead in his own camp the next morning. His soul never got back. [64]

In contrast to the foregoing instances where conjuring was undertaken to kill someone, I was told that, in former days, attempts sometimes were made to bring the dead or moribund back to life.[106] The conjurer would dispatch his helpers to the Land of the Dead and attempt to lure the departed soul back to its body. The soul would be heard speaking in the conjuring lodge but no one would understand it except the conjurer. The son of Owl (conjurer B) said that his father had attempted this many times, especially with children. Sometimes he had been successful.

Because of the strength derived from his supernatural helpers, a conjurer is able to deal effectively with dangers of a supernatural order that threaten the whole community. If at any

---

[106] Cf. Skinner (3) pp. 194-95. Among the Menomini the soul is coaxed back to the body "by whistling on a wooden tube." The soul approaches the tube, is caught and imprisoned there by the conjurer. This receptacle is then fastened to the patient's breast and kept there for four days, during which time the patient must lie quiet and no noise is permitted in the camp lest the soul be frightened away and not return to the body. I do not know whether a similar procedure applies to the Saulteaux. Skinner remarks that it is unique in North America but has a parallel in Malaysia.

time a camp, especially in winter, is menaced with the approach of a *windigo* the only protection is conjuring. Now a *windigo*, of the type here referred to, is a cannibal giant of immense proportions, taller than the highest stand of trees. Such beings are the focus of the most intense fear that the Saulteaux know. Since a *windigo* is "made out of a sorcerer's dream" the only protection that is available is the exercise of greater power on the part of another sorcerer to divert the monster from his course or to kill him in open combat. There are men who have accomplished the latter but not in the conjuring lodge. If a *windigo* is discovered approaching a community the conjurer, if his spiritual helpers are strong enough, may ward him off and thus save the lives of the human beings who are threatened.

One of my informants was living on the Poplar River several decades ago when such an occasion arose. During a terrific blizzard a *windigo* was reputed to be advancing from the north. The Indians were so terrified that they moved their wigwams to the south side of the river for several days. During all this [65] time their strongest conjurer was at work day and night overcoming the giant cannibal which was threatening them.[107]

Although the Berens River Saulteaux have no tradition of the warpath, conjuring in former times was one of the means employed elsewhere for obtaining knowledge of the enemy's movements. From the psychological standpoint, therefore, the conjurer was an important instrument of morale in so far as he was able to establish confidence in the face of danger and at the same time to supply information that could be taken as the basis of action, For practical maneuvers of defense and offense undoubtedly were, in part, determined by the clairvoyant powers and prognostications of the conjurer.[108] In our earliest account of conjuring Champlam describes its use on the warpath in order to find out whether the enemy will be overcome. And in the eighteenth century we have the famous account of a seance at Sault St. Marie witnessed by

---

[107] This function of the conjurer is also reported by Mason for the Oxford House Cree. A woman informant said that in her mother's time the spirits "had warned the people living down near the lake in front of the [Hudson's Bay Co.] post that a *witiko* was heading that way. All the people moved their tipis back into the bush near where Mrs. Smith's tent now is, and left two conjurers in their hide wigwam to keep the *witiko* away. The boss at the post gave the two old men smokes and liquor to keep the *witiko* away so the people wouldn't leave the post.... They sat in the tent smoking' and drinking and making medicine against this *witiko* while the people waited upon the hill for the results- Soon they heard a noise like an aeroplane, and gulls and geese in the air, a great whirring noise, and then it passed off to one side and was gone. This was the *witiko* and it had been driven off by the conjurers."

[108] Fortunately, we have the personal statement of one Ojibwa conjurer on this point (as reported by W.M. Johnson, see Hardinge, p. 486). Wau-chus-co says, "The occasion was urgent, and our chief was afraid that our foes would attack us unawares, and we were also destitute of provisions." Upon entering the lodge the spirits immediately manifested themselves and his fellow Indians [cried out;

"Tell us; Tell us! Where are our enemies?" ... Soon the vision of my thinking mind, or spirit, embraced a large extent of country which I had never seen before. Every object was plainly before me. Our enemies were there in their villages, unsuspicious of danger. Their acts and conversation were made known to me. Game abounded in another direction. All this I told. Next day we procured food in abundance, and a few days afterwards a dozen scalps graced our return to the cross village.

Alexander Henry.[109] The occasion for this was a message from Sir William Johnson inviting the Indians to attend a conference with the Six Nations. The Ojibwa and other [66] Indians at the Sault feared a trap so there was a resort to conjuring in order to discover the best course to pursue. Mikīnák was sent east to find out what he could about the plans of the white men. He journeyed all the way to Fort Niagara and Montreal and after "a quarter of an hour elapsed in silence" he returned and "delivered a lengthy speech," says Henry.

At Fort Niagara he had seen no great numbers of soldiers; but on descending the St. Lawrence as low as Montreal, he had found the river covered with boats, and the boats filled with soldiers, in number like the leaves of the trees. He had met them on their way up the river to make war upon the Indians. The question was then asked:
"If the Indians visit Sir William Johnson, will they be received as friends?" "Sir William Johnson," said the spirit (and after the spirit the priest), "will fill the canoes with presents; with blankets, kettles, guns, gunpowder and shot, and large barrels of rum such as the stoutest of the Indians will not be able to lift; and every man will return in safety to his family." At this the transport was universal, and, amid the clapping of hands, a hundred voices exclaimed: "I will go too! I will go too!"

Another function of the conjurer was to foretell when certain events would take place. A contemporary instance of this occurred at Little Grand Rapids in the early summer of 1940. No definite information had been received up until that time as to when the Indian Agent would arrive to make the annual Treaty payments, an event of great importance to these Indians. This uncertainty was most unusual since the date is usually set several months ahead. In consequence there was a great deal of discussion about the matter and much hearsay information was being bandied about. Conjurer J was asked to try to find out the date when the agent would arrive. The result was that he said the payments would be made so many nights from the time when he conjured. As it turned out he was mistaken. But he would have hit it closer if the date finally set had not been shifted ahead at the last minute.
In situations where food shortage or actual famine arose (especially in the past) a Saulteaux conjurer was called upon to direct the hunters to where game could be found. This [67] was an extremely important service, for "the silent enemy," hunger, constantly lurked in the background of what was at best a precarious existence. The threat of hunger or starvation, then, was another danger against which the conjurer was able to act as a buffer.[110] It should be

---

[109] Francis Parkman refers to it in his *Conspiracy of Pontiac* (1908) Vol. 2, pp. 165-66.

[110] Le Caron writes that the conjurer consulted the spirits in order to know whether they should soon have snow in great abundance, so as to have a successful moose and beaver hunt. He replied that he saw many moose, which were still a great way off, but which would soon come within seven or eight leagues of their cabins. This caused great joy to these poor benighted creatures.

The woman conjurer, Blue-Robed-Cloud-Woman, tells how she undertook her first séance because they were threatened with starvation. Advised by one of her helpers she directed the Indians to move west.

They had not proceeded far beyond the bounds of their former hunting circle, when they came upon the tracks of moose, and that day they killed a female and two young moose,

emphasized that this was distinctly a public service on account of the custom of food-sharing which existed among the Saulteaux and other northern peoples. There was no competition at the subsistence level. If any man found game it was divided with others. But if a particular hunter found that no animals came to his traps or he was unable to track moose or caribou, while his associates or neighbors had no difficulty in securing game then he might suspect sorcery directed against himself and employ a conjurer to find out who it was that was bewitching him. This was the situation in which Yellow Legs found himself and his revenge through the use of conjuring has already been described. Inquiries regarding prospective luck in hunting also may be made of a conjurer.[111] We even have one instance on record when an American garrison, apprehensive lest their winter [68] supplies already delayed a month might not arrive, called upon a conjurer.[112]

Sometimes a conjurer was asked to locate lost persons or articles.[113] One of my informants was present at a seance the purpose of which was to discover the whereabouts of a young man who had been missing for a week. His mother was worried and gave a conjurer tea and tobacco amounting to two dollars in order to locate her son. (The narrator commented that the amount given was very small.) After the conjuring performance had progressed for awhile the lost man was discovered. "Here he is," said the conjurer, and sure enough he spoke to his mother. He told her that he was all right and was camping at such and such a place. Two days later he arrived home. On the night of the seance he had been camping exactly where he had said he had been. But the performance took place when he was asleep and he did not know that his soul had been called into the conjuring tent.[114]

---

nearly full-grown. They pitched their encampment anew, and had abundance of animal food in this new position. My reputation was established by this success ....

(Schoolcraft (2), p. 172.) For the Oxford House Cree Mason was informed that "if the hunting were poor, they [the conjurers] were consulted as to the reasons, and what to do about it."

[111] Calkins says that the conjurer is "consulted by the Indians when they go out to hunt bear, to foretell whether success will crown their efforts." Flannery, p. 12, noted that in the Montagnais séance she witnessed "many of the questions were concerned with hunting." Cf. Black. That queries of this category are an old and integral part of the conjuring situation is evidenced by the fact that Le Jeune also mentions them (Vol. 6, p. 169).

[112] Wau-chus-co, the conjurer, himself told William M. Johnson about it (Hardinge, pp. 486-87). He "saw" that the expected vessel was disabled but was being repaired.

My sensations [*sic*] told me [he says'] that they would be ready in two days, and that in seven days the vessel would reach Macinac by the south channel, at that time an unusual route. I told all this to the inquirers. On the seventh day the vessel hove in sight by the south channel, and the captain of the schooner corroborated all I had said.

[113] Elsewhere we have instances of the conjurer locating domestic animals, (Densmore (3) p. 101; Mandelbaum) and money (Coleman, p. 51).

[114] At Oxford House, Leonard Mason was told that "if a York boat was late and the anxious relatives of the crew wondered what the trouble was, one of the crew would be called to the [conjuring] tent. When he arrived, his voice would be recognized and he would say whether they had been held up by the wind or low water, and not to worry, they would be home in a few days, etc." Jefferson reports a case in which a conjurer, asked to locate a lost girl, said

Cases are reported in which lost articles have been tossed out of the conjuring tent to their owners. Feats of this kind are attributed to *otcībámasis*,[115] one of the most famous conjurers of the last generation. While traveling up the Berens River to Grand Rapids by canoe, a woman who had a small child with her gave the baby some keys to play with. These keys belonged to a wooden chest that contained the family's belongings. The baby dropped the keys overboard near one [69] of the portages. When the party got to Grand Rapids *otcībámasis* was engaged to find the keys. It was not long after he had gone into the conjuring tent that he threw them out to the woman. The man who told me the anecdote commented that *mikznák* must have gone to the spot where the keys were dropped and obtained them for the conjurer. On another occasion, according to his son, *otcibamasis* was just coming out of a sweat bath when a man came to him in great distress. The latter had just come up the river and had lost his gun in the water. The old conjurer had a lodge erected and sent one of his *pawáganak* for the gun. He then handed it out to the man who had lost it. Sometimes, if a canoe overturned in the rapids *otcībámasis* would persuade *mīkinák* to fetch all of the goods to the conjuring lodge and he would hand them out.

Connected with the ability to locate and restore lost articles is a demonstration such as the following: The conjurer passed a knife out of the tent. It was marked by someone in the audience and then thrown into the bush. After some little time the conjurer handed the marked knife out of the tent. It was identified as the one thrown into the bush. The demonstration was repeated four times.[116]

The conjurer who did this (A) is still living and I was told the story by an eyewitness. Interestingly enough the man (M) who related the incident to me had conjured. Yet he was deeply impressed with the other man's powers, I suspect that we have here a real clue to the reason why conjuring as an institution can maintain its virility in a society where there is no fraternity of conjurers to conserve the secrets of the profession.[117] While all conjurers do certain standard things like [70] shaking the tent[118] which, under contemporary conditions, may become

---

she was dead. Three weeks later she turned up.

[115] The father of conjurer B.

[116] The previously mentioned anecdotes pale beside two of those reported by Jenness (p. 68). In one case a conjurer sent his spirit helpers "with a load of furs 60 miles to a trading post, whence they brought back several cases of whiskey within an hour"; in the other, it is said that once when some Indians had exhausted their supply of flour and bacon a conjurer, upon receiving four marten skins "produced in exchange for them a 50-pound sack of flour which his *medewadji* (helpers) had brought from Penetanguishene 100 miles away." Cf. Flannery (2) p. 16, who refers to a conjurer said to have had fresh blueberries brought to the lodge in the dead of winter.

[117] Referring to the Ojibwa, Hoffman [(l) p. 157] writes, "There is no association whatever between the members of this profession, and each practices [70] his art singly and alone whenever a demand is made and the fee presented ... His renown depends upon his own audacity and the opinion of the tribe." Cf. Schoolcraft (1) I, p. 359.

[118] 117 Although some of the Berens River Saulteaux had heard of the famous "Davenport trick," none of their conjurers was credited with it. But this trick appears to have been part of the repertoire of many Ojibwa-Saulteaux conjurers of old. The conjurer is either trussed up securely with rope or enveloped in a skin or blanket and then tied, before being thrust into the conjuring lodge, which begins to shake, nevertheless. There are several accounts of

the subject of a limited amount of skepticism, some conjurers apparently invent or acquire new tricks. [71]

These enhance their personal reputations and probably support the native theory of conjuring even in the minds of other conjurers who are unable to duplicate them, although they may have tricks of their own.

L, a conjurer himself, told me that one of his contemporaries, D, was a fake, while in the same conversation he extolled another man, F, as the best conjurer at Grand Rapids. He asserted that this man could conjure in a lodge made of forty poles and twenty hoops. L said that he did

---

such performances in which a wager was offered to the conjurer and he collected it. Hoffman (1), pp. 276-77, quotes the details of one such case witnessed at Leech Lake, Minnesota about 1858 by Paul Beaulieu. There was a committee of twelve appointed on which one clergyman served. But this gentleman, when the tent began to shake almost at once, despite the care that had been exercised in tying up the conjurer, said it was the work of the Devil and left. In this case the conjurer not only escaped from the ropes but while still in the lodge he told Beaulieu, who had laid the wager, to go to a house nearby and he would find the rope! It was there and the Indian collected his hundred dollars. Duncan Cameron likewise made a wager with a conjurer who claimed he could get free of a net wrapped about him and tied with ropes. "In about 16 minutes he began to shake his rattle, which made me think his hands were free, and 6 minutes after, he threw out the net and desired me to examine it and say whether it was cut; finding the net all right I paid the wager." Another eyewitness account is to be found in Coleman (p. 51). Cooper's informant at the Lake of the Woods said his grandfather did it. More circumstantial references for Ojibwa peoples are to be found in Schoolcraft (1) V, p. 421; McDonnell, Hargrave, Skinner and Densmore (1) pp. 123-24, (3) pp. 104-05. The conjurer, reputedly a Cree, who astonished Carver so much was bound up in a skin with ropes around it. Cf. Franklin, Jefferson, Mandelbaum. Among the James Bay Montagnais Flannery (1), p. 14, reports the absence of this trick and it is not referred to by Le Jeune, so that it is not a universal feature of conjuring like the shaking tent and in any given locality it may not have been in the repertoire of all conjurers. It was not observed by Kane, McKenney, Black, Winchell, Kohl's informant, or Godsell. The only conjurer from whom we have a personal statement about this trick says (Hardinge, p. 486); "I exerted my powers frequently amongst my tribe, and to satisfy the doubtful, permitted them to tie me as they thought proper. They would sometimes place me in the ches-a-kee lodge, which would then commence shaking, indicating the presence of the spirit. The cords with which I was tied would then drop from my limbs." Among the Cheyenne, Grinnell reports a special manner of tying a conjurer. For information on the technique of escaping from ropes and the Davenport brothers, see Carrington (2) Chap. 7, and Podmore, Vol. II, pp. 55-61. The Davenport brothers performed their trick in a cabinet resting on trestles. It had three doors, the center one having a lozenge-shaped opening. Inside were hung several musical instruments. The two brothers settled themselves inside the cabinet and were tied to their chairs by members of the audience. The doors were then closed but almost immediately an arm was thrust through the opening or a bell was thrown out of it into the audience, while inside the musical instruments were heard or heavy knocks or blows were audible. There were other variants but the general comparability of this performance to that of the Algonkian conjurers is obvious.

not see how this conjurer was able to enter such a lodge at all, the poles were so close. "But when the canvas is lifted, in he goes!" L spoke of another man, a young fellow, who can put his feet in the lodge, the rest of his body remaining outside, and yet it will shake. He said he saw him do it. Evidently L cannot duplicate either of these two feats, regardless of whether the facts as he stated them are correct or not.[119]

Further evidence in support of this interpretation can be cited in the case of the *Midewiwin* which has sometimes been looked upon as a society of shamans. On the Berens River and elsewhere in the Lake Winnipeg region the great *mīdé* especially a man who was an acknowledged leader of the ceremony, was one who was said to have performed miracles. These miracles were not acquired through payment or going through the various degrees; they were demonstrations of the power of a particular individual. Consequently, supported by the testimony of eyewitnesses, they are not attributed to shamans collectively, but a special miracle is connected with a particular *mīdé*. This is in harmony with native theories of supernatural blessings and with a mode of life which offers considerable latitude for the cultivation of individual versions of the basic cultural material. The basic philosophy of these people offers ample validation for unique powers of the individual, and the threshold of credulity remains low so long [72] as these powers are expressed in terms of familiar native patterns. And the respect, if not awe, which the demonstration of unique powers meets, is ample motivation for the individual who craves prestige. It is perhaps the major type of social recognition which this society has to offer. But it can only be won and maintained by actual demonstrations of magic power in competition with others. No doubt this is why it is said that conjurers are so jealous of one another.[120]

IX

---

[119] My interpreter heard of a man who lived at Albany years ago who was said to conjure in a lodge built in a couple of feet of water. Yet when he emerged he was perfectly dry. The miraculous aspect of this feat is only apparent when it is understood that the conjurer is supposed to remain at the bottom of the lodge during the entire séance. Actually, of course, there is no necessity for doing so.

[120] Which explains, in turn, why they frequently belittle each other. I have already mentioned the evaluation made by L of conjurer D. On another occasion B told me that D shakes the tent himself and has no real power. Not long ago, he said, the people left when D was conjuring. He did not know this and the tent kept shaking. Even though D was inside his *pawáganak* should have informed him of what was going on. The case of D is of particular interest because he suffers from deep-seated phobias. See the record of this man in Hallowell (5), where he is designated J.D. Cf. Hallowell (7).

ANSWERS TO SKEPTICS

WITHIN the framework of native theory any skepticism with respect to the presence of the spirits in the conjuring tent is out of place. On the contrary, a conjuring performance provides perceptual evidence of the reality of spiritual entities, and in aboriginal times conjurers, along with other types of shamans, undoubtedly enjoyed outstanding prestige. For the Ojibwa proper William Jones asserts that "nobody had so much influence as one who did the *tcisakiwim*, and formerly an equivalent statement would have been applicable to the Saulteaux.[121] But today many of these Indians are well aware that white traders and missionaries are of the opinion that the conjurer shakes the lodge with his own hands and that his voice is the voice of the spirits. Yet the conjurer, J, whose performance I have described, said to me with the greatest apparent sincerity, "Those were not human beings you heard speaking."[122] After having him expound a great deal of native theory to me and something of his own experiences, upon which there is a rigid taboo, I did not have the impudence to insult him by inquiring how it really was done.

One of the most interesting features in the history of this type of conjuring is the united front which the conjurers themselves have offered to those who have tried to secure detailed information about their modus operandi. We have a number of instances on record where converted conjurers, some practically [74] on their death beds, have been asked to explain how conjuring was done.[123] All of them have asserted that they were not personally responsible for the manifestations that occurred. This point was noted by Brinton[124] years ago and it has been taken up and stressed as an argument in favor of the authenticity of the phenomena produced in the references made to conjuring in the Spiritualist literature.[125] The statements of these conjurers are important as psychological documents and I shall quote selections from them here.

One of them is given by Kohl, but neither the name of his white informant who interviewed the conjurer nor the name of the latter is given. The Old Indian is quoted as saying:

> "I have become a Christian, I am old, I am sick, I cannot live much longer, and I can do no other than speak the truth. Believe me, I did not deceive you at that time. I did not move the lodge. It was shaken by the power of the spirits. Nor did I speak with a double tongue. I only repeated to you what the spirits said to me. I heard their voices. The top of the lodge was filled with them, and before me the sky and wide lands lay expanded. I could see a great distance around me, and believed I could recognize the

---

[121] Cf. Schoolcraft (1) I, p. 359; V, p. 405. So far as the Saulteaux are concerned, a great deal might be said about the role of the conjurer in relation to effective leadership in a culture where chieftainship was lacking until after the treaties with the Dominion Government. But this topic deserves separate and more extended treatment.

[122] Once when I was discussing the acquisition of songs in general with a man who happened to be a conjurer (L), I asked him whether each conjurer had his own special songs. I was immediately informed that a conjurer does not sing. It is always the *pawdganak* that are heard.

[123] See Kohl, p. 280; Hardinge (Johnson), pp. 486-87; Schoolcraft (2) pp. 169, 172; Densmore (1) p. 124. Cf. LeJeune, Vol. 12, p. 17.

[124] Brinton, pp. 309 ff.

[125] Cf., e.g., Bozzano, p. 21.

most distant objects." The old dying *jossakid* said this with such an expression of simple truth and firm conviction, that it seemed to me, at least, that he did not consider himself a deceiver, and believed in the efficacy of his magic arts and the reality of his visions.

Another statement comes from Wau-chus-co, who died near Mackinac in 1840. He had been a Christian for ten years previous to his death. In his early days he was a *mide* and a *wabanowinim* as well as a conjurer.[126] Among other things Johnson reports him as saying:

I possessed a power which I cannot explain or describe to you. I never attempted to move the lodge. I held communication with supernatural beings, or thinking minds, or spirits which acted upon my mind, or soul, and revealed to me such knowledge as I have described to you.... [75]

Schoolcraft is more categorical. He writes:

In reply to our inquiry as to the mode of procedure, he stated that his first essay, after entering the lodge, was to strike the drum and commence his incantations. At this time his personal manitos assumed their agency, and received, it is to be inferred, a satanic energy. Not that he affects that there was any visible form assumed. But he felt their spirit-like presence. He represents the agitation of the lodge to be due to currents of air, having the irregular and gyratory power of a whirlwind. He does not pretend that his responses were guided by truth, but on the contrary, affirms that they were given under the influence of the evil spirit.

The statement of another converted conjurer is quoted by Densmore. This old man essayed no explanation because he said he was "an entirely different being at that time." Finally, there is the statement of the famous woman conjurer whose "confessions" Schoolcraft obtained after she became a member of the Methodist Episcopal Church. In describing her first attempt at conjuring, Blue-Robed-Cloud-Woman says that after entering the lodge which she had ordered to be built of ten different kinds of saplings, she knelt down with her head near the ground and began singing.

The lodge commenced shaking violently, by supernatural means. I knew this, by the compressed current of air above, and the noise of motion. This being regarded by me, and by all without, as a proof of the presence of the spirits I consulted, I ceased beating and singing, and lay still, waiting for questions, in the position I had first assumed.

In view of such statements, is it possible to maintain that these conjurers were deliberate imposters, charlatans and frauds? I think not. Nor is it necessary to conclude with the Spiritualists that they told all they knew, and to draw the inference that the movements of the tent and the vocal phenomena actually were due to supernormal forces. The problem is much more

---

[126] This man was interviewed by both W.M. Johnson (see Hardinge, pp. 486 ff.) and Schoolcraft (2) pp. 206-10.

complex than either of these antithetical solutions suggest. To my mind the essential point is this:

As individuals these conjurers had played a role that was set by their culture. And they had played it successfully. [76]

Their personal statements, in fact, reflect the thoroughness with which they had identified themselves with it, and consequently the depth of their personal convictions. Not only had they dreamed the appropriate dreams that validated their role in their own eyes; we must assume that they unconsciously invested the act of conjuring with an emotional aura which was experienced as if some objective forces were involved. Such an emotional vortex is not an unfamiliar psychological phenomenon and while it may verge toward the abnormal in certain types of personality, individuals with creative artistic gifts are well acquainted with it. In Western culture, in fact, we still have a tradition that the poet or musician becomes "inspired." To play a role successfully that is thoroughly validated by the ideology and values of any human society is only to act a part in the sense that we all act a part. The successful conjurer thoroughly identifies himself with his role. The approved means are part of the total situation and inseparable from it. When, as outsiders, we raise questions about insincerity and fraud, therefore, it simply indicates that we find it impossible to penetrate and understand the behavioral world in which these Indians lived.

In rejecting, as we are inclined to do, all the a priori assumptions upon which their belief system is based and in terms of which their behavioral world is organized, we are actually indicting the foundations of their culture, which is irrelevant to the problem of how conjuring functions within that culture. Within the cultural system of the Saulteaux, for example, *conjuring as an institution* serves a variety of functions and is an integral part of Saulteaux society as a going concern. From the standpoint of these Indians themselves, therefore, it is not conjuring as an institution that can be challenged for it embodies too many beliefs and values that are basic to the operation of the social order as a whole. All that is possible is to differentiate between genuine conjurers and those thought to lack the necessary supernatural validation for their task.

It was not until 1940, after I had spent a number of seasons with the Saulteaux and written this monograph, that I had an intimate conversation with an Indian that illuminates this [77] differentiation in a very striking manner and bears out the deductions cited above which I had made previously.

This man, whom I shall call M, had conjured only once. What he tried to do was to discover the hidden cause of a young woman's illness. He found that she was sick because her father had used "bad" medicine to make a man he disliked suffer. The illness of the woman was an automatic penalty for her father's aggression. The outcome of the conjuring performance was that the old man not only confessed he had done wrong but immediately fetched the "bad" medicine and turned it over to the conjurer. The woman recovered so that conjuring in this instance was a perfect success.

Imagine my surprise, then, when M spontaneously told me not to believe for one moment that the conjuring lodge was shaken by spirits or that the voices heard were not the vocalizations of the conjurer himself. Such statements, if removed from the context of our total conversation, would suggest that this man was quite clearly an impostor. Yet this is by no means the case. When we consider other things which he also told me in the same conversation I believe that an integral psychological picture is produced which is realistic, despite the fact that it contains features that seem inconsistent from our point of view. It demonstrates, I believe, the insight that can be gained through one man's actual unpretentiousness and thoroughgoing honesty. We can discern a little more clearly how conjuring works as viewed from the standpoint of the conjurer himself.

M was not an impostor from the native point of view, nor from the standpoint of his own ego, because he had a dream revelation that validated his conjuring. M said he had this dream for the first time when he was a baby, in fact he was still on the cradle-board. It was later repeated several times. M dreamed of the West Wind, the main one that blows in the conjuring lodge, he said. He also dreamed of the lodge itself and of growing up to be a man who conjured. (Parenthetically, I may add that M's father was a well-known conjurer.)   In his dream, *wisakedjak* came to M and told him of a sick woman who still had years of life ahead other – if he conjured. [78]

After M was married and had two children there was a sick woman in camp whom he recognized as the one he had been told about and he knew he could cure her. So M had a conjuring lodge of eight poles made. He ordered that they be planted very deep in the ground and he said the lodge was not easy to move from the outside.

But as soon as I got inside [he said] and put my hand on one of the posts it seemed as if the lodge were very easy to move. It is something like beating a drum; it was almost as if it shook itself. I knew just what to do, what songs to sing and everything else. There are more than thirty different songs. The inside of the lodge was not dark; it was as light as day. I saw *wisakedjak* plainly before me there. He told me what was the matter with the woman. So I said to her father, "You have done something wrong. You have used medicine you got in the *midewiwin* for bad purposes. You made a man suffer illness for three winters." I told him to give up the medicine at once or else his daughter would die. So the old man gave up the medicine.

If we take this account at its face value, as I believe we must, it is obvious how M's experience was colored by the behavioral world in which he was brought up. No skepticism, is evident with respect to the fundamental beliefs of Saulteaux society. M had full confidence in the validity of his dream experiences and their significance for subsequent action. And I see no reason to doubt his vision of *wisakedjak* in the conjuring lodge nor the illumination in the lodge of which he speaks. Yet we know that psychologically speaking these were of the nature of projections. But from the standpoint of his behavioral world they were as "real" as anything could be. M was caught up in the whole situation. In fact his success in putting over such a performance without previous experience might almost class as a miracle in itself. But I may add that M is an unusually capable individual in all departments of Saulteaux life and, as estimated from the Rorschach record I obtained, he undoubtedly is a man of very superior mental endowments. Consequently I am ready to believe that the observation of conjuring performances over a long period of years, particularly since his father was a conjurer, may easily [79] have prepared him for the one performance which he undertook. On this occasion he was genuinely "inspired."

M, then, is anything but an impostor despite his perfectly honest statements of the mechanics of tent shaking. Actually, he played the game according to the rules. He had a dream blessing, he conjured without formal tutelage at the proper time and he cured the woman because of the power obtained through his dream blessing. These features are essentially those called for in the cultural blue-print of conjuring in Saulteaux society. The mechanics of shaking the lodge are subordinate to these and unless we believe in the possibility of supernatural forces ourselves it must be assumed that the Saulteaux conjurer must integrate the material means employed in manipulating the lodge with his personal inspiration and beliefs. In the case of M, of course, the effectiveness of conjuring as an institution was supported by the cure effected. And M himself stressed this fact; he did not deny it. Consequently I believe that in the last analysis the point to be emphasized is M's honesty – an honesty, that is to say, of belief as well as of action. It is for this reason that his statements give us a psychologically realistic picture of the Saulteaux conjurer. We have illuminated for us the various factors in the situation that must be reconciled.

At the same time it must be clear that although M was honest with me, he might have been inclined to be less so if he had been a practicing conjurer, or if contemporary Saulteaux culture were less undermined through acculturation.   For I believe we must assume that conjuring, as a going concern, of necessity must receive support from the belief that supernaturals manifest themselves in the conjuring lodge according to the prevailing notions already described. But it may be doubted if the conjurer, no matter what his state of mind at the time of any particular performance, can fully believe what the spectators believe. Ordinarily he must maintain a professional reserve on certain points.

The importance of the traditional view of the mechanics of the agitation of the lodge emerges quite clearly in the way in which expressed doubts usually are met. [80]

The Saulteaux readily admit that certain individuals have either shaken the conjuring tent, or tried to shake it, with their own hands.[127] But it is pointed out that the information divulged by these men had proved false or that their "deceit" had been punished by illness. Skepticism is directed toward individuals who practice conjuring rather than toward the institution itself. In support of conjuring, on the other hand, the Saulteaux cite cases which, if taken at their face value, do meet the challenge of the outsider and for the Indians themselves completely settle the issue.

Cases are pointed out, for example, where extremely old men have been known to conjure for hours. The skeptic is asked how this is possible, since these men obviously did not have enough strength of their own for such continuous exertion. Then there is the case of the one-armed conjurer who used to shake a tent for six hours at a stretch. Another conjurer, the great-grandfather of my interpreter, had had the fingers of his left hand shot off. Only the thumb remained. When he wished his pipe filled while in the conjuring lodge, he always handed it out with his right hand. But the tent would continue shaking just the same.

Old Yellow Legs is said to have had four lodges built on one occasion. He put an article of his clothing in three of them and entered the fourth himself. As soon as he was inside, all four lodges began to shake. The son-in-law of conjurer L told me that the latter in his younger days had been known to throw his coat into the conjuring lodge and it would begin to shake at once

---

[127] Densmore (1) p. 124, refers to such a case. This man is said to have had the lodge built on the sandy shore of a lake so that it could be swayed more easily, Her informant said,

Once this man was giving an exhibition and he climbed up inside the lodge to shake it. Of course he had to do this because he was not a regular juggler and did not know how to do it right. He was almost at the top and was swaying it back and forth when some boys pulled up the poles and threw the man and his lodge into the water. No one paid any attention to the man after that.

even though he himself remained outside. An old man across Lake Winnipeg at Jack Head told me the following anecdote about his father. On one occasion when he was conjuring some white people were present. They were overheard to say that it was the conjurer who was doing [81] the singing, not the spirits. So my informant's uncle, who knew a little English, called out to his brother, the conjurer, and told him what the white people said. An agreement was made to repeat the performance the next night and the four white men told the conjurer that they would give him five dollars apiece if he convinced them that he did not do the singing. So the conjurer ordered a lodge of forty poles built the next day and to each corner had ropes attached. These were tied to stakes in the ground like a tent so that the structure could not be shaken. When everything was ready the conjurer first walked around the lodge and shook it a little from the outside. It was very firm. Then he told the *skabéwis* to raise the canvas covering. Taking off the new black broadcloth coat he was wearing he folded it up and shoved it into the lodge which began shaking at once. Then he sat down outside a little distance from the lodge. It not only continued to shake, but the *pawáganak* came in and sang just the same. So the white men paid him the money they promised.[128]

In another case the conjurer was bound with ropes and placed *outside* the conjuring lodge, but in contact with it. It shook just the same. And finally, another man was named who conjured with only the upper part of the structure covered. He could be seen by the audience kneeling on the ground while the tent was moving.

Since at any time a man may be accused of deception for one reason or another, this possibility must operate as a fairly severe selective agency in the adoption of this "calling." And in a very real sense it is a "calling." Besides, it is necessary that the conjurer give a convincing performance in order to maintain his status. Severe comparisons are made between the conjuring of different men. To meet the demands required [82] undoubtedly necessitates considerable skill. The conjurer also must have physical stamina, for in first-class performances the tent is scarcely ever still and at the same time singing and talking go on in different voices. Yet in the performances I have seen there was little reflection in the "voices" of the contemporaneous physical exertion supposedly necessary to keep the tent in motion. While I heard no ventriloquism of a high order, it is easy to imagine how effective this would be. The conjurer must also have a good memory for songs, some sense of dramatic impersonation, and be nimble-minded in order to carry on repartee. If, in addition, we are willing to admit that the best conjurers of old may have possessed some canny psychological insights that produced an impression of clairvoyance, their high repute is easily intelligible. Such an institution would afford a very effective instrument for the expression of the psychic gifts of individuals or actual dissociative manifestations.

---

[128] This reputed effectiveness of an article of the conjurer's wearing apparel is a very widespread belief. See, e.g., Jenness, Black. Speck says he was told that a Montagnais conjurer would sometimes place his hat inside the lodge which would then begin to shake before he made his entrance. John Du Bay (quoted in Justice Larrabee's letter) claimed that on several different occasions he saw a conjurer place his moccasins in one lodge, his leggings in another, while he entered the third himself – "immediately the three lodges would commence swaying from side to side, as if shaken by someone from within, and voices would be heard issuing from one or the other, and often from all three lodges at the same time."

The reputation of conjurers among their fellow Indians becomes even more intelligible if we take into account the opinion of white men who do not share the dogmas of the natives. Not all of these have been skeptics, as the citations given from Spiritualist literature testify. Even Father Le Jeune, after several years close association with the Montagnais and Algonquins, seriously raises the question "whether these Sorcerers really have communication with the Devil."

> If what I am about to tell is true [he writes in 1637] there is no doubt that the Demons sometimes manifest themselves to them; but I have believed until now that in reality the devil deluded them, filling their understandings with error and their wills with malice, though I persuaded myself that he did not reveal himself visibly, and that all the things their Sorcerers did were only Deceptions they contrived, in order to derive therefrom some profit. I am now beginning to doubt, even to incline to the other side ..,

following which he gives his reasons, none of which are any more convincing than those given by the Indians themselves.[129] But his considered convictions make it understandable why native belief in the institution persisted, and why it is that, as [83] Densmore says,[130] "Whatever may be the mechanical explanation of the tipi shaking, its greatest interest lies in the influence it exerted on the minds of the Indians, an influence affecting every phase of their lives."

X

---

[129] Vol. 12, p. 17.

[130] Densmore, (4) p. 314, advanced the idea "that the lower hoops may hold the poles in place after the manner of barrel hoops and that the upper hoops may be larger than the circle of poles and manipulated by cords attached to the body of the juggler." Personally, I do not see how this would work in the case of the lodge diagrammed or the one photographed. Flannery [(1) p. 16] likewise rejects Densmore's explanation in the case of the Montagnais lodge. And what of the lodges reputedly built with only one hoop at the top? I do think, however, that the fact that the poles are slanted inwards when put in the ground is a feature that should be taken into account in seeking an explanation of the potential mobility of the conjuring lodge. It would appear that this gives it a higher potential mobility than if they were driven perpendiculary into the earth. Unfortunately we have no data of importance on the distribution of this detail. All that I can say personally is that the Berens River conjuring lodges built in this fashion were extremely easy to set in motion. They readily responded to the slightest pressure from without, as I can testify.

SOCIAL FUNCTIONS OF CONJURING

IN addition to its ostensible and immediate purpose as denned by the occasions upon which it is practiced, conjuring as an institution plays an important role in Saulteaux society from a more inclusive point of view. It reinforces values and beliefs that make Saulteaux society a going concern.

In the first place, it provides tangible validation of basic concepts about the nature of the ynamic entities of the cosmos, familiar in belief and myth. By means of it the *pawáganak* become objectified to men through a direct appeal to auditory experience; at the same time they are individualized by a qualitative differentiation of the "voices" issuing from the lodge. Each voice can be identified with the personality, hence the "real" existence of the *pawágan* from whom it is believed to issue. This auditory association is also promoted by the adoption of the characteristic vocal peculiarities of certain *pawáganak* as heard in the conjuring tent, by story tellers. A narrator, for instance, will imitate the vocal peculiarities of *mikīnák* in repeating the myths in which the Great Turtle appears. The songs sung by each *pawágan* also aid in establishing the latter's identity and individuality. Consequently, to doubt the existence of the *pawáganak* is almost tantamount to doubting the evidence of one's senses.

This objectification and differentiation of the personalities of spiritual beings likewise humanizes them, and this effect is enhanced by the intimacy established between the audience attending a conjuring performance and the *pawáganak*. These spiritual beings are not only heard, but rapport is established between them and the human beings present, principally by the repartee that goes on between members of the audience and *mikīnák*. I fancy that there is an important psychological principle involved here. Objectification, without the [86] encouragement of rapport through conversation which promotes a certain sense of intimacy, might tend to set up a cool and detached appraisal of the spirits which might lead to skepticism and disbelief. In short, the situation as denned is ideally adapted to promote the ends which it undoubtedly serves. Tangible support is likewise given to the belief that the souls of human beings survive death when the spirits of the dead are invoked in the conjuring lodge. And in the seance described, one of these spirits spoke of how pleasant a place the Land of the Dead was.

There is one spiritual being, however, who is never invoked in the conjurer's lodge. This is *kadabendjiget*, the high god. "He" remains remote and aloof from direct contact with the lives of men. His name is seldom mentioned, he is regarded with awe and it is unthinkable that he should enter into intimate and tangible relations with man. But even in this case the conjuring lodge as an institution supports native beliefs in a negative fashion. The high god is conspicuous by his absence, this fact emphasizing his status.

In the second place, by implicitly exposing the dangers involved in a violation of the mores in certain instances, conjuring lends indirect support to the social structure. And directly it reinforces the sanction which is one of the motivating forces for conformity. This sanction operates through the belief that illness will inevitably follow deviations from established codes of conduct.[131] Murder, deceit, incest and the minor sexual perversions, even unnecessarily cruel treatment of animals, are under a disease sanction. Since a conjurer is called upon from time to time to fathom the hidden sources of illness, the exposure of moral turpitude as the basic cause in some instances serves to remind the community of its potency. The disease sanction is thus

---

[131] See Hallowell (8).

upheld, and a warning provided for those who may be inclined to depart from traditional patterns of conduct.

In the third place, the very existence of conjuring as an institution, and the possibility of resorting to it when consumed with fear, apprehension, or worry, creates a sense of [87] security and confidence in the face of the hazards of life. If game is scarce and famine threatens, a conjurer can be appealed to and, with the aid of his supernatural helpers, he may be able to direct the hunter to the place where game may be found. By similar means it is possible for him to secure news about the health or circumstances of absent persons which will alleviate apprehension. Furthermore, a powerful conjurer is able to protect a whole community or specific individuals from malevolent influences. He can determine the source of magically projected illness and even retaliate in kind if he is strong enough.[132] Or he may protect a whole community from the ravages of a *windigo*.

Since conjuring performances are always carried out in public, the concrete demonstration in case after case of the way in which the dynamic forces of the universe can be mobilized for the benefit of man creates a sense of security and confidence. Perhaps this is the reason one old pagan remarked to me that the Christian religion might be all right for the next life, but that the Indian religion was better for this one.

Finally, a conjuring performance provides diversion and entertainment for those assembled to witness it, despite the fact that this is not its ostensible purpose. It might even be characterized as a form of dramatic art, confined like radio performances to the auditory level. Dramatic qualities must be particularly striking in those instances where two conjurers are struggling for power or where a *windigo* is being fought.[133] I believe that the Saulteaux themselves are not insensible to esthetic qualities in these performances. This is evidenced in [88] their evaluations of the seances of different conjurers. They do not rate them exclusively in terms of the truths revealed or the proximate ends believed to be achieved. A conjurer, for example, who can bring a lot of *pawáganak* into the tent is not only considered stronger in power than one who commands fewer spirits, but the performance of the former is judged to be *better*. That is to say, the Indians appear to enjoy a performance where there is a great variety of *pawáganak* present,[134] where the spirits are well characterized and where there are funny things said. This requires considerable artistic skill on the part of the conjurer. A good ventriloquist will undoubtedly outrank a poor one since voice manipulation is so essential to success. It is fair

---

[132] Jenness (p. 68) says,

> The Indians on Parry Island today live in constant fear of witchcraft, to which they attribute many deaths, believing that it has greatly increased since conjurers disappeared from their midst. Formerly, they say, the conjurer could punish the sorcerer by summoning his soul into the *djiskan*, where one of the helping spirits, at the request of the dead man's relatives, would kill it with a sharpened stick of cedar.

[133] Black refers to a struggle between a conjurer and the spirits of the bear and the lynx in which the former was victorious. Since Black did not understand the language his statement needs elucidation since the spirits were reputedly "killed" in this demonstration of the conjurer's powers. However, from the description given the dramatic effect was evidently impressive.

[134] Members of the audience will sometimes cry out *timóskina* (keep it full) – i.e., of *pawáganak*.

to say that a conjuring performance which is thoroughly satisfying and convincing to the Indians is one which is on a higher artistic level than one they deem unsatisfactory. One of the criticisms of the performance described was that the conjurer did not bring in enough spirits, although, as I have said, his prognostications all proved correct.

In view of these wider social functions it is not difficult to understand why conjuring has persisted up until the present day even in communities where the Indians have been Christianized and in other respects influenced by occidental culture. To my mind, the occurrence of conjuring in such cases is an index of the vitality of native beliefs, attitudes and values despite a veneer of acculturation. When conjuring entirely disappears we can be certain that the behavioral world of these Indians, as constituted in terms of their aboriginal belief system, already will have collapsed. Other institutions of occidental origin will have arisen to perform social functions relative to the new order of life which conjuring previously exercised in Saulteaux society.

Because Pete Hallowell annotated and evaluated this bibliography,
it and other bibliographies included herein
could not be amalgamated at the very end
and so remain attached to their own texts.

ANNOTATED BIBLIOGRAPHY

* Individuals contributing first-hand observations of conjuring performances.
† f Valuable data obtained at second hand from Indian or white informants.
‡ { Primary sources that mention conjuring without contributing details of importance.

BARAGA, R. R. A Theoretical and Practical Grammar of the Otchipwe Language for the use of Missionaries and other Persons Living among the Indians. 2nd ed. Montreal, 1878.

BEAULIEU, PAUL. * Ojibwa of mixed blood, interpreter at White Earth Agency, Minnesota, who gave W.J. Hoffman and Col. Garrick Mallery an account of a seance he witnessed at Leech Lake, Minnesota, about 1858. See Hoffman (1) p. 277.

BELCOURT, G. A. ‡ "Department of Hudson's Bay," Collection of the Minnesota Historical Society, Vol. 1 (1902), p. 185. (Originally published in the Annals for 1853.) Belcourt entered missionary work in the West in 1831.

BENEDICT, RUTH. The Concept of the Guardian Spirit in North America, Memoirs, American Anthropological Association, No. 29, 1923.

BLACK, A.K. * "Shaking the Wigwam," The Beaver, Dec. 1934. Manager, Nipigon House Post (White Sands Ojibwa), 1929.

BLUMENSOHN, JULES. "The Fast among North American Indians," *American Anthropologist*, Vol. 35 (1933), pp. 451-69.

BOAS, FRANZ. "America and the Old World," Proceedings, *International Congress of Americanists*. Goteborg, 1925, pp. 21-28.

BOGORAS, W. The Chuckchee, Memoirs, *American Museum of Natural History*, Vol. 7, 1909.

BOZZANO, ERNEST. Des Manifestations supranormales chez les peoples sauvages. Bibliotheque de philosophic spiritualiste moderne et des sciences psychique, Paris, 1927.

BRINTON, D. G. The Myths of the New World. 3rd ed. Philadelphia, 1905. [90]

CALKINS, HIRAM. † "Indian Nomenclature of Northern Wisconsin, with a Sketch of the Manners and Customs of the Chippewas," First Annual Report and Collections of the State Historical Society of Wisconsin, Vol. 1 (1855), pp. 123-24. Information, obtained by the author from William Cross who lived for many years among the Ojibwa, pertains to a conjurer named Mah-ca-da-o-gung-a, the Black Nail. (The relevant quotation is also to be found in Hoffman (2) p. 146.)

CAMERON, DUNCAN.* "The Nipigon Country, 1804." See Masson, Vol. 2, pp. 262, 270.

CARRINGTON, H. (1) The Psychic World. New York, 1937. A history of psychic phenomena with an account of native practices throughout the world. See Part II, Psychic Phenomena among Primitive Peoples. Quotation from Kohl via Howitt, pp. 232 ff.

——.' (2) The Physical Phenomena of Spiritualism, Fraudelent and Genuine. New York, 1920. See Chap. VII, "Rope-Tying Tests."

CARVER, J. * Travels through the Interior Parts of North America in the Years 7766, 7767 and 1768. 2nd ed. London, 1779. Pp. 123-29.

CHAMBERLAIN, A.F. "Indians of the Eastern Provinces of Canada," Annual Archeological Report, 1905. Appendix to the Report of the Minister of Education, Ontario. Toronto, 1906. Montagnais-Naskapi, p.131.

CHAMPLAIN, SAMUEL DE. * Works of Samuel de Champlain, ed. H.P. Biggar, Toronto, Publications of the Champlain Society, 1932. Vol. IV, pp. 85-86.

CHARLEVOIX, P.F.X. Journal of a Voyage to North America . London, 1761. Vol. 2.

COLBMAN, SISTER BERNARD, † "The Religion of the Ojibwa of Northern Minnesota," *Primitive Man*, Vol. 10 (1937), pp. 50-53.

COOPER, JOHN M. † *Notes on the Ethnology of the Otchipwe of Lake of the Woods and Rainy Lake*, Catholic University of America: Anthropological Series, No. 3, 1936. Pp. 9-10; 25-26.

CROSS, WILLIAM. * Source of Calkins' information.

DENSMORE, FRANCES. † (1) "Chippewa Music," Bul. 45, Bureau of American Ethnology (1910), pp. 123-25.

—. † (2) "Chippewa Customs," Bul. 86, ibid. (1929), pp. 45-46.

—. * (3) "Menommee Music," Bul. 102, ibid. (1932), pp. 101-05.

—. * (4) "An Explanation of a Trick Performed by Indian Jugglers," *American Anthropologist,* Vol. 34 (1932), pp. 310-14. Cf. the author's condensed observations of the same séance in (3) p.103. [91]

Documents Relating to the Early History of Hudson Bay, ed. J. B. Tyrrell. † Publications of the Champlain Society, 1931. Pp. 228-29; 389. Contains accounts of De la Potherie and Oldmixon.

Du BAY, JOHN. * Agent of the American Fur Co. Quoted in a letter from Judge Larrabee to Governor Tallmadge. See Emma Hardinge, pp. 484-85.

EVANS, I.H.N. The Negritos of Malaya. Cambridge, 1937.

FLANNERY, REGINA. * (1) "The Shaking-tent Rite among the Montagnais of James Bay," *Primitive Man*, Vol. 12 (1939), pp. 11-16.

—. † (2) "The Cultural Position of the Spanish River Indians [North Shore Ojibwa]," ibid., Vol. 13 (1940), pp. 1-25.

FRANKLIN, JOHN. Narrative of a Journey to the Shores of the Polar Sea, in the Years 1819-20-21 and 22. Philadelphia, 1824. Pp. 57 ff. John Richardson * wrote the chapter on the Cumberland House Cree in which reference to a seance occurs. The conjurer was tied up by a white man and could not get loose.

FRAZER, J.G. Totemism and Exogamy. A Treatise on Certain Early Forms of Superstition and Society. London, 1910. Vol. 3, p. 454.

GODSELL, P.H. * "The Ojibwa Indian," Canadian Geographical Journal, Jan. 1932. This author's account of a performance is generalized but it is probable that he has been an eyewitness to conjuring on more than one occasion.

GRINNELL, G.B. *The Cheyenne Indians.* 2 vols., New Haven, 1923. See Vol. 2, p. 114.

HALLOWELL, "Pete" Alfred IRVING   (1) "Some Empirical Aspects of Northern Saulteaux Religion," American Anthropologist, Vol. 36 (1934), pp. 389-404.

—, † (2) "Psychic Stresses and Culture Patterns," *American Journal of Psychi*atry, Vol. 92 (1936), pp. 1291-1310.

—. † (3) "Shabwan: A Dissocial Indian Girl," *American Journal of Orthopsychiatry*, Vol. 8 (1938), pp. 329-40.

—, † (4) "Sin, Sex and Sickness in Saulteaux Belief," British Journal of Medical Psychology, Vol. 18 (1939), pp. 191-97.

—, (5) "Fear and Anxiety as Cultural and Individual Variables in a Primitive Society," Journal of Social Psychology, Vol. 9 (1938), pp. 25-27.

—, † (6) "Spirits of the Dead in Saulteaux Life and Thought," Journal of the Royal Anthropological Institute of Great Britain and Ireland, Vol. 70, Pt. 1 (1940), pp. 29-51. [92]

——, (7) "Aggression in Saulteaux Society," Psychiatry, Vol. 3 (1940), pp. 396-407.

—, (8) "The Social Function of Anxiety in a Primitive Society," American Sociological Review, Vol. 6 (1941), pp. 869-81.

HARDINGE, EMMA † History of Modern American Spiritualism. New York, 1870. Pp. 483-87. Contains Henry's account of the seance at Sault Ste. Marie, Judge Larrabee's letter to Governor Tallmadge giving the observations of John Du Bay and William A. Johnson's interview with a conjurer published in the Detroit Daily Tribune, 1859.

HARGRAVE, J.J. ‡ Red River. Montreal, 1871. The author came out to Red River (Manitoba) in 1861. He gives an account of events during his residence.

HENNEPIN, Louis. † A New Discovery of a Vast Country in America. Reprinted from the 2nd London issue of 1698, etc., ed. R.G. Thwaites, 2 vols., Chicago, 1903. Pp. 557-78.

HAUPT, HERMAN, JR. * Source of information in Winchell.

HENRY, ALEXANDER. * Travels and Adventures in Canada and the Indian Territories between the Years 1760 and 1776. New York, 1809. (Cited as Henry, since there is only one reference given to Henry, the Younger.)

HENRY, ALEXANDER (THE YOUNGER). * New Light on the Early History of the Greater Northwest. The MS Journals of Alexander Henry and David Thompson, 1799-1814. Ed. with commentary by E. Coues. New York, 1897. Pp. 199-200.

HIND, H.Y. ‡ Explorations in the Interior of the Labrador Peninsula. 1 vols. London, 1863. Vol. 2, p. 102, A brief categorical statement based on observations of the Catholic missionary, Pere Amaud.

HOFFMAN, W.J. † (1) "The Midewiwin or 'Grand Medicine Society' of the Ojibwa," Seventh Annual Report, Bureau of American Ethnology, (1891), pp. 156-58; 251-54. John Beaulieu's account, p. 277.

—. † (2) "The Menomini Indians," Fourteenth Annual Report, ibid. (1896), pp. 138-48. Contains quotations from Charlevoix, Lahontan, De la Potherie, Carver, Peter Jones, Maurault, Calkins.

HOWITT, WILLIAM The History of the Supernatural in All Ages and Nations, and in All Churches, Christian and Pagan; Demonstrating a Universal Faith. 2 vols., London, 1863. Chap. 17, "The Supernatural amongst the American Indians," Quotes Kohl in full, pp. 402-06. [93]

JEFFERSON, ROBERT † Fifty Years on the Saskatchewan, Canadian North-West Society Publications, Vol. 1, No. 5, Battleford, Saskatchewan, 1929. Pp. 74-76.

JENNESS, DIAMOND. † *The Ojibwa Indians of Parry Island, Their Social and Religious Life.* National Museum of Canada, Bul. 78, Anthropological Series 17, Ottawa, 1935. Pp. 65-68.

The Jesuit Relations and Allied Documents, ed. R.G. Thwaites. Le Jeune's Relation, Vol. 6 (1633-34) and Vol. 12 (1637).

JOHNSON, WILLIAM M. † Gives the account of an interview with Wau-chus-co, an Ojibwa conjurer, who died on Round Island near Mackinac in 1840. Quoted by Emma Hardinge from the Detroit Daily Tribune, 1859, pp. 485-87. Additional information about the same conjurer is to be found in Schoolcraft (1) pp. 206 ft.

JONES, PETER ‡ History of the Ojibway Indians. London, 1861. p.151.

JONES, WILLIAM ‡ "Central Algonkian," *Annual Archeological Report*, 1905. Appendix to Report of the Minister of Education, Ontario. Toronto, 1906. Ojibwa, p. 145.

KANE, PAUL * Wanderings of an Artist among the Indians of North America from Canada to Vancouver's Island and Oregon through the Hudson's Bay Company's Territory. London, 1859, p. 439. The seance described took place at Dog Head near the narrows of Lake Winnipeg. This is a point about fifty miles south of the Berens River.

KEATING, W.H. ‡ Narrative of an Expedition to the Source of St. Peter's River, Lake Winnepeek, Lake of the Woods, etc. Performed in the Year 1823. 2 vols. London, 1825. Vol. 2, p. 159.

KOHL, J.G. † Kitchi-Gami. Wanderings Round Lake Superior. London, 1860, Pp. 278-80. This author bases his information on what he was told by a white man married to an Indian woman. This informant briefly describes a performance witnessed and the interview he had with the conjurer thirty years later after the Indian had become a Christian and was on his deathbed.

KÖHLER, W "Psychological Remarks on Some Questions of Anthropology," *American Journal of Psychology*, Vol. 50 (1937), pp. 271-88.

LAHONTAN, BARON DE New Voyages to North-America, ed. R.G. Thwaites. 2 vols. (reprint of the English edition of 1703). Chicago, 1905. Vol. 2, p. 468.

LANDES, Ruth. † (1) Ojibwa Sociology. New York, 1937.

—. † (2) The Ojibwa Woman. New York, 1938. [94]

LAWRENCE, E. Spiritualism among Civilised and Savage Races, London, 1921. P. 68.

LE CARON, JOSEPH. * (Recollect Missionary.) Letter written in 1618 to the Father Provincial of Paris. Le Caron had been at Tadoussac, Province of Quebec, (see next reference.)

LECLERQ, CHRISTIAN First Establishment of the Faith in New France, Trans. By J.D.G. Shea. 2 vols. First published in 1691. New York, 1881. Letter (1618) of Father Joseph Le Caron to the Father Provincial of Paris.

LEH, LEONARD L "The Shaman in Aboriginal North American Society," University of Colorado Studies, Vol. 21 (1934), No. 4, pp. 199-263.

LE JEUNE * See Jesuit Relations, Vol. 6, pp. 163-73; Vol. 12, pp. 17-23.

LOEB, E.M "Shaman and Seer," *American Anthropologist*, Vol. 31 (1929), pp.60-84.

McDONNELL, JOHN. † "Some Account of the Red River (about 1797)." See Masson, Vol. 1, p. 276.

McKENNEY, THOMAS L * Sketches of a Tour to the Lakes, of the Character and Customs of the Chippeway Indians and of Incidents Connected with the Treaty of Fond du Lac. Baltimore, 1827, pPp. 269, 328-30.

MANDELBAUM, DAVID G † The Plains Cree, Anthropological Papers, American Museum of Natural History, Vol. 37 (1940). Part II, pp. 261-62.

MASON, LEONARD † MS notes on Oxford House Cree, Manitoba (1940).

MASSON, R.L Les Bourgeois de la Compagnie du Nord-Ouest. 2 vols. Quebec, 1890. Contains accounts of Cameron and Mc Donnell.

MAURAUL, T.J.A ‡ Histoire des Abenaki. Quebec, 1866. Pp. 29-30.

NELSON, ALLAN * Notes on Saulteaux of Little Grand Rapids, Manitoba (1936).

OLDMIXON, JOHN † See Documents Relating to the Early History of Hudson Bay. P. 389.

OSGOOD, C "The Ethnography of the Great Bear Lake Indians," Annual Report, 1931, rational Museum of Canada. Ottawa, 1933. p. 48.

OESTERREICH, T.K Possession, Demoniacal and Other. New York, 1930.

PODMORE, FRANK Modern Spiritualism. 2 vols. London, 1902. [95]

POTHERIE, DE LA † *See Documents Relating to the Early History of Hudson Bay. Pp. 228-29.*

RAUDOT, ANTOINE DENIS ‡ Memoir concerning the different Indian nations of North America. Letter 31, dated Quebec, 1709. "These savages have among them some that are called jugglers. These people pretend to speak to the devil, and he tells them things that they ask him; to invoke him they place themselves in a cabin of bark or skin where they give frightful yells; the devil appears to them and sometimes beats them badly; this cabin while they are there trembles with so much force that one would think it was going to turn over." See W. Vernon Kinietz, "The Indians of the Western Great Lakes 1615-1760," *Occasional Contributions from the Museum of Anthropology of the University of Michigan*, No. 10, 1940. Appendix (p. 354).

RAY, VERNE F *The Conjuring Complex in the Plateau and the Plains.* Sapir Memorial Volume, Menasha, Wisconsin, 1941.

ROY, M * (Cass Lake) Source of statements by Coleman. He helped build the lodge of a conjurer at Knife Lake.

ROSSIGNOL, M.F "The Religion of the Saskatchewan and Western Manitoba Cree," *Primitive Man*, Vol. 11 (1938), p. 70.

SAGARD, GABRIEL ‡ The Long Journey to the Country of the Hurons, ed, with Introduction and Notes by George M. Wrong and translated into English by H.H. Langton. Toronto, Publications of the Champlain Society, 1939, Vol. XXV. Reference (p. 64) to "those magicians who profess to converse with the devil in little round towers isolated and apart (the editor notes that in his Histoire Sagard adds 'in the woods or in the very midst of their lodges') which they build on purpose to receive oracles in them and to predict or learn something from their master." The people referred to are the Nipissings (see note p. 561). Sagard made his journey in 1623-24; he was a Recollect missionary.

SCHBESTA, P Among the Forest Dwarfs of Malaya. (Translation of *Bei den Urwaldzwergen von Malaya*, Leipzig, 1927.) London, n.d.

SCHOOLCRAFT, HENRY R † (I) Archives of Aboriginal Knowledge. Philadelphia, 1860. Volume I contains a reference to the Ottawa conjurer, Chus-co or Wau-chus-co, and pictographic material obtained from him (Plate 49 B opposite, p. 352); autobiographical account of the early life of Blue-Robed-Cloud-Woman. It was narrated in Ojibwa to Mrs. Schoolcraft when this woman was about forty-one years old and had been converted. Other biographical details of her life are given as well as a pictograph representing [96] the dream or vision in which she obtained conjuring powers (Plate 55).

Volume V (pp. 405 and 421 ff.) contains a generalized account of conjuring with some interesting details. It is oriented to Plate 32, fig. 1 (wrongly cited in the text as Plate 34), which is a pictorial representation of a conjuring lodge, the conjurer, singers, the audience and the spirits themselves. I cannot discover any reference to the source of this drawing.

——. † (2) The American Indians, their History, Conditions and Prospects, etc. New revised edition, Philadelphia, 1851. Contains the short autobiography of the woman conjurer (pp. 169-74) but not the other data found in (1); an interview with the Ottawa conjurer, Chus-co (p. 206 ff.).

SHIROKOGOROFF, S.M (1) "What is Shamanism?" *China Journal of Science and Arts.* Vol. 2 (1924).

——. (2) *Psychomental Complex of the Tungus.* London, 1935.

SKINNER, A ‡ (1) "Notes on the Eastern Cree and Northern Saulteaux," Anthropological Papers, American Museum of Natural History, Vol. 9, Part I (1911), pp. 14, 67, 153.

——. (2) "Political Organization, Cults, and Ceremonies of the Plains-Ojibwa and Plains-Cree Indians," *ibid.* Vol. 11, Part VI, p. 505. Brief passing mention that Bungi (= Plains Ojibwa = Saulteaux) "have a cult called *Djisakid*, the members of which are dissociated, but who build the conical [sic] conjuring lodge and prophesy."

——. † (3) "Associations and Ceremonies of the Menomini Indians," *ibid.* Vol. 13, Part II (1915), pp. 192-97.

SPECK, FRANK G † MS notes on Montagnais-Naskapi conjuring.

VESME, CAESAR DE *History of Experimental Spiritualism*, Vol. 1: *Primitive Man.* London, 1931. See Chap. 7, "North American Indians."

WINCHELL, N.H † The Aborigines of Minnesota, Collated, Augmented and Described by N. H. Winchell. Minnesota Historical Society, 1911. Pp. 611-12. Apparently the information on conjuring is based on the observations of Herman Haupt, Jr., a corresponding member of the Minnesota Historical Society. An unpublished MS on the Dakota and Ojibwa "as seen by him on the occasion of numerous visits during the years from 1879-1890" (p. 411) was utilized. Haupt's sketches of many objects are scattered throughout the volume and on page 611 a pen-and-ink sketch of a conjuring lodge is reproduced.

Florence R. Kluckhohn
Roy Webb

Diamond Jenness   The Ojibway Indians of Parry Island, Their Social and religious Life. National Museum of Canada, Bulletin 78, anthropological Series 17, Ottawa 1935.

Leonard Mason MS notes on Oxford House Cree Manitoba, 1940.

Alanson Skinner   Associations and Ceremonies of the Menomini Indians.   Anthropological Papers, American Museum of Natural History, Vol 13, part II 1915.

Frank Speck Ms notes on Montagnais-Naskapi conjuring.

PUBLICATIONS OF THE
PHILADELPHIA ANTHROPOLOGICAL SOCIETY

Volume II

The Role of Conjuring in Saulteaux Society

By

ALFRED IRVING HALLOWELL

Philadelphia

UNIVERSITY OF PENNSYLVANIA PRESS
London: Humphrey Milford: Oxford University Press

1942

In spite of the fact that the bundle owner could use his bundle for the benefit of other persons, professional shamanism was very strong.

The contents of the bundle and its preparation were prescribed by the supernaturals to the youth at his spirit quest. Bags were owned by every man and by many women. Owners were constantly singing to their bags and receiving instructions from them. Indeed, these bundles are very common to this day.

A medicine bundle is never sold. Neither can its power be transferred to another by gift unless the owner knows he is going to die. He might *in conspecfu mortis* give his bundle to a man he likes, and who he thinks is "smart" enough to use it, but for the most part bundles are buried with their owners.

TALKING TO ANIMALS

The power to talk to animals was of great value. This was especially true of dogs, whose power in scouting made them invaluable in war.

SHAMANISM

Shamanism is far from dead among the Ktunaxa. Anthropologists who have earned the Indians' trust may actually see shamans at work. Several quite young men have become shamans recently, and others have expressed willingness to "go behind the blanket" if they can get powers. One becomes a shaman, as recounted a few pages back, entirely at the will of the supernaturals. One will be "called" and given specific instructions.

There were ordinarily several practitioners about, but should the village lose its only shaman, the community would do all in its power to acquire another. They felt that the spirits realized their consternation and would look about for a likely boy with whom to become familiar. Strangely enough, young shamans are preferred to old ones. They are fresh from their medicine experience and are more charged with power. Use blunts the power, and unless an old man can get recharged, he might lose his shamanistic ability completely. Ktunaxa shamanism is pragmatic. If a shaman loses a patient, it is a sign that his powers are weak and he loses public confidence.

People do not hate or fear shamans. They were and are respected figures. Yet in spite of this, there was a sinister note in Ktunaxa shamanism lacking among the Salishans. Shamans could be induced to kill an enemy for a client, although this was somewhat dangerous. If a man should think his illness the result of malevolent shamanism, he would go to another one for cure. After this one had sung and cured his client, he would know if the source of the illness had been some other shaman's enchantment. The shaman [174] would then ask his client if he wanted the malevolent shaman killed. This was easy to accomplish if the answer were in the affirmative. The Kutenai gave up asking shamans to kill after the coming of the priests.

Due to the respect and power accorded shamans, a father hoped that his son would be given this power at his first experience. There was never any doubt as to the boy's subsequent religious role. If he were to be a practicing shaman or just an ordinary layman, his spirit would tell him and advise him what to do. He was told just what kind of a shaman he was to be, "guide shaman" or hunting adviser, Sun Dance leader, or the greatest of all, a shaman "behind the blanket," and warned not to step outside his specialization,

The blanket shamans were and are the greatest. It is they to whom the people turn when they need help. It is they who help find lost articles, heal the sick, foretell the future.

Blanket shamanism is undoubtedly one of the most interesting forms of the phenomenon and in the Ktunaxa mind their own contribution. They consider the practice among any other tribe the result of direct diffusion from the Ktunaxa. They are aware of the phenomenon of culture borrowing in religious matters, as the Bluejay cult of the Flathead is at present growing among them. The resemblance of the Ktunaxa séance to that of the Eskimo and the Ojibwa has been interestingly remarked elsewhere.

While almost anything is likely to happen during a blanket shamanizing, the general pattern is as follows:

The lodge is set up in either a tipi or a modern house. A rope is tied from one lodge pole, skipping the second, and made fast to the third, just high enough to be above the shaman's head when he retires behind the blanket-If a modern dwelling is used, a corner of a room is roped off to provide the hidden space.

A blanket is then hung so as to curtain off a space from the people's view. A string of deer hoof rattles is then hung down the middle of the blanket from a cord. Lasso Stasso, the shaman of Elmo, does not practice behind the blanket but lays it flat on the floor behind him.

The shaman enters the lodge and strips to the breech clout. He has purified himself beforetime in the manner to be described. He proceeds to paint his face according to his instructions. He then sits on the floor with his back to the blanket facing the people. A long, light ruffle is beaten on the drum either by the shaman or a delegated assistant. The shaman sings the song of the spirit invoked and blows long blasts on his whistle. When he thinks that a spirit has come behind the blanket, he retires there himself. It is not hard to know that the spirits have come. One can hear them walking on the roof. [175] Furthermore, the blanket begins to shake, sometimes violently, so that the rattles are sounded.

The shaman emerges from behind the blanket and shows that his thumbs have been tied behind his back. Sometimes the spirit completely hog-ties him, so that he must roll out. At other times, in order to test his powers, he has someone bind and tie him as firmly as possible before the people's eyes. He then rolls behind the blanket and in about two seconds comes out entirely free. The spirit almost always prefers to tie the shaman, so that he rolls out in order to have someone put his bone whistle in his mouth. He then retires behind the blanket to whistle until several spirits come. In the meantime the people keep the song going. One can hear the shaman talking to the spirits, imitating their twittering, and can hear the spirits respond.

The shaman comes from behind the partition to be untied and to smoke several times, the specific number varying with the individual shaman. An ex-shaman of Tobacco Plains whose powers are now blunted says that he always went behind the blanket and came back four times.

Generally but not always the shaman has a rope tied around his waist. Retiring behind the blanket, he throws the free end of the rope over it so the people may see it. Soon they observe that the rope has lost all tension, since it has cut the shaman in two. They hear his two halves hit the floor.

As many as four spirits might attend the séance. Owl is especially sought. It is he who shakes the blanket. The audience changes the song and drum rhythm with the arrival of each new spirit.

The Owls then pick up the shaman and fly a long way off with him, where they deposit him and return. There is now presumably no human agent behind the blanket, yet it shakes and voices issue forth. More and more spirits flock in, if the séance is a success. It is useless to tell of the number of Ktunaxa who claim to have seen the blanket raised and have seen absolutely nothing behind it to produce the voices. Such a contention is all but universal.

When this stage of the séance is reached, the people bring their pipes to the blanket to pray. An official sits on the left side of the blanket's face to light the pipes for the people. He hands a pipe back of the blanket, where a spirit takes it and smokes. After the spirit has blown a few puffs, he hands the pipe back over the top where it is received by the owner. The supernatural who has smoked then advises his client. It is often very hard to understand the spirits, since they mumble far more often than they shriek. Often they speak in an archaic Kutenaian which is not understood today. Sometimes they speak pure gibberish, so that a second shaman must be asked for the interpretation. Ordinarily, however, they only speak softly, so [176] that the official just mentioned is just a man with keen ears who can hear their remarks and relay them to the client.

When the séance is over, the supernaturals bring the shaman back, and he rolls or walks from behind the blanket in a befuddled condition. He smokes and soon recovers.

It has been said that one need not be a shaman to attempt a blanket séance, that any person who has an ordinary spirit may try. Actually there is a keen sense of who is and is not a shaman at such a time. No layman would ever unbidden attempt to go behind the blanket, either publicly or alone. It sometimes happens, however, that in the early part of the séance the officiating shaman will come from behind the blanket and invite some specific man, hitherto considered a layman, to come with him behind the partition. If the layman has the normal experience of the blanket shamans at that time, he comes forth a blanket shaman, not a layman. This is done at the specific instruction of the spirits. Without this the attempt would be futile or perhaps fatal.

Bull Robe maintains that shamans were always paid for their services, but this is consistently denied by all other informants. These latter are most probably right, for this would fit the pattern of shamanism in the neighboring Plateau peoples. It is true, however, that the younger modern Montana shamans expect fees for their services, certainly from a white man. As indicated, shamanistic powers decrease with use, so the shaman feels that the fee is no more than his right. Shamans certainly are not paid at Tobacco Plains.

Shamans are supposed to know when they are about to die. They are supposed to die quickly, too, without knowing more than a few days' sickness.

Following is a partial vocabulary regarding shamanism:

Shaman's power in general	*g'nup'kaka*
Shaman in general	ᵤ*wámu*, or *wámɔ*
particularly one who does not go behind the blanket	
Shamanizing behind the blanket	*kumnakanıkıtnámu*

The concept of purity is strong in Kutenai religion. Before each rite the shaman must purify his mind. Before the rite he must purify himself with Juniper smoke. A fire fed with juniper burns before the blanket continually during that ceremony. No person of impure action or thought is supposed to witness the rites. Those known to have had recent intercourse are enjoined to stay away, and every effort is made to keep intoxicated men away. The supernaturals hate impurity in all its forms and are supposed to sicken or even kill a shaman if an impure man or one who has recently tasted whiskey is near.

THE CURTAINED STAGE
A STUDY OF KTUNAXA CONJURING PRACTICES

Claude Schaeffer

Purpose of Conjuring
(note)

The occasions for which conjuring was employed varied throughout its New World range of occurrence. The most extensive list of purposes served by the séance has been recorded for the Saulteaux. This forest-dwelling group utilized clairvoyance to secure information on the location of game, about the welfare of distant people, determine and treat the cause of illness, detect sorcery and moral transgressions, exorcise the former and identify the latter, restore the dead to life, ward off a *windigo*, foretell the occurrence of certain events, locate lost persons or objects and obtain knowledge of an enemy's whereabouts (Hallowell 1942: 53-72). While these and other objectives were pursued at times by conjurors of the Plains tribes, the last appears to have been an important reason for performing the rite. It has been recorded for the Sarsi, Atsina, Plains Cree, Kiowa, and in the Plateau, the Colville and Ktunaxa. One observer's remarks are pertinent in this connection: "the conjuror was an important instrument of morale in so far as he was able to establish confidence in the face of danger and at the same time to supply information that could be taken as the basis of action" (Hallowell 1942: 65). To be able to foresee the enemy was an important qualification of the leader of the Plains Cree war party, since he was expected to know where the hostile camps were located and plan the attack accordingly (Mandelbaum 1940: 261). Among the Kiowa, conjuring was held, among other purposes, to predict success of a war party (Collier 1944: 46). If Colville raiders intended to go out to fight in the spring, they wanted the power and advice of their spirit intermediary, and his forecast of defeat would prevent the them from going (Cline and others 1938: 152). The major purpose of Ktunaxa conjuring in earlier days was to determine the location and intention of enemy war parties. If signs of hostile scouts were observed near camp, a séance was immediately held to determine if the enemy was after scalps or horses. A conjuror always accompanied the bison hunting party to the plains (Schaeffer, Ktunaxa, ms).

(over)

< Note: Unique phrasing of Ktunaxa conjuring No obvious relationship with Blackfeet rite Traits in common with Plains Cree rite Possibility that Ktunaxa conjuring and old complex among Ktunaxa, cf Ray's pioneer study, etc; Collier's conclusions >

INTRODUCTION

The Ktunaxa Indians, together with the Colville of eastern Washington, are unique among the Plateau tribes of northwestern North America in their knowledge and use of the conjuring rite. Among the Ktunaxa, at least, conjuring represented one of the most important properties in their socio-ceremonial complex. The rite was an institutionalized means of obtaining the aid of different classes of spiritual entities by invoking their presence and communicating human desires to them" (Hallowell 1942: p. 9). By this means the Ktunaxa believed that information was made available to them that was previously withheld by barriers of time add space. The types of information sought referred to the location and intention of enemies, the whereabouts of game, the cause and treatment of illness and the recovery of lost people or strayed animals.

The conjuring rite among the Ktunaxa was called *q!aq!anamnam*, "cutting a person in two," and refers, of course, to the Houdini trick by which the rite is opened and by means of which the conjuror is believed to be cut in two. The conjuror is called *q!aq!ał* "the one cut in two." Modern Ktunaxa commonly speak of the conjuring rite as "putting up the blanket" after the blanket screen behind which the conjuror retires and the spirits are believed to come and go.

The Ktunaxa conjuring rite has been described by a number of earlier field workers among that tribe. In the following paragraphs I have commented on the amount and quality of that material and have attempted to evaluate it. Where the data of these earlier workers differ from my own, I have indicated so in the text.

The earliest account of Ktunaxa conjuring was based upon information collected in 1888 and published the following year by Franz Boas (1889: 855). Since this represents the initial attempt by a modern ethnologist to record data on the Ktunaxa, the material has historic as well as cultural interest. That portion of the account discussing the Houdini trick is reproduced first below:

> The Shamans of the Kutonaqa are also initiated in the woods after long fasting. They cure sick people and prophesy the result of hunting and war parties. It this is to be done, the shaman ties a rope around his waist and goes into the medicine-lodge, where he is covered with an elkskin. After a short while he appears, his thumbs tied together by a knot which is very difficult to open. He re-enters the lodge, and after a short time reappears, his thumbs being untied. After he has been tied a second time he is put into a blanket which is firmly tied together like a bag. The line which is tied around his waist, and to which his thumbs are fastened, may be seen protruding from the place where the blanket is tied together. Then the men pull at the protruding end of the rope, which gives way; the blanket is removed, and the shaman is seen to lie under it. This performance is called *K'eqnamnam* (somebody cut in two).

The balance of the Boas' account is concerned with the séance proper:

> The Shaman remains silent and re-enters the lodge, in which rattles made of pieces of bone are heard. Suddenly something is heard falling down. Three times this noise is repeated, and then singing is heard in the lodge. It is supposed that the shaman has invoked souls of certain people whom he wished to see, and that their arrival produced the noise. From these he obtains the information and instructions which he later on

communicates to the people.

Alexander F. Chamberlain carried on field work among the Ktunaxa in 1891 and collected rather indirectly some information on conjuring. After reproducing the above noted data of Boas, Chamberlain (1901: 95-6) stated that one member of the tribe gave the following free translation of a medicine song:

> An Indian is crouching in the corner of his lodge beneath blankets invoking the spirits. Soon the spirit enters through the top of the lodge, passes beneath the blanket, and enters the Indian, who then flies away on high; by-and-by returns, and, sitting under the blanket, causes the spirit to depart again.

This informant, according to Chamberlain, applied the term *kEk•aqnamnam* to the whole procedure under the blanket. According to another Ktunaxa, the "spirits" assume the form of some beast or bird, in which state the adept can summon them, and commune with them. The Kootenay "medium" gets behind a blanket in the tepee, as noted above, and summons the spirit to him, and while under the blanket, imitates the voice, etc., of the beast or bird in whose form the spirit appears. The "spirit" is supposed to "fall down" through the smoke hole of the lodge. The advent of the blanket (*seet* or *tłamatł*) has driven out the elkskin (*aqk•o'ktla gitlk•ᵗatles*) which was formerly the cover under which the shaman ensconced himself. With many Indian tribes the elk has always been great or good "medicine"; hence, perhaps the use of its skin here. In accordance with the general democratic character of Kootenay institutions, the coming and going of "spirits" is not bound up with intervention of the shaman, whose art has, nevertheless, been looked upon, in recent times, as more efficacious. Probably at an earlier stage in the history of these people, all persons of a seasonable age could "traffic with the spirits." It would not be surprising if not a little of the paraphernalia and *modus operandi* of the "medicine-man" among the Kootenays turns out to be borrowed from neighboring tribes.

Although the published an extended account of the Ktunaxa Sun Dance, Edward S. Curtis seems to have passed over any reference to the conjuring rite of this tribe.

The first description of Ktunaxa conjuring recognizable as such was published by Verne F. Ray in 1939. < sources informants Pete Andrew & Madeline One Thumb ? > His account, based upon a brief field trip among the Elmo Ktunaxa, is accurate and includes roost of the major features of the rite. Two years later Doctor Ray made use of his Ktunaxa data in a comparative analysis of conjuring in the Eastern Plateau, Northern Plains, and Central, and Eastern Woodlands. We shall have occasion to refer to this excellent study later in this work.

In 1941 Harry Turney-High presented a more detailed account of conjuring as part of his monograph on the Ktunaxa Indians. In it he covers many of the traits composing the mechanics of this complex. Most of his data, I believe, were obtained from the Elmo Ktunaxa. Dr Turney-High's description differs from mine in a number of places and I have called attention to such discrepancies in the appropriate places below. Turney-High nowhere makes use of the terms "conjuror" or "conjuring" but includes all clairvoyant data under the rubric of "shamanism."

The foregoing accounts of Ktunaxa conjuring suffice, perhaps, to make brief, general comparisons with related ceremonies among other tribes. However, they fail to give us much of an idea of the wealth of detail, the rich symbolism and the psychological values built up by skilled conjurors over the years. They do not acquaint us with the supernatural background of the rite, the spiritual characters involved and the relationship of these beings to mankind. They do not shed much insight upon the personality of the conjuror nor define his role in the native community. They omit detailed discussions of such topics as skepticism, treatment of the sick, the Houdini trick and the quest for conjuring power. Finally they do not mention the statecraft exercised by skilled conjurors during his task of satisfying the economic, therapeutic or psychological need of the petitioner, while maintaining the interest and cooperation of spectators during the ten or twelve hour, ceremonial period. I have attempted to shed light upon these various matters from the standpoint of field data collected over a number of years.

My own interest in Ktunaxa Kutenai conjuring goes back to the summers of 1934, 1935 and 1937, when I was sent into the field by Dr. Clark Wissler, of Yale University, and the American Museum of Natural History, New York, to collect data on various aspects of Ktunaxa history and culture. During those years I visited all of the Ktunaxa communities in Montana, Idaho and British Columbia and discussed native ceremonialism with the oldest members of the tribe. I discussed the subject of clairvoyance with a number of Ktunaxa conjurors, all of whom I found willing to talk openly and frankly of their calling to a serious listener. In 1935-36 I spent eight months on the Flathead Reservation working for the Bureau of Indian Affairs in connection with the Wheeler-Howard Program on the Flathead Reservation. During that period I was able to gather at odd moments more information from the Ktunaxa at Elmo on conjuring. In the summer of 1947 and again the following year I re-visited the Ktunaxa at Bonners Ferry and at Elmo to open up other lines of investigation. Since then, in 1952 and in 1963, 1964 and l965, I have made a number of brief trips to the same areas as duties at the Museum of the Plains Indian permitted.

Conjuring seems to have been practiced by all of the Ktunaxa groups, except possibly for the Michel Prairie people, for whom we lack adequate data.

Among Ktunaxa religionists who shared their knowledge of clairvoyance with me were Stanley Como and Abel Sebastian of St. Mary's Reserve, B.C.; Chief Paul David, Joe David and Pauline of the Tobacco Plains Reserve, B.C.; Abraham and Susanne Bullrobe, and Baptiste Matthias, of Elmo, Montana; Francis Adams and Simon Francis of Bonners Ferry, Idaho; and of Creston, B.C. Of the above informants, Como, Joe David, Sebastian, Pauline, Bullrobe and Frances Adams were or had been at one time practicing conjurors. The remaining Ktunaxa had attended many séances performed by these and other conjurors. With the exception of one or two, all of the foregoing individuals have passed to that land in which there are no "barriers of time or space" to penetrate.

A word should be said here as to the strong, religious conservatism of the Ktunaxa. This characteristic does not mean, fortunately, that the Ktunaxa will not discuss native religion with strangers or we would know nothing of their ceremonio-religious life. It does mean that they refuse the writer and other non-Indians as well an opportunity to witness the performance of various religious rites and ceremonies. This has been the experience of most students, I believe, who have attempted to carry on ethnological work among members of this tribe. Certainly it has been mine. This tendency is due, I think, to several factors. One, of course, is the very limited amount of intermarriage between Ktunaxa and white in Idaho and Montana, and even less in British Columbia. This factor, in contrast to the advanced state of miscegenation among the Montana Piegan, has helped to preserve the pagan ceremonialism. All this, of course, is a rather roundabout way of saying that I have never witnessed a conjuring performance of the Ktunaxa.

I RITE'S EARLIER FORM AND PURPOSE

I have secured a small amount of information on the earlier form and purpose of conjuring among the Ktunaxa and have set it off as such below. This separation has seemed advisable so as not to confuse data of the earlier with that of more recent period. The dividing lines are rather arbitrary, based as they are upon particular events that I believe affected conjuring strongly in one way or another. The coming of the first white traders probably influenced Ktunaxa culture and hence, their ceremonial life, strongly. The next event in point of time and emphasis is the arrival of Father De Smet and his establishment of Christianity among the Ktunaxa. Years later the virtual extermination of Plains bison removed a resource of considerable value to Upper Ktunaxa economy. At about the same time (1884) the establishment of intertribal peace by Major Macleod marked the end of Blackfoot raids upon the Ktunaxa, and thus removed one ostensible purpose of conjuring. Thereafter clairvoyance among these Indians could not help being affected by innovations. Below I have set forth the data on the method and purpose of conjuring that preceded these culture-affecting events.

The major purpose: of the conjuring rite in earlier times, according to modern Indian informants, was to determine by clairvoyance the location and intention of enemy war parties. If signs of hostile scouts were observed about camp, a séance was held to determine if the enemy were after "blood" (scalps) or "goods'* (horses).

A séance was held by the Ktunaxa before leaving for the bison hunt in the eastern foothills of the Rockies and there, the Ktunaxa were warned of the whereabouts of the Blackfoot and other hostile tribes. The *nupíka,* it was believed, would instruct the Ktunaxa what trail to take, where to camp and hunt to avoid meeting the foe.

Joe Dennis, of Tobacco Plains, thought that possession and use of the conjuring rite made the Ktunaxa better able to resist the numerically-superior Blackfoot.

A diviner with strong clairvoyant power was generally able to use his ability to 1) locate game, 2) secure wealth by successfully raiding for horses, and 3) cure the sick.

The spirits were questioned in the séance about the location and intentions of the enemy, about illness and physical infirmities, about the scarcity of game, approach of food scarcity, epidemics and similar crises.

If a group of Ktunaxa set out upon a raid and the leader's power was not considered especially strong, a conjuror would be asked to accompany the party to determine its chances of success. Often the leader of such a party would possess clairvoyant power.

In earlier times a young conjuror, before setting out on a raid, would be asked to hold a séance. If he succeeded, his spirits would speak for him and defend his actions. They would say," He and we are one; we are in his body. He will return safely. Do not worry about him." The *nupíka* would then announce the number of séances to be held before starting out and the interval between them, i.e. four with seven days between. Many people would attend his next performance. He must demonstrate his power by returning successful from his raid. < Clarify with Simon ! >

In earlier days, according to Susanne Bullrobe, the lodge in which the séance was given, would be violently shaken as an indication that the enemy would be encountered. When this occurred it was regarded as a warning of danger. The movement of the lodge was said to be caused by spirits entering and leaving the lodge.

Informants describe the apparently greater power of conjurors in earlier days and the magical feats they carried out.

A powerful seer then could merely go outside, walk around his lodge, and summon his spirits upon reaching his lodge entrance.

Similarly, a conjuror with great power would have a thong fastened about and <u>outside</u> his arms. Then he would merely go outside, walk around his lodge and re-enter with the thong passed <u>beneath</u> his arms.

Likewise in those days a conjuror could summon the *nupíka* by merely walking to his lodge door, shaking the two poles besides the entrance, and then shaking the two, rear foundation poles.

The Ktunaxa séance was formerly held in an ordinary, conical skin-, or among the downriver groups, mat-covered lodge. A rawhide thong was tied between the two, rear foundation poles of the structure at a height of about six feet from the ground. From this was suspended a tanned, body robe of bison hide to serve as a screen. Pauline, a conjuror of Tobacco Plains, declared that two robes were fastened together with wooden skewers in the same way as with woolen blankets in modern times. The "medicine pole," to which the lodge cover was attached, was located between these two, foundation poles and was the one by which the *nupíka* were believed to descend to the area behind the screen. In the center of the robe, on the side facing the audience, a small bunch of deer-hoofs were suspended from a thong, the ends of which passed through two holes in the robe to the inner side. The deer-hoofs served, of course, as rattles during the time of the performance.

In the case of an old conjuror of Tobacco Plains, according to information obtained from Pauline, a stiff, untanned bison hide was merely leaned against a horizontal thong or pole in the rear of the conjuror's lodge as a substitute for the tanned, body robe to serve as a screen. This variant practice does not seem to have been general. < A variant of the vertical, hide screen described above. >

On the basis of tribal tradition the Ktunaxa tend to trace the existence of conjuring back to the pre-1840 period. Prior to that date Three Moons, a prominent Lower Ktunaxa warrior and ritualist, is said by Simon Francis to have foretold the coming of the Black Robes during his visions in the conjuring rite and Sun Dance Ceremony. He is believed to have died at an advanced age prior to the arrival of father Jean De Smet among the Ktunaxa in the early 1840's. If Ktunaxa tradition is reliable on this point the possibility exists that this association might establish, conjecturally at least, the existence of conjuring among the Ktunaxa by and possibly before, the beginning of last century.

(over)

Presumably the two sons of Three Moons, Big Archer and Caterpillar, served as conjurors. They were baptized Thomas and Moses, respectively and played a prominent part in favoring the introduction of Christianity among the Lower Ktunaxa.

II CONJURING IN RECENT TIMES

In general the principal purpose of conjuring was concerned with ascertaining the number and location of enemy raiders, with hunting, sickness and location of beings and objects of secondary importance. With the extermination of the Plains bison and the establishment of intertribal peace about 1885, the warfare and raiding purpose disappeared and use in hunting, treating sickness and locating lost, strayed or stolen became primary objectives. Of these, hunting became secondary and finally disappeared with the establishment and enforcement of state game laws about 1900. So we are left with treating the sick, locating the lost and possibly in accumulating property by gambling.

In late years the séance has been held for any one of a variety of purposes, including the following: to learn the location of game; to discover the cause of ill-luck in hunting or gathering; to amass property; to treat the sick, to avert crises, such as epidemics, etc.; and in general, to secure aid from the supernaturals in some human endeavor.

(over)

< Some shamans and warriors could foretell future by means other than conjuring; these competitive systems led to rivalry between practitioners of several systems. >

Often a séance was used to confirm or disprove the validity of a dream. Thus if a person should dream that a relative had been killed by a cougar or grizzly bear. If confirmed by the *nupíka* in a séance, the dreamer, to avert the tragedy, would be required to kill the particular animal indicated. If he failed, nothing, according to Ktunaxa belief, could avert the tragedy.

In recent times when a person with power becomes old and has but a short time to live, his guardian spirit departs from his body. In former days the spirit would have been transferred to a younger relative but this is often close impossible today, particularly if the owner has no relatives. The supernatural now looks for a new owner, the Ktunaxa say, and if none is found, it will enter a séance. Behind the blanket the ownerless spirit will say, "I'm traveling about in mourning. I came in for a smell of the juniper incense. I'm looking for a lodge, i.e., an owner. If I can't find any, I'll stop in at different séances to receive a pipe, i.e. a smoke. At this time I'm ready to grant petitions. I'll name myself and help you. If anyone is sick, sing loud and strong the song I give you and I'll help that one. My power will be as great as if I belonged to someone." At present there are many ownerless *nupíka* of this kind. Conjurors often acquire additional spirits in this manner.

At present young Ktunaxa who have been baptized, find it difficult to obtain a spirit, as the latter cannot approach such a person.

We can assume, I believe, that the conjuring rite was held at frequent intervals among the various Ktunaxa groups until the break down of their respective economies under White settlement, for the Upper Ktunaxa economic demoralization got under way around 1880-85 with the extermination of the bison from the Plains. This event, of course, rendered excursions across the Rocky Mountains unnecessary and meant a shift in their subsistence pattern to deer, elk, moose, mountain goat, and bighorn sheep. Also at about this same time peace was made between the Ktunaxa and the Blackfoot, Assiniboine and other Plains tribes, thus ending hostilities that had persisted for generations. Thereafter the practice of conjuring tapered off and the purposes for which it had been held, also changed.

As for the Lover Ktunaxa, conjuring up until about 1905 played an important role in the fall hunt of the Bonners Ferry Indians. The hunting party started out on horseback up the Kootenai River in September and returned, after several snowfalls, the latter part of November. The hunting party was made up of younger, able-bodied men and women. Before 1900 runners would report back to the home camp on the results of the séances held at intervals during the fall hunt, and give the names of those youths who had excelled in hunting. In these rites the *nupíka* are said to have predicted the location of game.

In 1927 the Superintendent of the Coeur d'Alene Indian Agency is said to have attempted to sell the allotments of the Bonners Ferry Ktunaxa, according to Simon Francis, and place each family on a five-acre tract. The returns from the land sale were then to be used to build each family a house at the present Mission Reserve site. The Superintendent was threatened by a Ktunaxa conjuror.

III RECENT HISTORY OF CONJURING

Modern Seers

At St. Mary's Reserve, in 1935, Stanley Como had recently given up conjuring because of the disapproval of the authorities at St. Eugene's Mission. Abel Sebastian was the conjuror there with whom I worked and who posed for certain photographs relating to conjuring.

About this time the body of a boy killed by a fall from his horse was said to have been located by a seer on St. Mary's Reserve.

Séances held on this reserve were concerned mainly with hunting activities.

For the Columbia Lakes Ktunaxa, I vas informed by the Indians of St, Mary's Reserve in 1935 that there were no practicing conjurors among the members of this group. Further that there had been no shamans there during the lifetime of Chief Louis Arbell.

Among the Tobacco Plains Ktunaxa, Not-a-Grizzly, chief of this group during the early part of last century and killed by the Piegan, was a good conjuror. He took a stiff bison hide, rolled it into a cylinder and tied it to the poles of his lodge. He would then enter the cylinder screen for the séance, instead of using a blanket suspended between lodge poles. He also had men wrap him into a robe and tie it with a series of half hitches; he would then free himself from the robe. He would hold a séance before leaving for the bison range in order to foretell an attack by enemies. Only two men used the vertical, hide cylinder as a conjuring booth, Not-a-Grizzly and a Flathead, Siła, who married a Ktunaxa woman. The latter was a powerful conjuror and father of Mrs. Couture and Peter Caye of Elmo, Montana.

Pauline, who gave me much information on clairvoyance at Tobacco Plains in 1934 and 1936, was described by other Ktunaxa as having *nupíka*, which placed difficult injunctions upon petitioners during the séance. He was said to have predicted that an Indian would be appointed Canadian Minister of Indian Affairs, etc.

Abraham Shotnana is a contemporary conjuror at Tobacco Plains but the Ktunaxa consider him untrustworthy and undependable because of his excessive use of alcohol.

Michel Hump-back is recalled as an earlier conjuror at this reserve.

Siałi was a conjuror noted for his strong power some years ago at Tobacco Plains.

Joe David was said to be an adept at conjuring in his younger days. He was also a shaman and Sun Dance leader in later life, after the pagan rites were revived.

Andrew Bear Hat was a prominent conjuror.

There have been a number of conjurors among the Ktunaxa of the Flathead Reservation down through the years.

Alexander Andrew, nephew of Lame Joe, was a conjuror, *wamu* and Sun Dance leader. He was the first to start up the pagan rites at Elmo.

Lame Joe was a conjuror and a shaman.

Looking Glass (*Hewankorn*) was a conjuror at Elmo. His *nupíka* were said to impose such difficult injunctions upon petitioners that only rarely could they be carried out.

Alec Couture was a conjuror but was killed as a law enforcement officer in a fight with some young Ktunaxa.

Abraham Bullrobe, Mathias Finlay and Lassoo Stasso were conjurors at Elmo in recent years.

Moses Mathias, son of Baptiste Mathias, is said to have ceased conjuring.

Ambrose Gravelle thought that the Stasso boys were conjuring.

Conjuring has been slowly dying out at Bonners Ferry, according to Simon Francis. There have been few séances since 1935-40, although there were three seers among the group at that period. The three had held performances during their earlier years but had gradually ceased, perhaps because of drinking. Simon added that there is no more religion – pagan or Christian – at Bonners Ferry and only the elderly attend church.

The last conjuror, according to Simon, was Michel Michel Timu, Jr. He married at Elmo and started to hold séances there. When his wife died, he returned to Bonners Ferry.

Francis Adams was regarded as a fair clairvoyant.

Louis Abraham, son of Tamia Abraham, was an adept at conjuring.

Second Chief David, and his half-brother, Paul, were both conjurors.

Nicola Jerome, son of Jerome *Kiyakał,* was a skilled clairvoyant as well as travel leader of the hunting parties around 1880-90. Because of other interests he usually turned his performances over to Michel Timu.

Among the Creston, B.C., Ktunaxa, séances were said to have been held in 1935 principally to secure good fortune in gambling!

On the St. Mary's Reserve, it was believed that the population decline among the Creston Ktunaxa was due to the latter engaging in shamanistic warfare during séances with Colviile medicine men. Catholicism has brought a decline in supernatural power among the Creston Ktunaxa but has not adversely affected the Colville. The same informant claimed that Ktunaxa conjurors fought among themselves during séances.

IV THE SPIRITUAL BACKGROUND

In order to understand the function and scope of the conjuring rite among the Ktunaxa, it is necessary to have an understanding of their spiritual realm, including the hierarchy of the spirits, the importance of an unusual, native doctrine and the relationship of these beings and tenets to the clairvoyant performance itself. < protective spirit >

The Ktunaxa believe in a universe subject to the divine law of the Supreme Being, in which he set forth in the beginning all that was to be. He had made the world island at the same time that he created the Sun, Moon, Stars and all the other supernaturals. He had decreed from the beginning that mankind would some day appear on earth. At this time the pre-existing spirits would retire before the new comers, abandoning their new anthropomorphic forms in favor of new faunal or avian guises, and turn the world over to mankind.

At the peak of the Ktunaxa spiritual hierarchy was the Supreme Being, who had made the world at the same time that he had created all of the other supernatural beings. The Sun, Moon and Dawn were considered to be his visible representatives. Through his identification with the Sun and the Dawn, the Sun Dance Spirit was considered able to approach the Supreme Being with a petition from a human suppliant submitted in the conjuring lodge. Bullhead, the messenger-intermediary, was often the supernatural being designated to bring back this decision. Below these two anthropomorphic beings were arrayed the entire host of lesser spiritual entities, who had earlier assumed their faunal and avian forms before giving way to mankind. < Re-write – We may examine the data regarding Ktunaxa deities and religious concepts in greater detail >

Supreme Being

If we can accept native testimony on this subject, the Ktunaxa appear to have believed in a Supreme Being in pre-missionary times. This deity, known as the Master Spirit (*kuiɫka nupíka*), [2] was a remote, vaguely-defined being, whom neither humans nor ordinary supernaturals could directly approach. He is believed to have made the world at the same time that he created the othr supernatural beings. The Sun, Moon and Dawn were considered to be his visual representatives. < Disagreement over Supreme Being concept (C-131) Contrast with Christian God! >

The Ktunaxa seem able to distinguish clearly between their old concept of the Master Spirit and the idea of the Christian God introduced by the early Catholic missionaries. They say that they learned for the first time of the white man's God from Father Jean De Smet and his fellow priests. The latter urged the Indians to cease their sinful praying to the Sun and other supernaturals, as there was another and greater Being above all. In discussing the whereabouts of their Deity, the Catholic priests pointed upward, which led the Ktunaxa to conclude that He dwelt on high. Prior to this event they had no conception, of course, of Heaven, Hell and Purgatory.

The Ktunaxa attempt to distinguish between their *kuiɫka nupíka* and the Christian God is borne out, I believe, by the native terms applied to the latter. Among the Lower Ktunaxa, the white men's God became known as *yakásin kínawaski*, "the leader who made (owns) us." The Upper Ktunaxa, on the other hand, spoke of him as *yakasin ki•nmi•ki*, "the leader who made (owns) himself." The more the Ktunaxa could learn of this new Deity, the more they became convinced that he could only be their own *kuiɫka nupíka*. It therefore became easy for them to accept the religious teachings of the Black Robes.

Doctrine of Predestination

We have already referred to the Ktunaxa belief in the determination by the Supreme Being that some time mankind would appear on earth and displace the pre-existing spiritual beings. This was but one of the decrees of the Supreme Being from the beginning of time respecting all subsequent events. Another was the granting of power to the "little *nupíka*" to appear visibly to and assist mankind. Still a third was the Supreme Being's ordaining of the time and place of each man's death. A person has so many days of life, the Ktunaxa believe, and there is no power capable of increasing it. A spirit may be able to extend this period by a few days but not longer. A shaman may dream, for example, that a friend will die but he can do nothing to aid him, unless he dreams that he can be helped. Although the lesser spirits through their clairvoyant power have foreknowledge of these events, they are forbidden by the Master Spirit to attempt to change them. The *nupíka* themselves are subject to the ordinances of the Creator, since they were made by Him and must live according to His counsels. Hence they refuse to transgress the Higher Law by attempting to prolong an individual's life. This tenet of predetermination accounts for much of the organization and activity during the séance, since any serious petition, in native theory, must be dispatched to the Supreme Being for decision.

The comments of a native, religious thinker on this subject are of interest here. The *nupíka* according to the conjuror, Stanley Como, have the power of clairvoyance, but their Creator has forbid them to exceed in any way his decrees. Thus the Master Spirit has foreordained the time and place of every man's death. As the final hour approaches, the *nupíka* publicly state in the conjuring rite, "We cannot go beyond the law of our Maker, who has decreed the hour of every individual's death. We cannot transgress the Higher Law by attempting to prolong a person's life. We ourselves are subject to the Master Spirit. We were created by Him and must live according to His law."

Major Spirits

A number of the more important and powerful spirits in the Ktunaxa hierarchy regularly appeared in the séances of both Upper and Lower Ktunaxa groups. Usually conceived in anthropomorphic form, they were the Sun Dance Spirit (*Kukłukinam*), Bullhead or Sculpin (*q!iq!um*), the messenger, and *wisiyał*, the spirit of the sweathouse. These three beings were believed to reside far to the east in the home of the Sun, word of whom was brought the Ktunaxa by the two youths, who are believed to have journeyed to the Sun. The term "grandfather" was applied by the Indians to both Bullhead and the Sweathouse Spirit.

In Pauline's séances at Tobacco Plains, the False Dawn (but not the intervening Darkness), the Dawn, the Sun and the Sun Dance Spirit would, one by one, arrive behind the blanket screen in that order.

Sun Dance Spirit

The Sun Dance Spirit (*Kukłukinam*) regularly entered the séance of the Lower Ktunaxa but rarely that of the upriver groups. Among the former his entrance at the beginning of the divinatory rite was explained on the basis of his being the intermediary messenger to the Supreme Being. At Bonners Ferry séances he arrives first to receive the petitioner's request and relay it to the Master Spirit. Upon his arrival *Kukłukinam* will inquire," What is your reason for putting up the blanket?" The sponsor of the séance arises and presents, with an offering of tobacco, his petition, *Kukłukinam* departs with the request and is succeeded, one by one, by other supernaturals. One of these towards the close of the séance will bring the expected reply to the petition from the Supreme Being. Upon entering the conjuring lodge, *Kukłukinam* may instruct the spectators to purify themselves in the smoke of juniper incense. Among the Upper Ktunaxa *Kukłukinam* appeared rarely to inform people that "a lodge was to be erected to him, i.e., notice of a Sun Dance performance. He might then on condition that the spectators arose and danced in the style of the Sun Dance, grant a request.

Kukłukinam, the Ktunaxa believed, never appeared to adolescents to grant them supernatural power. Instead he went around "to eliminate sickness, to keep each family's campfire burning, and to help people stay well." He would enter a séance and announce, "If a person falls sick, it does not mean that I lack power, but only that he became ill before I arrived. I'm always glad when a person recovers. You have been given the incense coals and my power is in the juniper incense. Each camp must keep the coals alive. Cense yourselves to obtain my aid help, whenever there is sickness in camp. I will be there to help you." Thus despite the Church's opposition to the Medicine Lodge Ceremony, *Kukłukinam* is felt to be at hand any time sickness threatens the Ktunaxa.

A séance was occasionally held to obtain information regarding a projected Medicine Lodge Ceremony. Thus a person, who had obtained a spiritual blessing during his vision quest but who had never demonstrated his power publicly in curing, warfare or leading a ceremony, was known as a *knupqaqaqa*, " ? ". His power would be known to but one or two people. Most individuals were said to be in this category. *Kukłukinam* might appear to such a person in a dream and instruct him to "put up the Medicine Lodge." The individual thus selected would turn to a former Medicine Lodge leader (*kanquxonałka*) and both would consult a conjuror. The latter would hold a séance, during which *Kukłukinam* would give further details and, if necessary, explain the dream.

Bullhead

Bullhead or Sculpin (*q!iq!um*) is considered by the Ktunaxa one of the more important spirits in the conjuring rite." [4] I have discussed the role of this supernatural in Ktunaxa mythology and religion elsewhere (Schaefer 1949: 7-8). By many Ktunaxa, Bullhead is thought to be the grandfather (*kepapa*) of the spirits as well as of mankind, and is so addressed.

In the séance Bullhead acts as both messenger and as intermediary [5] between the other supernaturals and mankind. If misfortune is predicted for a member of the company, the suppliant may request Bullhead to intercede in his behalf. Bullhead then leaves the lodge to discuss the matter with the particular spirit and returns with an answer. The reply may be favorable or unfavorable; if the former, an injunction may be placed upon the petitioner. If he is to avoid the predicted misfortune, he must carry out the injunction as instructed. Thus if it appears to be in store for the Ktunaxa, Bullhead may ask the audience to dance in order to avert it. Again a petitioner's request may be granted on condition that the spectators circle the lodge in the manner of the Black-tail Deer Dance. And again in the case of a recent death in the community, this spirit may request the audience to dance in order to "banish sorrow" and "make people happy again".

Another role carried by Bullhead in the séance is that of interpreter. The greater number of petitions are presented to him because he can clarify the remarks of the supernaturals. Often he is thus able to make clear an otherwise ambiguous remark made by an earlier spirit.

Bullhead usually enters the séance towards its close. At this time he will announce the return of the conjuror, stating, for example, that after three more *nupíka* have come and gone, the conjuror will arrive.

The supernaturals, according to modern Ktunaxa, are uniformly serious during their visits to the conjuring lodge. Bullhead is an exception, however, inasmuch as he jokes good-naturedly a great deal during his stay and the younger Ktunaxa exchange jests with him. The older Ktunaxa, however, listen closely to even his raillery for some covert meaning of importance.

During the séance Bullhead often sends a young boy down to the stream to dip up water and upon his return, asks him what he has seen. Or he will send him down to bring up his (Bullhead's) canoe, which turns out to be no longer than a matchstick.

Some of the younger Ktunaxa characterize Bullhead as the "newsboy". During the séance he brings the latest word of people in other bands, warns of the approach of strangers, and contributes news of general interest.

In appearance Bullhead is said to resemble a dwarfish, old man, with a protruding stomach. His clothing is described as being made of fawnskins and each of his mittens fashioned of the hides of two yearling deer. He always arrives at the place of the séance in a canoe, as he dislikes to walk far on land.

Sweatlodge Spirit

The Spirit of the Sweatlodge (*wisíyał*) represented one of the more important supernaturals of the Ktunaxa. Although most petitions were presented to this spirit in the sweatlodge, he also visited the conjuring lodge. There he was said to grant requests for acquiring wealth and recovery from illness. Hunters and gamblers were among those who solicited his aid.

The Sweatlodge Spirit is said to live among the Ktunaxa. As he is the last of the seven, major spirits, one informant believed that he possessed the seven powers of each major spirit, making "seven sevens" or forty-nine in all.

wisíyał never grants power to anyone but people still seek his favor.

Subordinate Spirits

The less important supernaturals, who were known to the Ktunaxa in their faunal, avian or even inanimate guise, were known collectively in the séance as *nupíkanana,* "little spirits," or *nupíkanananaintek,* "all little spirits."

There is a leader of the *nupíka,* who is believed to communicate with the higher supernaturals. Simon Francis did not know whether it was the same entity among all conjurors.

Of the lesser, spiritual entities the Owl, Ghost, and Woodpecker Spirits played the most important parts in the conjuring performance. Informants clamed that other supernaturals directed the Owl, Ghost and Woodpecker Spirits to carry out their specified tasks of assisting the conjuror in his departure from and return to the lodge. Hence he did not have to acquire specific powers from these particular spirits for his clairvoyant activities.

The Ktunaxa attempted to incorporate their taxonomic concepts of the faunal world in the séance but in a vague and rather ill-defined way. Specifically this was the tendency to refer petitioners' requests to the leader of the four groups of faunal beings. Thus the eagle was considered by some the leader of the avian group; the woodpecker, by others. Grizzly, perhaps, as the leader of the "clawed group" of animals and Two-pointed Buck as head of the animal group with hooves. Once an individual had obtained power from the leader of a group, he had the rest of the creatures in that category as his spiritual helpers.

There was not, however, a spiritual master of conjuring among the Ktunaxa such as Hallowell (1942: 23) found among the Saulteaux.

The Owl Spirits

The Ktunaxa share the wide-spread belief among Indians that owls speak to them in human language and relate happenings that have taken place elsewhere or are about to occur locally. Thus people were sometimes warned of the approaching death of a relative or friend. A hunting party, it was said, was occasionally informed by this means of a death in the main camp. It was believed that misfortune predicted in this way might be averted by firing a gun in the general direction of the harbinger of evil. The Great Horned Owl is described as the particular species that carried news in this way.

Once at Big Meadows, Susanne Bullrobe related, Charley Andrews said that an owl imitated a dog's bark and then began to curse in English. Shortly after a Ktunaxa named Bird Dog was killed and the owl, it was believed, had foretold his death.

Modern Ktunaxa differ considerably as to the number and species of Owl Spirits controlled by the conjuror and participating in carrying him from, and to the lodge. [6] This failure ofagreement probably reflects individual and perhaps, even group variation among clairvoyants. One informant stated that usually from four to five birds undertook the task. Abel Sebastian, of St. Mary's, claimed that there were nine owls of different species to serve the transportation needs of the seer. Simon Francis, of Bonners Ferry, claimed that the number of these super-naturals varied from seven, "twice-seven," or rarely, "thrice-seven." Any number below seven, he added, reflected but slight power on the part of the conjuror.

According to Susanne Bullrobe, the conjuror was carried from the lodge by three Great Horned Owls (*kupi*). Seven owls were said to enter the lodge, one by one, and then leave immediately. Their arrival was signalled by the sound of striking the lodgepoles, next the shaking of the dew-claw rattles on the blanket surface, and finally, by the sound of a thud on the floor. Then three other owls enter, singing their song in which the audience joins. After the entrance of the third, the conjuror is carried from the lodge. Informants state that the birds lift the clairvoyant by a thong, one end of which was fastened to his forelock, the other to both of his big toes. Using the same arrangement, they return with him towards the end of the session.

In any case we can imagine something of the interest and expectancy of the audience, especially the younger people, as they carefully listened for the arrival and departure of these supernaturals and counted their numbers.

Informants {consultants} did not believe that the Owl Spirits specifically granted power to the conjuror but rather were directed by other *nupíka* to carry out their aerial activities.

The story is related of a Ktunaxa who was waiting at a salt lick for game. He heard the sounds caused by a number of Owl Spirits carrying the body of a conjuror through the air. The noise they made frightened away some elk approaching the lick. Later the hunter reproached the seer for spoiling his chance to get some fresh meat.

When a person is supported in the air by the supernaturals, as when a conjuror is taken from the lodge, it is spoken of as *knupqaqaɫetkin*, "spirit aid". The spirits are believed to move constantly through the air and to transport themselves and humans by such power.

< There were said to be seven songs of the Grizzly Bear, one for the male and female, and one each for the six children. Grizzly Bear always has two cubs, hence four in family (Susanne Bullrobe) >

Ghost Spirits

The Ghost or Skeleton Spirit (*qałqa*) represented an important character in the Ktunaxa

(over)

< Certain *qałqa* may also grant petitions to acquire wealth and others to cure certain illnesses. Petitions to locate missing people or animals were usually made to the ghost Spirit in the séance. It was believed that a request made to this spirit would determine if the missing one was still alive. If a lost horse was close at hand, the ghost could easily direct the owner to it. If, however, the animal had strayed for some distance and crossed a number of roads or streams, the ghost might have recourse to the altar in order to inform a person of {its location} >

According to Ktunaxa belief, there were two kinds of ghost spirits, 1) a benevolent spirit that could confer power upon humans; and 2) an inimical one, that attempted to frighten or even harm people. The latter was thought to be the spirit of an evil person, who remained a wanderer on earth seeking to injure people. [6a] It is important to note that a ghost did not represent the spirit of a particular dead friend or relative. Rather it was a generalized concept of a ghost, i.e. an impersonal being emanating, say, from a dead, unidentified person or even animal, whose physical remains rested somewhere off in the forest. In fact, informants agreed that no clairvoyant possessed sufficient power to summon the spirit of a particular deceased individual to the conjuring lodge. This limitation to the Ktunaxa seer's power is in direct contrast to Blackfoot conjuring practices, in which a conjuror was believed able to summon the spirit of a specific dead relative to his aid.

Both were known as *qałqa* and the evil spirit as *sanqałqa*. < The latter was often seen in the vicinity of a cemetery and it would attempt to frighten people by disarranging their clothing.

The benevolent ghost was said to be invisible. Hence if the blanket screen was raised during his presence, nothing was to be seen. In addition, to his song, rendered in a characteristically hoarse voice, he could also be identified during the séance by the rattling of his bones. >

There was the usual disagreement among Ktunaxa informants as to the number of ghost spirits and the number controlled by any seer. According to Simon Francis, although there were said to be seven ghost spirits, the average diviner had power to control but two or three. Only rarely did a conjuror at Bonners Ferry have power from all seven. Bullrobe, a former conjuror of the Flathead Ktunaxa, stated that there were seven benevolent ghosts, which would enter the conjuring lodge in succession. However, he added, if one over this number arrived, the audience could be certain that it was a *sánqałqa*. The identification would be positive if the seventh ghost began to criticize its predecessors. If that occurred, Bullhead, the messenger, was thought to call attention to its true identity. Such a spirit had no song of its own but bragged continually about itself and refused to cooperate with other spirits.

If many *qałqa* entered the conjuring lodge, the Ktunaxa regarded it as a forewarning of a fellow tribesman's death.

The conjurors, Little Abraham, of Bonners Ferry, and Pauline, of Tobacco Plains, rarely had a ghost enter their conjuring performances and then only upon serious occasions when death threatened someone in the community. If a ghost arrived behind the blanket, Pauline would advise those present to ask that it try to avert the tragedy. At Tobacco Plains one *qałqa* and rarely two, would enter the séance. The Ghost Spirit can be identified by the sound of rattling bones and by certain songs.

Occasionally several strands of hair in the mane of a horse were found to be curled up into a circle. Such a knot was believed to have been tied by a ghost. It was called *qałqa kanałikamuis,* "ghost's stirrups," and the knot was said to have been used by the ghost in riding upon the horse's neck. A ghost was said to prefer a prized horse for riding upon the horse's neck. A ghost was said to prefer a prized horse for riding, but Alec Gravelle, of Tobacco Plains, has found "ghost stirrups" upon one or two of his old mares.

Ambrose Gravelle related an incident of a ghost encountered by Peter Paul and his wife, Ann Mary, of the Flathead Ktunaxa. They were driving back to Niarada from a hunting trip to Elmo. Suddenly along the highway they heard the sound of loud laughter behind them. Looking back they saw a *qałqa*, with its skeleton frame curved into a circle and rolling along the side of the road. Although their car was travelling about forty miles an hour, the bony skeleton quickly passed them laughing and gesturing in high glee. Peter Paul smiled at sight of the apparition and said to his wife, "Maybe I can pass him and find out how fast he is really going." His wife replied, "This is no laughing matter. This may foreshadow someone's death." Three months later Peter Paul himself was dead.

Ambrose Gravelle related on incident of his wife's uncle, Joe Dennis, and his encounter with a ghost. The conjuror, Looking Glass, was holding a séance at Dayton. Joe Dennis, then a boy about sixteen, was sitting in the doorway of the conjuring lodge and leaning against one of the entrance poles.

When the ghost (*qałqa*) entered, it warned the spectators not to lean against the lodgepoles at the entrance. But the lodge was crowded and Joe could not move from his position because of the people. The ghost again issued its warning from behind the blanket. Joe became irritated since there was nothing he could do. The spectators started to move away, some criticizing Joe for not moving. He became angrier then and was determined not to stir from the spot. The ghost then said," If you don't move, I'll move you."

A second *qałqa* then entered behind the blanket, which was observed by Joe but not by the other spectators. The two *qałqa* then made their way around the circumference of the lodge, one on each side, towards the entrance. Joe suddenly felt a cold chill run down his back. An infant was lying asleep near the edge of the lodge. The child started to cry. Joe shouted," You shouldn't allow the *nupíka* to do this. You will kill the child." He then turned and left the lodge. The infant died within three days, while Joe was ill for six months with an irritation extending from his head down along his spine, a headache and a general run-down condition.

One day while Joe and his parents were returning from Jennings, he said, "You go on and I'll catch up with you. I want to see my uncle, Bear Hat". Joe took a short cut and came upon two lodges, one of which was occupied by old *suksał* (meaning unknown). He remained there that night. Nearby was a lodge of Bonners Ferry Ktunaxa, Little Abraham and his family. Joe left next day and travelled up Wolf Creek and ran across some relatives there. Then he returned and came across the same two lodges. Kustata and his wife were in one lodge and a séance was being held next door. Joe entered the lodge where the conjuring performance was taking place. Little Abraham was the seer and the séance was well along. Joe sat down at the entrance. All at once *qałqa* entered. This was a departure from the usual pattern of Little Abraham's séance. Little Abraham was ignorant of Joe's earlier experience and, besides, *qałqa* never entered his séance. *qałqa* spoke to Joe, saying, "I didn't talk to you recently to make you feel bad. If anyone tries to scare you, scare them back. Thus you wouldn't have become sick." Joe felt a shock at being struck by the *qałqa*. The *nupíka* of Bear Hat, however, had once told Joe if anyone attempted to frighten him, he was to scare them back. Thus he was reminded by a different conjuror of the power given him by *qałqa* as a child.

The following account of a séance involving the presence of ghost spirits in a séance was related by Abraham Bullrobe. It took place during his youth. Although lengthy, the detail makes it seem worth quoting in full:

> There were two adjacent camps of Ktunaxa during this particular winter. Game was scarce. The people decided "to put up the blanket." It was difficult to get the performance going properly. The *nupíka* came and left the lodge quickly and would not accept the pipe offerings. Bullhead entered and predicted that one of the spectators would die within a few days. He explained, "It's too late to prevent this but the explosion of a gun will cause the person's death." The spectators insisted that Bullhead prevent the catastrophe and finally, he consented to try. He left, promising to secure a decision from the *nupíka* as to whether the accident could be averted.
>
> After a time Bullhead returned and said, "I'm going to tell you what the *nupíka* have decided. Remember that there are seven Ghost Spirits, which are friendly, and one which is not. During our conference the latter was unfavorable and insisted that this man must die. This Ghost has been against you for ages. If you listen to him, you will come to harm. Now the spirits will enter and you must count the number of Ghosts as they arrive. When the eighth enters, then one of you must have a gun ready and shoot him through the blanket". Bullhead then left.
>
> The Ktunaxa talked the matter over. They realized that shooting through the blanket was a most unusual occurrence. However, one old man had heard something similar from his parents and he agreed to take the risk, if that was the only way to save the victim. The Ghosts came and went and, finally, the seventh entered, saying, "Now look out for the next, whom you must shoot." The eighth entered the lodge, rattling his bones loudly. The old man shot through the blanket, causing a human scapula to fly over the top of the blanket and drop near the campfire. Upon inspection it was seen to have a bullet hole in it. Bullhead returned and said "The *nupíka* are very glad that the eighth Skeleton has been killed. You have fired the bullet that was intended for one of you. Now that person is safe, I have some advice for you. Tomorrow only one of you is to go hunting. He must follow the trail until he comes upon a deer. If he can kill it, then you are out of danger. The hunter must return with the kill at once, have the meat cooked, and served to all of you. Thereafter game will be plentiful."
>
> Things turned out exactly, it was said, as Bullhead had predicted. The deer was killed and while the people feasted, the snow became soft and by morning, a 'chinook wind' had arrived bringing rain. Thereafter many deer were killed close to camp.

The Woodpecker Spirit

The Woodpecker Spirit (*yamakpał*) was believed to protect the conjuror during his absence from the lodge. As soon as the seer was carried out by the Owl Spirits, the Woodpecker Spirit followed in order to protect him.

This spirit was said to be the last to enter the conjuring lodge during a séance. While there he seldom accepts a smoke and usually departs if a pipe is offered him, his arrival indicates to the audience that the séance is soon coming to a close and that the conjuror's return may soon be expected.

Some informants believe that there were two Woodpecker Spirit – a male and a female.

The Woodpecker Spirit is believed to have great power for curing.

Lesser Spirits

Certain of the *nupíka* are believed to occur in groups of seven in the conjuring performance. At Bonners Ferry such groups include Two-pointed Buck, Three-pointed Deer, the Flute Spirits, Grizzly Bears, Ghosts and Crazy Dogs. They are said to be the only spirits differing one from another in age and sex. These spiritual beings may enter as a group or more frequently, in succession.

When the Deer Spirits enter the séance followed by the Flute Spirits, it is an indication that the conjuror is about to return to the lodge.

Of the seven Flute Spirits, the first or second to enter may bring back the strap by means of which the seer is believed to be carried from the lodge. These spirits are regarded as female and the notes of the flute can be heard above the sound of the audience singing.

Two-pointed Buck, the Grizzly Bears, the Sun, and Flute Spirits are said to attend every séance held by the Bonners Ferry Ktunaxa.

Frog, *watak*, an important figure in Ktunaxa mythology, was considered the grandmother of all the spirits as well as of mankind. Her song, like those of a few other spirits, was said to be the same for all conjurors. She is good natured and willing to help people during the séance.

If the conjuror should have power from the Grizzly Bear, that spirit could be expected to enter the séance. There were said to be seven songs of the Grizzly Bear Spirits, one for the male-female, and one each for the six cubs. The Black Bear might also appear as a guardian for some conjurors.

The Gun Spirit enters the conjuring lodge and sings its song, as also does the Steamboat Spirit, with its sounds of escaping steam and steam whistle. When firearms were first introduced among the Ktunaxa, an informant stated, one conjuror introduced the Gun Spirit, with its song, into the divining rite.

In former times the Spirit of the Bison was said to enter the conjuring lodge.

The Horse Spirit comes behind the blanket and can be identified by what is described as a beautiful song.

Dog Spirits enter the conjuring lodge and sing the Crazy Dog song.

Moose, elk, caribou, bighorn and mountain goat Spirits enter the divining lodge but seldom and then only for a conjuror with power to summon all animal spirits.

The Loon Spirit had been heard by Susanne Bullrobe to enter a séance once; also a magpie.

In the séance the *nupíka* always address the Ktunaxa by their native names.

The Crow and Raven (*qóqen*) were said by Bullrobe to have great power for curing in the conjuring lodge. If these Spirits appear to a person and grant him power, he ıs ınstructed to make a drum. If a sick person goes to a séance for treatment, the *nupíka* enter and state that one is coming, who will treat the sick person. The spirit indicated is Crow. Baptiste Mathias, of the Flathead Ktunaxa, has such a drum, which he beats to summon the spirits.

Ambrose Gravelle related the following incident involving the Raven Spirit:

Once near Tobacco Plains, Ignatius Jack's father bought a .44 Winchester rifle from some Stony Indians. The Ktunaxa were shooting at a target with the gun. Jack's father slipped the gun into a buckskin case, slung it over his shoulder, and set out for home.

Upon removing the gun later, he discovered that the rear sight was missing. He went to Michel Humpback and asked, "Could you locate that sight for me in a séance? I 'll pay you for it." Michel replied that he would try and asked something moderate in payment. Jack suggested his blanket and Michel replied, "That's what I meant."

The séance was arranged for that evening in Jack's father's lodge. His blanket was employed as a screen in the performance. *Q!iq!um* entered, after several *nupíka* had come and gone. By this time Jack was becoming anxious. *Q!iq!um* said, "The *nupíka* have located the sight but they are afraid to touch it. However there is one coming who can handle it. Now that *nupíka* is there and he will bring it. He is not afraid of metal." *Q'iq'um* then left.

Another spirit now entered, saying, "I was coming to show you the spot where the gunsight is lying. And I'd be there when you find it. The identity of this spirit was unknown. "Now the spirit is coming with the sight. Reach your hands above the dew-claw rattles on the blanket and grasp the sight behind the blanket. Get several others to help you as it will hit you hard." Things turned out as the spirit had predicted. Joe David, a large, strong individual, volunteered to grasp the sight, he reached for it and the shock threw him into the air. Twice he tried to feel the sight in his clenched fist but without success. Finally he felt it on the third attempt and opened his fist to reveal the sight. *Q!iq!um* returned and accused the Stony Indians of sending their *nupíka* to steal the sight. "The thief knows it and will not be around to bother you." Raven was the spirit < written along side: that recovered the sight>. The other *nupíka* were unable to handle it because it had been sent magically by a Stony shaman.

Certain spirits are thought by some conjurors to be paired off as male and female. Simon Francis stated that his father, a conjuror, kept this idea a secret from everyone but his wife. If a male spirit enters and the female fails to follow immediately, it is an indication of trouble. The conjurors wife or a close friend must then take steps to avert the impending trouble. Abel Sebastian, a conjuror of St. Mary's Reserve, believed that his *nupíka* entered successively and in mated pairs – the male first, followed by the female.

There were but few mythical beings associated with the séance. Ambrose Gravelle spoke of a conjuror named *Toutcak*, "Thumb", who had received his power from the giant Otter. He weighed about 200 pounds and was Abraham Bullrobe's father's brother. He was of the Tobacco Plains Ktunaxa but intermarried among the Elmo Ktunaxa. When brought back to the séance, he was soaking wet from his power animal's habitat the underground river, *Kiłwiaki*, "the heart of water."

Yaukekam, son of Redstone, is an anthropomorphic spirit from the mythological period, who enters the séance and always asks for salmon eggs to eat.

At the end of the period set by his spiritual guardian, the diviner must then use his clairvoyant power entirely for the welfare of his people, particularly in times of adversity. This might take place at the age of 25, 30 or even later in life. Now his attitude and behaviour changed and he adopted a quiet, reserved mode of life. His previously accumulated wealth now began to dissipate. The loss of property was an overt indication to fellow tribesmen that the diviner no longer worked for his own personal interest. Now he became unaware of what took place during his séances. Such events must be related to him by others later. People might win horses, robes or furs through his clairvoyant powers but only rarely did he share in them. Thus a spirit might direct during a séance that a certain captured horse be given the clairvoyant but this happened only rarely. It is for this reason, as we have noted, that the *nupíka* have given him the name of "poor in all ways."

Long ago the conjurors and the members of the Crazy Dog Society were friendly rivals. The latter would evince skepticism at the séances and upon being convinced by the diviners. Leaders of the Sun Dance and Grizzly Bear Ceremonies represented the other two, informal groups. The members of each would assist one another.

V ACQUIRING CONJURING POWER

Generally speaking the power quest of the Ktunaxa conformed to that of their Salishan-speaking neighbors to the south and west.

Spiritual power to perform the conjuring rite was often granted a youth during his first vision quest. Among the Ktunaxa a youth's first quest for power took place in his pre-adolescent days, Less frequently, as will be noted later, a nature person might have such power conferred upon him.

Power for divination could be conferred upon a person, it is important to note, by any supernatural being, an animal, a bird or even the spirit of an inanimate object. Matthias Finlay, a conjuror of Elmo, is said to have obtained power in his youth from a small, cedar tree (*nisinat*). Abraham Bullrobe, also of Elmo, played at conjuring as a child, using his pet dogs as an audience. His parents were reproved at supernatural a séance for allowing him to do so. However, he received power to conjure, possibly from one of his dogs and held séances later in his life.

The guardian spirit experience of Pauline, a conjuror of Tobacco Plains, illustrates several points of interest. When he was four years old, his mother died and his father remarried. The family was hunting east of Flathead Lake. On the return he was sent to bed early by his step-mother and awakened to hear people singing nearby. Walking over to the adjacent lodge, he entered to find a séance in progress. A voice coming from the blanket, spoke to him, "Boy, get a pail and go down to the stream for water so people can drink!" He found a bucket and walked down to the river. Stooping over to fill it, he saw nothing but gravel. So he walked farther out. Filling the bucket, he returned to the lodge. There Bullhead again spoke to him, "Boy, you tried to dip water from my canoe (see p. 98). That is why you were unable to get any." The Spirit then asked the child what he had seen. Pauline told him and was warned not to divulge this information to anyone. Such was the beginning, Pauline remarked, of his conjuring career. At this time he was considered too young to be visited by a supernatural.

The novice, even after he has obtained conjuring power, will be unable to hold a séance until the Owl and the Ghost Spirits confer their powers upon him. The services of the former, informants state, are required to transport the seer to and from the conjuring lodge; while the Ghost is believed to control the exit and entrance of the seer to the lodge. Some Ktunaxa would add to this spiritual pair the Woodpecker Spirit, which is thought to protect the diviner during his absence from the lodge.

The spiritual being will bestow a song upon his human protégé, the singing of which will serve to summon the spirit at his need. The repetition of this song at the séance of the seer will serve to fix it in the minds of his fellow tribesmen and to identify it with this particular spirit. Some conjurors will go on to acquire two or three additional spirits; a few, four or five. The songs of these supernaturals were sung in succession by the diviner and his audience at the start of the séance to bring the former's spirits to the performance.

The *akúkłiłimi*

The Ktunaxa concept of the *akúkłiłimi*, "one's own ground," should be discussed here. A youth in search of a spiritual guardian is often sent to a locality believed frequented by supernaturals. There were a number of these places scattered throughout Ktunaxa territory. Often a parent or a grandparent would sponsor the novice's quest, give him a token to be carried along and direct him to the place where he himself had received spiritual power. Sometimes, in this case, the Ktunaxa believe, a spirit will enter the token and transport the youth to the *akúkłiłimi*.

Here the neophyte spends several days fasting until a supernatural appears and grants him power. Thereafter this particular locality will have significance for him as the place frequented by his spirit guardian. The relevance of the concept here is that the diviner, upon "being carried" from the conjuring lodge, was believed to be transported first to his *akúkłiłimi*.

Immanent spirit concept

We can discuss next what I have called the "immanent spirit" or "in-dwelling spirit" concept of the Ktunaxa. Upon first confronting a spiritual being during his quest a youth is believed to become paralyzed with fear and lose consciousness. During this period the spirit is said to place an object within the novice's body and then to enter that object to remain with his protege throughout his life. The novice, of course, learns in what part of his body the spirit resides, as the latter will communicate later with bin in case of danger. This information he will later pass on to his wife so that she can strike him there if the need arises. In earlier times an elderly person would often ask a relative to do this as a temporary restorative. Thereafter no one will touch this spot or even seat himself closely on this side of the person for fear of rendering him unconsciousness. In fact, during an emergency, someone will be asked to slap the person on this spot. The effect is such that he will be nearly knocked unconsciousness but it will bring the supernatural to his aid. Shortly before the person's death the supernatural is believed to leave his body. In earlier times such a departing spirit would have been transferred to a young relative.
< Densmore, Mandan-Hidatsa, 43, 45, etc; Jenness, Sekani, p.69; See Goddard, Beaver, p262 >

If a person with power is struck by a bullet, Stanley Como stated, the *nupíka* within his body will cradle the missile without causing harm to the person until his declining years. When about to die and the *nupíka* ready to leave his body, the individual will begin to feel for the first time the affect of the bullet. Thus old warriors who were wounded during their youth and never felt it throughout mature life, are bothered in their final years.

When a person with power sings his guardian spirit song, his *nupíka* is believed to leave his body and enter his power token placed before him. Otherwise there would be no efficacy in the token.

Because of his youth a novice will be instructed by his tutelary spirit, the Ktunaxa believe, not to attempt to hold a séance until he reaches maturity. Usually the appointed time is set to coincide with some personal event, such as the novice's marriage, birth of his first child or the like. Matthias Finley, of the Flathead Ktunaxa, was thus instructed not to perform his first séance until he had reached a certain age. There was also a belief that if a novice began to conjure earlier, he might soon exhaust his power.

If the young conjuror-to-be held his initial séance before the appointed time, the Ktunaxa believed that he would be punished for his disobedience with death within two years. Sometimes if a person attempted a trial performance too soon, the *nupíka* themselves, it was said, would refuse to assist in the rite.

As we noted earlier, a mature person may occasionally be granted power for divination. Thus the father of Abel Sebastian, of the St. Mary's Reserve, and already married, walked outside his lodge one day and returned with his thumbs tied behind his back. This was the first intimation that he possessed clairvoyant power.

Occasionally two youths who had become intimate friends (*suwútimo*) would be visited by the same spirit and both receive power for conjuring. Friends with such common power were known as *kasí•tops*. In such a case one would assist the other in later life in arranging séances. We have a detailed account of such a spiritual co-visitation from the late Chief Paul David, of Tobacco Plains. In 1935 when I recorded the episode, Chief Paul remarked that because of his advanced age and the fact that his guardian spirit was about to desert him, he felt free to fully reveal his youthful visitation. Although of extended length the account seems worth quoting in full for its significant details on this point.

When he was about nine years old, Paul David was out riding double with his *suwútimo* in the St. Eugene's Mission area, near present Cranbrook, B.C. It was winter and the snow was deep. Suddenly the horse stopped and refused to move despite the blows given him by the two boys. Suddenly Paul felt as if he was being seized by someone, began to get dizzy and then lost consciousness. He recovered his senses to find himself across the Rockies, near Three Buttes, still on the horse and on one of the buttes. Again he lost consciousness and recovered to find himself back at the Mission. He discovered that he and his friend were tied with the bridle (*atsíka*) with the hands of both tied behind them to their belts by their thumbs. The voice of Ghost (*qałqa*) was heard talking to them.

Again Paul lost his senses and regained them at a place called *yakávisúkwe* to see their horse upon the very edge of a waterfall. This time Owl's voice was heard before Paul again lost consciousness. Again he recovered to find himself at the Mission. Here a voice spoke to the boys and granted them power, saying, "Twenty-five years from now, you may put up the blanket." Thus Paul and his friend received power from the same spirit. They were instructed to hold a séance three times, the first time Paul being tied up and his friend going behind the blanket, the second time Paul going behind the blanket, and the last occasion the same as the first. Thereafter each one could hold separate performances. The spirit disappeared.

Their horse now proved without difficulty and the boys were soon back in camp. After their experience they were unable to speak but managed to make a noise heard by an old man. Upon glancing at them he exclaimed," My children have seen a spirit. Get up and make a tire so that they can cense themselves!" The youths were taken from the horse by relatives, who found it difficult to remove the bridle so tightly had it been knotted. The boy» started to relate their experience but were immediately halted by Paul's father.

Many years later – twenty-three to be exact – Paul's friend was thrown from his hone and killed. This accident, of course, prevented him from carrying out the instructions of the spirit to hold a joint séance with his friend at the age of thirty-four. Paul added that he saw the Owl and Ghost Spirits as well as the unnamed one, which actually granted him power to conjure and cure the sick. Now at his advanced age he feels at times as if his spirit was about to leave his body, apparently located at the back of his neck.

Most of the younger Ktunaxa of recent decades are said to have acquired their supernatural power for conjuring, the Sun Dance, and treating the sick through the transfer of *nupíka* from an older relative. This is considered to be an easy way of obtaining power.

Some supernaturals that do not really belong to the conjuror, may enter his séance. Since members of the audience already know the identity and number of his supernaturals by their songs, the spectators immediately become aware of the entrance of the strange *nupíka*. The possibilities situations of this and similar aberrant situations offer many opportunities entertaining and even amusing séances to the imaginative and skilled diviner.

< Develop this and 2 following an opportunity for imaginative seer to stage unique shows, etc. >

A strange *nupíka* may enter the conjuring lodge. If it does not offer any reason for entering, its presence may portend trouble. To learn its purpose certain of the spectators will begin to question succeeding spirits. Such an event may mean, for example, that another conjuror is in danger of death and hence, his spirit has already begun to seek another owner. A *nupíka* obtained so easily, however, is not considered an indication of strong supernatural power.

Again a wandering spirit may enter a séance. The strange *nupíka*nupíkamay have belonged to a conjuror, who recently died. The supernatural will say, "I'm a wanderer. Long ago I used to go behind the blanket of so-and-so," naming its former owner. The ownerless spirit may then remain to be adopted by the present conjuror.

Abuse of Conjuring Power

Hallowell (1942: 25) has referred briefly to the occasional abuse of divining power among the Saulteaux Indians. He points out that there must be a real need for the séance and that it must not be done too frequently or for fun or to show off. I gained the impression that these same limitations held for Ktunaxa conjurors.

In this connection a spirit will instruct his protégé that he should not publicly display his clairvoyant power until he reaches a certain age, or has so many children, etc. If he disobeys and holds a performance earlier, the supernatural will appear to him in a dream or vision and say, "You have disobeyed my instructions and you will have to pay for your disobedience by giving up one of your children or even yourself." The life of the child then rather than that of the diviner is believed taken by the spirit as a sacrifice. If the spirit so decides, the man, his wife or his child may die or as an alternative, he may lose his power altogether. In the last case he will try to acquire other power but would not return to his *akúkłiłimi*. My sacrificing his wife or child, he may be able to retain his original power but it would never be as strong.

Recently, at St. Mary's Reserve, a youth began to conjure too soon and was then required to postpone this activity for three years. He lost some of his power, in addition, and has difficulty recovering his strength upon being brought back into the lodge.

Mary White-pete, of St. Mary's Reserve, related an incident in which & spirit belonging to a conjuror entered the divining lodge and spoke of his protege misusing his supernatural power. The Spirit said," I never told the person who owns this blanket, to boast of me. I instructed him to act differently. He was directed to make use of me for curing the sick and helping others." This informant declared some that a supernatural never grants power for evil but/people make the wrong use of their power. She added that in boasting of his power, a person will say, "I'm powerful. I can do anything," She pointed out that a person with power should be humble, *kúmnakatwinátek*, as instructed by the *nupíka*.

If a conjuror mis-uses his power during a séance, for example, the spirits will notify the company of that fact and according to my informant, publicly state that the diviner will have but a short time to live. Thereafter the seer will be unable to hold another séance.

An example of the mis-use of clairvoyant power given me was the following incident:

A Ktunaxa conjuror remained behind the blanket for a day and a half and was brought back by the Owl Spirits during the daytime. He did this to convince people of his power. Bullrobe and other members of the audience were awaiting his return to the lodge. In broad daylight they claimed to have seen his shadow through the lodge canvas passing overhead, after which he then arrived back of the blanket. Those outside the lodge insisted they had seen his body carried through the air. Shortly after he disappeared and was never heard from again. This was considered a supernatural punishment for gross misuse of his power.

The following account of a Lower Ktunaxa séance in which a seer was said to have abused his power, was related to me by Simon Francis. It took place about 1927.

The incident took place during one séance Simon attended. The diviner's name was Paul, now deceased. About 11 o'clock the *nupíka* inquired if anyone in the audience could see anything on the dew-claw rattles, Simon was unable to detect anything. The seer was teasing the people and hurting their feelings. The *nupíka* came and went. Finally Paul said, "Some of you have seen it. One of you get up and take it." One young woman went over and reached out her hands to the rattles. Her hand was instantly drawn to them and closed over them. She staggered back and complained of the pain. Everyone witnessed this. The *nupíka* left when this occurred and it was a few moments before one of them returned. There was no conjuror in the audience so nothing could be done. The victim was very ill and couldn't free her hand. She began to cry. Then a spirit entered and explained that the conjuror was being brought back to take care of the emergency. (In this case *yamakpał* doesn't come behind the blanket). The blanket was raised and the diviner came out. He was supposed to remove tile object from her hands. All at once her hand opened and the conjuror staggered back and went under the blanket and was again taken from the lodge. This closed the incident. There was no explanation and the séance ended. *Yamakpał* entered. A noise was heard as if heavy boards were being pried loose. The conjuror cried out in pain. The blanket was now seen to be pushed out from the corner by the conjuror's head as he re-entered behind it, belly side up. His assistants lifted the blanket and the conjuror could be seen projecting through the wall of the cabin but there was no hole visible. The assistants quickly dropped the blanket and a few seconds later, the seer was heard to drop to the floor. His assistants quickly took the blanket down but there was no hole visible in the cabin wall. People thought that the conjuror went too far in displaying his power. Evidently the young woman had made fun of Paul's power at one time and he took this method of punishing her. She was just being "pinched."

Conjuror's Compensation

There was considerable variation among diviners in respect to payment made for services. Some, such as Joe David, Stanley Como and Pauline were loath to accept fees but others, such as Looking Glass, expected compensation. Pauline would refuse money but at times would ask that it be given to his wife or another person, Paul, the conjuror at Bonners Ferry, would ask that payment be made to some individual he would name. In the case of treatment of a patient in a séance, some conjurors would expect to be paid. Others might ask that a gift be attached to a wooden hoop for the spirit, *Kítnokokíniyał*. The feeling among the Ktunaxa was in general that payment made a diviner should not be exorbitant but in keeping with the spirits' name for such a person, *kłmnakani kítnanai,* "poor in all ways." The above statement conforms in general, I think, to data gathered on the subject by Dr. Turney-High (1941: 176).

For a certain period of time after he was allowed to practice the conjuror, like other young men so blessed, was free to derive personal advantage from his calling. During this period of, say, ten or fifteen years, he was said to be cognizant of what the *nupíka* were saying in the séance and able to turn such information to his own advantage. During this period he could make use of his clairvoyant powers before starting out on a raid, to gamble in the wheel and dart, or stick games, to trap for fur-bearers or to engage in other types of wealth accumulation. As a result he was sometimes able to amass considerable property during the time of individual enterprise. When that period came to an end, however, the diviner was expected to employ his gifts for the benefit of his people. If war should break out with a neighboring tribe, he would be expected to employ his clairvoyant ability in defence {defense} of his people. Similarly, he was supposed to put his diviniatory powers to use in other fields for the good of his tribe.

Even more important to the conjuror than the wealth thus accumulated, however, was the wealth-gathering power itself. Because of the semi-nomadic and uncertain life of the Ktunaxa and the difficulty of transporting and storing property, there was a definite limit to the amount of property that a person could accumulate. Even the number of horses that one man could look after, was limited. Often if an individual had forty or fifty head, they might all be driven off in one night by enemy raiders. Then the owner would have to start over again to collect a herd. As a result there was felt to be little security in possessing property in early times. Those people, however, who had supernatural power to gather property, whether by gambling, raiding, trapping or other means, were reasonably certain, if they were unfortunate enough to lose their possessions, of accumulating more. So the power to amass property was considered more important than property itself. This explains, perhaps, the preoccupation of the Ktunaxa with gambling as observed and recorded by early white travellers in fur trade annals and elsewhere. [8]

VI CONJURING PERSONAGES

The conjuror vas known by the term *q!aq!ał*, "one who is cut in two," this term is derived from the name of the conjuring rite.   Having received supernatural power for divining in his youth, the novice was obliged to wait to exercise his power until he reached maturity.   Men who followed this calling were said to range in age from post-adolescense to middle-age.   The role was generally assumed by a younger son, the male parent and older brothers confining themselves to ceremonial parts in the Sun Dance and other Ktunaxa ceremonies.

Not all young men were conjurors in earlier days.   Some were given power for warfare; others for curing the sick.   Those who received supernatural power for warfare were accorded higher honor by their fellow tribesmen, as they fought in the open with the aid of their spiritual guardians.   In respect to a conjuror, however, the spirits were considered fighting for him (in shamanistic conflict).   A conjuror was never expected to fight in person against an enemy for this reason. Less honor was therefore given him.

The mature conjuror claims to realize nothing of what takes place within the conjuring lodge during his "absence."   It is believed that he is first taken to his *akukłiłimi*, the locality where he was first visited by his tutelary spirit.   Thereafter, as we saw in the vision quest account of Paul David, the conjuror is believed to lose and regain consciousness repeatedly to find himself each time in a hazardous place.   Among such places, for example, were the side of a steep canyon, the top branch of a tall tree, or the brink of a waterfall.   Sometimes the novice experienced the sensation of passing entirely through a large rock or a giant tree.   The inference here, of course, is that the conjuror is in physical danger constantly during his absence from the divining lodge.   Such is borne out by the testimony of clairvoyants on this point.

I recorded several accounts of conjurors bearing upon their séance experience:

William Gingres, my late interpreter of the Flathead Ktunaxa, once asked a conjuror about his sensations while absent from the lodge. The latter replied, "At times I regain consciousness to find myself in the top of a tall tree. As soon as I move, I lose my senses and regain them to find myself a tall cliff. Occasionally I am able to recognize certain physical features of the country about me."

During his absence from a séance, Pauline remarked that he usually regained consciousness on top of Chief Mountain in Glacier National Park to find himself fastened to a rock by his conjuring belt. If he so much as breathed, however, he felt that the strap would become loose and let him fall to the rocks far below. He next awakened to find himself in a precarious position on a high peak in the Rockies east of St. Ignatius (Montana). Again he recovered his senses on a great rock at another high point near Tatum Creek. And again on a high butte near Hot Springs (Montana).

According to conjurors' testimony, the sense of danger to the diviner was heightened by skepticism on the part of members of his audience. The seer, Pauline, emphasized the point that it seemed to become more hazardous for him if anyone among the spectators indicated doubt as to the validity of his séance. We shall have occasion to refer to the matter of skepticism later.

It is uncertain in native ideology as to whether the conjuror's body or spirit is removed upon his departure from the lodge. {Sources} Informants claimed that it was necessary for the conjuror's body to remain behind the blanket during the séance. But in the case of a diviner with great power, he may just throw his moccasin behind the blanket. Then while he remained among the spectators, the *nupíka* would come and go behind the blanket. Turney-High (1941: 174) refers to something like this in speaking of the conjuror, Lasso Stasso, of Elmo, who "does not practice behind the blanket but lays it flat on the floor behind him."

Unlike other persons with spiritual powers, the conjuror was said never to lose his gift for clairvoyance in his old age. Although he may no longer conduct a séance, he still retains his supernatural power to do so. This notion appears to contradict Paul David's belief that he was about to lose his spirit guardian.

Status of Conjuror

The more skilled and successful conjurors among the Ktunaxa were in the main anything but charlatans and frauds. They were excellent judges of human nature and men of knowledge concerning their environment as well as their band, tribe and adjacent peoples. They knew their fellow tribesmen intimately, both physically and psychologically, and as a result could formulate good advice to reply to questions about sickness, hunting conditions, gambling and the other interests and activities of the Ktunaxa. They were informed as to the numbers and seasonal locations of fish and game animals and hence could advise people upon matters of food procurement. They had a working knowledge of the principles of stagecraft and hence could vary their séances so as to lend additional interest for spectators.

It is probable that most questions put to the spirits in Ktunaxa séances were requests for advice and that relatively few petitioners were really concerned with questions of the future.

It might be said, we believe, that the body of conjurors represented a single, regulating and arbitrating authority equipped to deal, on a native level, with crucial problems, disputes and emergencies in their contemporary world. We feel that they acted so as to focus the scattered light of public opinion upon the problems of the individual Ktunaxa, such do as do our ministers, physicians, psychiatrists, welfare workers, etc.

Conjurors like leaders of the Sun Dance Ceremony, were said to live to an advanced age. In the winter of 1935-36 I was told by Abraham Bullrobe that the old chief, Kustata (Gustave), at Elmo had been promised by Bullhead that if he succeeded in putting up his blanket seven more times before Spring, he would continue to live for a few more years. The ability of the *nupíka* to lengthen his life was declining, it was said, because of his advanced age. The old chief died in 1942.

The role of conjuring calls for considerable endurance and resistance to cold on the part of the diviner. He may be behind the blanket from seven to ten hours often in freezing weather and with nothing but a breechcloth in the way of clothing.

The possession of conjuring power in the recent reservation period has made for certain difficulties among administrative and law and order officials. Simon Francis, a former Indian Service police officer, claimed that conjurors had such confidence in their clairvoyant powers and lack of fear of the authorities that they were difficult to deal with during the breakdown and demoralization accompanying Ktunaxa acculturation. He spoke as a former law and order officer on the Bonners Ferry Reserve, he stated that many diviners were inclined to drink immoderately, indulge in sexual immorality, etc.

< Write up important role of conjurors in earlier culture and contrast with recent reservation conditions and changes. >

The story of the exchange of two conjurors during a séance was told me by Simon

Francis, of Bonners Ferry, B.C.

David, a conjuror of Creston, BC, had an intimate friend at Libby. At this time the *akukłiłimi* had removed to the Flathead reservation but still hunted in the Libby area.

Siałłis, was a close friend of David's and the father of old man Caye of Elmo. In a séance the *nupíka* reported that *Siałłis* was conjuring at Elmo while David performed at Creston. They stated, "One of these days we'll give you a surprise!"

During a séance at Creston the *nupíka* promised the surprise. They came and went behind the blanket. Finally one entered and said, "Prepare yourselves! Fill up the pipe!" the same instructions were given in the séance at Libby. After a certain spirit leaves, "*Siałłis* will be brought to the lodge for a smoke and David will appear in the lodge at Libby. Tie a small piece of plug tobacco (used at this time) to *Siałłis'* toe! The same thing will be done at Libby. Thus you will exchange smokes. This is a good sign. It means peace. Nothing harmful will happen to you in the near future."

The seer was heard approaching, the blanket was lifted, and he was brought out. The *nupíka* had warned them that the conjuror in each séance would announce some news. They told *Siałłis* that they would fasten a piece of tobacco to his toe. He was given a smoke.

Everything turned out as the *nupíka* had said. *Siałłis* had said, "We're having trouble about hunting in the Libby area (Simon had forgotten David's announcement at Libby). The blanket was again lifted, *Siałłis* put under it and he was then taken from the lodge. After a few *nupíka* had come and gone, David returned with a piece of tobacco tied to his toe. So the Lower Ktunaxa smoked the tobacco of the Upper Ktunaxa, and vice versa.

The Assistants

In addition to the conjuror there were three assistants, who played important roles in the conjuring rite. Two of them, the Pipe Lighter and Pipe Receiver, were responsible for making arrangements for the séance. They arranged for a place to hold it and made the necessary arrangements for the performance. Immediately before the séance they spread out the conjuror's equipment on the floor, arranged the blanket screen, and saw that everything was in readiness. During the séance the same, two helpers assisted the diviner in preparing for the several steps of the Houdini trick and also prepared him to "be transported" from the lodge. After the seer is bound they aid him in going behind and returning from the blanket and in taking a drink or a smoke. They also assist suppliants in presenting requests and tobacco offerings to the *nupíka* during the séance.

< Did assistants eventually become conjurors? Did conjuror teach them? >

The Pipe Lighter (*tsukupxa*, "light the pipe") is seated at the left of the exterior or audience side of the conjuring blanket. Besides those tasks enumerated above, it is his duty to light with a coal from the fire the petitioners' pipes as each is handed to him. He then takes several puffs to make sure the pipe is lit and then passes it across to his colleague, the Pipe Receiver.

The Pipe Receiver (*kłamatakułłas*, "return the pipe") is seated at the right side of the blanket and opposite the Pipe Lighter. It is he, as we have seen, who accepts the pipes, one by one, from the Pipe Lighter, checks again to see that they are lit and then presents them, individually, to the *nupíka* behind the blanket. After the *nupíka* presumably has finished smoking and returns the pipe, this functionary takes it and returns it to its owner.

Interpreter

The Interpreter (*kutsinⱡiⱡat*, " ? ") had the duty of translating the statements of the *nupíka* during the séance, and of explaining the significance of any unusual phrase or movement. If he is a unable to understand some of the *nupíka*'s remarks, he calls upon Bullhead for aid. As we have seen elsewhere the statements of the *nupíka*'s during the séance may vary from plain, ordinary human speech to their own spirit language, the latter incomprehensible to humans and translatable only by Bullhead. [10]

The Trial Séance

The novice will hold his first séance at the time indicated by his tutelary spirit. Previously, as we have noted, he will have received a token from his supernatural guardian, such as a claw, feather, hoof or other object. He will also have prepared his *atsika* or braided thong, by which his body, in native theory, will be severed in half; a bone whistle; a set of deer-hoof rattles, and the remainder of his equipment. From the preparations thus made, his relatives and friends will recognize the nature of his calling, and one or more of them will assist the young conjuror in his first performance.

The novice, according to informants, may be required to undergo a test of his powers during his first séance. The following data were contributed by Stanley Como on this topic: If another conjuror is holding a performance at the same time in another camp, he may attempt to drive the novice back into his own lodge. If this occurs the young diviner often had his *nupíka* stolen from him. This would hold true particularly if the tyro falsely claims clairvoyant power that he doesn't possess. If he thus loses his spiritual guardian, he will never succeed in subsequent séances. If it so happened that he possessed the necessary powers but was giving the séance before the appointed time, he would be able to conjure later but would never recover his stolen spirit.

The novice will attempt, it was said, to recover his stolen spirit from his rival. If he has falsely claimed divinatory power, however, he will never be able to do so. If his rival already has a spirit similar to the one stolen, the novice will never be able to reclaim it. However, if the opposing seer has none resembling the stolen spirit, the neophyte may easily regain it. While recovering his own spirit, he may also be able to seize one from his opponent, providing the latter's supernatural accompanied the stolen one. Such a spirit can never be recovered.

After this initial performance to publicly demonstrate his power, the young conjuror will never again be tested by a diviner of his own tribe. Henceforth he will be recognized as possessing the powers necessary for divination and will be allowed to practice his profession freely.

Women as Conjurors

There were but few women conjurors among the Ktunaxa in earlier times. The names of a few, prominent female clairvoyants, however, haw come down to us.

One named Bull Woman (*niⱡsik paⱡki*) was mentioned by Susanne Bullrobe. She was an

Akiyinik and lived before Susanne's time. Two youths attending a séance of Bull Woman were said to wonder among themselves whether she wore a breechcloth like a male diviner. She laughed, and asked one to remove his own and said she would wear it. Apparently the *nupíka* had communicated their thoughts to her.

In 1935 when I visited the St. Mary's Ktunaxa, the wife of Frank Whitehead was said to possess conjuring power. Shortly before my visit she found, while on a hunting trip, seven knots tied in her moccasin string, an omen of the impending death of a near relative.

Conjuring was practiced by both sexes among certain tribes of this area but probably fewer women than men followed this pursuit. As one authority has pointed out for the Saulteaux, "while women might conjure", it was extremely difficult for them to achieve the same recognized status as the men ... "Although my data are incomplete on this point, female conjurors have been noted for the Blackfeet, Atsina, Crow and Kiowa." The Ktunaxa of the Plateau, and Saulteaux of the Woodlands should be added to this group.

VII CONJUROR'S EQUIPMENT

The paraphernalia of the Ktunaxa conjuror was represented by the following objects:

1.	Bone whistle	*kústał*
2	Deer-hoof rattles	*aakíłq!ołukp*
3.	Thong for con juror*s forelock	?
4.	Thong to bind conjuror's thumbs	?
5.	Belt to confine conjuror's arms	*akamałnam* 'corral', *aaktsíka*
6.	Rope used to "divide" conjuror	*watsnïyałnam* 'next to body'
7.	Two blankets used for conjuring screen	*aakłaho*
8.	Blanket pins to fasten blankets	*akinka•wok*
9.	Power token of his spiritual guardian	*ka•nupika* 'my spirit'
10.	sucking tube	*gagah wanmu*

Some informants would add to this list, 9) cup in which conjuror's whistle is placed, and 10) the incense coals. Some of the above objects were regarded as spirits and were thought to possess spiritual identity and power of their own.

Deer-hoof Rattles

The bunch of deer-hoof rattles (*akiłq!ałukp*) affixed to the front or exterior side of the blanket screen served as an indicator of the presence of spirits in the séance. A number of deer-hoofs were fastened to two leather thongs, each about a foot long. The ends of these thongs were then run through two holes made in the center of the blanket about three feet above the floor. The thongs are tied together so that the rattles hang down rather loosely against the surface of the blanket. The ends of the thongs are suspended from the inner surface of the screen. The number of hoofs on the thong vary from one diviner to another, and were indicated by the spirit from whom clairvoyant power was obtained. The usual number was ??

According to the conjuror, Stanley Como, there were seven invisible knots (*yenowis nupíka*) tied in the deer-hoof rattles' thongs on the inner side of the blanket. The conjuror, according to this authority, is believed to leave" the lodge on one of these knots, the particular one of which is selected by the *nupíka* themselves. There is a connection between each of the respective knots and the degree of ambiguity of the *nupíkas*' language. When the *nupíka* make use of the first knot in the thongs, they speak in ordinary, everyday human speech. For the second knot, they talk somewhat differently from humans and are in use harder to understand. As the number of knots in use increase, their language becomes more difficult to understand, until with the 6th and 7th their speech becomes utterly unintelligible to even the interpreter and the services of Bullhead are required. We will speak of this matter again in connection with the séance itself.

Whistle

The whistle (*kustał*), usually made of the wing bone of an eagle or hawk, was the ordinary variety used in this area. It was used to summon the spirits in the conjuring rite and in other ceremonials of the Ktunaxa. Infrequently it was placed behind the blanket screen and "blown by the *nupíka*" as an indication of their presence.

Incidentally a drum was never taken into a séance unless the seer had been given specific instructions for its use by his guardian. Its use in this way was apparently infrequent. [16]

Songs

Up until the removal of the conjuror from the lodge, the songs used and were his personal, guardian's song or songs, the *q!aq!anamnam* song, the song of the Owls. With the arrival of the *nupíka* proper, the song or songs of each spirit was sung by the audience as long as each, individual spirit remains inside the lodge.

Conjuror's Forelock Thong

The short, leather thong was used to tie up the diviner's forelock of hair before the start of the séance. When not in use, the thong was usually tied to the diviner's bone whistle; a few shamans wore it affixed constantly to their forelock. The thong was ?? inches in length and called ??

Thong for Conjuror's Thumbs

This thong was known as ?? According to Simon Francis, it was commonly kept laced in holes of the ordinary waist belt of the diviner.

Belt for Conjuror's Arms

In earlier days the heavy thong (*akamaɫnam*, "corral") used in binding the conjuror's arms to his body was the same thong used in supporting his leggings and breechcloth. With the adoption of modern dress, it was replaced by a commercial leather belt with metal buckle. Two small holes were bored into it midway in the rear, to which the thong securing the diviner's thumbs was fastened.

The thong-belt apparently held a symbolical significance for the conjuror, which may be of some age. Pauline, of Tobacco Plains, stated that it represented the "corral" or "pound" of the conjuror's body, which was representative of driving game animals into an enclosure; in the same way all disease objects inside a patient, could be driven within an enclosure and then removed by the diviner. The term was also applied to a "barricade" used to withstand enemy attack.

In another sense the *akamaɫnam* met a psychological, protective role of the conjuror. Thus Pauline referred to the part played by his belt in fastening him securely to a rock in a hazardous place and preventing him from falling with resulting injury or death, while "absent" from the lodge.

Rope for "dividing" the Conjuror

The braided thong and later, rope (*atsika*) was used in the Houdini trick of apparently severing the conjuror's body. Formerly two thongs ten to fifteen feet long were employed for this purpose. A loop was made in the end large enough to slip over the conjuror's head. The same rope is also thrown behind the blanket and was said to be used by the Owls in carrying the conjuror from the lodge. The braided rope used in the conjuring rite was identical with the pack strap employed by hunters to drag game home. It was wrapped around the hunter's waist and the ends tied. Thus this one object served a dual function, an example of economy employed by northern-forest, nomadic peoples. The same name was applied to the dual uses of the same object.

Conjuring blankets

In recent times the screen shielding the conjuror from the view of his audience consisted, as we have mentioned earlier, of two ordinary wool blankets (*aklaho*, "body robe"). There were suspended from a horizontal, wood post fastened across the corner of the room in the small, log cabins occupied by the reservation Ktunaxa. The blankets served as a screen behind which the diviner retired to be "removed" from the lodge and behind which his spirits then came and went.
< Blanket thongs too high to be manipulated by conjurors's mouth? >

Blanket pins

There were seven wood pins or skewers (*akinka•wok*) used to fasten the two blankets together and to the horizontal post, as shown in the accompanying sketch (Fig.). The method depicted in the figure on the left was said by Joe David, of Tobacco Plains, to have been used many years ago by a Ktunaxa conjuror, named *Siała*, of the same group. He was noted for his great, supernatural power in divining. The method of inserting the pins shown in the figure to the right was that claimed to have been used by Ktunaxa conjurors in the 1930's at Tobacco Plains, Some diviners preferred to fasten the blankets together by a method probably old and widespread among the Indians of the Plateau. This was the us e of several, small round stones placed against the overlap of the two blankets and thongs then looped around them and knotted. A few clairvoyants preferred to use a metal awl to puncture holes in the blankets in order to pass through the wooden skewers and thongs holding the deer-hoof rattles.

Ground Plan of Conjuring Performance

The plan shows the location of officials and arrangement of paraphernalia. This is the show house, as it were, of the divinatory rite. < gap = entrance faces East >

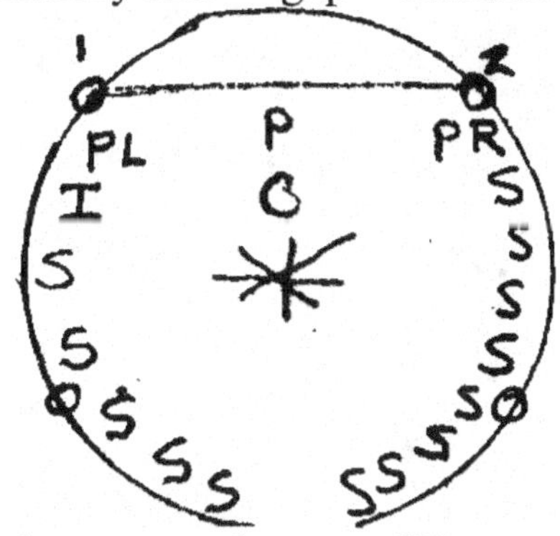

PL = pipe lighter	C = incense coals	< Where cup of water, thongs?
R = pipe returner	+ = camp fire	Pipes, interpreter? >
P = petitioner's place	S= spectators	
I = interpreter	1,2 = rear foundation poles supporting blanket	

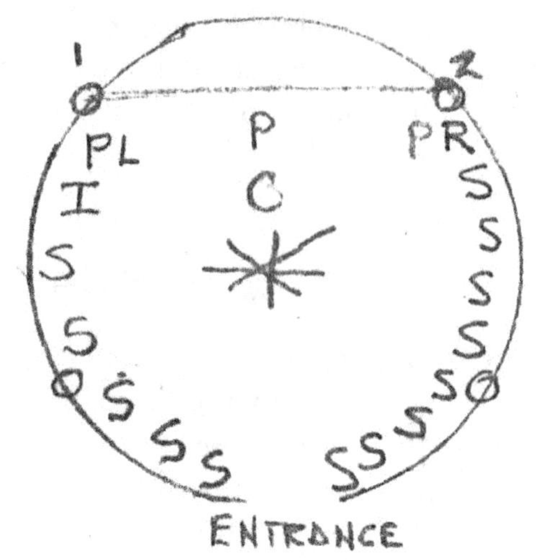

East

PL = Pipe lighter
R = Pipe returner
P = Petitioner's place
I = Interpreter
C = Incense coals
✳ = Camp Fire
S = Spectators
1,2 = Rear foundation poles
Supporting blanket.

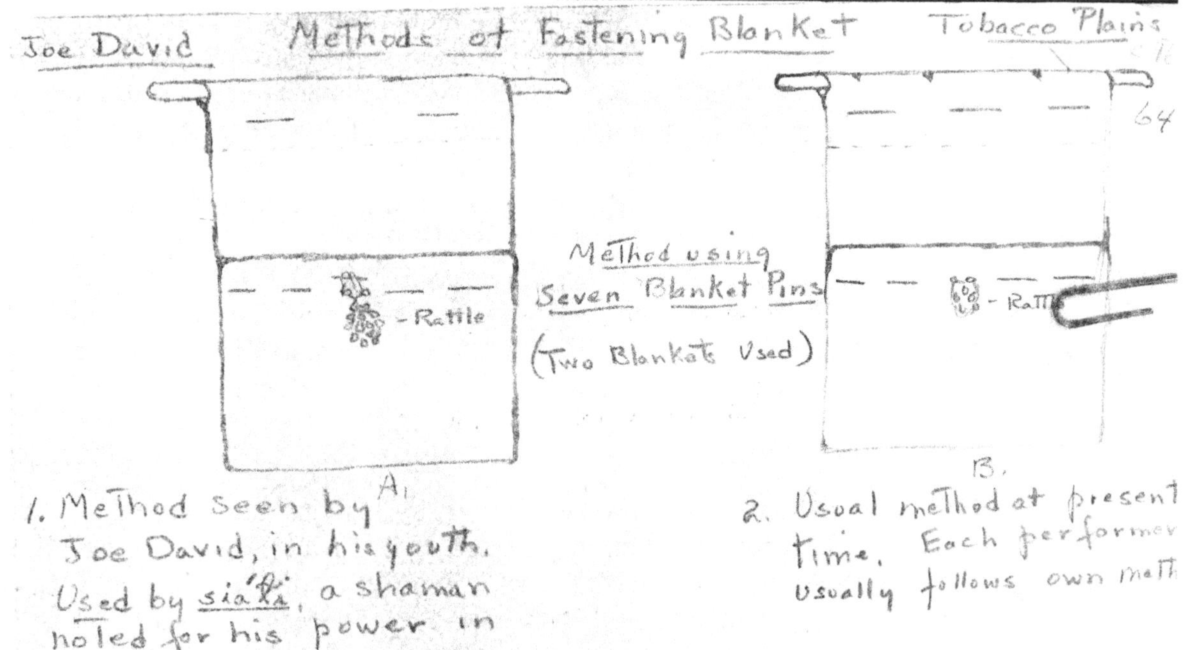

Tobacco offerings

Tobacco, which was cultivated by the Ktunaxa in earlier times represented in both its native and later commercial forms a product of value. Thus when it was used to reinforce a request made of the spirits in the séance, it represented a sacrifice made to obtain divine aid. The use of tobacco in the conjuring rite will be discussed below, a practice which differs but little from pipe offerings made in the Sun Dance Ceremony.

A quantity of tobacco in a pouch and a number of pipes contributed for the séance, were placed on the floor before the conjuring screen. In recent times commercial pipes have been offered Bullhead. He accepts the innovation, saying, "We should not accept this modern pipe. But because you are poor, we will do so."

All of the *nupíka* who came to the séance, Baptiste Mathias claimed, liked to smoke.

In former times the spectators were not permitted to smoke individually during the séance. Now people in the audience have been free to smoke cigarettes at any time but they are required first to point the lighted cigarette towards the Pipe Lighter, then towards the Pipe Receiver, after which they are free to smoke. The movement from left to right (clockwise) corresponds to the Sun's movement and the spectators dance movement is in the same direction.

Some conjurors may allow cigarettes or commercial pipes to be smoked in a séance but will not touch either themselves. A cigarette can only be lighted in a séance from a pipe being passed around among the spectators.

Incense fire

The use of incense in the divinatory rite appears to have been less important than in the Sun Dance Ceremony.

The incense fire (*akok!płułał*, "juniper") is kept alive constantly in a metal pan placed on the floor before the blanket screen. Twigs of the Rocky Mountain Juniper (*Juniperus scapulorum Sarg.*) provide material for incense here as well as in the Sun Dance Ceremony.

If there is a sick person to be taken behind the blanket for treatment or diagnosis, the patient is first incensed. Juniper is placed upon the coals, then both hands are held in the smoke and passed over the face, body and limbs. Then one arid the other foot are held briefly in the smoke. The curative power of the supernaturals is believed to be transmitted to the sick, via the smoke on the incense.

The diviner in the same manner incenses himself before going behind the blanket.

Occasionally the Sun Dance Spirit (*Kukłukinam*) may ask all those present in the séance to cense themselves. This is done it is said, to show respect for the Spirit. After all have used the incense, it is felt that the company is united into a close-knit group with common interests. All participants in the Sun Dance Ceremony do this immediately upon arriving at the site.

Shoes must be removed but moccasins may be worn while smudging the feet.

Food

Occasionally a conjuror < who? > may be required by his spiritual patron to distribute small portions of cooked meat or other food among the spectators during the singing of the first song in the séance. A few may even be required to serve a full meal at the conclusion of the rite.

Apparently certain of the *nupíka* that enter the conjuror's lodge are served food, at least among the St. Mary's Reserve Ktunaxa. Thus in the episode related by Stanley Como, it was noted that *Yaukekam,* son of Red Stone, and a character of the mythological period, regularly asks for salmon eggs.

The *Akukłiłimi*

Although it seems to have been used more often in the absence of a conjuror, occasionally a diviner might be instructed by the Ghost or another spirit to prepare a "ground map" to depict the whereabouts of lost people or strayed animals. East of the Rockies the Ktunaxa were said to determine the location by this method. It was given the same name, *Akukłiłimi,* as the locality in which a person's first spiritual visitation took place. The use of such maps goes back so far that modern Ktunaxa were rather hazy as to details. < check Chamberlain here ? > The map, it seems, was a small rectangle of ground located between the two, rear foundation poles and directly under the "spirit pole" of the diviner's lodge. According to Stanley Como, no physical features were drawn in the surface of the ground. The Elmo Ktunaxa, however, claim to have drawn the natural features of the locality in prepared soil or ashes of the map. [17] It was then covered overnight with a small hide. Upon examination the next morning, the trail of the lost horse or person was said to be discernible on the surface of the map.

Modern substitutions

Here we may point out some of the substitutions made in original properties of the Conjuring rite in late years, instead of a china or metal cup, a small coiled basket of native manufacture and filled with water, was formerly used as a receptacle for the diviner's whistle. The skin- or mat-covered lodge in which the séance was formerly held, was heated by a central campfire; when necessary, this source of light could be dampened to make the lodge interior practically dark. The modern cabin, which has replaced this earlier structure, is heated by a wood stove and lighted by a kerosene lamp.

< Whistle receptacle used at Tobacco Plains? No baskets. In the following description of a séance the terms "cabin," lamp", "stove", etc, with the understanding that these are modern objects and replace the earlier term "lodge", "campfire", etc. >

VIII THE CONJURING PERFORMANCE

Initiation of the rite

The séance must be requested of the diviner by a client, who is sick or otherwise in need of aid from the supernaturals. Rarely, if ever, does a diviner hold a performance of his own volition.

The person in need, according to Simon Francis, goes to a seer and says, "I want to throw you under a blanket." Upon hearing this, the conjuror cannot refuse, except for a very good reason. The diviner replies," you prepare the place," So arrangements are made to hold it at the sponsor's lodge or cabin, or at the home of the conjuror. < offer of payment ? describe how arrangements are made ? >

A séance should be requested for a serious and specific reason, which should be of sufficient importance to justify the performance. Otherwise the conjuror may be adversely affected.

The séance is held at night and most sessions are concluded before morning. It starts usually around 7:00 or 8:00 P.M. Less frequently a séance may continue until daybreak or even until 9:00 or 10:00 A.M. the following morning. If the need was really serious and required the attention of many spirits, the performance may continue all night and be concluded the following night.

The selection of the place for the séance and other arrangements are made by the conjuror's assistants, never by the conjuror himself.

Both men and women are free to attend the session. People may go merely as spectators or with the idea of submitting a petition to the spirits.

Small children are not encouraged and usually not permitted to attend the séance or treatment of a sick person by a shaman. In earlier days such affairs were considered unsuitable for little children. [12] Francis recalled that he attended his first séance at the age of seven. The practice has been liberalized in recent years.

In former times no one could attend a conjuring performance unless he was dressed in native costume – breechcloth, blanket and moccasins for men and buckskin dresses and moccasins for women.

More recently, as we have indicated earlier, the séance has usually been held in an Indian cabin on the reservation. Across a corner of the building at a height that no one can see the conjuror's head, a wooden pole is nailed horizontally. The two blankets, which will form the screen, are suspended from this pole. Strings are attached midway up the sides of the blanket vertically so that it can be firmly tied at a certain point in the performance to the nails driven in the walls < of the cabin >.

In the center of the floor, usually beside the stove, the various properties required by the conjuror are arranged. A quantity of tobacco in a pouch and a number of pipes for the session, are placed upon the floor before the blanket screen. A small cup of water into which the conjuror will place his bird-bone whistle, stands nearby. There is also a metal pan containing hot embers for burning incense of juniper twigs. The room is lighted by a kerosene light, which at the proper moment can be turned low.

Procedures in each séance vary slightly between different conjurors of the same band and somewhat more between those of different Ktunaxa bands. Such differences were largely due to varying reasons for holding the performances as well as to diverse spiritual gifts conferred upon different practitioners. Other differences were no doubt due to slightly different physical environments, the resultant of their natural resources and their reflection in the economies of the several bands.

Two or more séances may have been given on the same night in different bands or among separate camps of the same band. If there happened to be a séance given by two hands of Ktunaxa on the same night, the spirits, it is said, would so inform the participants in each group. In entering and departing from the conjuring tent the *nupíka* would explain that they had to travel back and forth between the two performances.

On one occasion, < according to Bullrobe, > séances were being held simultaneously by the Bonners Ferry, and the Tobacco Plains groups. The latter were camped at modern Fortine, Montana. The respective conjurors of each performance were exchanged for a brief period. The Bonners Ferry diviner appeared in the ceremony at Fortine, smoked with the spectators, and told them of events downriver. Bullhead remarked in the Tobacco Plains rite that many of the Ktunaxa seemed skeptical of the power of the conjuror. In order to prove the validity of the rite he offered to keep the Bonners Ferry seer at Fortine overnight and allow him to walk about camp the next day. The spectators at Tobacco Plains declined the offer, however, and the rite came to a close.

The Houdini trick forms an integral and important preliminary step in the Ktunaxa séance, Hallowell (1942: 70, fn.) discusses it under the name of the Davenport trick" and states that although some of the Berens River Saulteaux had heard of it, none of their conjurors were credited with it, lie goes on to say that "the conjuror is either trussed up securely with rope or enveloped in a skin or blanket and then tied before being thrust into the conjuring lodge." The diviner, in native theory, is freed from his bonds by the spirits. The variant methods mentioned by Hallowell of 1) being trussed up with rope, or 2) enveloped in a skin or blanket, were both practiced by the Ktunaxa, the former being more common, at least, in recent times. In our description below of the Houdini trick, we will consider tie two preliminary steps of having the conjuror's thumbs tied and arms bound as part of the Houdini trick series.

The three steps in the Houdini trick series, as performed in the Ktunaxa séance, will be briefly indicated here. Each step may be repeated several times or varied slightly.

1) The diviner goes behind the blanket and emerges with his thumbs behind his back and fastened to his belt.
2) With his thumbs still secured as above, the diviner goes under the blanket with his arms confined to his body by a leather strap and emerges with it transferred beneath one of both of his arms.
3) The Houdini trick proper involves a rope looped beneath the arms of the diviner, each end of which is then pulled by one of his assistants so as to apparently divide his body into two parts.

The Ktunaxa variant of the Houdini trick in earlier days consisted of wrapping tire conjuror in a bison or elk robe, tying him tightly with thongs, and then having him effecting his release without outside aid. The account of this practice was related to me by Pauline, a conjuror of Tobacco Plains, who had it from one of his grandparents. The Ktunaxa same practice was said to have been used by an old/conjuror more recently on the Flathead Reservation. Pauline's account ran as follows:

The conjuror's hands were first fastened behind his back to the thong supporting his leggings and breechcloth. The bird-bone whistle was next placed between his big and adjacent toe on the right or left foot, depending upon instructions from his guardian spirit. Then a bison robe was wrapped around him so that only his feet and head protruded. Then the first loop of a long thong was placed about his ankles in a half hitch and a series of half hitches taken around the robe up as far as his neck. The end of this thong was then moved down and slipped under the first loop and drawn tight, thus pulling the conjuror's body around in an arc, with his head extending down towards his feet. Another thong (*akamałnam*) was then arranged and tied so as to join his forelock and his toes, forming a crude sort of loop by which the conjuror, in native theory, could be lifted by the spirits and carried from the lodge. The screen was then raised and the diviner thus trussed up, was placed behind it with the free end of the binding thong carried up and over the top of the blanket. Meanwhile the campfire had been dampened down so that the lodge was nearly dark. At the appropriate moment an assistant pulled on the end of the thong, the sound of the whistle was heard, and the line, as originally tied around the buffalo robe, came free. The whistle, however, remained behind the screen to be blown by the spirits as they entered the lodge. No additional details are known of this method.

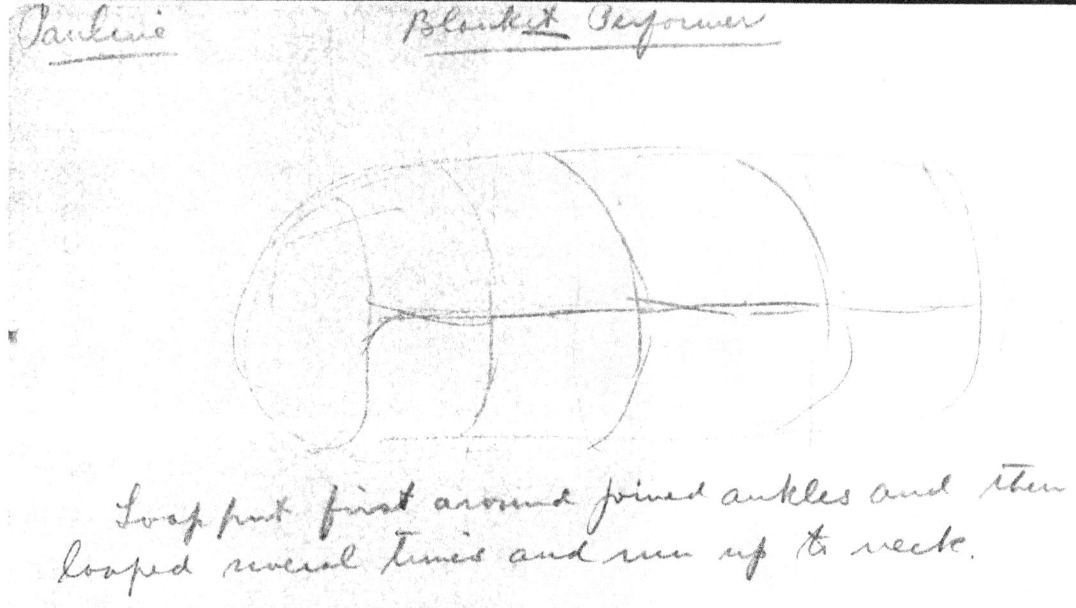

< Loop put first around joined ankles and then looped several times and run up to neck. >
We have previously noted the statement of one Ktunaxa conjuror that he was taught the Houdini trick by the Owl and Ghost Spirits,

The Séance

The following description may be taken as generally representative of the conjuring rite among the various Ktunaxa bands in modern times. The order in which I have set down various, minor preliminary steps may have varied somewhat for one conjuror to another, and from band to band. The broad pattern, 1 believe, is characteristic of the several Ktunaxa bands.

The different articles used by the conjuror are spread out on the cabin floor before the blanket screen. These include the belt, rope and various thongs used in the Houdini trick. Here also is the cup of water in which the conjuror's whistle has been placed as well as a pan holding hot coals for burning incense of juniper twigs. Also on the floor are a number of tobacco pipes and a quantity of tobacco.

The petitioner, conjuror, assistants, and spectators will have made their way to the conjuring lodge or cabin arranged for the séance. The performance usually starts around 7:00 or 8:00 o'clock in the evening.

The Houdini Trick

The conjuror cane to his place before the blanket facing the spectators, who have arranged themselves around the rear portion of the lodge or cahin. He seats himself aid begins to sing his guardian spirit song. The audience joins in the singing. They may repeat the same song or follow it with one or more songs, if the conjuror has additional, supernatural helpers.

< T-H says conjuror paints face! True of all conjurors? When? >

The conjuror now ties up his forelock by means of the short thong used for that purpose. He then attaches the thong carrying the dew-claw rattles, bear claws or other power tokens to the center of the blanket. The number of these objects on the thong varies according to instructions earlier received from his tutelary spirit.

The conjuror next removed his clothing, except for his shirt and breechcloth." He then picks up his whistle from the cup of water, censes it in the juniper smoke, puts it in his mouth, and blows it. The singing continues. At first, the seer cannot strike the right pitch but he continues to give repeated blasts. At times he removes it from his mouth to continue singing. Once satisfied that he has the correct pitch, he blows it almost ceaselessly. The sound of the whistle and the singing are to notify the *nupíka* of the séance. Often the diviner will also summon them by calling, "*Nupíkanintek*, the people are thinking of you. You must come and tell them of the future. If there is any misfortune in store, come and tell them." or he may grasp each side of the blanket screen with outstretched arms and cry, "*Nupíka*! Get in line and come to the right place. We are putting up the blanket." Again he calls, "You, Spirits, are asked by the people to be here tonight. You are invited to accept tobacco by the people."

(*First Step*)

The conjuror now turns his back to the audience. He places both hands briefly in the smoke of the burning juniper and then rubs them over his face, limbs and body. In order to find out if the Spirits have arrived, he now goes behind the blanket. He walks over to it, the Assistants being seated at each side. As a signal he touches the blanket lightly with his foot. An Assistant then lifts the blanket and the conjuror then steps behind it. The singing continues. Soon the deer-hoof rattles can be heard to vibrate vigorously, an indication that the first spirit has arrived. Again the conjuror touches the blanket with his foot, it is raised and he steps forth.

< Contrast with later arrival of Spirits after conjuror leaves. Which spirit? >

Procedures vary somewhat among different conjurors at this point. At Bonners Ferry the diviner will emerge with his hands behind his back, his thumbs tied together by a thong passed through holes in his belt. The assistants closely examine the knots. Usually there is a tight, double knot binding the thumbs, an indication the spirit is ready to assist in the séance. Here my informant interjected that the diviner had not been behind the blanket long enough to have tied his thumbs himself. If there is only one knot or if the thong is only loosely tied, it is an indication that something is wrong. The assistants then untie the thong and the preliminaries, including the singing of each song, must then be repeated. If the conjuror does not succeed the second or third time, he is said to give up the attempt, so informs the spectators, and allows some other diviner to take his place. A failure such as this probably does not occur very often.

< Where has the thong for tying thumbs been kept ? >

Among the St. Mary's Ktunaxa, however, the conjuror during his initial period behind the blanket, is said to be able to foresee coming events and to judge of their seriousness. This clairvoyant ability is known as *tcikatłikłihamek*, " ? ". He emerges and then goes under the blanket once more. The second time the *nupíka* are believed to be there, as indicated by the vibrating rattles, and then are thought to tie his thumbs to his belt. The diviner comes out and his assistants inform him as to the number of knots tied in the thongs binding his thumbs. Some conjurors will not return behind the blanket to have additional knots tied; others, such as Stanley Como, will do so in order to better cope with a serious problem confronting them in the petitioner's request. In extreme cases, a conjuror may go under the blanket seven times to amass a total of seven knots.

In order to comprehend the preceding paragraph, we must discuss a native concept involving seven, invisible knots believed to be tied in the thongs connecting the deer-hoof rattles to the blanket. These knots are thought to belong to the *nupíka* and are never conferred upon the conjuror. There is said to be a direct, numerical correlation between these seven, invisible knots and certain other groups of phenomena in the séance. The latter are 1) the increasing degree of difficulty in the aid required of the *nupíka* by the petitioner, 2) the increasing degree of obscurity in the language employed by the *nupíka* in the séance, and 3) the increasing number of knots tied in the thongs confining the seer's thumbs.

The interrelations of these various factors may be briefly discussed here. The conjuror is believed to be taken from the lodge on one of the seven, invisible knots of the deer-hoof rattles' thong, the particular one depending upon the seriousness of the petitioner's case. The *nupíka* are said to select the particular knot on which the seer is to be removed from the lodge; if the latter believes that he needs more, he will go ' under the blanket to obtain them. The equivalent of the number of knots he needs and obtains are the knots tied in the thongs binding his thumbs. Usually there are from three to seven knots at the conjuror's thumbs. Finally the degree of unintelligibility of the *nupíka*'s language is directly related to the number of knots employed by the conjuror. If he is to be taken from the lodge on the first knot, the spirits will speak in ordinary, human language. Their speech thereafter becomes increasingly difficult for humans to understand in proportion to the number of knots, until the services of Bullhead, the spirit interpreter, are required to unravel the complete incomprehensibility accompanying the 6th and 7th knots.

(Second Step)

It was now time for the second step of the Houdini trick. Once the knots in the thong confining his thumbs were tight, the conjuror was ready for the next part. The audience continued to sing. The diviner walked over to the incense coals and censed each foot again in the smoke. Again he faced the blanket. The whistle had been retained in his mouth all this time. < blowing ? > Facing to one side, he again went behind the blanket. If the deer-hoof rattles began to move, the conjuror came out, re-censed each foot, and went behind the blanket again but this time facing the <u>opposite</u> direction. Again the rattles on the front of the blanket were heard to move. The conjuror came out and again censed his feet. His hands remain tied behind his back throughout this period.

Next the belt was picked up from the floor by the assistants and buckled about and <u>outside</u> the conjuror's arms, confining them tightly to his body. The buckle was placed to the rear, apparently beyond the diviner's reach. He again went under the blanket, the rattles began to vibrate, he stepped out, and the belt was now seen to be tightly fastened about his chest but <u>beneath</u> one or sometimes both arms. It was removed by the assistants and again fastened <u>outside</u> both arms as before. The conjuror smudged his feet and again went behind the blanket, this time facing the <u>opposite</u> direction. The rattles vibrate, and he came out once more with the belt <u>beneath</u> his arms. The conjuror repeated this routine movement for the third time and if he came out with the belt fastened transferred from outside to <u>beneath</u> his arms, everything was proceeding satisfactorily. The belt was now removed and placed on the floor. Ray (1939: 116-17) omits mention of this second step in his account of the Houdini complex.

(Third Step)

The Houdini trick proper was next in order. The piece of rope was now picked up by the Assistants. Blowing his whistle constantly, the conjuror again censed his feet and then went under the blanket. He may go under from either side or from underneath it. He signaled {How?} in some manner to his assistants. The latter who have been waiting with the looped rope, raised it above and over the top of the blanket screen, and drop the loop. < Arrangement of rope ? > Each, however, retained hold of one end. < How ? > Immediately the rattles began to vibrate and within a few seconds, my informant stated, the conjuror kicked the blanket as a signal. The assistants, each continuing to hold one end of the rope, raised the blanket. There the conjuror was to be seen with the rope around his waist <u>inside</u> his arms. If everything seemed satisfactory, the assistants let the blanket drop.

The diviner now stepped out from behind the blanket with his back to the audience, walked backwards around the incense coals, and then forward to peer at the blanket as if searching for something on its surface. The assistants kept the ends of the rope taut. The conjuror then reversed his position, bent over and let the whistle fall from his mouth into the cup of water. He again turned around, tapped the blanket with his foot and as it was raised, went behind it. The assistants continued to retain hold of the ends of the rope and kept it taut. The seer again signals. An Assistant then removed the whistle from the cup and placed it between the toes of the conjuror's right foot, thrust out from beneath the blanket.

The audience now began to sing the q!aq!anamnam song, as an indication that the diviner's body was about be "divided" in the feat of legerdemain to follow. It was sung in diminished volume. In a few minutes the diviner was heard to cough several times, which then gave way to the sound of repeated blasts on the whistle. Soon these sounds were heard to merge into a continuous blowing of the whistle. Now the spectators sang even more softly.

Now the assistants stepped to each side of the lodge entrance, each holding his end of the rope taut. When the whistling reached the proper pitch and volume, each assistant pulled on the end of the rope to lift the conjuror from the ground into the air. Sometimes the outline of his body was seen defined against the blanket so that it was observed by the audience to swing to a horizontal position and then rise towards the top of the blanket. Suddenly, however, the rope came free and was jerked out from over the top of the blanket to fall to the floor below. It was evident to those present that the conjuror's body had just been severed in two. Sometimes the outline of the two parts of his body could be seen against the blanket as falling separately to the floor. The effect of this dramatic episode was sometimes heightened by the sounds of two separate thuds on the floor. The sound of the whistle ceased and people stopped singing. In former times the camp-fire was extinguished at this point; now the flame of the lamp is turned low. The lodge was in near darkness.

After a time loud exhalations of breath are heard coming from behind the blanket. One of the assistants now turned up the lamp and returns to his regular place. The whistle, which had previously been placed between the conjuror's toes, could now be found in one of two places. Usually it lay within a loop in the center of the rope fastened around the conjuror's body. The rope is examined by an assistant to determine if the whistle was there. If not, he informed his colleague, who turned around to see if it had been placed in the cup of water. If not there, it had been retained behind the blanket to be blown by the *nupíka*. Now the blanket was raised to reveal the conjuror, who had presumably been restored whole and unharmed by the spirits, seated in the corner of the cabin. The assistants lifted him, one grasping his body beneath the knees, the other under the arms and carried him to a place beside the stove.

Someone in the audience had previously filled the pipes with tobacco. An assistant picked up a pipe, lighted it and stuck the stem in the conjuror's mouth. The latter took several puffs, signalled for its removal and then blew the smoke upward. In the same manner he blew smoke towards each of the four directions, in succession, and finally, to the ground. The pipe was then handed to the other assistant, who started it circulating among the spectators.

Conjuror "Removed" from the Lodge

Now preparations were made for the diviner to be "taken" from the lodge. He might first ask for a drink of water, which was given him from the cup containing the whistle. He took a small amount, washed out his mouth, gargled and spat out the remainder into a waste can. He was then raised, carried under the blanket and placed in a seated position with his back in the corner, or in the case of a canvas lodge, against the lodgepole. The blanket was then allowed to fall into place.

The audience now started to sing the Owl Song to summon those spirits to carry the conjuror from the lodge. At this point, it was said, the effort the company put into the song, the better indication that they were working earnestly for tire diviner. The lamp was again turned low. Now the blanket was tied down securely by the assistants to the cabin walls by the thongs attached for that purpose. They also threw the rope previously used, behind the screen. After several moments the sound of breaking wood could be detected and an object was heard to strike the blanket. The rattles began to vibrate. Now, the spectators exclaimed, "Hoyi...! Hoyi,..! Hoyi..,! Hoyi,.,! Hoyi... [10] Thuds and grunting sounds were heard at intervals coming from behind the blanket, indicating that the Owl Spirits were entering the cabin. Now the sound of bird wings could be heard within the cabin. The thuds were counted by the spectators to determine the number of these spirits controlled by the diviner. There was usually a long interval between the arrival of the first and second Owl Spirit but thereafter they entered with increasing rapidity. One end of the thong, the Ktunaxa believe, was tied to the seer's forelock and the other to his big toes. This thong was grasped, according to modern informants, by the Owls as they rose in the air lifting the conjuror's body from the dwelling. Now the conjuror could be heard to moan as if in pain. The outline of his body could be seen to rise against the blanket and as it neared the top, it disappeared. Now the noise of the conjuror breaking through the upper part of the cabin wall or roof was heard. The sound of splitting wood, of tearing canvas or of tearing tule stalks were said to accompany the seer's departure, depending upon the material of the conjuring structure. The rattles have ceased to move. The singing stops. The conjuror has been "carried" from the cabin!

The Intermission

After the diviner had been "removed" from the cabin, the lamp was again turned up and people felt free to relax and talk. They were now free to refer jokingly to mistakes in procedure made by one or other of the assistants. This period of relaxation lasted but for a few minutes. Suddenly an object was heard to strike the blanket. The spectators now exclaimed, "Hoyi,.! Hoyi..! Hoyi..! Hoyi..!, "which my informant explained, was equivalent to the English 'amen', or 'so be it'. All conversation, levity and above all, skepticism on the part of the spectators, was supposed to cease. The spirits had begun to arrive.

Arrival and Departure of the Spirits

Various *nupíka,* now entered the conjuring lodge, one by one, and remained behind the blanket for from five to fifteen minutes. Usually each spirit announced its identity as it entered, saying, "I'm the Otter." In addition each sang: its individual song, which, of course, was familiar to the spectators and in which they joined.

The spirits' entrance and departure from the lodge was signalized by an appropriate sound behind the blanket. Turney-High (1941: 174) stated that the spirits can be heard walking on the roof of the cabin. During the time they were in the lodge, they were believed to perch upon the knots in the thongs supporting the deer-hoof rattles on the interior side of blanket.

While they were present the rattles were shaken slowly and continuously but prior to their entrance and exit, were shaken vigorously. As long as the rattles were moving, the spectators were aware that a spirit was present.

During the séance a spirit may enter and say," This is my blanket! (*akłaha*). I am the one who gave this person power to perform the ceremony." In this way people came to learn the source and nature of a conjuror's power.

When a spirit arrived in the conjuring lodge, the interpreter asked it to sing its song, adding that the audience will join in. Thus the arrival and identity of each spirit became known to the spectators. The company joined in singing the song, which is continued until the spirit left the lodge. The songs of most *nupíka* differed from one seer to another.

However, the songs of Grizzly Bear, Otter, Ghost, Bullhead, Owl, Woodpecker, Flute, Frog and the Sun Dance Spirit were said to be the same among all conjurors.

With Bullhead as the well known exception, the various supernaturals are serious and never joke in the conjuring rite. If, however, one spirit after another continually jokes about one person in the audience, it is regarded as an indication of trouble. In such a case Bullhead will be asked to ascertain the cause.

The *nupíka* speak in a way that differs from ordinary, human speech and hence can be understood only with great difficulty by lay persons. To indicate time intervals, for example, they may speak of "two-three days," meaning six days, etc. It is the duty of the Interpreter to translate ambiguous statements made by the spirits. Any that are unintelligible to him, must be referred to Bullhead.

Most spirits speak in a high, falsetto voice resembling somewhat that of a small child.

At Bonners Ferry séances, the first spirit to arrive is the Sun Dance Spirit (*Kukłukinam*). As the intermediary between the people and the Supreme Being, he is the one to receive the petitioner's request and convey it to the *Kuiłkap nupíka* for decision. On his arrival at the séance *Kukłuknam* inquires, "Why have you people put up the blanket?"

The Suppliant's Petition

In response to the first *nupíka*'s inquiry as to the reason for the séance, the petitioner arises, picks up a pipe from the floor and steps forward to the blanket. [17] Grasping the stem in both hands he extends it towards the blanket and states his request. In presenting their petitions most people speak loud enough so as to be heard clearly by all those present. One who spoke so low as to be inaudible, would come under suspicion of seeking benefits detrimental to his fellow tribesmen. After presenting his request the suppliant steps back, hands the pipe to the Assistant of the left – the Pipe Lighter – and takes his seat.

The Pipe Lighter lights the pipe and takes several puffs to insure that it is drawing well. Then he hands it to his colleague to the right of the blanket. The latter accepts it and also makes sure that it is well lighted. Then he rises to his feet to present the pipe to "the spirit" behind the blanket. Usually the pipe is passed and returned across the top of the blanket. In the case of the spirit, Bullhead, however, the pipe is handed around to the left side of the blanket and in returned, vis the right side, i.e. in the direction of the Sun's course.

Occasionally one of the *nupíka* will ask that the pipe be handed across unlit, so that he can light it himself.

The Pipe Receiver, on the other hand, may ask the concealed spirit how he wishes the pipe passed to him. The latter may reply, "Hold the pipe over the incense coals, then puff once to the east, to the west, to the Sun (overhead), and then to the earth, after which pass it to me." Such instructions may then be translated by the Interpreter to mean long life for the petitioner. There are a number of different procedures used in passing the pipe, the significance of which is made known to the spectators by the Interpreter. The spirit behind the blanket presumably has now accepted the pipe offering and the assistant resumes his seat.

Both assistants now watch the blanket screen closely and as soon as the pipe is thrust out, the one on the right receives it and then hands it to the petitioner. The latter takes several puffs and then passes it to his neighbor. It circulates among the company until empty, whence it is returned to the Pipe Lighter. After the pipe has cooled, someone in the audience refills it. The spirit which has entered and smoked, leaves the lodge and is replaced by another.

Upon accepting the pipe the spirit is believed able to "read the mind" [9] of the suppliant, and judge if his petition is important and necessary. If not, the Ktunaxa believe the spirit will refuse to grant his request.

When the pipe is returned the petitioner examines it carefully to determine if any covert sign has been left upon it by the supernatural. Such a sign may reveal whether his request will be granted. The slightest movement or word of the *nupíka* during the séance may therefore be of significance. If any indication is revealed and not understood by the petitioner, he inquires as to its meaning of the Interpreter. The latter attempts to explain the significance of any covert sign and make it meaningful to the spectators. It is usually an ominous sign if the pipe goes out or is rejected by a spirit; this is believed to indicate that a relative of the person will die in the near future. Sparks seen dropping from the pipe bowl foreshadow similar unhappy events. If a spirit fails to wait upon a petitioner's request and leaves the lodge, it is considered an unfavorable omen. The suppliant will then inquire as to the meaning of this hasty departure of the next spirit to enter, who will in most cases, enlighten him. Then the suppliant will wait upon Bullhead's arrival to request his aid as an intermediary in averting the impending event.

Anyone among the spectators is free at any time to pick up a pipe, step forward and submit a request to the *nupíka*. Some people prefer to wait upon the arrival of a favorite spirit. Usually the requests are for food, clothing or improved health. On the other hand a spirit may refuse to consider a certain petition, adding that the third or fourth to enter thereafter will do so.

The spectators will immediately recognize if someone has displeased the spirits and they will inquire as to the cause, in case a spirit refuses to accept a petitioner's pipe. The spirit will usually give the reason for his action, so that the person responsible will know of it. In 1947 there were said to be two Ktunaxa families < names ? > on the Flathead Reservation, which failed to heed the *nupíka*. As a result, members of the families, one by one, began to die off. In this way they lost six or seven children.

Older people especially watch the movements of the pipe closely as it is returned to the petitioner. After the Pipe Lighter passes it across the blanket and it is accepted, it may re-appear above the blanket, moving back and forth with smoke curling from the bowl. Or the bowl may be so tilted as to be nearly upside down with tobacco spilling from it. These unusual actions are believed to have significance and are discussed next day by the Ktunaxa in an attempt to resolve their meaning.

Similarly unusual movements of the deer-hoof rattles on the front of the blanket quickly attract the attention and interest of the spectators. If they are shaken so vigorously as to nearly lift the blanket off the floor, the eyes of all spectators are immediately drawn to them. Or if the rattles are nearly hidden as if grasped by a person's hand behind the blanket, it is considered an ill omen. Most observers interpret it as a warning from the *nupíka* of an imminent death in the band. Further, the rattles in this case may indicate upon being released, i.e, thrown to the right, left, or directly ahead, the direction from which the bad news will come. If the death will occur within the camp, the rattles will indicate that by failing vertically on the blanket.

Meanwhile the conjuror, if he has arrived at the time in which he works for the welfare of the group, claims to know nothing of events inside the lodge during his "absence." He states that he is first taken by the spirits to his *akukłiłimi*, the locality of his spiritual visitation. Thereafter, as we learned in the account of Paul David (p. 108), he says that he loses and regains consciousness repeatedly to find himself each time in a hazardous place. Thus the conjuror insists that he is in physical danger constantly during his absence from the lodge. This sense of peril is apparently heightened by an attitude of skepticism on the part of the company.

< Conjuror can disclaim knowledge of data disclosed during séance? >

< Treatment of the Sick >

< Answers to petitions presented by members of the audience are brought by a spirit towards the close of the séance. Children are cautioned to stay awake in order to learn the outcome. At Bonners Ferry *Qíqom* is often selected to return with the reply. He may say, "*Qíqom* you did such and such a thing to cause the trouble affecting you now". Of if due to sorcery, the *nupíka* will reveal the author. >

Injunctions and Penance

The injunction imposed upon a petitioner, if not difficult, is at least inconvenient to carry out and in that respect, may be said to resemble the penance of the Catholic Church. If sincerely and faithfully carried out, the petitioner feels reasonably sure that his prayer will be answered. Thus the *nupíka* may require that one or all of the petitioners take a sweat bath after the performance as part of the injunction to have their requests realized.

Young people, who through ignorance disparage the spirits, are forgiven but must undergo penance for doing so. Adults are seldom forgiven as it was believed that they should have been aware of their sin, and hence there was no way of earning forgiveness.

The *nupíka* continue to come and go in the séance and are offered tobacco by petitioners to support their requests. Some notion of the length of the session has already been disclosed to participants, according to Simon Francis, by the number of attendant Owl Spirits. If only seven Owls enter the lodge, the performance will be concluded by about 1:00 A.M.; if fourteen, it may go on until around 3:00 A.M.; but if twenty-one, the séance will continue until sun-up. A skilled seer will usually "remain away" from the lodge until dawn. In earlier times the spectators would remain until the rite ended. More recently, some conjurors insist upon everyone staying until the end; others do not.

Conclusion of Séance

Indications that the séance is drawing to a close become evident upon the arrival of certain spirits. At Bonners Ferry performances, Simon Francis stated, when the Skunk, Grizzly, Frog, and Muskrat Spirits enter, it is an intimation that the performance will soon end. At another time he declared that if the Deer Spirit entered and was followed by the seven Flute Spirits, the rite would soon end. The children are now awakened. Usually the first or second Flute Spirit will bring back the rope used to carry the conjuror from the lodge. One end of it is thrown over the top of the blanket by the spirit. The assistants, if drowsy, may fail to notice it but the end is moved back and forth until it attracts their attention. Then one of them pulls it down and puts it in its regular place on the floor.

Finally the Owl Spirits can be heard approaching the lodge carrying the conjuror. The sound of his coughing becomes louder and louder as he approaches. The Owls are followed by the two Woodpecker Spirits. Although there is no noise made to indicate that the conjuror is being "thrown into" the lodge, the company is made aware of it, however, by seeing the outline of his head forming against the inner side of the blanket, followed next by his chest, hips, and finally, his feet, his face is revealed in outline as if looking upward; while his body is shown as being suspended and held only by the blanket. The assistants wait until his loud, fast breathing has become normal, tie is heard to exclaim, "I'm alright." His thumbs are still tied to his belt and the strap may lie across one shoulder and be buckled at one side. The singing of the Woodpecker Song now ceases.

The conjuror is now brought out from behind the blanket.

The spirits towards the end of the ceremony may decide that another session will be required in "two-three" (six) days or a similar period.

If the situation is serious and requires the attention of many *nupíka*, the performance may last all night and be continued the following night.

IX MODERN PURPOSES OF CONJURING

< Recovering lost animals or missing humans > The following incident involving a missing person was related by Stanley Como:

A Kutenal went fishing but failed to return. As his body could not be found, people thought him dead. Some time later a conjuror entered camp and the missing man's wife asked his help in searching for the body. He agreed to hold a séance. Many *nupíka* entered the lodge. The first to arrive said, "There's one coming who will tell you everything." This spirit entered, saying, "If you had not called upon me, you would never have located your husband's body. Walk down to where the river forks and near by is a small island. On the island is a log sticking out from the ground. If you see a bird on that log, which calls, jumps to the ground, and then flies towards the east and calls again, it will indicate that the body is there."
The next day one person went to the spot described, saw the bird, which behaved as the spirit predicted. The people dug in this place and found the man's booty. The stranger was offered payment but he refused, saying that he merely wanted to help people.

Some years ago several Canadian Ktunaxa went across the Rockies to trade with the Stony Indians in Alberta. An episode resulting from their visit was narrate by Stanley Como:

One Ktunaxa traded a horse for a new gun but on the way home, lost the rear sight from it. One of the company was a conjuror, who arranged a séance so that the *nupíka* might search for the missing object. During tile performance the spirits entered and said, "If you hadn't thought about us, you would have lost the horse, which you traded. Only certain spirits have power to handle metal." Then *q!o!om* entered, saying, "You lost your rifle sight in the water and while I can't touch metal, I will recover it with my paddle. Then the other spirits will find it where I have thrown it. After I leave, the second spirit to enter will return your lost gun sight." He left and another entered the lodge, saying, "Four of you stand up, two men and two women. Now the sight will be put in the hands of one of the women. Don't drop it! When I give it to you, pass it from one to another of you four. The last one may display it." When the first person received the sight from the Spirit, he almost fell from the shock of the supernatural power and had to be supported by the others. This occurred in lessening degree with each of the others, until the last held the sight in the incense smoke and then opened his hand to reveal the missing sight to the company.

Abraham Shotnana, the conjurer of Tobacco Plains, held a séance to discover the cause of Abraham Bullrobe's disappearance and, if dead, the whereabouts of his body. In the scarce the *nupíka* came and went behind the blanket, during which they discussed how to locate his remains.
Q!iq!um entered, saying that two *nupíka* were fighting one another, the third and fourth thereafter to enter. *Q!iq!um* said, We do not know what to do about them. Its up to them and up to you people."
Grizzly Bear entered, saying," I'm a *nupíka*, who remembers things for a long time. No matter how long the period is, I get my revenue." The Ktunaxa realized what the Bear was

talking about and now knew that Bullrobe had been killed by a human. Further, that if the Ktunaxa wished to punish his slayer, Grizzly Spirit would see to it. Chief Paul David replied to the Spirit with a pipe offering." We do not want another death caused by this person! Or to cause his death'! I want to recover the remains of Bullrobe, bury them, make the sign of the cross, and forget the entire affair."

Grizzly Bear left and was succeeded by the Ghost Spirit. *Qałqa* said, "I'm a *nupíka*. I like to see one death and no more." Chief Paul arose and said, "That's what I want. Show us where the body is located, so that we can bury it." Ghost retorted," That's the way I like it. Bullrobe is dead! You'll have' to wait! One! Two! Three! And you'll find the body! Then it will be as we have said. There will be no additional deaths from this cause."

Ambrose Gravelle then inquired," You said One! Two! Three! What did you mean?" *Qałqa* replied," We call this séance Number One! Tomorrow at noon build a sweathouse! As many of you as possible, enter. You and *kumnakanikitnamu* enter! We will call that Number Two! Tomorrow night hold another séance! Then we'll let you know exactly what will take place!" The séance was concluded.

The next day the Ktunaxa built and entered the sweathouse. That night a séance was held. The *nupíka* said," Go up to where the search for Bullrobe ended! Go there with three men, turn around and return on the trail! You will discover something that you will recognize! Continue on! Farther on, you will see a carcass! Its a creature with paws! That's lead Number Two! Continue walking! Suddenly, you will see a stump! You're looking for a dead body! Why do you have to run away? That's a body there! What do you expect to see? Why are you running away from it? There will still be One! Two! Three!" All this was said by *Q!iq!um*. Ambrose realized then that Bullrobe's body would not be found.

Ambrose, Louis Gingres, and two others went up to the place described by the *nupíka*. Ambrose and the two others continued on. The two hung back but Ambrose walked on. Soon the two men turned back. They were frightened at the idea of finding the body. Ambrose accused them of cowardice, and said," I should have asked *Q!iq!um* to let me come alone."

Shotnana, the conjuror, told Ambrose to wait three months for another séance. But the conjuror failed to return at the appointed time. Later he returned and said," Its three and a half years since Bullrobe disappeared. *Qałtqa* did not want the body found and the death avenged. We should have held the séance on the exact day of the third anniversary. Now the bones are scattered and cannot be identified. However Chief Paul and some others did not want the death avenged.

Disease and its Treatment

Before discussing Ktunaxa concepts of disease, their causes and treatment, we might first consider the importance placed by them upon health and long life, Good health represented one of the most important values in Ktunaxa magico-religious activities, and a prominent place was given to its quest in Ktunaxa ceremonialism. In the Sun Dance the first of the final, three nights was given over to petitioning the super-naturals for improvement of a person's health, or if already good, for its continuation. Similarly the séance represented an important mechanism for bringing a person's ill-health to the attention of the spirits. Much of the Ktunaxa New Year's rites were given over to ceremonies centering about one's state of health for the coming year.

< Native terms for good health? Long life? >

In his definitive study of Plateau Indian cultures, Verne Ray (1942: 246) stated that there were two concepts of disease causation among the Ktunaxa. These were 1) an intrusive material object caused by a malignant shaman, and 2) personal spirit loss as a result of a) mistreatment, or b) sufficient thrown away when angry. I have found sufficient evidence of the first a), and of b) of the second but there are fewer indications of guardian spirit loss by deliberate desertion. What might have confused matters for Ray in this connection was the Ktunaxa concept of what we have called the "immanent spirit", a belief that a person's guardian spirit actually dwelt within that person's body. Although the spirit was believed to leave the person's body shortly before death, we have found no widespread indication of any belief in deliberate desertion by the spirit.

<written in vertical: Followed by Mikwam tale >

The only instance I found of deliberate desertion of an individual by his power spirit was the following related by Susanne Bullrobe:

Years ago her father once said to her," I don't know for sure but I think something is wrong. I saw the spirit given to *Mikwam* 'floating' around here. I think he has power from Coyote. I saw Coyote going through here and he was leaving, so *Mikwam* no longer has control of him."

Bullrobe happened to be in *Mikwam's* lodge, when someone told the old man that if he indeed had power from Coyote, it might be leaving the country. Further, that this could be established in a séance that evening. *Mikwam* retorted, "That is not true. I have power from Coyote but I would be the first to know if it is leaving me. But that is not the case." The incident took place at New Year's and about ten days later *Mikwam* was found frozen to death in the hills. As his power came from Coyote, an animal known for its endurance and ability to travel in any blizzard, the Ktunaxa concluded that *Mikwam*'s power had deserted him shortly before his death.

In treating sickness, the *nupíka* will treat the patient standing near or even behind the blanket; *or* by a shaman (*wamu*), or by the conjuror in front of the blanket.

If the *nupíka* learn that sickness threatens one or more families in a camp, Stanley Como explained, they will appear in the séance. One of the first spirits to enter will warn the audience, "One of you is in danger." After several *nupíka* have come and gone, one will enter and call upon the threatened person by name to stepforward and present him with a smoke. In this way the identity of the person becomes known. The Spirit then says, "I'm going to help you. I smoke your pipe and take seven puffs (or twice-seven, etc.). A puff is being taken for every family of the camp. If you had forgotten me, you would be in danger. I'll try to avert it. The Spirit then advises the person as to the necessary steps to take in the immediate future; this *is* often difficult, so that if a person does become ill, he will realize that it is the result of failure to carry out the injunction correctly. For example, he may be directed to smudge himself every day for a certain period; or to take a certain number of bites of food bites only at a meal; or take a smoke very early in the morning for a time, taking so many puffs and directing them toward the east. Any spirit may impose such a regimen to avert sickness. If the procedure is correctly followed, the person will not fall ill.

If a séance is put up to avert an epidemic in camp, the conjuror or some other religionist may have dreamed of the threat. The diviner cannot refuse to hold the performance. He prays, "I wish the sickness may be taken away for the welfare of the people. There is too much suffering and sorrow.

< Ambrose Gravelle related an account of this serious? illness years ago >

When Alec Gravelle was about seven years old, he took sick one morning and became paralyzed. The father of Joe Dennis, uncle of the boy's mother, learned of it and summoned the conjuror, Pauline. Pauline came, examined the boy and decided to hold a séance for him.

After Pauline went under the blanket. Alec was placed behind it in accordance with instructions from the *nupíka*. Several spirits came and went. Then one spirit asked that boy be removed. *Q!iq!um* entered and said, "This is something you should constantly remember. There's nothing to be afraid of. You must always think of the *nupíka*. If they cannot help you, they will say so. They may even send you to a white physician. But always consult the spirits first. If you don't want them, go to a white physician. As today, your son could have been crippled for life. But we can help Alec and restore him to health. This sickness is spreading over the country both among Indians and whites." Ambrose was thus led to suspect polio as the cause of Alec's sickness, as it was present in Eureka at the time and its victims were crippled.

The following day Alec was back on his feet. "Tomorrow morning at sunrise, pray to the sun for the life of your child. Then help him to go outdoors, put him on his feet and he will be able to walk." Early in the morning, Alec felt a movement in his limbs but his father declined to take him outdoors before the sun rose above the eastern mountains. By the following morning the youth was back on his feet. As a result, < Alec, now a grown man, > believes strongly in the power of the *nupíka*.

The Hoop Spirit, *Kitnokokiniyał*, may enter the séance and warn one among the spectators that he would be in critical danger from sickness or accident at sow future time. To avert this hazard, he was instructed to sacrifice tobacco, a favorite dog, or some other belonging of value, tie a personal article, such as a piece of clothing to the sacrifice, place all of it within a wooden hoop and hang the latter to a tree. If this was done, the person was relieved from the threatened danger. Some people doubted the power of this spirit and failed to heed his warning. Such a person was expected to die within the space of three years.

Among the Lower Ktunaxa, disease was believed to be an invisible spirit, which could assume the form of a human or an animal. It was called *ksanełonetsamat*) " ? ". Children were taught to place a bucket of water on each side of the lodge entrance to prevent the disease spirit from entering. Children, it was believed, were attacked first by the disease spirit and it was the child's duty to prevent entry of this spirit after everyone was asleep. The disease spirit forms itself into a corporeal entity outside the lodge and then crawls on all fours inside. It crawls on its belly under the lodge door. It is believed to know the identity of the lodge occupants and may be in search of a certain person. Once inside, it rises to a level of about four feet and feels around the interior. If it touches water on each side of the entrance, it will not eat but leave. The same water is used for this purpose as for household use. (Coiled basket containers were employed before the introduction of metal pails). It was Simon's responsibility to keep these two water buckets filled.

(over)

Treatment of the Sick

< Return to old draft after rewriting > The conjuror occupied something of a special role

in Ktunaxa shamanism. Without entering into a discussion of the broad subject of shamanism, we can confine our attention to the relationship of conjuring to sickness, and the treatment of the sick. In previous sections we referred briefly to the conjuror's acquisition of shamanistic power, the nature of that power and the rights and duties of the conjuror as shaman. Here we may briefly discuss the types of illnesses among the Ktunaxa ad the methods of treatment by Ktunaxa conjurors.

Some conjurors had been granted power to cure the sick or more accurately, certain types of sickness; others lacked such power. A diviner's method of treating a patient reflected, of course, the type of powers he had received from his spirit guardian. Some conjurors would treat a person's illness openly, by sucking or blowing; others would take the patient behind the blanket for treatment by the *nupíka*. A few seem to have been granted power for both.

In a serious case a conjuror will usually work on the patient in the open but if unsuccessful, will take him behind the blanket.

A sick-person on the other hand usually selected a conjuror whom he felt best qualified to treat his illness. If the case seemed to warrant it, the conjuror would call upon a number of his colleagues (*wámunintek*) to come together and assist him in the treatment.

If a patient requests treatment from a conjuror and states, "I want your blanket." The latter cannot refuse to use this method. During the séance, however, the *nupíka* usually will clarify the situation by announcing that the conjuror can treat the client in the open rather than behind the blanket. Whichever method is selected does not necessarily mean
that one requires more supernatural power than another.

A sick person was often taken to a séance in order to bring him into direct contact with the diagnostic and curative powers of the supernaturals. Here the patient's request for assistance was usually carried by *Kukłúkinam* to the Master Spirit. If an answer favorable to his recovery was returned, consideration was then given to identification and treatment of the cause. If it was learned from the spirits, however, that the sickness had been ordained by the Master Spirit, it was made known to the patient that nothing could be done for him. This was later confirmed by the conjuror. In the case of a favorable prognosis, the spirits usually asked that patient, after being incensed, be taken behind the blanket. There < the cause of > his sickness could be identified and proper remedial measures suggested by the *nupíka*. The conjuror, often aided in serious cases by several of his colleagues, took an active part in the supernaturally-recommended therapy.

Confession

In the case of illness which resisted treatment and cure, the Ktunaxa practiced a form of penance, which involved the patient's confession to a shaman, of past remarks and deeds accompanied by an admission of contrition, and the performance by the patient of an act of satisfaction. < The reparation seems to have been self-imposed and the first step of the process. > With the knowledge of the person's past in mind and his permission to do so, the shaman could now trace back his recital of acts and statements to determine if any one of them had given offense to a person with power for sorcery. If the source of the illness could be determined and identified, the conjuror would then take stops to deal with the malignant shaman.

The following account of native confession and its associated practices, was related to me by Simon Francis. The information had been handed down from his father, a conjuror, who died while Simon was young.

The native version of confession was known as *ktsanatkaha•me•k*, "one confesses". [18] When a person is ill and believes strongly in the old, native religion, he must do the following: Taking a blanket or some other valuable object, he must seek the aid of a shaman. Arriving at his lodge he sits down with the conjuror and tells him about his illness. Perhaps he has been treated before but unsuccessfully. This time he makes an offering.

The conjuror will then ask the patient to go back as far as he can in his memory and recall any serious remark or action that nay have given offense to someone. The sick person must relate fully and sincerely everything of this kind that he can remember, if he is to be helped. Most of the incidents recalled were never intended to injure anyone but one or two here and there may have been intentionally malicious. If the patient can recall any of the latter type, he must relate them to the conjuror. At the same time he inquires if such may not have been responsible for his trouble. Before departing, he says, "I offer this blanket as a sacrifice. I confess because my sickness may be the result of my wrongdoing." The patient thus expresses willingness to acknowledge his past errors.

Now the sick person, it is believed, stands a good chance of recovery.

The conjuror has the necessary information by which to trace back the patient's life to earlier years. He "works" on the confession of his client to determine if the illness derived from some past offense. First he traces back the remarks made by the patient, then his actions. He may also look into the past illnesses of the patient and members of his family. Then he looks around /?/. If he finds the illness due to the actions of another person, it may represent a case of sorcery. If he determines this to be the case, he will reveal it unless there is good reason for not doing so.

If the cause of the sickness does not lie in the earthly realm, the conjuror will attempt to trace its cause among the spirits. Presumably the patient would be taken behind the blanket for this purpose. Thus it may be learned from the spirits that the sickness has been ordained by the master Spirit. In this case the conjurer will make it clear that nothing can be done for the patient. The spirits will confirm this by saying, "A black robe will come and administer the last rites of the Church.

It was emphasized by my informant that the patient must sincerely believe in the *nupíka,* if the conjuror is to help him. If the sick one is a skeptic, nothing much can be done for him. A patient may admit to a limited belief in the *nupíka* as well as an irregular attendance at conjuring performances. If these lapses are believed responsible for his sickness, the patient will admit his past errors, saying "I take back all that I have said and done." However repentance must be real.

< Confession If a person was dying, a shaman was called. He would inquire, "What causes your sickness? Have you ever spoken to anyone in the past who might have sent this sickness?" Then the sick person would try to recall everything that might have been responsible for his illness and then to relate it to the shaman. >

A conjuring performance was once given on behalf of Charles Allard, a prominent stockman in the Flathead Valley. This incident was related to me by Ambrose Gravelle, of Tobacco Plains, as taking place about 1900.

It had been a cold, stormy winter and Allard needed moderate weather if he was to save his cattle. He went to Looking Glass, a Ktunaxa conjuror at Elmo, and asked him to try to bring more temperate weather. The conjuror agreed to try.

Looking Glass "put up the blanket" and the *nupíka* told the audience that Looking Glass himself must do the work but that they would help. Upon his return to the lodge, according to their instructions, the seer must be untied, say nothing, and two men must grasp his arms, run with him to a waterhole in Flathead Lake, each pour a bucket of cold water over him, leave him there and return to the lodge. Thus the seer would be virtually naked and dripping water in below-zero temperature weather. Upon the conjuror's return to the lodge a distance of over one hundred yards, his assistants must examine him to make sure that the water running from his body was not frozen, as this would indicate colder weather.

Things turned out as the *nupíka* had said. As the conjuror entered the lodge, water could be seen dripping from his body. It had not frozen. Someone then went out to check the weather and found that the temperature was rising and rain was beginning to fall. Thus a Chinook had arrived and the snow was beginning to melt.

Charlie Allard, now very pleased, offered Looking Glass a payment of $5.00. The conjuror was dissatisfied at the smallness of the payment and told Allard so in Ktunaxa. The following day a fine cow of Allard's fell and split its pelvis on the ice of Flathead Lake. Allard then went to Looking Glass, told him to shoot the animal and {share it.}

< Look up tale of injured white youth who was helped by conjuror. >

X MORAL ASPECTS OF CONJURING

The *nupíka*, according to Mary White Pete, never grant power for evil but people make use of the spiritual power granted them for harmful ends. A person with power should be humble (*kumnakatiwina•te•k*, " ? ", as instructed by the spirits.

The *nupíka* will reprove people for wrong doing in the conjuring rite. This has occurred recently when warnings were given to the younger Ktunaxa at Bonners Ferry for over-indulgence in alcohol. The spirits would say, "We work for you, i.e. in the séance. Our work is no different than that of the regular authorities, who try to protect you. We ask you to refrain from wrong doing. If you persist, you will hurt no one but yourself."

Several spirits, in succession, will talk in this vein. Then a spectator will ask the *nupíka* to indicate more clearly what is meant. They reply that they were referring to the young people drinking. The young men were going too far in doing this. The consequences would be that some time they would be found dead somewhere. They added, "We once lived where you live now. We never indulged in drinking parties like you do. We never die. We still are spirits. Too many of you young people now occupying our former home, are ruining your health by drinking." They issue warnings for misdemeanors other than drinking. Parents re-emphasize these warnings behave, at least for a time. Simon Francis, who was Indian police officer during the 1940's, grants that supernatural assistance of this kind has been useful in maintaining law and order on the Bonners Ferry Reserve.

Mary White Pete described a conjuring performance once held by Stanley Como, who was present at the recital. Mary's son was sent to jail for drunkenness and her husband wanted Como to hold a séance to find a way to obtain his son's release from prison. A spirit entered and said, "Your son is doing this purposely. He will have to pay a fine and you will thus lose some of your property. He will be released." The prisoner's son was ill and was summoned 'by the spirits to cense himself. They said," This boy is very sick. His father, upon being released, must stop drinking. If he doesn't, the boy will die." The father, however, did not mend his ways and the child died.

There is an old conjuror of Bonners Ferry, who claimed that a white man shot at him point blank. Because of his spiritual power, the gun only inflicted a powder burn. The conjuror, according to Simon Francis, constantly boasts of this feat in his séances. Because of the diviner's lack of fear and indifference to the priest's teachings, his grandchildren are very independent, constantly in trouble, aid refuse to attend school. For this reason Simon criticized the modern practice of pagan rites as making certain Ktunaxa over-confident and without respect for the Government or Church.

XI PUBLIC SKEPTICISM

According to certain conjurors with whom I have talked, the sense of danger experienced by seers was heightened by skepticism on the part of spectators during the séance, Pauline emphasized the point that it seemed to become more hazardous for him if anyone in the audience evidenced doubt as to the authenticity of his performance.

It is probable that disbelief and doubt have increased down the years, especially as a result of Christian missionary influence. The loss of former native convictions has gone apace with the increasing settlement and industrialization of the Ktunaxa country.

< Increased greatly in recent times with increasing acculturation although there probably was a modicum in earlier days. Increases hazard to conjuror during his feigned absence from séance. Characteristic of Siouian séances ? >

We have already referred to the dislike of skepticism among conjurors as to the sincerity of their divinatory performance and their expressed feelings that it increased their physical danger during their absence from the lodge.

If a sick person is a skeptic and doesn't believe in the old pagan practices, the Ktunaxa believe that he could not be successfully treated by native methods of Indian shamans.

If anyone in the séance doubts the conjuror's power, the latter becomes aware of it by "reading the heart" of the doubter. He thinks to himself, "I'll convince him of my power," and when the rope is pulled free, his body falls to the ground in two parts as revealed in outline against the blanket. If he wants to demonstrate his power, people outside the lodge hold an end and tie rope is jerked from his body without anyone knowing how it is accomplished. The rope end is held by one in < ? >, passes under and then over the top of the blanket and the conjuror, who walks around the incense coals and then the rope is removed from around his blanket. This is one way of demonstrating one's power.

After Stanley Como had the rope for the Houdini trick attached to his body and believed that someone doubted his power, he would give additional proof of it by having the *nupíka* remove the rope in full view of the audience as he walked around the incense coals.

Stanley Como related an incident of a Ktunaxa named *e•kłam*, who was believed to have secured power for gambling from the Devil, while bathing at Hot Springs, B.C. He blackened his face with charcoal before playing and won a large sum of money thereafter.

The Tobacco Plains Ktunaxa were attacked by sickness. One of them, *nak!i*, heard the voice of *Kitnokoniniyał*, the Hoop Spirit, while hunting. The spirit spoke, "I'm *Kitnokoniniyał*. When you return to camp, have the conjuring rite held. This sickness is dangerous and will attack everyone. Those who are only slightly sick, should go and cense themselves. Those who can't get about, should send a piece of their clothing to be censed." The man did as he was told. Those who could walk, circled the incense and were cured.

When told of the Spirit's advice, only *e•kłam* refused to send a garment, although his wife sent a handkerchief. Although very ill, he crawled over to the séance and upon entering, told the spirit," You've lied to the people." He accused the conjuror, saying, "Its you who are talking behind the blanket, not the spirits." The Spirit then behind the blanket, invited him over to see if there was anything behind the blanket. The doubter crawled over and was just ready to thrust aside the blanket when it rolled up and nothing was to be seen behind it. He returned home and sent his wife back to offer two horses to the spirits, if they could cure him. The same spirit, Ghost, that was behind the blanket before when he was there, said, "There is no payment due the Ghost," i.e. the man will not get well. She returned with the message and in a few minutes, his nose began to bleed and shortly after *e•kłam* died.

Another incident involving a skeptic was recounted by Stanley Como:

In the séance certain spirits enter and after being given something to eat, leave. During one performance a certain spirit regularly asked for, and was given dried salmon eggs to eat. The following day the conjuror was found asleep and in his mouth, which hung open, could be seen remnants of salmon eggs. One Ktunaxa questioned the conjuror's power, claiming that he rather then the spirit, was behind the blanket and ate the eggs. The skeptic told a friend and they agreed to expose the diviner at the next séance. As the proper spirit entered, they walked over and were about to lift the blanket, when it rolled up apparently of its own accord. The pipe had already been passed behind it. There they could see a rock upon which small, juniper trees were growing and in the branches was the pipe with smoke rolling from it as the spirit smoked. It was *Yaukekam*, a mythological character, who is represented by a rock and who always asks for salmon eggs. He inquired of the doubters if they were convinced that it was a spirit rather than the conjuror behind the blanket.

Some cases of unbelief were so serious, if we are to credit native testimony, as to cost the skeptic his life. Stanley Como related an incident of such among the St. Mary's Ktunaxa, that was said to have happened shortly before 1935.

A conjuror there was doubted by some people including a prominent Flathead, named "Fast Eater." One time the latter declared that at the next séance, "He would show him up! That he lied to the people as it was he, not the spirits, behind the blanket." Other Ktunaxa heard of the threat and waited to see the outcome at the séance. The Ghost Spirit, who was, of course, aware of the Flathead's intentions, arrived at the séance and was talking to the people. Fast Eater, telling the audience, "I'm going to do what I promised," walked towards the blanket, which to his surprise, immediately rolled up. The Ghost continued talking in a hoarse voice, above the rolled-up blanket, saying to Fast Eater, "Reach for me and take me out." The Flathead felt the entire blanket with his hands but was unable to find the Ghost. He then turned around and left the lodge. At once sounds of the Ghost attacking the doubter could be heard outside. The noise ceased and the spectators went out to find his dead body. The Flathead was struck dead because of his incredulity.

Simon Francis related the following account of skepticism among the Lower Ktunaxa:

Jerome was a very old conjuror at Bonners Ferry. The younger Ktunaxa laughed at him because he snored behind the blanket and thus they doubted that he was really taken from the lodge. Their parents warned them not to ridicule the old man. Some of the younger people asked Jerome for a séance. It was held and the *nupíka* entered and announced that the diviner would return for a smoke. He was taken out from behind the blanket, and given a smoke, < and returned behind the screen >.   One of the young Ktunaxa then inquired why Jerome snored behind the blanket? The spirit replied, "You'll see something in a moment!" Then Jerome was heard some distance away, coughing even while he snored behind the blanket.   Then his coughing was heard coming from different directions and finally, Jerome entered through the lodge entrance. The older Ktunaxa advised," Light a pipe and hand it to him." The blanket rolled up, Jerome was transported to the space behind the blanket and the blanket rolled down. Thereafter no one teased the old diviner.

The following account of skepticism was given me by < ?? >

The eldest daughter of a Ktunaxa family did not believe that the conjurors could cure sickness and wanted to test them out. She was the cause of the young diviner's death (p.), as he was urged by this girl to over-exercise his power by remaining outside the lodge until after daybreak. One of her sister's was a diviner too. She and her mother were evilly-disposed but the remainder of her family were well-intentioned people. One time she pretended she was sick and asked that a diviner hold a séance for her. The *nupíka* entered, examined her, and stated that she was not ill at all. They were not angry, however, over her disbelief. The girl continued to ask that a séance be held for her and then the Spirits became angry. They said to her, "Maybe you do not know what sickness is. We will show you what it is and then if you do not come to us, it will go hard with you. Your whole family will die since you are breaking all the rules." The girl paid no attention to the warning. The first to die was her grandfather; then her father; then her three brothers. The first, two relatives to die, did believe in the pagan religion but their lives were taken anyway. Next her two sisters died and only she and her mother were left alive. These two requested a séance, offered the pipe to the *nupíka,* and publicly apologized for their disbelief. Their apologies were accepted and both the girl and her mother were spared.

Simon Francis, who claimed that very old conjurors in late years displayed their powers too openly in the séance, related the following account of skepticism:

An old conjuror named Paul, mentioned earlier as the half brother of Assistant Chief David, was described by the Spirits in a séance, as returning for a smoke. The young Ktunaxa were accustomed to make fun of him on account of his age. Paul complained that crashing through the wood wall of the cabin in departing from and returning to the séance, hurt him too much. One time the boys lifted the blanket and saw Paul midway through the cabin wall with his legs and feet still hanging outside. He groaned and then cried aloud in pain. The older Ktunaxa present shouted to the boys to drop the blanket, as their actions were hurting the conjuror. They did so and his body was heard to fall to the floor.
Paul, according to Simon, was unable to stand criticism and doubt and he would cause his critics to become ill. After the above incident Simon never cared to attend séances.

Modern conjuring in some tribes has been met with skepticism on the part of some native spectators. Within the framework of Salteaux theory, doubt in regard to the visitation of spirits is, according to an authority, out of place. In recent years many Indians are aware that white traders and missionaries have questioned the manipulation of the shaking tent and the voices therein are assignable to the spirits. Accordingly, there is recognition of the existing disbelief on the part of conjurors in some tribes. Among the Atsina, for example, the binding of the diviner was often turned over to a skeptic." A Montana Cree conjuror was tied up only if there were doubtful persons present. A Dakota seer cautioned against anyone expressing uncertainty during the séance. In Ktunaxa séances magical feats were occasionally presented during performances to convince unbelievers.

XII Sorcery and Shamanistic Conflict

We may consider briefly the < maleficient > category of witchcraft or sorcery – illness caused by the introduction in a person's body of some material object (*q!oq!ot*) by a malignant shaman. Such an object might be a human hair, a small piece of bone, an insect or some other small, foreign object. If an object of this kind was found to be the cause of a person's illness, the spirit returning with an answer from the Master Spirit, will identify the sorcerer responsible.

We have an example of sorcery in the case of Mary White Pete, of St. Mary's Reserve. At the age of fourteen she became very ill from this cause. The shaman responsible wished to marry her and her father had refused him. The sickness (*q!oq!ot*) had been diagnosed by the *nupíka* in a séance.

Mary was taken to a second séance for treatment by the spirits, *Kuktukinam*, the Sun Dance Spirit, entered and directed that she be taken behind the blanket. The Spirit then blew upon her five times once upon her back, once upon each foot, and once upon each breast. Then she was carried out and around the incense fire and passed twice through the juniper smoke, thus making a count of seven. In this way she went through the "seven marks" of *Kuktukinam*. The Spirit then told her," You will get well. You must look ahead to when the New Year's Dance is held; there you must shake your body, i.e. dance, so that your sickness is shaken off. Then turn around and go down the other side of the mountain and you will see green grass and flowers, i.e. Spring, and later still the ripening of berries, i.e. Summer. By that time you will have been cured. You will live to be an old woman."

Later, however, she became ill and was again placed behind the blanket, with but temporary relief. Her father then told her, "You're very sick. I'll give your body to the *wamu*." The shamans are able to "see" sickness-causing objects in a persons body and can remove them by sucking. Since the case was considered serious, seven shamans had been called in for treatment. She was placed behind the blanket and started working on her. They started to "chase" the sickness from her head down and would corner it in certain parts of her body. Each shaman worked with a whistle (*kustat*) in his mouth and once this was brought to the locality of the sickness, the latter was drawn away. Every sickness-causing object was removed from her body and when the shamans were finished, there was a considerable number of articles (*q!oq!ot*) beside the patient.

In a séance attended by Mary in 1935, she and her husband were told by the *nupíka*, "You two old people, your camp fire, i.e life, is burning very low. Its in danger of going out. Another person has asked us to do harm to you but we won't allow this to happen. We will put it aside, since we never advise the conjuror to make use of us in this way."

The Ktunaxa conjuror would at times aggressively assume the role of sorcerer in curing the sick or in former times, defending his people from attack by enemy shamans.

At one séance attended by Simon Francis at Bonners Ferry, the bone whistle of the diviner could be seen making its way horizontally across the blanket on its inner side. This was an indication, my informant explained, that the conjuror was angry and had put his spirits to work sending a material object of same kind into someone's body. Interestingly enough, the spectators present at the time disapproved of the diviner's actions as an exaggerated display of power for personal ends.

In working sorcery the Ktunaxa would approach the intended victim and inform him that he would die at an appointed time, i.e. when the first green grass appeared, and that he would meet his death in some prescribed way, i.e. drowning, attack by a bear, etc. The victim might avert his doom if he were willing to make amends of some kind.

In the case of those petitioners who speak so low in praying to the *nupíka* during the séance as to be inaudible to the audience, the suspicion of their concealing requests harmful to another person in the group, could easily arise. If the spectators happened to be singing quite loudly at the time, such a request might go unnoticed while the petitioner presented his pipe to a spirit. < method of treatment >

If a person feels ill from an intrusive object, he will become worse upon the approach of a shaman and the object itself will then begin to travel about his body. A shaman sings his song and performs a ritual act that will enable him to "locate" and to "see" the object. Then he selects a power token from his medicine bag, which will give him the power to handle the object. He then tries to drive it towards the patient's extremities, from which it can be removed more easily. Between it and the patient's body a pelt or thong is tied around the limb to act as a sort of tourniquet past which the object cannot move back into the body again. Finally it emerges into the closed hand of the shaman, who changes color, begins to tremble, while he or a colleague grips his arms above, so that the object cannot seek a hiding place within his own body. Another shaman removes the object from his clenched fist and holds it over the smoke of the incense coals until it is "dead." If, upon opening his hand, nothing is to be seen, the shaman again places his hand in the incense, this time the object will become visible.

The conjuror, in tracing back a patient's life revealed to him by confession, may find that his sickness has been caused by a sorcerer and will, unless there is some reason against it, frankly reveal it to the patient. He or one of his relatives may have ridiculed someone with power and his illness may have resulted from flat. The sorcery thus caused by a malignant shaman is called *kantsakinamnam*, " ? ". It is possible that the shaman responsible may not wish to bring about the patient's death but only punish him by making him suffer. Illness of this kind is called," ? ", "pinching".

In an ill-disposed person merely prayed that misfortune overtake the patient, this does not represent in Ktunaxa belief a real case of witchcraft. True sorcery is caused by a shaman, who has derived power from a specific spirit to cause illness in another person.

In a case of sorcery a diviner will hold a séance every seven days or oftener in order to work against the shaman responsible. As soon as the conjuror discovers the cause, his spirits will seek out the sorcerer's spirit causing the illness, isolate it from the others and drive it behind the blanket. Now he can either 1) take the offending spirit away from the sorcerer, or 2) remove the power of the offending spirit and release it, or 3) force the sorcerer to withdraw the offending spirit.

If the sorcerer has planned the death of his victim but the latter has admitted his error and offered a sacrifice, the conjuror will persist and strip the *nupíka* of power or else keep it for himself. If he succeeds, the patient will be cured; if not, the patient will become ill later on.

If the sorcerer does not withdraw, he will lose some of his *nupíka*, become ill and even die. In any case his power will never be as strong as before.

Bullrobe stated that among the Upper Ktunaxa there were no conflicts between conjurors during séances, such as stealing one's spirits, etc. Such practices were said to be more characteristic of the Lower Ktunaxa and the adjacent Salishan-speaking tribes.

If war was imminent, the *nupíka* might fight among themselves behind the blanket and the lodge poles would then be violently shaken.

Chief Baptiste Mathias, of Elmo was seized with an acute pain near his heart around 1929. After several shamans had worked on him, the intrusive object causing the trouble, was removed. It proved to be a large needle used in sewing grain sacks. Someone recommended that it be returned to the sender by supernatural means but Bullrobe suggested that it be merely taken to him as a sign of his failure.

In earlier days Blackfoot shamans, informants stated, would send their power spirits to fight against the Ktunaxa during séances.

Before inter-tribal peace was established, a violent shaking of the conjuring lodge also took place as *nupíka* of Blackfoot or Flathead shamans attempted to enter the séance and break it up. The lodge was violently shaken by the struggle between friendly and hostile spirits, while the conjuror was "absent" from the lodge.

About 1920, according to Abraham Bullrobe, Bullhead entered a séance at Elmo and warned those present to be prepared for an enemy, armed with a weapon, and about to enter the lodge. He instructed the men to attempt to disarm the enemy but to be careful not to get hurt. The shamans were told to be on guard and after the spirits had entered, the fourth one would be the armed enemy. Everyone should then be on guard. When the fourth spirit entered, the blanket began to shake and the shamans started to try to locate the hostile spirit. All jumped for it but when they opened their hands, they saw that they had missed. One of tie assistants was knocked unconscious by the spirit as it left the lodge; he saw it discharge an arrow and believed that he had been struck. In a few days this man died. Bullrobe was the Interpreter but remained seated and did not see the visitor. This was the second attempt of a hostile shaman and the Ktunaxa wanted to secure revenge. Bullrobe disapproved, however, pointing out that intertribal peace had been established.

Attacks by enemy shamans occurred more frequently in earlier times than at present. Since peaceful relations lave been established, the Ktunaxa make no effort to harm individuals of other tribes by supernatural power.

Elsewhere I have related the episode of David, Second Chief at Bonners Ferry, and his narrow escape years ago from a grizzly bear. David had been warned never to put castor on his person or clothing in high country for fear it would invite attack by a bear. His brother, Paul, some Ktunaxa believed, worked magic against David by causing the grizzly bear to attack him. David, however, claimed he himself was responsible for the narrow escape. He had seen Paul and his wife using red ochre mixed with castoreum. He asked for some and rubbed it on his face and moccasins. A bear then tracked David by the scent of the castor and nearly caught him. Word of this episode reached the ears of the Catholic missionaries, who exerted increasing pressure for abandonment of the pagan rites. The Ktunaxa belief in the animosity of the bear for the beaver goes back to a tale in Ktunaxa mythology.

Conclusion

According to Granville, when the Catholic priests entered the country, the Ktunaxa or some of them were forced to abandon "pagan" practices.

The *akiyinnik*, apparently, were not bothered too much after -?-

The Tobacco Plains Ktunaxa resumed conjuring again about 1917.

Ambrose as a child witnessed séances about 1906 at Elmo as it was resumed by *akiyinnik* at the time. The *akiyinnik* scattered out at this time as their land was being allotted in severalty. Ambrose's father wanted to take up land at Dayton but sold his allotment. He took up land at Elmo for Ambrose and latter's mother.

When Ambrose was 7 or 8, pagan practices, including gambling, died down for a time. This was for a period of 8 or 9 years and by 1915 conjuring started up again. Ambrose claimed that pagan ways never really died out at Elmo and that the Flathead never really dropped their Blue Jay Ceremony.

Ambrose went to St Ignatius from age 7 to 11 years (four years) and then attended public school at Elmo for three years. He also attended Chemawa for part of a year.

Could Ktunaxa conjuring be derived from Assiniboine (Stony) rather than Plains Cree? (See Kroeber, Culture Areas: 84).   Also Lowie 1909 (Stony!)

Boas, Franz 1890 First General Report on the Indians of British Columbia. (59th Annual Report of the British Association for the Advancement of Science for 1889: 810-893, London)

Chamberlain, Alexander 1901 Kootenai "Medicine-Men". Journal of American Folk-Lore 14 (53): 95-99.

Cline and others 1938 *The Sinkaietk or Southern Okanagon of Washington* (General Series in Anthropology # 6.

Collier, Donald 1944 Conjuring among the Kiowa. Primitive Man 17 (3-4): 45-49.

Densmore, Frances 1923 Mandan-Hidatsa Music, BAE Bulletin 80.

Goddard, Pliny Earle 1916 The Beaver Indians. American Museum of Natural History, Anthropological Papers 10: 201-293.

Hallowell, A.L 1942 The Role of Conjuring in Saulteaux Society. Philadelphia Anthropological Society Publications, Vol. 2, Philadelphia.Jenness, Diamond 1937 The Sekani Indians of British Columbia (National Museum of Canada, Bulletin, # 84).

Kroeber, A.L. 1939 *Cultural and Natural Areas of Native North America* (University of California Publications in American Archaeology and Ethnology, Vol. 38: 84.

Lowie, Robert H. *The Assiniboine* (Anthropological Papers, American Museum of Natural History, Vol. 4, pp. 1-270, 1909).

Mandelbaum, David G. *The Plains Cree* (Anthropological Papers, American Museum of Natural History, Vol. 37, pp. 155-316, 1940)

Ray, Verne 1939 Cultural Relations in the Plateau of Northwestern America. Southwest Museum: Publications of the Frederick Webb Hodge Anniversary Publication Fund # 3.

Ray, Verne 1942 Culture Element Distributions: XXII Plateau. University of California Anthropological Records 8 (2): 99-258+4, Berkeley.

Schaeffer, Ktunaxa ms

Turney-High, Harry H. 1941 Ethnography of the Kutenai. American Anthropological Association Memoirs # 56, Menasha, WI.

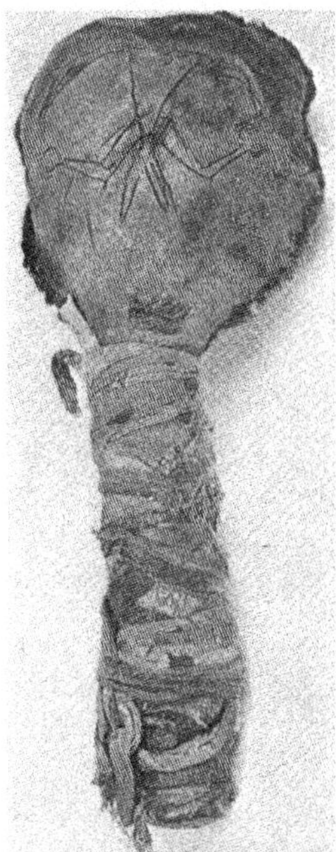

This rattle with a thunderbird design was used during Cree shaking tent rituals. It is part of Glenbow's ethnological collection, No. AP-939A.

Blackfoot Shaking Tent

Claude Schaeffer

Diffusion of the Ritual

The time and manner of the Skaking Tent rite's diffusion westward from the Central Woodlands is a question that has engaged the attention of students for a number of years. In 1941, after a pioneer survey and analysis of the ceremony through its then inadequately known range of distribution, Verne F. Ray (1941: 214) suggested the plains Cree as the transmitters of the comples to the Plains and [33] Plateau. However, not only was Dr. Ray then unaware of the rite's wide distribution among Northern Plains tribes but his knowledge of its intertribal extent and variety in that area was too limited to allow adequate analysis. Three years later Donald Collier (1944: 48), after pointing out that "materials on the conjuring complex in the Plains were still too fragmentary to permit a reliable historical reconstruction," warned that "diffusion of the complex [in this area] was no simple process, that there were cross lines of diffusion and that probably some form of conjuring existed in the Northern Plains before, or at least independently of the advent of the Plains Cree." That same year Father John Cooper (1944: 81) outlined some basic traits that served to distinguish Blackfoot-Atsina-Assiniboine conjuring from the Woodlands version. Our present analysis confirms Dr. Collier's suggestion that both the Northern Plains and Plateau versions of the conjuring rite were sufficiently different from the Woodlands pattern to indicate that the complex was of some antiquity in the west and probably existed there prior to the migration of the Cree.

If one were to venture some conjectures as to the history of the Shaking Lodge rite in the Northern Plains, the following factors and developments might be pointed out. At the start it is recognized in a general way approximately how and when this area was peopled by the precursors of the modern tribes. With the exception of the Kiowa and Sarsi, the antecedents of all recent residents of the Northern Plains were located in the prairies and woodlands to the east (Kroeber 1939:76-88). Here there were two great language divisions – Algonkian and Siouan. The Shaking Tent rite has undoubtedly been a cultural possession of the Woodland Algonkians for a considerable period of time (Cooper 1946: 296). The clairvoyant observance not only spread among neighboring Siouan peoples but extended eastward to the Montagnais and Naskapi, where accounts of explorers and missionaries attest its presence in the early 17th Century (Hallowell 1942: 40, 50).

Attracted early by the vast bison herds and stimulated later by the introduction of the horse, the prairie and taiga peoples began to expand into the western grasslands prior to and during the 18th Century. The Shaking Tent rite was probably carried westward by most if not all of these immigrants into their new homeland. At the start the predictive complex probably embraced certain basic traits, such as the true shaking lodge, multiple spirits, the trussed conjuror ostensibly freed by supernaturals, use of an unintelligible language and apparent return of the spirits with the information desired. Gradually changes were introduced in the complex to accommodate the new environment or beliefs and practices of local origin. Animal hides were substituted for birchbark as cover material for the conjuring lodge and the latter was reduced in size to fit inside the conical, skin tipi. In time some groups would substitute a vertical hide for the miniature booth as a means of concealment, except when on the hunt or war trail. Most conjurors would abandon the earlier method of embedding the conjuring lodge poles in the ground while retaining the practice of manipulating the lodge. Among some tribes the ceremony would be utilized more and more for protection in the ever increasing intertribal warfare. [34]

The initial bearers of the Shaking Tent rite westward were probably those dialectically most divergent and hence earliest Algonkian migrants – the Blackfoot and Arapaho. While authorities differ as to their length of residence in the plains, traditions locate the Peigan in the valley of the North Saskatchewan, near the Eagle Hills, in the early decades of the 18th Century. Directly to the east, near present Saskatoon, were the Atsina, who had separated from the Arapaho some time before. The Blackfoot and Atsina had become close friends and allies and their conjuring performances would come in time to resemble one another closely. From the Eagle Hills, the Peigan would make their way southwestward to the foothills of the Alberta Rockies. Here Fidler and Mackay would witness separate séances around 1795, which featured the true shaking lodge, the vertical hide curtain, and probably the ghost helper concept.

Immediately east of the Atsina in their habitat around Saskatoon were the Algonkian Plains Cree and Siouan-speaking Assiniboine (Lewis 1942: 12). The western-most bands of forest Cree, after obtaining firearms in 1670, had shifted westward into the grasslands to become native entrepreneurs and buffalo-hunters. They were accompanied by the Assiniboine, who likewise left the Yanktonai Dakota, to join their allies in their westward movement. Although the Shaking Tent ceremony of the Plains Cree seems never to have diverged from its basic Woodland pattern, the Assiniboine rite, like that of the Dakota, probably already had been modified to a prairie-Siouan version. Contacts between Blackfoot-Atsina and Assiniboine at this period could have resulted in the adoption of the ghost helper concept by the two Algonkian tribes.

Another Siouan-speaking group, the Crow Indians, early ventured to give up farming for a nomadic, bison-hunting life. Upon their separation from the Hidatsa probably in the early 1700's, the Skull Bundle may have represented their major clairvoyant observance. The Shaking Tent rite may have been a later acquisition from the Cheyenne, as Dr. Robert H. Lowie was inclined to think.[135] If these assumptions are correct, the Crow may have been an alternate source of the ghost helper concept for Blackfoot-Atsina-Kiowa conjuring and for the Blackfoot Ghost Dance bundle.

The two remaining conjuring tribes of the Northwestern Plains, the Kiowa and Sarsi, were fairly late recipients of the clairvoyant ceremony. The Kiowa, originally a southern Plains [Southwest] people, claim to have migrated north to the extreme headwaters of the Missouri River. Moving down from the mountains, they formed an alliance with the Crow Indians (Hodge 1907: 1, 699 quoting Mooney). It was undoubtedly at this time that they took over certain cultural traits, including no doubt the Shaking Tent ceremony, from the Crow.[136]22 Similarly, the Sarsi, a northwest Athapascan group, left their kinsmen in the northern forests to take up a Plains-type of life with their allies, the Blackfoot. The latter were most probably the source of Plains traits, including their little known version of the Shaking Tent ceremony (Jenness 1933: 31). [20]

---

[135] Collier (1944: 48) accepts the Kiowa possession of certain traits of the Shaking Tent rite as some confirmation of the Kiowa and Interior Salish tradition of a former northwestern habitat.

[136] Personal communication of the late Dr. John M. Cooper, 4/4/42.

Blackfoot

Binding Techniques

The binding of the conjuror and his subsequent release, supposedly through supernatural aid, was one of the most widely distributed of all traits associated with the conjuring complex. It was practiced by native peoples extending from the state of Washington to the Atlantic Coast. This feat of legerdemain, which has come to be known as the Houdini trick, has been found to occur among the Kutenai, Blackfoot, Atsina, Assiniboine, Dakota, Plains Cree, Cheyenne, Cree, Ojibwa, Montagnais and Naskapi (Hurt and Howard 1952: 295). To this list may be added the Mandan (Bowers 1950: 180), Sauk (Skinner 1923: 54) and Colville (Cline and Others 1938: 152). The Arikara could also be added through the testimony of Father Pierre DeSmet (Chittenden and Richardson 1905: 1, 250) but whether this tribe also practiced conjuring is unknown. I have been unable to find any reference to binding the conjuror among the Crow or Kiowa. Incidentally, the custom has been reported for the Central Eskimo (Boas 1888: 593-94).

Apparently the purpose of binding the conjuror was to immobilize him so that his release seemed possible only through supernatural intervention. Thus the practice served to validate the medium's [21] possession of spiritual power for clairvoyant purposes. Tribal accounts of binding describe a method of fastening the conjuror's hands, even the fingers of each hand, with thongs behind his back. Most descriptions, however, are so generalized as to afford an inadequate account of the binding technique. It is not unlikely, however, that one or more of what appear to be distinctive techniques of binding diffused westward as part of the Shaking Tent complex. One of the better described instances is that of the Cheyenne, in which the medium was tied with four bowstrings. Each finger of each hand was tied separately to the next finger in a hard knot and the ends of the bowstring on each hand tied together behind his back so that his hands were tightly bound there. His feet were tied together in the same way, each toe being secured to the next in a hard knot, and the feet fastened together by the bowstrings (Grinnell 1923: 11, 112-15). Both Fidler's and Mackay's accounts of the binding techniques of the earlier Blackfoot may refer to this method. A somewhat different technique of arranging the thongs was followed by the Plains Cree. Here the conjuror's hands, palms out, were placed behind his back and similar fingers were tied together (Mandelbaum 1940: 261). There was no mention of binding the feet.

The remainder of the Northern Plains groups followed binding techniques involving intertwining with thongs or sinew the conjuror's fingers of each, or of both hands behind his back, and in some instances the toes of his feet. In the case of the Atsina performer, "the four fingers of each hand were tied together by interlacing them [somewhat after the technique of wrapped or twined basketry], the hands were tied behind the back" (Cooper 1944: 65). This is apparently a duplication of the Cheyenne method. Among the Dakota the conjuror's assistant tied his hands behind his back with a short rawhide thong (Fugle 1966: 6). Other observers of Dakota divination have noted that "even individual fingers and toes are bound together" (Hurt and Howard 1952: 290). The Assiniboine conjuror's "fingers and toes [were] laced together with smaller thongs and hands fastened behind his back by tying the thumbs together" (Kennedy 1961: 163). In neither the Dakota nor Assiniboine cases, however, can we be certain from the accounts of the exact techniques employed. Among the Saulteaux, although no modern diviner was credited with the Houdini trick, the practice was part of the repertoire of many conjurors of old. Here the performer was either trussed up securely with rope or enveloped in a skin or blanket and tied (Hallowell 1942: 70, fn. 117).[137]

Regarding the Shaking Tent rite of the Plateau, the binding procedures were quite different from those of the Plains. Among the Ktunaxa and Colville, conjuring concepts varied from those of the east, leading to differences in techniques. Instead of ostensibly being freed by spiritual aid from bonds securing his hands and feet, the Ktunaxa diviner must also elicit supernatural help in freeing himself from a line passed about his mid-section in such a way that it seemingly divides his body into two parts. After going behind the vertical [22] screen, the performer emerges with his thumbs fastened by buckskin laces behind his back to his belt. With his hands still bound, the performer's arms are tightly secured to his body by a leather strap fastened by an assistant. He then goes behind the blanket and soon reappears with the strap passed beneath one or both arms. The conjuror again goes behind the screen. Then his two assistants reach over the top and drop a looped rope over his head to his waist, each meanwhile holding on to one end of the rope. Almost immediately the curtain is raised to reveal the rope about the conjuror's waist but now inside his strapped-down arms. Meanwhile the assistants step back to the entrance area, each holding his end of the rope. At a signal, the assistants pull strongly on the ends of the rope, the outline of the conjuror's body can, be seen against the curtain to rise in the air, and suddenly fall back to the ground as if cut in two parts, and the rope comes entirely free. The conjuror has been "cut in two." However, the curtain is raised to reveal the performer safe and whole, restored apparently through the power of his spirits. The séance continues (Schaeffer, Kutenai ms).

In addition to being securely bound with thongs, the mediums of some tribes in this region were enveloped and tied within a blanket or robe before being thrust into the shaking tent. This practice has been noted for the Kutenai (Schaeffer, Kutenai ms.), the earlier Blackfoot (Fidler and Mackay), Atsina (Kroeber 1908: 223), Assiniboine (Kennedy 1961: 163), Cheyenne (Grinnell 1923: 11, 112-15), Arikara (Chittenden and Richardson 1905: I, 250), and Saulteaux (Hallowell 1942: 70, fn. 117). Rarely are we given a detailed description of wrapping and tying the performer in this case. In one Assiniboine séance (Kennedy 1961: 163), the conjuror was wrapped in a robe and a long thong wound about him from head to foot in a series of half hitches. This method of using half hitches was also the practice of the Dakota (Fugle 1966: 6), and the Kutenai (Schaeffer, Kutenai ms.). The Dakota term *yuwipi*, which is applied to the entire conjuring performance, is said to mean "wrapping" and refers to the wrapping and binding of the seer (Hurt and Howard 1952: 287). Information from the Saulteaux suggests that wrapping and tying the conjuror in a robe was an alternative to the more common method of merely binding him with thongs (Hallowell 1942: 70). An apparent alternative of the Cheyenne practice was to tie the bound medium to a stake driven into the ground or to a lodgepole (Densmore 1936: 56; Grinnell 1923: 11, 112-15).

The most characteristic feature of the Shaking Tent rite among the Woodland peoples was the manipulation of the old, divining lodge by the medium. The Saulteaux assign the cause of this movement to the winds, which are, in Hallowell's (1942: 23) words, "thus inextricably linked with conjuring." The westward flowing migrants, with the exception of the Plains Cree (Mandelbaum 1940: 261) and some earlier Blackfoot (Fidler), appear to have abandoned the old,

---

[137] In the conjuring rites of many Plains tribes, the thongs from which the medium frees himself, were disposed of in some peculiar, often striking fashion that could, of course, be credited to the spirits.

ground-implanted structure in favor of new forms of conjuring arrangements. Despite these adaptions, however, movement of the diving structure continued among virtually all conjuring peoples in the Northern Plains. Thus in the Blackfoot séance witnessed by Denny in the 1870s the lodge rocked violently. A Cheyenne [23] divining lodge, after the fire was extinguished, was shaken as if by a strong wind (Grinnell 1923: 11, 112-15). In a Crow séance the entire lodge shook violently during the reputed exit and return of the diviner in the form of an owl (Lowie 1922: 380-81). During an Assiniboine performance the top of the regular, canvas dwelling used for this purpose, shook (Cooper 1944: 78). Among the Atsina, as the ghost entered the tipi, always through the smokehole, the top and often the entire structure would shake severely (Cooper 1956: 261). In the case of the Kiowa, after the medium had smoked and prayed, a roaring noise was heard, the large tipi was shaken and filled with wind, and then the miniature tipi vibrated (Collier 1944: 47). The emphasis upon movement of the divining lodge extended into the Plateau. In former days the Ktunaxa conical lodge would shake violently as an indication that the spirits predicted the imminence of an enemy attack (Schaeffer, Kutenai ms.). In view of these data it is clear that the medium continued to manipulate the new structure much as in the earlier, eastern pattern. It is difficult to understand why some students of the ceremony have hesitated to apply the term "Shaking Tent" to the western forms of conjuring.

References Cited

Boas, Franz
  1888   The Central Eskimo. Bureau of American Ethnology, Annual Report 6, 390-669. Washington, D.C.
Bowers, Alfred W.
  1950 Mandan Social and Ceremonial Organization. University of Chicago Press.
  1965 Hidatsa Social and Ceremonial Organization. Bureau of American Ethnology, Bulletin 194, Washington, D.C.
Chittenden, H.M. and A.T. Richardson
  1905 Life, Letters and Travels of Father Pierre-Jean De Smet, S.J., New York, 4 vols.
Cline, W. and others
  1938 The Sinkaietk or Southern Okanagon of Washington. Leslie Spier, ed. General Series in Anthropology, 6, Menasha.
Collier, Donald
  1944 Conjuring Among the Kiowa. Primitive Man, Vol. 17, No. 3-4, 45-49, Washington, D.C.
Cooper, John M.
  1944 The Shaking Tent among Plains and Forest Algonquians. Primitive Man, Vol. 17 (3-4): 60-84, Washington, D.C.
  1946 Culture of the Northeastern Indian Hunters: A Reconstructive Interpretation. Frederick Johnson, ed. In Man in Northeastern North America, Papers, Robert S. Peabody Foundation for Archaeology Vol. 3: 272-305, Andover.
  1956 The Gros Venires of Montana: Part II Religion and Ritual. Regina Flannery, ed. Catholic University of America Anthropological Series # 16, Washington, D.C.
Dempsey, Hugh A.
  1968 Blackfoot Ghost Dance. Occasional Paper 3, Glenbow-Alberta Institute, Calgary.
Denig, E.T.
  1930 Indian Tribes of the Upper Missouri. J.N.B. Hewitt, ed. Bureau of American Ethnology, Annual Report 46: 375-628, Washington, D.C. [36]

Denny, Sir Cecil
1944 Blackfoot Magic. The Beaver, Outfit 275, Sept. 14-15, Winnipeg.
Densmore, Frances
1936 Cheyenne and Arapaho Music. Southwest Museum Papers # 10, Los Angeles.
Dusenberry, Verne
1962 The Montana Cree: A Study in Religious Persistence. University of Stockholm, Studies in Comparative Religion # 3, Stockholm.
Ewers, John C.
1958   The Blackfeet: Raiders on the Northwestern Plains. University of Oklahoma Press, Norman.
1967   Was There A Northwestern Plains Sub-culture? An Ethnographic Appraisal." Plains Anthropologist, Vol. 12 #36: 167-174, Lincoln.
Feraca, Stephen E.
1963 Wakinyan: Contemporary Teton Dakota Religion. Studies in Plains Anthropology and History, Museum of the Plains Indian, No. 2, Browning, Montana.
Fidler, Peter
1793 Journal, manuscript, E. 3/2. Hudson's Bay Co. Archives, London.
Fugle, Eugene
1966 The Nature and Function of the Lakota Night Cults. Museum News, South Dakota Museum, Vol. 27 (3-4), Vermillion, S.D.
Grinnell, George B.
1892 Blackfoot Lodge Tales. New York.
1923 The Cheyenne Indians. Two volumes, New Haven.
Haeberlin, H., and others
1928   Coiled Basketry in British Columbia and Surrounding Regions. Bureau of American Ethnology, Annual Report, 41, Washington, D.C.
Hallowell, A.L.
1940 The Spirits of the Dead in Saulteaux Life and Thought. Royal Anthropological Society, Journal, Vol. 70, Pt. 1: 29-51, London.
1942   The Role of Conjuring in Saulteaux Society. Philadelphia Anthropological Society Publications, Vol. 2, Philadelphia.
Hassrick, Royal B.
1964   The Sioux: Life and Customs of a Warrior Society. University of Oklahoma Press, Norman.
Hickerson, Harold
1960 The Feast of the Dead Among the Seventeenth Century Algonkians of the Upper Great Lakes. American Anthropologist, Vol. 62 # 1: 81-107, Menasha.
Hoebel, E. Adamson
1960 The Cheyennes: Indians of the Great Plains. George and Louise Spindler, eds. Case Studies in Cultural Anthropology, Stanford University, Palo Alto.
Hurt, Wesley R. Jr., and James H. Howard
1952 A Dakota Conjuring Ceremony. Southwest Journal of Anthropology, Vol. 8 # 1: 286-296, Albuquerque.
Jenness, Diamond
1938 The Sarcee Indians of Alberta. National Museum of Canada Bulletin # 90, Ottawa. [37]
Kennedy, Michael S, ed.

1961 The Assiniboines; As told to First Boy, James Larpentew Long. University of Oklahoma Press, Norman.

Kroeber, Alfred

1908 Ethnology of the Gros Venire. American Museum of Natural History, Anthropological Papers, Vol. 1, Part 4, New York.

1939 Cultural and Natural Areas of Native North America. University of California Press, Berkeley.

Lewis, Oscar

1942 The Effects of White Contact Upon Blackfoot Culture, With Special Reference To The Role of the Fur Trade. American Ethnological Society Monographs 6, New York.

Lowie, Robert H.

1909 The Assiniboine. American Museum of Natural History, Anthropological Papers, Vol. 4, Pt. 1, New York.

1922 The Religion of the Crow Indians. American Museum of Natural History, Anthropological Papers, Vol. 25, Part 2, New York.

1956 The Crow Indians. New York.

McClintock, Walter

1910 The Old North Trail. London.

MacGregor, J.G.

1966 Peter Fidler: Canada's Forgotten Surveyor, 1769-1822. Toronto.

Mackay, James

?? Indian Notes, Note 5. Manuscript in the Missouri Historical Society Library, St. Louis, Mo.

Mandelbaum, David

1940 The Plains Cree. American Museum of Natural History, Anthropological Papers, Vol. 37, Pt. 2, New York.

Ray, Verne

1941 Historic Backgrounds of the Conjuring Complex in the Plateau and the Plains. Language, Culture and Personality: Essays in Memory of Edward Sapir: 204-216, Menasha.

Schaeffer, Claude E. 1940 Kutenai ms.

1965 The Kutenai Female Berdache: Courier, Guide, Prophetess, and Warrior. Ethnohistory. Vol. 12 # 3: 193-236, Poughkeepsie.

1966 Bear Ceremoniaiism of the Kutenai Indians. Studies in Plains Anthropology and History, 4, Museum of the Plains Indian, Browning, Montana.

Schultz, James Willard

1916 Blackfoot Tales of Glacier National Park. New York.

Skinner, Alanson

1923 Observations on the Ethnology of the Sauk Indians. Public Museum of the City of Milwaukee, Bulletin, Vol. 5 # 1, Milwaukee.

Speck, Frank G.

1942 The Tutelo Spirit Adoption Ceremony. Pennsylvania Historical Commission, Harrisburg.

Tooker, Elisabeth

1964 An Ethnography of the Huron Indians, 1615-1649. Bureau of American Ethnology, Bulletin 190, Wash. D.C. [38]

Turney-High, Harry H.

1941 Ethnography of the Kutenai. American Anthropological Association Memoirs # 56, Menasha.

Uhlenbeck, C.C, and R.H. Van Gulik
  1934   A Blackfoot-English Vocabulary based on Material from the Southern Piegans. Verhandelingen Der Koninklijke Akademie Van Wetenschappen Te Amsterdam, 33 (2), Amsterdam.
Wildschut, William
  1960 Crow Indian Medicine Bundles. John C. Ewers, ed. Museum of the American Indian, Heye Foundation, Contributions, Vol. 17, New York.
Wissler, Clark
  1911   The Social Life of the Blackfoot Indians. American Museum of Natural History, Anthropological Papers, Vol. 7, Pt. 1, New York.
  1912 Ceremonial Bundles of the Blackfoot Indians. American Museum of Natural History, Anthropological Papers, Vol. 7, Pt. 2, New York.
  1913   Societies and Dance Associations of the Blackfoot Indians. American Museum of Natural History, Anthropological Papers, Vol. 11, Pt. 4, New York.

Cover pictures: Top left, Running Sun, Blood Indian; top centre, Blood mortuary tipi; bottom left, White Man Running Around, Blood Indian; bottom centre, Cree shaking tent rattle; bottom right, Mad Feathers, Peigan Indian.

Photo credits: Glenbow-Alberta Institute, 5, 7, 11, 14, 17, 23, 27, 28, 31 and 35; Geological Survey of Canada, 19.

BLACKFOOT SHAKING TENT   35

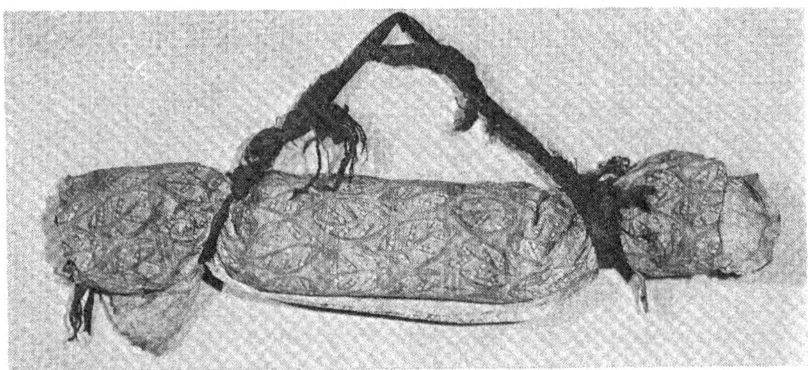

Important to Cree religious life was the "Carried on the Back" bundle which was used in the Round Dance. The above such bundle is from Glenbow's collections, No. AP-240.

Historic Backgrounds of the Conjuring Complex
in the Plateau and the Plains

Verne Ray

The nature of the conjuring ritual and the extent of the similarities in the various regions can only be understood in terms of specific procedure. Consequently a type picture from each area is in order.

The conjurers of the Parry Island Ojibwa (Georgian Bay, Lake Huron) have been described by Jenness.[138] Two classes were recognized, the *kusabindugeyu* and the *djasakid*. Procedures differed somewhat and the latter ranked higher than the former. Both received their power through adolescent visions and belonged to the category of shamans, not laymen. The principal spiritual source of power was Thunder; Owl and Whip-poor-will were of secondary importance.

The *kusabindugeyu* treated illnesses due to sorcery. He removed intrusive objects implanted by the sorcerer by a sucking technique in which several bone tubes were "swallowed," the last protruding from the mouth. With this tube placed against the patient's body he withdrew the disease object and deposited it in a container of clear water, together with the bones which he simultaneously regurgitated. The object removed was sometimes a small feather. He was also capable of retrieving a soul when stolen by a sorcerer; his clairvoyant powers enabled him to seek out the place of hiding. The same talent made it possible for him to discern the innermost thoughts of others.

The public performance involved the calling of spirits by means of singing and the use of a disc rattle. The appearance of each spirit was indicated by a dull thud of audible volume. The spirits did not speak, but merely "opened the seer's eyes so that he might behold the object of his quest."

The *djasakid* or *djiskid* used the "shaking tent" for the performance of his feats. This was a cylindrical lodge about four feet in diameter. The framework of poles and hoops was covered with birch bark or cloth. The ritual, which was held after dark, began when the shaman crawled inside the lodge and started speaking in an indistinguishable voice. Soon a thud was heard and the lodge swayed violently, marking the arrival of a spirit. This was repeated until a number of spirits had assembled. Among the sounds the voice of Turtle was heard; it was he who acted as intermediary between the other spirits and the shaman. At the top of the lodge, "covering it like a lid," was Thunder, and other spirits were perched upon the hoop near the top.

A present of tobacco was sometimes necessary before the spirits would begin their work. This was handed over the top of the lodge and soon tobacco smoke could be seen floating above. Shortly thereafter the spirits were heard conferring and soon one departed to carry out the mission at hand, perhaps to bring back a sorcerer's soul. The departure and subsequent return were marked by violent thuds and the swaying of the lodge. [206] Conversation ensued between the spirits and the audience as to the disposal of the captured soul. After the matter was settled the spirits departed, the audience disbanded, and the séance was ended.

The object of the performance was sometimes aid in hunting. The spirits were sent in

---

[138] Dr A.I. Hallowell, *The Ojibwa*, pp. 60-68.

search of moose and deer in much the same manner as though a soul were being sought. Success in the spiritual quest enabled hunters to find and kill the actual animals without difficulty. Conjurers are reported to have performed, upon occasion, remarkable feats of agility.

A conjurer has taken a man and lifted him high in the air with one hand; has loosened himself, unaided, from a network of ropes that bound him; has destroyed, with the aid of Thunder, evil serpents that preyed on the Indians' camps.

We may now turn to the Ojibwa of Minnesota and summarise the findings of Coleman, Densmore, and Hoffman.[139] Here the power of the conjurer was received in a dream rather than a vision. Thunder played no role; indeed, no specific spirit was segregated except Turtle, who acted as intermediary much in the manner we have seen. The talents of the conjurer included curing, the finding of lost articles and lost persons, the prediction of future events, and the performance of strange feats.

The curing power differed considerably from that of the Parry Islanders. Coleman strongly contrasts the conjurer and the medicine man, but Densmore mentions curing and describes an incident in which the *djasakid* swallowed and regurgitated bone tubes, then placed one against the throat of the patient and blew with great force, causing the congestion to "break." One or more of these bones was worn by the conjurer as a badge of his profession. Prognosis was definitely a field which the conjurer exploited but this was but one aspect of his ability to predict.

In preparation for the séance the "shaking tent" was constructed. The conjurer was bound hand and foot with rope or thongs and placed in the lodge. The appearance of the intermediary, the Turtle, was signalled by a loud whistling sound. The tent swayed violently as the spirits gathered and the voices of animals were heard to the accompaniment of the conjurer's rattle. The spectators were now asked if they wished to question the spirits. The questions put concerned prognosis, future events, and lost articles and persons. The successful conclusion of a search for a lost object or person was made known to the audience by a thud as of a heavy object hitting the ground. At the end of the performance the spirits departed and the conjurer called for a light to be provided. The audience could then see that he was free of his bonds; the ropes were often found entangled in the upper poles of the lodge or at some distant place.

The Cheyenne conjuring complex, as reported by Grinnell,[140] presents now familiar elements in typical arrangement. The talent was spiritually conferred in a dream. Any spirit [207] might confer this power, it seems, but relatively few persons were recipients. Only the Badger played a special role; he served as intermediary and his identity was made known by his voice. The conjurer was sometimes provided with a whistle and a pipe. Helpers occasionally beat upon parfleches. Usually a single spirit appeared at the séance but at some times many of them assembled; it was then that the intermediary functioned.

The séance was held at night: in a dwelling tipi in which many spectators and singers gathered. The performer unwrapped his sacred objects; then the fire was allowed to die.

---

[139]   Coleman, *Religion of the Ojibwa*, pp. 50-53; Densmore, *Chippewa Customs*, p. 45 f.; Densmore, *An Explanation of a {Miracle} Trick*; Hoffman, *Midē'wiwin*, pp. 176-78; cf. same, pp. 251-55, 276-78; cf. Skinner, *Political Organization*, p. 505; cf. Jones, *Central Algonkin*, p. 145 f.

[140]   *Cheyenne Indians*, Vol. 2, pp. 111-17.

Before the fire was out, the man who was calling the spirit was tied with four bowstrings. Each finger of each hand was tied separately to the next finger, in a hard knot, and the ends of the bowstrings on each hand were tied together, behind his back, so that his hands were tightly bound there. His feet were tied together in the same way, each toe being tied to the next one in a hard knot, and the feet bound together by the bowstrings. Thus tied, he sat in the back of the lodge, and sometimes he was tied to one of the lodge-poles. At times a little shelter shaped like a sweat-lodge, was built in the middle of the lodge, and the man was put in that.

After the fire had gone out, in some interval of the singing the lodge was shaken as if by a strong wind; the poles creaked, and suddenly in the lodge a strange voice was heard talking to the man. This secret helper was perhaps called to ask where there were buffalo; or where there were enemies; where missing people were; or even where lost horses might be found. Sometimes the secret helper told what was happening at a distance; or perhaps warned the camp of enemies near at hand. After the spirit had gone, and a light had again been made, the man was found to be untied, and the bow' strings were lying in the door, tied in innumerable knots.[141]

A sketch from the Plateau will serve to complete this descriptive survey. The Ktunaxa of southeastern British Columbia utilized the conjuring séance for the prediction of future events, particularly in wartime, the finding of lost objects, and the like. The performance served to bring the spirits into direct contact with the petitioner, thus making available immediate help and advice. The performer was not necessarily a shaman; anyone possessing a guardian spirit was privileged to attempt the contact. One's particular spirit was the effective agent in establishing the relationship, but that relationship was with the entire spirit world, not merely with the individual spirit. Owl was the central spirit figuring in the séance but did not serve as intermediary.

The performance was conducted in an ordinary tipi. The suppliant blew steadily on a whistle as he slowly disappeared behind a partition formed by a mat or blanket. He soon reappeared with his arms behind him, his thumbs tied to his belt. The knots were untied, he returned, and the same procedure was repeated seven times, or until seven knots were tied. The end of a long rope was then tied around the conjurer's waist. Thereupon he went behind the partition and threw the loose end of the rope over the pole from which the blanket was suspended. Soon the entire rope fell, in full view of the audience, and to the end of it was found tied a small whistle. Thus it was indicated that the performer had been "cut in two" by the rope; the two parts of the body were heard to fall with a thud. But the spirits soon reassembled the halves and the performer appeared, smoked briefly, and [208] returned. At this point the Owl spirit carried him away; the flight, as of a bird, was heard by the audience. The sound of a whistle was also audible; with it the conjurer called the spirits to take his place. The whistle used was that attached to the rope.

During these activities the audience drummed and sang spirit songs, and pipes were prepared and smudges lighted. Immediately thereafter the audience conversed with the spirits. One so desiring lighted a pipe and handed it over the partition. The spirits took seven puffs and returned the pipe. If the tobacco were no longer burning misfortune was portended. A second

---

[141] same, p. 113 f.

pipe was sometimes requested. The converser inquired directly of the spirits and answers were directly given, but in an unnatural voice. Following the questions the conjurer returned, his thumbs once more tied. The knots were loosed and the séance was concluded.

These sketches have not been selected to indicate extremes of distribution but rather to provide type pictures from the various areas. The western extreme is represented by the Colville of northeastern Washington.[142] The complex extends to the east as far as Labrador.[143]

It is now m order to examine the variations presented by the western examples. The Colville ceremony followed very closely the pattern of the Kutenai. However, only those possessing a specific spirit, that of a certain fish, became conjurers. It is perhaps significant that this spirit was called the director or leader of all other spirits; its place in the ceremony was analogous to that of Owl among the Ktunaxa. But it also performed the function of intermediary, answering the questions of the audience in a thick, muffled voice. In the questioning much emphasis was placed upon the finding of lost articles and persons. Marking the close of the séance, the spirits returned the conjurer, but he remained unconscious for several hours. He was brought to consciousness by a smudging process.

Cline states that the Colville conjurer was a shaman, but this may be questioned. Apparently no curing of any kind was involved in the séance. Furthermore, the performance was a part of the Winter Spirit Dances in which all persons possessing spirits participated. Cline tends to speak of any performer at the Winter Dance as a shaman. One minor point may be added: the conjurer's compartment was provided with a special aperture opening to the out doors for the entry of the spirits.[144]

The most significant difference between the performance of the Ktunaxa and that of the Colville appears to have been the presence of a spirit intermediary among the latter. However, the idea of the intermediary was also present in the Ktunaxa interpretation. The conjurer played this role so far as members of the audience were concerned. Throughout Ktunaxa [209] religious practise one's familiar spirit served to bring him in contact with all spiritual beings and permitted him to receive the benefits of this wider contact. It may be noted that this concept was quite foreign to all other parts of the Plateau but was wholly congenial to Ojibwa thought.[145]

Unique aspects not encountered among others sharing the séance include the bisection of the conjurer's body by the rope encircling him and the flight through the air. The latter was not inconsistent with the pattern of the complex. In all cases the spirits came and left by such a method; in some instances the upper portion of the lodge was left open or some other aperture was provided as an avenue of entrance and exit. The dramatic "cutting in two" appears to have

---

[142] Cline, *Southern Okanagon*, p. 153 f.

[143] Flannery, *Shaking-Tent Rite*, p. 14.

An excellent description for the Montagnais of James Bay, provided by Regina Flannery (op. cit.), indicates close parallelism on almost every point with Ojibwa practise. The most noticeable variation is the substitution of *Mistabeo* for Turtle as intermediary.

Skinner has recorded brief notes for the Cree and Salteaux (*Notes on the Eastern Cree*, pp. 67, 153); and Rossignol should be consulted (*Religion of the Saskatchewan*).

As noted above, the object here is not to examine the ramifications of the complex in the Woodlands but rather to seek the significance of its presence in the Far West.

[144] Cline, *Southern Okanagon*, p. 152 f.

[145] Cf. Ray, *Cultural Relations*, pp. 68 ff.

been a local interpretation of the trickery element of the séance. The placing of the cord around the waist possibly was related to the widespread practise in the Plateau and Puget Sound areas of holding a shaman, while engaged in treatment, by a rope similarly placed (so that he would not lose control of his actions while handling spirits).[146] But more probably the linkage was with the wrapping and tying of the conjurer among the Assiniboine and Gros Ventre, to be described later.

The feature most notably absent from the Colville and Ktunaxa séances was the shaking of the lodge. It is true that the huge Colville dance house was hardly susceptible to swaying but the partition might well have been vibrated. The Ktunaxa performance was held in a tipi which might quite conceivably have been swayed by one mechanism or another. It will be remembered that the Cheyenne performance sometimes involved the building of a hemispherical hut within the tipi. Several interpretations are possible to account for the absence of the shaking feature. The possibility of diffusion from west to east hardly merits serious consideration in the light of relative distributions and the organization of the complex. But: granting east to west diffusion, perhaps the idea spread before the addition of the "shaking tent" feature to the basic conjuring concept. This seems highly improbable since all eastern interpretations, and even that of the Cheyenne, involved shaking, and in most cases this feature was thoroughly integrated. Furthermore, evidence is to be presented below which indicates a recent diffusion. Consequently, the absence of the shaking feature is clearly a case of loss, either loss in the process of diffusion or a conscious discarding of the trait.[147]

The Cheyenne interpretation of the complex presents but few fundamental contrasts with that of the Colville-Kutenai. Any spirit might confer the conjuring power, as among the Ktunaxa. As in the north, the performer was definitely a layman, not a shaman. The highly specific and complex method of binding the conjurer stands out, but it will be recalled that the Colville- Ktunaxa method was identical in pattern although less elaborate. The Gros Ventre, too, shared this feature.

The Cheyenne ceremony lacked the involved ritual of exchanging a pipe of tobacco between the spirits and the questioners. Grinnell mentions, however, the presentation of a [210] pipe to the conjurer upon a specific occasion.[148] The exchange or presentation of tobacco or a pipe was characteristic of Ojibwa and Montagnais practise, hence it appears to have been a basic feature of the complex. The slight emphasis by the Cheyenne might mark a step in the discarding of the trait, while the Northwest practises would indicate local elaboration.

The Badger intermediary of the Cheyenne was unique. The fish spirit which played this role among the Colville was perhaps an equally independent selection, but a parallel did exist among the far distant Montagnais.[149] Among the Ojibwa the intermediary was in' variably Turtle, although the source of the conjurer's power was often Thunder. These are interpretations unknown in the west.

The possession by the Cheyenne of the "shaking tent" phase of the complex has been noted. Historically considered this fact is of utmost significance. It indicates more than any other single feature the intimacy of relationships between the Cheyenne ceremony and that of the

---

[146] Cf. Ray, *Sanpoil and Nespelem*, p. 206.

[147] Incidentally, rendering the term "shaking tent" inapplicable to the general complex.

[148] Cheyenne Indians, Vol. 2, p. 114.

[149] Flannery, *Shaking-Tent Rite*, pp. 12, 14.

Ojibwa. The Colville-Kutenai séance, on the other hand, exhibits its closest affinity with the more eastern form in the wholly typical assemblage of spirits at the call of the conjurer, and, incidentally, the signalling of arrival by a thud or a thumping sound. The "shaking tent" and the spirit assembly must be considered two of the most basic features of the complex. This is not to minimize the importance of the conjuring aspect; conjuring is common to all. Of these two central features the assembly of spirits is clearly the more fundamental. The "shaking tent" element is detachable without loss of identity; witness the Colville-Ktunaxa. Since the Cheyenne séance seems largely to have revolved around the calling of a single spirit, we might conclude that this gives the Colville-Ktunaxa affair the greater claim to closeness of relationship with the type ceremony. But this would be to overlook the fact that the Cheyenne conjurer was capable, at least upon occasion, of establishing contact with many spirits through the agency of his own particular spirit.[150] In other words, although the concept was minimized, it was known. This is strong evidence of diffusion as a part of the conjuring complex, since it was not typical of the Plains and was completely alien to the Plateau at large, being found only among the Ktunaxa and in the Colville séance. Consequently we must look upon the Cheyenne ceremony as bearing closer relation' ship to the type, since spirit assembly and "shaking tent" were both known, and the Colville-Ktunaxa complex as being one step farther removed. Although suggestive, this is far from definitive. Further illumination is provided by data on tribal movements to be offered a little later.

Two variants of the conjuring complex as found in the Plains remain to be considered, those of the Assiniboine and the Gros Ventre. The Assiniboine ceremony contrasts with those thus far encountered in the many modifications it exhibits; the Gros Ventre example is a mere fragment.

The Assiniboine ceremony differed not only in detail but in conceptual phrasing as well. Direct quotation from Lowie's informant will make this clear:

I dreamt of several men who told me I was wanted in a certain tent.... An old man was sitting inside. He said "My son, I am the one who has summoned you. I shall give you the painted lodge and teach you how to use it...." Then he told me I was to get the *waka^m* power to aid the sick. "Thus you will get plenty of horses and abundance of food, besides your family will always be well. When you doctor a patient, you must act as follows: Near the fireplace plant one end of a tree trunk not stripped of its foliage, and stick the other end into the flap-holes; get three or four dressed buffalo skins, and construct a little booth. Allow yourself to be tied hand and foot with buckskin thongs, then have tanned robes wrapped about you and tied from the outside. Have a rock put near the fireplace. It should be painted red and ought to rest on a clean piece of calico. Have a little dog suckling cooked and set near the fireplace. Two, or three, drummers are to sit on the right-hand side of the entrance; no one else must be admitted...." [After ritual preparations a spirit would speak.] A noise would be heard in the skies. The visitant was not to be seen, but only heard. He would ask what was the matter. "Then you must ask him for aid. He will first eat the pup. Then he will tell you whether the patient can be cured, and if so, how soon. If a cure is impossible, he will say so. He will disappear, but first he will free you in the twinkle of an eye, and hang your bonds

---

[150] Grinnell, *Cheyenne Indians*, Vol. 2, p. 115.

on the tops of the tipi-poles."[151]

Before discussing this remarkable variant, the obviously derivative Gros Ventre remnant may be presented:

There were some medicine-men who, having had their fingers tied, then had their knees fastened together and their hands secured behind their back. After this they were wrapped in a robe and the robe was wound about with a rope. Then such a medicine-man called his spirit. When it appeared, he was loosened instantaneously, and the robe and the rope were thrown at the man that tied him.[152]

The two fundamental conceptual features of the conjuring complex – assembly of spirits and the shaking tent – were clearly absent from the Assiniboine ceremony. However, the binding of the conjurer and subsequent spiritual release were practised. Further, it will be noted that the ropes were discovered exactly as among the Minnesota Ojibwa: at the top of the tipi poles. This highly arbitrary element points clearly to a common source. The wrapping of the conjurer in a blanket, however, is newly encountered and is doubtless a local interpretation. The Gros Ventre presumably borrowed the practise from the Assiniboine.

The fact that the Assiniboine conjurer was a shaman is surely significant. This was uniform practise to the east but was unknown to the west. However, the talent was conferred in a dream, a typical Plains phrasing. It goes without saying that the ritual flavor of the whole affair was in perfect accord with Plains taste.

Apparently the Assiniboine, in their contacts with the Plains-Ojibwa (or Cree), became thoroughly acquainted with the conjuring ritual, adopted the general framework and some of the most spectacular features, dropped the esoteric assembly of spirits, and adapted the whole to their own concept of a properly executed ceremony. Why the "shaking tent" feature was abandoned is uncertain. [212]

In comparing the type ceremony of the Ojibwa with the western interpretations generally, two points stand out in bold relief. First, the western distribution is irregular and discordant. The groups discussed above were the only ones possessing the ritual as far as I have been able to ascertain. It seems unlikely that the intensive ethnological work in the Plains left undiscovered any instance of this ceremony; if other Plains tribes shared the séance the references have been overlooked. All tribes of the Plateau except the Spokane (adjacent to the Colville) are sufficiently well known so that the complex could hardly have been overlooked.

Second, in the face of this sporadic distribution and the distances involved, the conformity of the individual variants to the general pattern is strikingly close, excepting only the Assiniboine.

How, then, are we to account for this uniformity of pattern and erratic distribution at one and the same time? I think the answer is to be found in the extensive movements of Algonkin peoples in recent times. It is generally recognized that large scale movements have carried Algonkin groups from their Woodland homes far westward into the Plains. For present purposes, however, we need precise statements, not general phrasings. We have these specific analyses as the result of the work of Strong, Wissler, and others.

---

[151] Lowie, *The Assiniboine*, p. 49.

[152] Kroeber, Ethnology of the Gros Ventre, p. 125.

That these Algonkin movements have not all occurred in the immediate past is indicated in the conclusions drawn by Strong in his analysis of Plains culture in the light of archaeology:

It is a Woodland culture of northeastern affiliations that occurs on the eastern border as the earliest known occupation of this sort in Nebraska. This was demonstrated by Stems' discoveries at the Walker Gilmore site; and the fact that Sterns creek culture is apparently related to the "Algonkian" and Lake Michigan cultures of Iowa and Wisconsin is undoubtedly significant...

In the light of the archaeological evidence it appears that the horse culture of historic times spread like a thin and strikingly uniform veneer over the central Plains, bringing with it many traits more typical of the forest hunting regions to the north than of the prehistoric Plains themselves. Given the horse, the Plains with their vast bison herds could not be resisted, and in the course of a century or two a new mode of life developed, involving many peoples that were apparently relative strangers to the region.[153]

It is possible, then, that the conjuring complex was carried westward at either a relatively early date or a very late date. An early diffusion would account for the sporadic distribution: the complex would have had ample time to disappear in intervening areas. But this same lapse of time would undoubtedly have led to a greater modification and differentiation of the western examples, particularly in view of the ideological conflict between the complex and general Plateau religious concepts.

Assuming a late diffusion, we may examine more minutely the recent movements. Wissler summarizes his findings relative to Algonkin migrations as follows:

[The study] reveals successive expansions of groups into the northern Plains largely by [213] Algonkin-speaking tribes: Blackfoot, Arapaho, Gros Ventre, Cheyenne, Ojibwa, and Cree. Thus, the repeated expansions in this area seem to have had a common source. The uniformity of this westward movement of Cree-like Algonkin is broken only by the Siouan-speaking Assiniboine. The historical data suggest that the Blackfoot first expanded into the area, followed by the Arapabo-Gros Ventre. The Cheyenne thrust was toward the southwest and to the Missouri. Later the Ojibwa followed on their heels. The Gros Ventre held most of the Saskatchewan area in 1754, but shortly thereafter began to contract their range and to decrease in population. At the same time the Assiniboine were expanding westward into the same area, reaching their maximum population about 1830. Following them, the Cree expanded westward, first along the north Saskatchewan, but gradually took to the plains in which their great expansion began after 1800 and culminated about 1875.[154]

With respect to the Cheyenne migration, Grinnell furnishes highly specific data. He explains that the movement proceeded band by band, with the laggards remaining in their older habitat until after 1800. This habitat was within the woodlands in Minnesota but quite near the

---

[153] Strong, *Plains Culture*, pp. 283, 185.
[154] Wissler, *Population Changes*, p. 18.

prairie. Here they were already separated from their linguistic relatives by an area of Siouan-speaking peoples. After arrival in the west a split occurred, beginning about 1830, which gave rise to the divisions Northern Cheyenne and Southern Cheyenne.[155]

Cheyenne speech is much closer to Central-Eastern Algonkin than is either Blackfoot or Arapaho. It is much more different, however, than it could have become during a separation of only two or three centuries. The purely linguistic inference thus is that the Cheyenne, though recent in the plains, lived, before that, somewhere apart from the Central Algonkins of the woodland; therefore most likely in the prairies.[156]

In the light of this evidence it seems reasonable to assume that the Cheyenne possessed the conjuring complex in their western habitat because they had brought it with them; that groups with whom they were in contact during the progress of their migrations did not take over the idea because those contacts were relatively brief and the concept not overly congenial; that the period of separation from Central Algonkins was sufficiently brief so that the conjuring complex retained its identity but at the same time was of ample duration to permit a waning of emphasis upon congregation of spirits and a shift in the nature of the conjurer from shaman to layman, thus bringing the complex closer into line with ideologies prevailing among the new neighbors.

If this interpretation is correct, the Colville-Ktunaxa could not have received their ceremony from the Cheyenne either directly or indirectly. Indirect reception would have demanded a wider diffusion; direct borrowing would have required a degree of contact between the two which we know did not exist.

This being the case, how are we to account for features common to the Cheyenne and the Colville-Kutenai, but lacking among the Central Algonkins? We find but two such features: the conjurer was a layman rather than a shaman; and a quite arbitrary method was used in tying him during the séance. The former is easily resolved. As explained above, this [214] was simply an adjustment which brought the ceremony into accord with a prominent principle of western religion; that is, the shaman was conceived as one who cured diseases by spiritual means, and anyone not so gifted was a layman no matter what marvelous supernatural powers of other kinds he possessed.

The second point is more involved. The same method of tying the fingers is suggested for the Gros Ventre. The Ktunaxa practise was perhaps closer to that of the Gros Ventre than the Cheyenne. Definitive comparisons are not possible because of the variant phrasings in the descriptions. The Ktunaxa achieved the elaboration of the Cheyenne in quite another context. The fingers and toes of the pubescent girl, during her isolation, were twined together so that they could not be separated. According to a superficial rationalization, this procedure insured against the stiffening of the fingers in later life.[157] It is possible that this was a somewhat general cultural practise and should be considered as such. Without further data a satisfying interpretation is elusive or impossible.

Nor could the Northwestern complex have been borrowed from the Assiniboine. The Kutenai ceremony was more closely related to the parent form than was that of the Assiniboine.

---

[155] Grinnell, *Cheyenne Indians*, Vol. I, pp. 1-46.

[156] Kroeber, *Cultural and Natural Areas*, p. 81.

[157] Ray, Cultural Relations, p. 56.

This was true of both conception and ritualistic structure. The Assiniboine lacked the significant congregation of spirits and the intermediary spirit.

Parenthetically it may be noted that a cultural inconsistency appears here. It was the Colville who emphasized the typical spirit intermediary, not the Ktunaxa. And yet there is no question that the former borrowed the complex from the latter. Apparently the Ktunaxa dropped the feature, at least in its typical form, after transmitting the ceremony to the Colville. This seems curious, since the Colville cling much more tenaciously to Plateau ideology than do the Kutenai. Perhaps for the Colville the complex was so markedly foreign that they reacted to it in an all-or-none fashion. Why both lacked the "shaking tent" is problematical. The Assiniboine, too, lacked this feature. Possibly the Plains Cree themselves had given it up in the Far West.

The Plains Cree emerge as donors of the Northwestern complex. This conclusion is necessarily indirectly reached, since adequate data are unavailable for the Plains Cree.[158] But recent contacts between the Ktunaxa and western Cree established an unbroken route of diffusion from the eastern Algonkins. We are thus provided a satisfying explanation for [215] the close kinship of eastern and western variants. The conclusion is thoroughly consistent with the positive findings throughout this analysis.

In the above study an attempt has been made to work out certain problems in consonance with Professor Sapir's precept that ethnological data must be treated "historically, that is, in terms of actual happenings, however inferred, that are conceived to have a specific sequence, a specific localisation, and specific relations among themselves." The degree to which this effort has been successful is largely attributable to the methodology employed, a methodology interpreted and clarified by Professor Sapir.

The reflection of the teachings of Professor Sapir is apparent in this paper, I trust. But the point deserving emphasis is that an equally profound impression is to be seen in the great bulk of comparable studies, and surely will continue to be seen in the work of the future.

Bibliography

Cline, Walter, and others *The Sinkaietk or Southern Okanagon of Washington* (General Series in Anthropology, No. 6, 1938).

Coleman, Bernard *The Religion of the Ojibwa of Northern Minnesota* (Primitive Man. Vol. 10,

---

[158] Mandelbaum's study, *The Plains Cree*, appeared subsequent to the writing of the above. He provides a full description of the conjuring complex (p. 261 f.), the details of which accord thoroughly with the interpretation here offered. The Plains Cree ritual followed closely the basic pattern of the eastern Algonkin ceremony. The "shaking tent" feature was present in a form resembling that of the Cheyenne. This suggests that the Cheyenne variant was linked more immediately with the (central ?) Cree than with the Ojibwa, although a dual indebtedness is not improbable.

Since the Plains Cree utilized the "shaking tent" it appears that the Kutenai were the first to discard it. However, Mandelbaum's data may not apply to the westernmost bands.

The Plains Cree, surprisingly, shared the unique method of tying the conjurer's fingers together. Thus they may have been the originators of this trait. However, the more general context in which this practise appears among the Kutenai still favors a western point of origin.

pp. 33-57 1937).

Densmore, Frances *Chippewa Customs* (Bulletin, Bureau of American Ethnology, No. 86, 1929).

   An Explanation of a Trick Performed by Indian Jugglers (American Anthropologist, Vol. 34, pp. 310-14, 1932).

Flannery, Regina *The Shading-Tent Rite among the Montagnais of James Bay* (Primitive Man, Vol. 12, pp. 11-16, 1939).

Grinnell, George Bird *The Cheyenne Indians: their History and Ways of Life* (2 vols,, New Haven, 1923).

Hoffman, W.J. *The Mide'wiwin or "Grand Medicine Society"* (Seventh Annual Report, Bureau of American Ethnology, pp. 143-300, 1891).

Jenness, Diamond *The Ojibwa Indians of Parry Island, their Social and Religious Life* (Bulletin, National Museum of Canada, No. 78, 1935).

Jones, William *The Central Algonkin* (Annual Archaeological Report, Toronto, 1905, pp. 136-46, 1906).

Kroeber, A.L. *Cultural and Natural Areas of Native North America* (University of California Publications in American Archaeology and Ethnology, Vol. 38, 1939).

   Ethnology of the Gros Ventre (Anthropological Papers, American Museum of Natural History. Vol. I, pp. 141-281, 1908).

Lowie, Robert H. *The Assiniboine* (Anthropological Papers, American Museum of Natural History, Vol. 4, pp. 1-270, 1909).

Mandelbaum, David G. *The Plains Cree* (Anthropological Papers, American Museum of Natural History, Vol. 37, pp. 155-316, 1940). [216]

Ray, Verne F. *The Bluejay Character in the Plateau Spirit Dance* (American Anthropologist, Vol. 39, pp. 593-602, 1937).

   Cultural Relations in the Plateau of Northwestern America (Publications of the Frederick Webb Hodge Anniversary Publication Fund, Vol. 3, 1939).

   The Sanpoil and Nespelem: Salishan Peoples of Northeastern Washington (University of Washington Publications in Anthropology, Vol. 5, 1932).

Rossignol, M. *The Religion of the Saskatchewan and Western Manitoba Cree* (Primitive Man, Vol. 11, pp. 67-71, 1938).

Sapir, Edward *Time Perspective in Aboriginal American Culture, a Study in Method* (Memoir, Canada Department of Mines, Geological Survey, No. 90; Anthropological Series, No. 13, 1916).

Skinner, Alanson *Notes on the Eastern Cree and Northern Salteaux* (Anthropological Papers, American Museum of Natural History, Vol. 9, pp. 1-177, 1911).

   Political Organization, Cults and Ceremonies of the Plains-Ojibway and Plains-Cree Indians (Anthropological Papers, American Museum of Natural History, Vol. 11, pp. 475-542, 1914).

Strong, W.D. *The Plains Culture in the Light of Archaeology* (American Anthropologist, Vol. 35, pp. 271-87, 1933).

Wissler, Clark *Population Changes among the Northern Plains Indians* (Yale University Publications in Anthropology, No. 1, 1936).

University of Washington
Seattle, Washington

Assiniboine

Edwin Thompson Denig

As [98/492] many as are believed to be *Wa-con*, or Divine, and are willing to run the risk attending the profession, do so. They are all called by the same general name of *Wa-con*, independent of their individual or real name. They affect to cure diseases, reveal future events, direct where lost articles are to be found, interpret dreams; etc. The ceremony attending any of these things (except sickness) is conducted by the medicine man, first being paid for his services. Afterwards he enters a small lodge built for the purpose, like the vapor bath and drums, rattles and sings alone the greater part of the night, returning his answer to those concerned in the morning. These answers partake of the nature of those of the ancient oracles, are ambiguous, with the view of evading decided failure.

They do not claim the power [99/493] of witchcraft, as this is a dangerous profession, but this power is ascribed to them by the other Indians.

The majority of these people believe, or say they believe, that some of these old conjurors can "shoot them with bad spells" (as they express it) at the distance of 100 miles off, and it is on the assumption that they are the cause of some of their deaths, that the lives of these professors are sometimes forfeited. "We believe their confidence in the powers of these priests and medicine men is pretty general, though some of them (the priests) are more divine or *Wa-con* than others. When an, Indian is sick they endeavor to cure him, as has been stated, and if unsuccessful and death ensues they usually keep out of sight until the first bursts of grief are over. Others of the same profession who have not been called to administer to the patient attend the funeral, their object being to secure whatever property they can by loud crying, cutting their hair and bodies, and other display of profound grief. Nothing resembling a prayer is said over the dead at the burial nor anything spoken. Indeed, on account of their loud lamentations it would be impossible to hear it if it were. Some weeks afterwards, however, other ceremonies take place regarding the dead which will be described in another place. The body is placed in the fork of a tree, on a scaffold, or occasionally interred on the top of a high hill. No device, inscription, or hieroglyphics are made at or near the place of interment by any of these nations.

As far as we have proceeded with their religion, belief is the general one, though it may be clothed in different language by different Indians, sometimes superstitious and fabulous, but our object has been to arrive at the philosophy of their religion by rejecting fables, etc., which do not bear upon the inquiry.

From this point all other religion diverges into different minor beliefs and superstitions according to the fancy of each individual. Many believe in certain evil spells and troubles brought on them by lesser spirits or ghosts and even of the spirits of monsters which have no existence nor ever had except in their dreams and morbid imagination. It appears that these ghosts are the cause of all petty malice, vexations, or bad luck, not being of sufficient consequence to attract the attention or induce the influence of *Wakonda*. To relate the different kinds of belief in these powers as each would explain it would require the labor of years, and it is somewhat difficult to generalize, owing to the prevailing differences. Under some of the answers that will follow regarding charms, amulets, ghosts, etc., will be detailed enough in conjunction with what has already been stated to form a tolerably connected idea of this feature of their faith.

Sorcery or witchcraft has already been noticed, but we may in addition state that the witchcraft imputed to some of their doctors [100/494] is their power to do evil at a great distance from the object, to produce death or disease, though they do not believe these persons can transform themselves into other shapes; think they can exercise the same power to do good if they choose, and do exercise it in curing the sick. It is in consequence of this belief that the doctor or divining man is punished in case of failure and death, as they think it is his unwillingness, not his inability, to cure "which produces the result. They do not burn them, but the "writer has seen several shot at different times by the relatives of the deceased, on the supposition they caused their death. This custom is in as great force now as it ever was.

The divining man has a chance to "become rich in horses and other property in a short time, as his fees depend on himself; but these advantages are more than counterbalanced by the risk attending the profession. The doctor, priest, conjuror, wizard, prophet, and divining man are all united in the same person; that is, to a divining man (*Wa-con*), or divining woman (*Wa-can*), these powers, or some of them, are ascribed, and they are believed to possess them in proportion as their success has been developed. Some are simply doctors of medicine, others in addition are conjurors and do tricks. Some go further, interpret dreams, reveal the future, find lost articles, etc. The whole united forms the entire divining man. The persons who profess and perform some of these things are tolerably numerous; but the effective diviner of established reputation, large practice, and possessing the whole of the foregoing powers are very few, perhaps not more than six or eight in the whole Assiniboine Nation. As has been observed, they form no distinct body and have but little influence in council unless they can add that of warrior to their many distinguished titles and degrees.

The whole of these Indians most sincerely believe in the theory of ghosts, that departed spirits have the power to make themselves visible and heard, that they can assume any shape they wish, of animals or men, and many will affirm that they have actually seen these apparitions and heard their whistlings and meanings. They are much afraid of these appearances, and under no consideration will go alone near a burial place after dark. They believe these apparitions have the power of striking the beholder with some disease, and many complaints are attributed to this cause. They therefore make feasts and prayers to them to remain quiet. Smaller evils and misfortunes are caused by their power, and a great many stories are nightly recounted in their lodges of the different shapes in which they appear.

Dreams are revelations of Great Mystery and have considerable influence over them, either in war expeditions or the chase.

Whence the Shaking[159]
Frances Densmore

TWO classes of men treat the sick among Algonquian tribes – doctors who administer herbs; and men who use magic and are commonly called jugglers. The former may be called a physical, and the latter a mental means of healing. That the two overlap in some cases is apart from our present consideration.

He who treats the sick by magic is in alliance with spirits and one phase of his work is the mysterious shaking of a little tipi constructed for the purpose. The juggler is tied with stout cords when placed in his little tipi and his first act is to free himself from this restraint, then he sings, pounds his drum and summons the spirits who are his advisors. The spirits make known their presence by a violent shaking of the tipi and by certain sounds which become familiar to those attending the performances but are understood only by the juggler. A spirit frequently summoned is the Great Turtle, said to make a whinnying sound. Hearing this sound, the people sitting outside the tipi may say, "We want the turtle to dance," and from within the tipi comes a sound like blunt sticks pounding on the ground. Then they say to one another, "The Great Turtle is dancing." The sounds seem to vary little through the years, as Parkman, in describing one of these séances, states that

> A low, feeble sound, like the whine of a young puppy, was next heard ... upon which the warriors... hailed it as the voice of the Great Turtle – the spirit who never lied.[160]

A Menomini informant said he had heard that the juggler produced these sounds by means of a small whistle but other Menomini, less independent in opinion, repudiated the idea. Certain songs are sung by the juggler as the spirits arrive and depart. The friends of the sick person, seated outside the tipi, hear the performance, and after the spirits have gone away the juggler emerges to announce the result of the conference. Perhaps the sick person has failed to fulfill the obligations of a dream, perhaps someone has "bewitched" him, or perhaps he is suffering from some peculiar ailment for which the spirits have prescribed a remedy. Such performances were also held to determine the location of lost articles, animals, or persons.

A juggler's performance was usually held at night, was expensive and impressive, and held a controlling hand over the Indians for many generations. [311] Only a few men remain who can perform this trick and, with the progress of enlightenment, the Indians have ceased to desire it, though it remains in a few isolated corners of the Indian country, especially on the north shore of Lake Superior. Members of the white race living near these Indians occasionally attend the dances and say that they hear, in the tipi, the voices of friends living at a distance, or long dead, and that many animals of the forest come at the call of the juggler. This performance among the Chippewa is described by Hoffman, who states that it was encountered by the Jesuit Fathers early in the seventeenth century and formed one of their greatest obstacles in Christianizing the

---

[159] An Explanation of a {Miracle} Trick Performed by Indian Jugglers by Frances Densmore, *American Anthropologist,* Vol. 34 (1932), pp. 310-14.

[160] Francis Parkman, The Conspiracy of Pontiac and the Indian War after the Conquest of Canada, 2: 165-166 (Boston), 1908.

Indians.[161] Hoffman also describes it among the Menomini and quotes a description of a dance witnessed by the Reverend Peter Jones.[162] The tipi figured by Hoffman is similar to a dwelling in construction, but much smaller and not so peaked at the top. The trick is mentioned by many early writers on the Indians but, so far as known, it has not been explained from the mechanical standpoint.

In July, 1930, the writer saw this trick at Grand Portage, Minnesota, an isolated Chippewa village on the north shore of Lake Superior, near the Canadian boundary. Although on friendly terms with the medicine-man, she was not invited to the séance and witnessed it by accident. The medicine-man was Sun-climbing-the-sky, whose magic power is held in high esteem by the Indians. He lives about 200 miles away but often comes to Grand Portage, and in the previous winter, according to report, he "made bad medicine" so effectively that it became necessary to send for another medicine-man to "straighten things out" and counteract his influence.

In the dusk of early evening the writer, accompanied by her sister, while crossing a meadow, was attracted by a strange sight in a grove of trees, about 300 feet away. A tall, slender tipi was swaying back and forth, though the air was still. Faintly came the sound of an Indian drum. Adjacent to the grove was a house where the juggler was visiting and had been seen, with his drum, less than half an hour before. No tipi was seen at that time, though the frame had probably been erected preparatory to putting on the cover. The situation was recognized at once as the famous shaking of a tipi. Standing still in the meadow, the writer and her sister watched the tipi sway with the regularity of a pendulum, back and forth, back and forth, moving exactly the same distance in each direction and stopping abruptly at each end of the arc. After continuing this for a few moments it stood motionless, a slender white figure in the shadow of the trees. [312 AMERICAN ANTHROPOLOGIST N.S., 34, 1932] Then it was shaken violently, seeming to be attacked by a convulsion. The covering at the top of the tipi streamed outward as though the structure might be blown to pieces. Then it stood still. A few Indians were moving quietly about, near the house and tipi. All around was the calm of early evening, and one felt that the strange behavior of the tipi must have been a matter of imagination. Suddenly the tipi began to move again, the top swaying back and forth, back and forth.

We moved to a place somewhat nearer, where our car was parked. The Indians were accustomed to seeing us with the car in this place, so our presence did not attract attention. There we listened and watched for a long time. The singing and drumming could be clearly heard, the songs resembling those of the Midewiwin (Grand Medicine) and the drum beats being rapid and evenly accented. The behavior of the tipi was the same that had been seen from the meadow. The only persons who passed by were a man and his little daughter, and we greeted them in the usual manner. They went on their way toward the grove and the vibrating tipi. The man had been ill for several weeks, and his illness was known to be a cause of anxiety.

A day or two afterward a doctor and nurse came from a town fifty miles away and visited the man, diagnosing his ailment as (apparently) typhoid fever and directing that he stay in bed. The same day a dance was held by the medicine-man at the sick man's house. A large number of Indians attended, the medicine-man sang, the people danced in a lodge like that of the Midewiwin, and the sick man's wife cooked food for the feast, using a huge kettle suspended over a fire. All this took place a few feet from the house where the sick man, obeying the doctor's orders, remained in his bed. The writer was invited to this dance and attended it, but did not mingle with the dancers. Many Indians, of all ages, were present.

---

[161] Walter James Hoffman, The Midewiwin or "Grand Medicine Society" of the Ojibwa, BAER 7: 251-252,1891.

[162] Walter James Hoffman, The Menomini Indians, BAE-R 14: 146-149, 1893.

The singing and drumming, like that at the tipi-shaking, resembled the custom of the Midewiwin. This dance was designated by an Indian as a "beneficial dance." It may be added that about two weeks later the writer talked about the tipi-shaking with the medicine-man who said he had summoned the spirits to ask whether his treatment of the sick man would be a success. He said that if the spirits "spoke loud and clear" he knew that his treatment would be successful but "if their voices were weak the man would surely die." In reply to an inquiry he said the man was getting well. No other inquiry was made as to the man's condition, but there did not seem to be any further anxiety about him.

The day after the shaking of the tipi an opportunity occurred for inspecting the paraphernalia. The writer had an errand at the house where the medicine-man was visiting and asked permission to see the place where the tipi stood. [313] Consent was readily granted on condition that no photographs be taken. The poles of the tipi were eight in number and were laid on the ground beside the folded cover of dingy white cloth or canvas, while against a tree were leaning numerous hoops to which a large number of stout cords were attached. These were near the circle of holes in which the tipi poles had been planted, within this circle being pine branches which had been pressed down by the juggler's body. This circle appeared to be about 30 inches in diameter, possibly three feet across. In the few moments at her disposal the writer observed chiefly the holes in which the tipi poles had stood. The edges of these holes were as clean as though pegs had been put in clay. The blades of grass around the edges were not disturbed nor the earth crumbled. A little stick was put down one of the holes and when measured was found to be more than a foot long. Courtesy did not permit a more detailed examination of the equipment.

Various items and comments drift toward a student who remains a considerable time in an Indian village, and it was learned that the juggler had used the equipment belonging to his host, who was himself a juggler and had given these demonstrations in the attic of a house, setting up his tipi there and shaking it in the approved manner. Two questions arose: If the frame of the tipi was shaken as violently as it appeared to be, why were the edges of the holes not disturbed? And how could such a structure be erected on a board floor?

As a possible explanation of this trick the writer suggests that the lower hoops may hold the poles in place after the manner of barrel hoops, and that the upper hoops may be larger than the circle of poles and manipulated by cords attached to the body of the juggler. These could be attached in such a manner that he could jerk them to one side or the other and continue to pound his drum. Although no measurements were taken, it appeared that some of the hoops were slightly larger than the circle of holes in the ground and it is always stated that the hoops were outside the poles. If the tipi cover were of proper texture and firmly fastened around the base of the framework, a jerking of the upper hoops would produce a violent agitation. The upper hoops could be attached to the poles by cords permitting them to hang loosely but not fall, while cords hanging down from the hoops could be attached to the juggler's body. The Indians stress the framework of poles, saying that such frames have been found in the woods and the poles were set so solidly that they could not be shaken. By the foregoing explanation there would be no need of shaking the poles as the agitation would be produced by the motion of the hoops beneath the cloth cover. For such a demonstration it would be important that the poles be solidly set, to withstand the jerking of the hoops against them. [314] Great secrecy attended the erection of the tipi and, as stated, the demonstration seldom took place in the daytime. Whatever may be the mechanical explanation of the tipi shaking, its greatest interest lies in the influence it exerted on the minds of the Indians, an influence affecting every phase of their lives.

Red Wing, Minnesota

Menomini

To present more intelligibly the ritualistic observances and pretensions of the several classes of shamans, the subject will be arranged under the following captions:

I *mitä'wit* or Grand Medicine society
II *tshi'saqka* or Juggler
III *wa'beno* or Men of the Dawn
IV Dreamers society

TSHI'SAQKA, OR JUGGLERS

The [138] greatest powers were always believed to be possessed by the *tshi'saqka*, though, on account of their greater number, the *mitä'wok* have been treated first.

The *tshi'saqka*, or juggler, class of shamans is limited, in the Menomini tribe, to very few individuals, probably not more than half a dozen professing the powers usually attributed to them. The jugglers were early mentioned by the Jesuits as being their greatest opponents in Christianizing the Indians; and as early as 1632 the Nipissing Indians of Canada had been designated as the nation of sorcerers. The Spaniards met with similar opposition when attempting to Christianize the Mexicans; and Father José de Acosta's description of one class of their sorcerers corresponds very closely to the accounts of pretensions of some of the Algonquian jugglers. He says:

There were an infinite number of these witches, divines, enchanters, and other false prophets. There remaines yet at this day of this infection, althogh [ok] they be secret, not daring publikely to exercise their sacrileges, divelis ceremonies, and superstitions, but their abuses and wickednes are discovered more at large and particularly in the confessions made by the Prelates of Peru.

There is a kinde of sorcerers amongst the Indians allowed by the Kings Yncas, which are, as it were, sooth-sayers, they take vpou them what forme and figure they please, flying farre through the aire in a short time, beholding all that was done. They talke with the Divell, who answereth them in certaine stones or other things which they reverence much. They serve as coniurers, to tell what hath passed in the farthest partes, before any newes can come. As it hath chanced since the Spaniards arrived there, that in the distance of two or three hundred leagues, they have knowne the mutinies, battailes, rebellions, and deaths, both of tyrants, and those of the King's partie, and of private men, the which have beene knowne the same day they changed or the day after, a tiling impossible by the course of nature. To worke this divination, they shut themselves into a house, and became drunk vntil they lost their sences, a day after they answered to that which was demanded. Some affirme they vse certaine vctims. The Indians say that the old women do commonly vse this office of witchcraft, and specially those of one Province, which they call Coaillo, and of another towne called Manchay, and of the Province of Huarochiri. They likewise shew what is become of things stolno and lost. There are of these kindes of Sorcerers in all partes, to whom commonly doe come the Anaconas, and Chinas, which serve the Spaniardes, and when they have lost any thing of their masters, or when they desire to know the successe of things past or to come, as when they goe to the Spaniardes citties for their private affaires, or for the publike, they demaund if their voyage shall be prosperous, if they shall be sicke, if they shall die, or return safe, if they shall obtaine that which they pretend: [139] and the witches or coniurers answer, yea, or no, having first spoken with the Divell, in an obscure place; so as those Anaconas do well heare the sound of the voyce, but they see not to whom these coniurers speake, neither do they vnderatand what they say.[163]

Jugglers were common in perhaps all of the Algonquian tribes, and indeed we have evidence of jugglery also among the Iroquois, for Charlevoix[164] says of the Hurons, whom he visited in 1635, that the jugglers had informed the Indians that the religion of the French was not applicable to them, and that they, furthermore, had a religion of their own. On account of this antagonism the missionary fathers were frequently compelled to perform their priestly offices in secret.

The Indians of Acadia are said to have had their jugglers, termed *autmoins*, and Charlevoix[165] says of them –

A sick person often takes it into his head that his disease is owing to witchcraft, in which case their whole attention is employed in discovering it, which is the juggler's province. This personage begins with causing himself to be sweated, and after he has quite fatigued himself with shouting, beating himself, and invoking his genius, the first out-of-the-way thing that comes into his head, is that to which he attributes the cause of the disease   There are some who, before they enter the stove, take a draft of a composition very proper, they say, for disposing them to receive the divine impulse, and they pretend that the advent of the spirit is made manifest by a rushing wind, which suddenly rises; or by a bellowing heard under the ground; or by the agitation and shaking of the stove. Then, full of his pretended divinity, and more like a person

---

[163] Acosta, Natural and Moral History of the Indies; in Hakluyt Society publications, vol. 61, pp.367-388, London, 1880 (from the English translation, edition of Ed. Grimston, 1604).

[164] *Histoire et description générale de la Nouvelle France*, tome i, p. 295 et seq,, Paris, 1744. "Ces Charlatans, qui craignoent de perdre la considération, oû les mettoit l'exercice de leur art, si les Missionnaires s'accrûditoient dans le Pays, entreprirent de les rendre odieux & méprisables, & ils n'eurent pas dans ces commencemens beaucoup de piene à y réussir; non-seulement parce qu'ils avoient à faire à une Nation excessivement superatitieuse & ombrageuse, mais encore parce que plusieurs s'etoient déja mis dans la tête, que la Religion des Francois ne leur convenoit point, & qu'elle leur seroit même funeste, si elle s'etablissoit parmi eux.

"Les Jongleurs vinreut donc aisément à bout de rendre suspectes toutes les demarches des Peres, & surtout leurs Prières, qu'ils faisoient regarder comme deS malefices; en sorte que ces Religeux étoient obliges de se cacher pour réciter leur Office, & pour s'acquitter des autres Exercices de devotion."

{"These charlatans that were afraid of loosing regard, whence they mastered the exercise of their art, if these missionaries that have appropriated the country, they undertook to make them odious and despicable and in the beginnings it was not hard to succeed not only because they had to deal with a nation that was excessively superstitious and obscured, but also because a lot of them already had in mind that the religion of the French wasn't suitable for them and would be fatal if it were established among them.

Therefore, jugglers easily mastered to make suspicious all the Father's mission and above all making their prayers look like curses, to that end that these religious had to perform their priestly offices in secret, and other exercises of devotion."} Translated by Marie Frutoso, Maxime Olmos, Donna Ellefson.

[165] Journal of a Voyage to North America, vol. ii, p. 177, London, 1761.

possessed by the devil than one inspired of Heaven, he pronounces in a positive tone of voice on the state of the patient, and sometimes guesses tolerably just.

The "stove" mentioned in the above quotation is the conical structure usually designated as the jugglery, a description of which will hereafter be given. "These *autmoins*," continues Charlevoix, "had much more authority than the other jugglers, although they were not possessed of greater ability, nor were they less impostors."

It appears from this remark that the class of shamans, known among the western Algonquian tribes as the *mitä^{iv}*, or *midē'*, was also represented among the eastern Indians of that stock, although the several classes are usually described under the designation of juggler or sorcerer.

Baron Lahontan, who was lord-lieutenant of the French colony of Placentia, in Newfoundland, and who visited the Algonquian tribes of [140] the northwest in the latter part of the seventeenth century, speaks of the treatment of the sick by the natives, and with reference to the shaman says:

A *Jongleur* is a sort of *Physician,* or rather a *Quack,* who being once cur'd of some dangerous Distemper, bus the Presumption and Folly to fancy that he is immortal, and possessed of the Power of curing all Diseases, by speaking to the Good and Evil Spirits. Now though every Body rallies upon these Fellows when they are absent, and looks upon 'em as Fools that have lost their Senses by some violent Distemper, yet they allow 'em to visit the Sick; whether it be to divert 'em with their Idle Stories, or to have an Opportunity of seeing them rave, skip about, cry, houl, and make grimaces and Wry Faces, as if they were possess'd. When all the Bustle is over, they demand a Feast of a Stag and some large Trouts for the Company, who are thus regal'd at once with Diversion and Good Cheer.

When the Quack comes to visit the Patient, he examines him very carefully; *If the Evil Spirit be here,* says he, "we *shall quicky disloge him.* This said, he withdraws by himself to a little Tent made on purpose, where he dances and sings houliug like an Owl; (which gives the Jesuits Occasion to say, *That the Devil converses with 'em.*) After he has made an end of this Quack Jargon, he comes and rubs the Patient in some part of his Body, and pulling some little Bones out of his Mouth, acquaints the Patient, *That these very Bones came out of his Body; that he ought to pluck up a good heart, in regard that his Distemper is but a Trifle; and in fine, that in order to accelerate the Cure, 'twill be convenient to send his own and his Relations Slaves to shoot Elks, Deer, &., to the end they may all eat of that sort of Meat, vpon which his Cure does absolutely depend.*

Commonly these Quacks bring 'em some Juices of Plants, which are a sort of Purges, and are called *Maskikik.* But the Patients choose to keep them by 'em rather than to drink them; for think all Purgatives inflame the Mass of the Blood, and weaken the Veins and Arteries by their violent Shocks.[166]

In his reference to the Indians (Ojibwa?) in the vicinity of Fort Nelson, on Hudson bay,

---

[166] New Voyages to North-America, vol. ii, pp. 47, 48, London, 1703.

M. de Bacqneville de la Potherie[167] remarks:

> Ils recounoisseut comme ces anciens heretiques un bon & un mauvais esprit. Ils appellent le premier le *Quichemanitou.* C'est le Dieu de prosperité. C'est celui dont ils imaginent recevoir tous les secours de la vie, qui préside dans tous les effets heureux de la nature. Le *Matchimanitou* an contraire est le Dieu fatal. Ils 1'adorent plus par crainte que par amour ...

> "Faire fumer le Soleil ne se pratique guere que dans des occaaions de grande consequence, & pour ce qui regarde leur culte ordinaire ils s'adreasent à leur *Manitou,* qui est proprement leur Dieu tutelaire. Ce *Manitou* est quelquefois un ongle de castor, le bout de la come d'un pied de Caribou, une petite peau d'hermine. J'en vis une attachée derriere le dos d'un Esquimau lorsque nous étiona dans le détroit qu'il ne voulut jamais me donner, quoiqu'il me traita generalement tous les habits dont il étoit vétu, un morceau de dents de vache marine, de nageoite de loup marin, & la plûpart reçoivent des Jongleurs ce *Manitou* qu'ils portent toûjours avec eux.

> Le démon paroit s'être emparé de 1'esprit de ces infortunez qui voulaut sçavoir l'évenement de quelques affaires, s'adresseut à leurs Jongleurs, qui sout, si je peux me servir de ce terme, des Sorciers. La Jonglerie se fait differemment. Elle se fait de cette maniere parmi plûpart des Sauvages qui viennent faire le traite. Le Jougleur fait une cabane en rond, faite de perches extrémement enforcées dans la terre, entourée de peau de Caribou on d'autres animaux, avec une ouverture en haut assez large pour passer un homme. Le Jongleur qui s'y renferme tout seui, chante, pleure, [141] s'agite, se tourmente. fait des invocations & des imprécations, à peu prés comme la Sibille dout parle Virgile, qui poussée de 1'esprit d'Apollon rendoit ses Oracles avec cette même fureur.

> At Phoebi nondum patiens, immanis in antro.
> Bacchatur vates, magnum si pectore possit,
> Excussisse Deum: tanto magis ille fatigat,
> Os rabidum ? fera corda domans, fingit que premendo.
>
> *– Virgil, I, 6, v. 77.*

> II fait au M*atchimanitou* les demandes qu'il souhaite. Celui-ci voulaut donner réponse, l'on entend tout à bruit sourd comme une roche qui tombe, & toutes ces perches sont agitées avec une violence si surprenante, qui l'on croiroit que tout est renversé. Le Jugleur reçoit ainsi l'oracle: & cette confiance qu'ils ont aux veritez qu'il prononce sonvent, sont autant d'obstacles à tout ce que 1'on peut leur reprocher sur la fausse erreur où ils sont: aussi se donnent ils de garde, qu'aucun François n'entre dans 1'endroit où se fait la Jouglerie.

{ They recognize as the ancient heretic a good and bad spirit. They call the first one *GichiManitu.* It is the god of prosperity. It is the one they imagine from whom they will receive all the support for life, who preside in all the good things of nature. The *MachiManitu* on the contrary is the fatal god (of death). They adore him more from

---

[167] *Histoire de l'Amérique Septentrionale*, vol. i., p. 121 et seq., Paris, 1753.

fear than from love.

Offering (tobacco) smoke to the Sun is only practiced on occasions of grand consequence and regarding their ordinary cults/rites they are speaking to their (own) Manitou who is properly their tutelary god. This *Manitou* (amulet) is sometimes a beaver claw, the hoof of a Caribou foot, a little skin of an ermine. I saw one (ermine) attached on the back of an Eskimo while we were in the strait that he has never wanted to give me, whereas he generally traded me all the clothes (made beaver cloaks) he wore, a piece of tooth of a sea wolf, and most of them receive from Jongleurs this Manitou that they always are wearing.

The demon seems to seize the spirit of those unfortunates that, while wanting to predict the outcome of some business, speak to their Jongleurs, who are, if I can use this term, sorcerers. Jonglerie is done differently. It is done in that way among most of the Sauvages to come to make that request (inquiry). The Jongleur builds a round hut, made of poles deeply embedded in the ground and covered with caribou or other animal hides, with an opening large enough at the top for a man to enter. The Jongleur who is enclosed by himself, sings, cries, [141] agitates, torments himself, makes invocations and imprecations, quite as the Sybil of whom Virgil talks about, who uplifted by Apollo's spirit make his Oracles with this same furor.

> (But the wild prophetess raged in her cavern, not yet)
> submitting to Phoebus, as if she might shake the great god
> from her spirit: yet he exhausted her raving mouth
> all the more, taming her wild heart, shaping her by constraint.
> *Aeneid*, Virgil (70-19 BCE), Book VI: lines 56-97: The Sibyl's Prophecy[168]

He demands of the *MachiManitou* what he wishes/desires. The following tries to give an answer, (when) suddenly one can hear a loud sound, like a rock that falls, and all these poles agitate with violence so surprising, that one can believe that everything is (turned) upside down.

At the moment the Jongleur received the oracle, they had such confidence in the truths he often predicts as to create many obstacles toward (understanding) everything (that) one could reproach (them) about this false error of their existence: also they are wary that none of the French enter the locale where the Jonglerie is done.}

Hennepin[169] speaks of the religion and sorcerers of the tribes of the Saint Lawrence and those living about the great lakes, as follows:

We have been all too sadly convinced, that almost all the Salvages in general have no notion of a God, and that they are not able to comprehend the most ordinary Arguments on that Subject; others will have a Spirit that commands, say they, in the Air. Some among 'em look upon the Skies a kind of Divinity; others as an *Otkon* or *Manitou*, either

---

[168] Virgil (70-19 BCE), *Aenied*, written over a decade (29 and 19 BCE) in 9,896 lines of dactylic hexameter, telling of Trojan Aeneas's voyage to Italy to become a founder of Rome.

[169] A continuation of the New Discovery, etc., p. 58 et seq., London, 1689.

Good or Evil.

These People admit of some sort of Genius in all things; they all believe there is a Master of Life, as they call him, but hereof they made various applications; some of them have a lean Raven, which they carry always along with them, and which they say is the Master of their Life; others have an Owl, and some again a Bone, *a Sea*-Shell, or some such thing.

There is no Nation among 'em which has not a sort of Juglers or Conjuerers, which some look upon to be Wizards, but in my Opinion there is no Great reason to believe 'em such, or to think that their Practice favours any thing of a Communication with the Devil.

These Impostors cause themselves to be reverenced as Prophets which fore-tell Futurity. They will needs be look'd upon to have an unlimited Power. They boast of being able to make it Wet or Dry; to cause a Calm or a Storm; to render Land Fruitful or Barren; and, in a Word, to make Hunters Fortunate or Unfortunate. They also pretend to Physick, and to apply Medicines, but which are such, for the most part as having little Virtue at all in 'em, especially to Cure that Distemper which they pretend to.

It is impossible to imagine, the horrible Howlings and strange Contortions that those Jugglers make of their Bodies, when they are disposing themselves to Conjure, or raise their Enchantments.

Carver gives a description of a Killistino, or Cree, juggler's performance, which will further illustrate the method of procedure as followed by this division of the Algonquian peoples. The narrator had been expecting the arrival of the traders, as provisions were getting very low, and, while in a state of anxiety, the "chief priest" of the tribe said he would endeavor to obtain a conference with the Great Spirit, and thus ascertain when the traders would come. Carver[170,] says:

I paid little attention to this declaration, supposing that it would he productive of some juggling trick, just sufficiently covered to deceive the ignorant Indians. [142] But the king of that tribe, telling me that this was chiefly undertaken by the priest to alleviate my anxiety, and at the same time to convince me how much interest he had with the Great Spirit, I thought it necessary to restrain my animadversions on his design.

The following evening was fixed upon for this spiritual conference. When everything had been properly prepared, the king came to me and led me to a capacious tent, the covering of which was drawn up, so as to render what was transacting within visible to those who stood without. We found the tent surrounded by a great number of the Indians, but we readily gained admission, and seated ourselves on skins laid on the ground for that purpose.

In the centre I observed that there was a place of an oblong shape, which was composed of stakes stuck in the ground, with intervals between, so as to form a kind of chest or coffin, large enough to contain the body of a man. These were of a middle size, and placed at such a distance from each other that whatever lay within them was readily

---

[170] Travels through the interior of North America in the years 1766, 1767; and 1768, p. 123 et seq., London, 1778.

to be discerned.... In a few minutes the priest entered, when, an amazingly large elk's skin being spread on the ground just at my feet, he laid himself down upon it, after having stripped himself of every garment except that which he wore close about his middle. Being now prostrate on his back, he first laid hold of one side of the skin and folded it over him, and then the other, leaving only his head uncovered. This was no sooner done than two of the young men who stood by took about 40 yards of strong cord, made also of an elk's hide, and rolled it tight round his body, so that he was completely swathed within the skin. Being thus bound up like an Egyptian mummy, one took him by the heels and the other by the head and lifted him over the pales into the inclosure. I could now also discern him as plain as I had hitherto done, and I took care not to turn my eyes a moment from the object before me, that I might the more readily detect the artifice, for such I doubted not but that it would turn out to be.

The priest had not lain in this situation more than a few seconds when he began to mutter. This he continued to do for some time, and then by degrees grew louder and louder till at length he spoke articulately; however, what he uttered was in such a mixed jargon of the Chippeway, Ottawaw, and Killistine languages that I could understand but very little of it. Having continued in this tone for a considerable while, he at last exerted his voice to its utmost pitch, sometimes raving and sometimes praying, till he had worked himself into sch an agitation that he foamed at his mouth.

After having remained near three-quarters of an hour in the place, and continued his vociferation with unabated vigor, he seemed quite exhausted, and remained speechless. But in an instant he sprung upon his feet, notwithstanding at the time he was put in, it appeared impossible for him to move either his legs or arms, and shaking of his covering, as quick as if the bands with which it had been bound were burned asunder, he began to address those who stood around in a firm and audible voice. "My brothers," said he, "the Great Spirit has deigned to hold a talk with his servant at my earnest request. He has not, indeed, told me when the persons we expect will be here, but to-morrow, soon after the sun has reached his highest point in the heavens, a canoe will arrive, and the people in that will inform us when the traders will come." Having said this, he stepped out of the inclosure, and after he had put on his robes, dismissed the assembly. I own I was greatly astonished at what I had seen, but, as I observed that every eye in the company was fixed on me with a view to discover my sentiments, I carefully concealed every emotion.

The next day the sun shone bright, and long before noon all the Indiana were gathered together on the eminence that overlooked the lake. The old king came to me and asked me whether I had so much confidence in what the priest had foretold as to join his people on the hill and wait for the completion of it. I told him that I was at a loss what opinion to form of the prediction, but that I would readily attend him. On this, we walked together to the place where the others were assembled. [143] Every eye was again fixed by turns on me and on the lake; when, just as the sun had reached his zenith, agreeable to what the priest had foretold, a canoe came round a point of land about a league distant. The Indians no sooner beheld it than they sent up an universal shout, and by their looks seemed to triumph in the interest their priest thus evidently had with the Great Spirit.

In less than an hour the canoe reached the shore, when I attended the king and chiefs to receive those who were on hoard.... The king inquired of them whether they had seen anything of the traders? The men replied that they had parted from them a few days before, and that they proposed being here the second day from the present. They accordingly arrived at that time, greatly to our Satisfaction....

This story I acknowledge appears to carry with it marks of great credulity in .the relator. But no one is less tinctured with that weakness than myself. The circumstances of it I own are of a very extraordinary nature; however, as I can vouch for their being free from either exaggeration or misrepresentation, being myself a cool and dispassionate observer of them all, I thought it necessary to give them to the public, ... but leaving them to draw from it what conclusions they please.

Thus it will be observed that the Juggler, after having been carefully wrapped and tied, was placed within his *tshi'saqkan* or jugglery, which, in Carver's description is likened to a chest or a coffin. The Juggler, at this day, enters his jugglery alone and unassisted, although it is reported that some of the Ojibwa performers will permit themselves to be securely tied, placed within the Jugglery, and a moment later be at liberty and the cords at some other locality. Further information in regard to this subject, as relating to the Ojibwa, has already been presented in a paper entitled "The Midē'wiwin or Grand Medicine society of the Ojibwa," published in the seventh annual report of the Bureau of Ethnology.

The power of prophecy and prevision is claimed by the juggler, and the citation of an instance of this, from the work of Peter Jones,[171] may not be without interest. The author mentioned was a Protestant Episcopal clergyman and a member of the Misasauga tribe of the Ojibwa nation, of Canada. He thus remarks:

I have sometimes been inclined to think that, if witchcraft still exists in the world, it is to be found among the aborigines of America. They seem to possess a power which, it would appear, may be fairly imputed, to the agency of au evil spirit.

The conjurers not only pretend to have the powers already specified, but they profess also to have the gift of foretelling future events. The following curious account on this subject I received from a respectable gentleman who had spent most of his life in the Indian country, and who is therefore well acquainted with their character and pretensions. He is now one of the Government Indian agents in Upper Canada.

The following account is then given by this author:

In the year 1804, wintering with the Winnebagoes on the Rock river, I had occasion to send three of my men to another wintering house for some flour which I had left there in the fall, on my way up the river. The distance being about one and a half days' journey from where I lived, they were expected to return in about three days. On the sixth day after their absence, I was about sending in quest of them, when some Indians, arriving from the spot, said that they had seen nothing of them. I could now use no means to ascertain where they were. The plains were extensive, [144] the paths numerous, and the tracks they had made were the next moment covered boy the drift snow. Patience was my only resource, and, at length I gave them up for lost.

---

[171] Hist. of the Ojebway Indians, p. 147 et *seq.,* London, [1843 ?].

On the fourteenth night after their departure, as several Indians were smoking their pipes, and telling stories of their war parties, hunting, etc., an old fellow, who was a daily visitor, came in. My interpreter, a Canadian named Felix, pressed me, as he had frequently done before, to employ this conjurer, as he could inform me about the men in question. The dread of being laughed at had hitherto prevented my acceding to his importunities: but now, excited by curiosity, I gave the old man, a quarter-pound of tobacco and two yards of ribbon, telling him that if he gave me a true account of them, I would, when I ascertained the fact, give him a bottle of rum.... The old fellow withdrew, and the other Indians retired to their lodges.

A few minutes after, I heard *Wahwu*n (an egg) begin a lamentable song, his voice increasing to such a degree that I really thought h would have injured himself. The whole forest appeared to be in agitation, as if the trees were knocking against each other, then all would be silent for a few seconds; again the old fellow would scream and yell as if he were in great distress. A chill seized me and my hair stood on end; the interpreter and I stared at each other without power to express our feelings.

The narrative states that finally everything became quiet, and the next morning the Indian was sent for, for an explanation.

"I went," said he, "to smoke the pipe with your men last night, and found them cooking some elk meat which they got from an Ottawa Indian. On leaving this place they took the wrong road on the top of the hill; they traveled hard on and did not know for two days that they were lost. When they discovered their situation they were much alarmed, and, having nothing more to eat, were afraid they would starve to death. They walked on without knowing which way they were going until the seventh day, when they were met near the Illinois river by the Ottawa before named, who was out hunting. He took them to his lodge, fed them well, and wanted to detain them some days until they had recovered their strength, but they would not stay. He then gave them some elk meat for their journey home, and sent his son to put them into the right road. They will go to Lagothenes for the flour you sent them, and will be at home in three days." I then asked him what kind of place they were encamped in when he was there. He said "they had made a shelter by the side of a large oak tree that had been torn up by the roots, and which had fallen with the head towards the rising sun."

All this I noted down, and from the circumstantial manner in which he related every particular – though he could not possibly have had any personal communication with or from them by any other Indians – I began to hope my men were safe and that I should again see them.

Suffice it to say that on the appointed day the men returned, and, upon being asked to give an account of their experience, they told exactly what the Indian had before stated, not omitting the tree or any other circumstance.

In an account of the life and customs of the Indians of Canada in 1723, found in the archives of France by the Honorable Lewis Cass,[1721] while minister to that country, the narrator

---

[172] Cass MS., translated by Charles Whittlesey, in Coll. Hist. Soc. of Wisconsin for 1856, vol. iii,

says:

> They perform a thousand tricks of magic, pretending they can bring back dead animals to life, cause an otter to run across the lodge, or a bear to walk in there. [145] They do this by means of young girls and noises that are apparently under ground. With an arrow they pretend to stab the naked body of a man. To show the blood flowing, they lay upon the supposed wound, very adroitly, the juice of a red root. The arrow has its stem so made that when it strikes the body, instead of entering it, it slides within itself. The pretended wound is rubbed with a salve composed of roots, and by this means the injured man is cured upon the spot. This is done to prove the virtue of their medicines. They cure gun-shot wounds in the same way, before the whole tribe. But, in truth, the ball is made of earth, rubbed over with lead, which they break in pieces in the barrel of the piece as it is driven down.

The locality referred to appears to be near Mackinaw, and may refer either to the Ojibwa or to the Ottawa Indians. The Abbe J.A. Maurault,[173] says regarding the subject:

> La jonglerie était en grande vénération chez ces sauvages, et les jongleurs jouissaient d'une trés-grande influence auprés d'eux. Ces pauvres gens, extrémement superstitieux, avaieut une telle confiance aux sortiléges de ces imposteurs qu'ils se soumettaient aveuglement à toutes leurs ordonnancs, les considérant comme venant de l'autre monde. Les jongleurs, suivant eux, évoquaient les Esprits du Mal, qu'ils appelaient "Madaôdos," avaient le pouvoir de les vaincre, prédisaient 1 beau temps et 1 mauvais temps, l'heureus on la mauvaise fortune dans la chasse, les accidents qui devaient arriver dans un voyage, le résultat d'une expédition cotre l'ennemi, et mille autre choses. Les sauvages avait une telle confiance aux sentences des jongleurs qu'ils n'entreprenaient jamais une chose de quelqu'importance sans les consulter.
>
> Chaque sauvage recevait d'eux certains objete, qui étaient appelés "Madaôdos." Ces objets étaient des petites pierres, ou des os, ou des morceaux de certains bois, ou autres choses semblables. Les Sauvages conservaient ces objets dans des sacs, et les considéraient comme un grand préservatif centre les attaques des Esprits du Mal. Plusieurs conservaient un grand nombre de ces " Madaôdos."
>
> La jonglerie solennelle était une chose qui inspirait de l'horreur. Elle se faisait dans les circonstances importantes comme à la veille d'une guerre, pour en connaître d'avance le résultat. Voici comment se faisait cette jonglerie. Le Jongleur s'enfermait seul dans une petite cabane, faite ordinairement d'écorces de bonleau. Alors, il évoquait hautement l'Esprit du Mal. Il passait quelque fois plusieurs heures dans cette cabane à se débattre et à crier comme un dàmon. Les sauvages se tenaieut à une certaine distance de la loge aux sortiléges, attendant avec une grande anxiété la prophétie favorable ou défavorable. Lorsque le jongleur en était rendu à un tel état d'épuisement qu'il ne pouvait plus crier, il sortait de sa loge, le corps tout ruisselant de sueurs, et annonçait le résultat de son sortilege. Sa parole était alors reçue comme venant du ciel.

---

pp. 145, 146, 1857.

[173] Histoire des Abenakis, Quebec, 1866, pp. 29-32.

Les jongleurs soignaient les malades, prédisaient leur guérison ou leur mort, évoquaient et chassient les "Madaôdos," qui les tourmentaient et les faisaient souffrir.

Lorsqu'un jongleur était appelé auprés d'un malade, il déclarait ordinairement de suite qu'un "Madaôdos" voulait faire mourir ce malade. Il sortait alors du wiguam, faisant mine d'aller à la recherche de cet Esprit; puis revenait bieutôt, et annonçait qu'il était caché sous terre, à un endroit qu'il indiquait, mais qu'il saurait bien 1'en arracher et le détuire. Voici ce qu'il faisait alors. Il enfonçait profondémeut dans le sol un poteau, auqnel il attachait une longue corde, par le moyen de laquelle les sauvages devaient réunir leurs efforts pour 1'arracher. Ordinairement les premiers efforts des sauvages étaient inutiles. Alora le jongleur, faisant mine d'aller menacer le "Madaôdo" obstiné, remuait la terre au pied du poteau, qui, aprés plusieurs essais, était enfin arrache. Le jongleur, tout rayonnant de joie, montrait alors aux sauvages étonnes des arêtes de poisson, des os ou antres objets, fixés à 1'extremité [146] du poteau qui sortait de terre, disant que ces objeta étaient les restes du " Madaôdo" qu'il venait de détruire. Les sauvages, ignorant que le jongleur avait lui-même préalablement fixé ces objets au poteau, admiraient ce grand prodige.

Si la maludie ne diminuait pas à la suite de ce sortilegé, le jougleur annoncait que le malade mourrait dans trois ou quatre jours. Alors, le pauvre malade, effrayé par cette prédiction, et convaincu désormais qu'il allait mourir, refusait de prendre nourriture, et mourait d'inanition, à peu prés au temps fixé par le jongleur.

{ The Jonglerie was much venerated by the Sauvages, and the Jongleurs enjoyed a very great influence over them. These poor people, extremely superstitious, had such a confidence in the curses (edicts) of these impostors that they blindly submitted themselves to their ordinances, considering them as coming from an other world. The Jongleurs, according to them, evoked the Bad Spirit that they called "Madaôdos," had the power to defeat them, predicted the good and the bad fortunes in hunting, (an) accident that could happen on a voyage, the result of an expedition against the enemy, and a thousand other things. The Sauvages had such confidences in the pronouncements of Jongleurs that they never undertook anything important without consulting them.

Each Sauvage received from them certain objects, called "Madaôdo." These objects were little rocks, or bones, or pieces of certain woods, or other similar things. The Sauvages kept these objects in bundles and considered them as a great deterrent against the attacks of the Bad Spirit. Many kept a large number of these "Madaôdo."

The formal Jonglerie was something that inspired horror. It was made at/in important circumstances such as the night before a war/battle, to be aware of the result. This is how this Jonglerie is done. The Jongleur locked himself alone inside a little hut, ordinarily made with birch bark. Then he greatly evoked the Bad Spirit. He sometimes spent several hours in this hut debating and screaming like a demon. The Sauvages kept a certain distance from the hut of curses, waiting with great anxiety the favorable or unfavorable prophecy. When the Jongleur has reached a state of such exhaustion that he was unable to scream, he went out of his hut, his body streaming sweat, and announced the result of his cure/effort. His word was then received as coming from the sky/ above.

The Jongleur cured patients, cured their malady or their (impeding) death, evoked and hunted (out) the "Madaôdos" that tormented them and made them suffer.

When a Jongleur was called at one person's bedside, he typically declared that a "Madaôdo" wanted that person to die. He then came out the wigwam, pretending to go find this Spirit, came back quickly, and announced that he was hiding underground, in a place he was indicated, but he would know how to tear it out and destroy it. Here it was he was then doing. He was burying a pole deeply into the ground, to which he attached a long rope, and the Sauvages had to work together to tear it off. Usually, the first efforts of the Sauvages were useless. So, the Jongleur, pretending to go threaten the stubborn "Madaôdo", stirred the ground at the bottom of the pole, so that, after several tries, it was finally torn off. The Jongleur, radiating with happiness, then showed the Sauvages fishbones, bones or other objects, attached to the end of the pole that came out of the ground, saying that these objects were the remains of the "Mataôdo" he has just destroyed. The Sauvages, unaware that the Jongleur had previously attached these objects to the pole himself, admired this miracle.

If the disease didn't decrease after this curse, the Jongleur announced that the patient would die in three to four days. So, the unfortunate patient, scared by this predilection, and now convinced he will die, refused to take food, and died of starvation, roughly around the time predicted by the Jongleur.}

Mr Hiram Calkins[174] mentions the performance of an Ojibwa who lived on Wisconsin river, near the Menomini country, which apparently embraced the pretensions of both the *tshi'saqka* and the *wa'beno*:

The chief medicine man or conjurer is *Mab-ca-da-o-gung*, or The Black Nail, who performed the feat of descending the Long Falls in his canoe, and is represented by the other Indians as being a great medicine man. He is always called upon, far and near, in cases of sickness, or in the absence of relatives, to foretell whether the sickness will prove fatal or whether the friends will return in safety, and at what time. He is also consulted by the Indiens when they go out to hunt the bear, to foretell whether success will crown their efforts. Before performing these services, he is always paid by the Indians with such articles as they have, which generally consist of tobacco, steel-traps, kettles, broadcloth, calico, and a variety of other commodities. He usually performs after dark, in a wigwam just large enough to admit of his standing erect. This lodge or wigwam is tightly covered with mats, so as entirely to exclude all light and the prying curiosity of all outsiders. Having no light within the lodge, the acts and utterances of the medicine man or conjurer are regarded as mysterious, and credulously received by the wondering crowd surrounding the tent. He first prepares himself in his family wigwam by stripping off all his clothing, when he emerges singing, and the Indians outside join him in the song with their drums, and accompany him to the lodge, which he enters alone. Upon entering, the lodge commences shaking violently, which is supposed by the Indians outside to be caused by the spirits. The shaking of the lodge produces a great noise by the rattling of bells and deers' hoofs fastened to the poles of the lodge at the top, and at the same time three voices are distinctly heard intermingled with this noise. One is a very heavy hoarse voice, which the Indians are made to

---

[174] Coll. Hist. Soc. of Wisconsin for 1854, vol. i, pp. 123, 124, 1855.

believe is that of the Great Spirit; another is a very fine voice, represented to be that of a Small Spirit, while the third is that of the medicine man himself. He pretends that the Great Spirit converses in the heavy voice to the lesser spirit, unintelligibly to the conjurer, and the lesser spirit interprets it to him, and he communicates the intelligence to his brethren without, The ceremony last about three hours, when he comes out in a high state of perspiration, supposed by the superstitious Indians to be produced by mental excitement.

The structure described by the Reverend Peter Jones,[1753] which he saw occupied by a juggler while the latter was engaged in consulting the *ma'nidos*, was "made by putting seven poles in the ground to the depth of about a cubit, in a circle of about 3 or 4 feet in diameter, and about 6 feet high, with one or more hoops tied fast to the poles to keep them in a circle. The sides were covered with birch bark, but the top was left open. Into this the pow-wow had entered, and was chanting a song to the spirit with whom he wished to converse. The *jeesuhkon* began to shake as if filled with wind."

The Menomini structure is about the same size as that above named, but not so large as 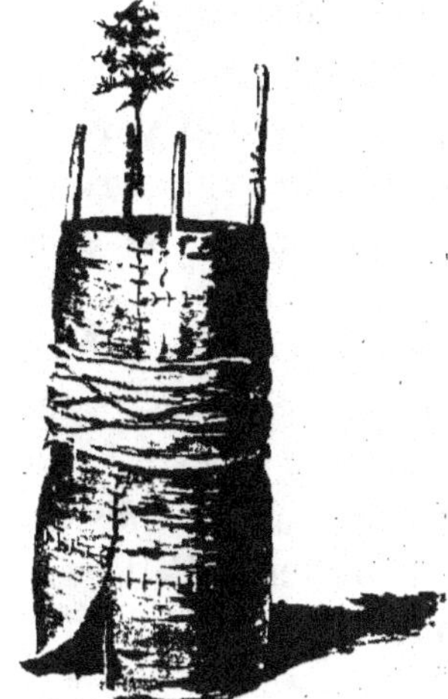 the jugglery usually erected by the Ojibwa of northern [147] Minnesota. The Menomini *tshi'saqkan* is composed of four upright poles from 6 to 8 feet high, securely planted in the ground at the east, south, west, and north sides of a circle measuring 3 to 4 feet in diameter. These poles are from 4 to 6 inches thick. Around them is wrapped bark, and sometimes even pieces of cloth, to make the interior invisible from without (figure 20).

The *tshi'saqka* sometimes enters this place when he wants to consult the *ma'nidos* about the future. The latter come here and tell him what he wishes to know. To invoke their presence, he first enters the inclosure, then facing the east, addresses the *ma'nidos* who are supposed to abide in that direction, that they come to him; then he faces the south, and invokes the presence of the *ma'nidos* from that

FIG. 20 – *Tshi'saqkan* or jugglery. direction; then he talks to the ma'nidos who live in the west; and finally he turns to the north, and appeals to the *ma'nidos* of that region.

The following data are obtained from Menomini Indians who are members of the Mitä'wit, as well as from others who have laid aside their aboriginal beliefs and embraced Christianity. Although the structures exist at the present day, no prophecies have been made in this manner [148] for some years, but the *ma'nidos* have been consulted for remedies wherewith to combat violent symptoms of disease supposed to have been caused by angry or jealous rivals.

Then the *tshi'saqka* lies on the ground and begins to chant, during which time the *ma'nidos* begin to arrive. Their arrival is made known to those outside by the air swaying the top of the structure, and the wind also can be felt and heard.

The *ma'nidos* are next heard dropping upon the ground within, and their voices can be distinguished. Presently the assistant, or perhaps the one who desires information, goes to the *tshi'saqkan* and taps – with a stick or other object – upon the four upright poles in regular order, beginning at the east, then passing to the south, the west, and the north, and asks if all the

---

[175] *Op. cit.*, p. 115.

ma'nidos have arrived. The *tshi'saqka* replies that all have arrived save one – his own personal *ma'nido*. Then the *tshi'saqka* sings and drums again, and presently a voice is heard above the *tshi'saqkan*, resembling the voice of the *tshi'saqka*. Their voices are similar, and the conversation between them is heard by all those seated or standing near by.

The rattle employed by the juggler, both in the jugglery and when exorcising demons, is shown in figure 21.

Fig. 21 - Juggler's rattle.　　The *Miqkä'no* – the turtle – is the most powerful of all the *ma'nidos*, and he, as the speaker for the others, is consulted for information; but should the *tshi'saqk*a ask too many, or any injudicious questions, the personal *ma'nido* will be heard above the *tshi'saqkan*, in the same tone of voice as the interrogation, advising the latter to be careful, or not to be incautious in his demands.

When such a service has been performed in the interest of a sick person, the friends and family of the sick believe that the illness has been caused by the anger of an enemy through the influence of another *tshi'saqka*. The one consulted by the friends of the sick man is expected to reveal the name of the injuring conjurer, and to bring his shade into the *tshi'saqkan*. This is done, and the *Miqkä'no* is then the *ma'nido* who kicks the shade of the conjurer almost to death; if he is too much hurt and loses consciousness, the other *ma'nidos* bring his shade back to life, so that he is able to respond to the questions of the *tshi'saqka*, who asks him how and why he caused the illness of the person. The shade of the conjurer then relates how he did this wrong, and the reason therefore, and he is then told to restore him to health. If the conjurer promises to do this, all is well, and the patient is expected to recover in a short time.

If the conjurer refuses to comply with the demands of the *tshi'saqka*, the latter asks for a cedar knife, which the assistant throws into the [149] structure, when the *Miqkä'no* takes it and stabs the conjurer's shade to death. The bloody knife is then thrown out into the crowd, but it falls on the ground without touching any one, no matter how large the crowd may be. As the knife falls near one of the friends or relations of the sick, the person is by this token called on to kill the conjurer. In a short time, perhaps after a lapse of several weeks, the conjurer is found in his own wigwam stabbed to death.

When the tutelary daimon of the conjurer reveals the nature of the remedies used by him in having caused the illness of any one, he often reveals the remedy necessary to cure him; then the *tshi'saqka* may prepare it and give it himself. People always pay the *tshi'saqka* in presents of cloth, robes, furs, or any other objects which they may possess and which may be regarded by the *tshi'saqka* as a satisfactory return for his services.

The method of removing disease by sucking the cause thereof through bone tubes has been fully described in my paper on the Ojibwa Midē'wiwin, before mentioned. The juggler, after taking a vapor bath, returns to his everyday wigwam, seats himself upon a blanket, and awaits the arrival of the patient, if the latter is in condition to be brought.

When the patient is laid down near the juggler, the latter has also before him a basin or bowl containing some water, and several bone tubes varying in length from 2 to 5 inches, and from one-third to one-half an inch in diameter. An assistant drums upon the tambourine drum, as the juggler uses the rattle with one hand, while with the other he grasps a tube which he places over the part of the patient's body affected by the presence of a demon, or by some substance put there by another sorcerer, juggler, or *wa'beno*. After chanting for a short time, the operator places his mouth to the tube and sucks violently; then assuming his former position he strikes the bone, which projects from his mouth, with the palm of his hand and apparently drives it down his throat. Then he goes through a similar performance until the disappearance of the second, the third, and every other tube that he may have. After considerable contortion and retching, he pretends to vomit into the basin the poison which had been extracted from the patient, the bones also making their appearance.

Alexander Henry, who was among the Ojibwa Indians at Mackinaw, and also through the surrounding country, over one hundred years ago, says:

I was once present at a performance of this kind, in which the patient was a female child of about 12 years of age. Several of the elder chiefs were invited to the scene, and the same compliment was paid to myself on account of the medical skill for which it was pleased to give me credit.

The physician (so to call him) seated himself on the ground, and before him, on a new stroud blanket, was placed a basin of water, in which were three bones, the larger ones, as it appeared to me, of a swan's wing. In his hand he had his *shishiquoi*, or rattle, with which he beat time to his medicine-song. The sick child lay [150] on a blanket near the physician. She appeared to have much fever and a severe oppression of the lungs, breathing with difficulty, and betraying symptoms of the last stage of consumption.

After singing for some time, the physician took one of the bones out of the basin. The bone was hollow, and one end being applied to the breast of the patient, he put the other into his mouth, in order to remove the disorder by suction. Having persevered in this as long as he thought proper, be suddenly seemed to force the bone into his month and swallow it. He now acted the part of one suffering severe pain, but presently finding relief he made a long speech, and after this returned to singing and to the accompaniment of his rattle. With the latter, during his song, he struck his head, breast, sides, and back, at the same time straining as if to vomit forth the bone.

Relinquishing this attempt, he applied himself to suction a second time, and with the second of the three bones; and this also he soon seemed to swallow.

Upon its disappearance lie began to distort himself in the most frightful manner, using every gesture which could convey the idea of pain. At length be succeeded, or pretended to succeed, in throwing up one of the bones. This was handed about to the spectators and strictly examined, but nothing remarkable could be discovered. Upon this, he went back to his song and rattle, and after some time threw up the second of the two bones. In the groove of this the physician, upon examination, found and displayed to all present a small white substance resembling a piece of the quill of a feather. It was passed round the company, from one to the other, and declared by the physician to be the thing causing the disorder of his patient.

The multitude believe that these physicians, whom the French call jongleurs, or jugglers, can inflict as well as remove disorders. They believe that by drawing the figure of any person in sand or ashes, or on clay, or by considering any object as the figure of a person, and then pricking it with a sharp stick or other substance, or doing in any other manner that which done to a living body would cause pain or injury, the individual represented, or supposed to be represented, will suffer accordingly. On the other hand, the mischief being done, another physician, of equal pretensions, can by suction remove it. Unfortunately, however, the operations which I have described were not successful in the instance referred to, for on the day after they had taken place the girl died.[176]

The office of "rainmaker" is also held by a conspicuous juggler, when one of sufficient ability is supposed to abide with the tribe. When in times of great drought the chief demands rain for the benefit of the crops and disappearing streams, the juggler is commanded to cause the necessary rainfall; or, when too much rain has fallen, his powers are likewise called into requisition to stay the storm. The rainmaker is found in various tribes in which but little evidence of the existence of other pretenders is met with, though reference is made by Father Juan Bautista, in a work published at Mexico, as early as the year 1600,[177] that –

There are magicians who call themselves *teciuhtlazque*, and also by the term *nanahualtin*, who conjure the clouds when there is danger of hail, so that the crops may not be injured. They can also make a stick look like a serpent, a mat like a centipede, a piece of stone like a scorpion, and similar deceptions. Others of these *nanahualtin* will transform themselves to all appearances (segun la aparencia), into a tiger, a dog, or a weasel. Others again will take the form of an owl, a cock, or a [151] weasel; and when one is preparing to seize them, they will appear now as a cock now as an owl, and again as a weasel. These call themselves *nanahualtin*.

In this connection it maybe said that the powers of both the juggler and the *wa'beno* of the Algonquian tribes appear to be combined. It is quite probable, however, that more specific distinctions might have been observed to exist between the two professions had more thorough investigation and careful discrimination been made, though this is always a difficult proceeding with shamans when attempted by ecclesiastics, the so-called agents of the *Kishä' Ma'nido* of a common enemy.

---

[176] Travels and Adventures (1760-1776), pp. 119-121, New York, 1809.

[177] Quoted from Brinton's Nagnalism, A Study in Native American Folk-Lore and History, in Proc. Am. Philosophical Soc., vol. xxxiii, p. 14, Philadelphia, 1884.

Spirit Lodge[178]

The Proto-Tsistsistas spirit lodge, as expressed in Tsistsistas {Cheyenne} time, was of four types: (1) the lodge where spirits were called for [59] information or advice regarding important matters; (2) the lodge where spirit allies were called before medicine hunts and from which they were released after the slain animals' spirits had been formally freed and sent away; (3) the lodge from which the *omotome* {immortal gift of breath} of the deceased were released after the conclusion of the secondary burial or where a *hematasowna* {soul} might be joined with an *omotome* to be kept temporarily by a person or persons of the family of the deceased; and (4) the lodge where a sick person was healed or where a person physically "dead" was revived by calling his *hematasooma,* already free, back into his body.

The wolf lodge of the Massaum must also be seen as a spirit lodge where the *maheyuno* {sacred guardians of universe} and *maiyun* {spirits} were called and where some spirits were joined with the physical forms of impersonators who played roles in me sacred drama.

The old Proto-Tsistsistas and Tsistsistas concept of the spirit lodge derives from the configuration of the sacred mountain (e.g., *Nowah'wus,* Bear Butte) that itself is a spirit lodge and that is associated with *maheonoxsz,* the sacred caves, and *heszevoxsz,* the underground caverns where the animal spirits reside.

Two Tsistsistas terms for the spirit lodge ritual are *nisimatozom* (from *nisimatoz,* "bringing a spirit ally," or "conjuring" a spirit helper, and *om,* "lodge") and *wxeeom* (from *mxee,* "apparition," "manifestation from the spirit world," and *om,* "lodge").

The first of the four types of spirit lodge performances listed has survived to the present. It is related, as is to be expected, to the "shaking tent rite" of other Algonquian groups (e.g., see Burgessc 1944; Cooper 1944; Flannery 1944), indicating a common origin.

In this *mxeewn,* the shaman causes spirits to come to the lodge and to express themselves there. In its most dramatic form, sketched later, the shaman places himself at the mercy of the spirits; without their swift intervention, he would not survive the ordeal. He neither becomes "possessed" nor ecstatic. He does not perform tricks and does not speak in voices, although his speech apparatus might be used by the spirits directly at other times. He does not send out from the spirit lodge forces of his *hematasooma,* as he would during game-calling ceremonies.

This ritual was conducted by a shaman following a request by a member or members of his group or, on the last day of the *Maxhoetonstov,* the Ceremony of the Sacred Arrows, as a regular feature integrated with the ceremony. There were many variations of this performance, all dependent on a specific shaman's style that in turn [60] was dependent on the spirits' tolerance. Reduced to essentials, the main events were the following:

A large lodge, the *mxeeom,* consisting of two or three regular tipi covers, was raised in the evening facing cast. Behind it a bundle of tall willows or saplings was tied to a pole on which offerings of cloth were exposed (compare the Evenk's *kamlanye* and *turu* pole with gifts of cloth outside the spirit lodge). Near dawn, at the end of the ritual, these offerings were distributed in camp. Because they had been touched by the spirits during the night they had acquired protective power.

---

[178] Karl Schlesier *The Wolves of Heaven ~ Cheyenne Shamanism, Ceremonies, and Prehistoric Origins.* U Oklahoma 1987.

Inside the lodge a fire was started after nightfall, and many witnesses assembled, sitting in a tight circle along the inner wall of the lodge. On the west side of the fireplace, a small buffalo-skin tipi was erected; sometimes, instead, a small sweat lodge was built there. A line of coals extended from the entrance of the buffalo tipi across the fire to the east entrance of the large lodge; on these, sweetgrass was burned all night. The shaman entered wearing a breechclout and moccasins; he was usually painted red.

He was tied barefoot within the packed circle of witnesses. He was tied with four bowstrings: each finger of each hand separately to the next finger, both hands tied together behind his back; each toe of each foot separately to the next toe; both feet tied together and tied securely to his bound hands. This operation was executed by sceptics who were called up and charged to tic the shaman as hard as their strength permitted. Their efforts were closely watched by the people present.

In a bent, inextricable position he was placed inside the buffalo tipi; sometimes, when no interior lodge was used he was tied to a tipi pole (Grinnell 1923, 2:113). A rope was tied around his neck and, extending through the pole frame of the buffalo tipi, was held by either four or eight men sitting next to it on opposite sides. A painted rattle and an eagle-bone whistle were placed near the shaman before the buffalo tipi was closed.

The fires had died down. The shaman sang one summoning song to call one of his spirit helpers. When he had ended, the assistants raised him inside the buffalo tipi by pulling hard on the rope. When the men dropped him he lay dead.

The helping spirit, traveling with the speed of thought, entered at the top of the *mxeeom* and rushed down to free and revive his shaman associate. The rope slackened. He came with the force of a whirlwind and caused the large lodge to vibrate violently. The whistle sounded, [61] the rattle bounced among the lodge poles, and lightning flashes lit the dark.

Then the spirit helper spoke. He identified himself by name. If he was the spirit self of a person who had died within the memory of persons present, he was recognized by voice. He answered questions and informed on missing persons or objects and predicted future events.

Some spirits who came were *maiyun;* some were celestial spirits. All of a shaman's spirit helpers could come one after another. All arrived with a terrifying display of power. Animal voices approached from below ground and from the night sky. The spirits left after the shaman, who sometimes had remained silent after the inviting songs, released them with a parting song. Their departure was as impressive as their arrival had been. The fire was started again, and the shaman left the buffalo tipi. The bowstrings with which he had been tied were found knotted into a ball, sometimes in an observer's clothing.

During the spirit lodge ritual of the 1908 *Maxhoetonstov*, as outlined by William Somers, a participant, to Truman Michelson (in Powell 1969, 2: 889-90), four inviting songs were sung nor by the shaman, Bull Thigh, but by "medicine people, both men and women." The spirits who were called were not Bull Thigh's spirit helpers but seven celestial spirits. They advised on tribal affairs and prophesied the Tsistsistas future. Bull Thigh, in this performance not permitted to call *on his* personal spirit allies, faced certain death by hanging in the small tipi if the first of the spirits had not responded quickly to the summoning calls of the medicine people.

The spirit lodge has remained an integral part of the *Maxhoetonstov* from *Motseyoef*'s {Sweet Medicine} original instruction of this ceremony to the present. *Motseyoef*, who was prominent in Proto-Tsistsistas and Tsistsistas history, was a famous spirit lodge conductor.

Some shamans, during a spirit lodge ritual or at other occasions, were able, with the aid of *maiyun* helpers, to dissolve physical form temporarily, thus making themselves invisible and, after moving their *hematasooma* to another location, to reconnect the two there. Castaneda (1979: 301-10) surprised readers by describing an action with a similar outcome in which he says he participated. Tsistsistas memory retains the names of persons who could perform such feats. Grinnell (1923, 2: 114-17) mentions Stone Forehead and Ice in this context, and publishes Ice's personal account and interpretation in full! (see also Curtis 1911: 123-24).

Tsistsistas lore also recounts many instances in which shamans [62] called on their spirit allies in emergencies in broad daylight, in view of many witnesses, and caused them to move objects, cover the Tsistsistas against enemies, or change weather conditions to hide people in flight.

CONURING AMONG THE KIOWA
DONALD COLLIER
Chicago Natural History Museum

RECENTLY several discussions have called attention to the occurrence of the conjuring complex in the Plains and the Plateau; and on the basis of the distribution in these areas of features of the complex, certain historical conclusions have been drawn.[179]

There seems to be no question of the historical connection between the western forms of conjuring and the conjuring or shaking tent ceremony of the northern Algonkians. In the latter, a shaman practices clairvoyance with the aid of supernatural helpers, such as Thunder, Turtle and Owl. These spirits are summoned to a specially constructed cylindrical lodge or booth and make their presence known by thumping and talking, by shaking the booth, and often by casting loose the ropes with which the shaman is bound. In the Plains, there are several variations from Woodland conjuring practices, such as the substitution of a miniature tipi or a curtain for the conjuring booth, and the invocation of human ghosts instead of animal spirits and other supernaturals.

Although there is no published reference to conjuring among [46] the Kiowa, this tribe possessed a full-fledged conjuring rite. following summary is drawn from the statements of two and two female informants gathered by the Laboratory anthropology field party to the Kiowa in 1935, of which the anthropology field party to the Kiowa in 1935, of which the writer was a member.[180]

Among the Kiowa, the owl played an important role in conjuring performances in which a shaman summoned the spirits of the dead. The owl, especially the horned owl, was powerful and greatly feared. Owls were thought to be souls of the dead. Owl-power was especially associated with sorcery, and owls were believed to be connected with evil whirlwinds that caused paralysis when blowing over sleeping persons. Owl shamans were particularly successful in curing various kinds of paralysis which came from whirlwinds, bewitching by owls, or owl sorcery perpetrated by another shaman. Some owl shamans could predict the future by interpreting the hooting of owls.

Only a few owl shamans possessed the special power required to summon spirits in a seance. A few women had this power, but it was held mostly by men.

The seance was held for the purpose of predicting the success of a war party, or to locate an enemy war party, to secure news of overdue warriors, or to find lost horses. The performance might be held on the initiative of the shaman or upon the request of a client, who offered a pipe to the shaman at the time the request was made. The rite was held at night in a darkened tipi. On the west side opposite the door was placed a miniature tipi one to three feet high. The spectators sat in the other part of the large tipi. At some performances it was necessary for them to lie face downward with heads covered. To peek was dangerous, for it would anger the spirit, who might

---

[179] 1 V.F. Ray, Historic Background of the Conjuring Complex in the Plateau and the Plains, in Language. Culture and Personality, pp. 204-216; A.I. Hallowell, The Role of Conjuring in Saulteaux Society, Pubs. Philadelphia Anthrop. Soc., Vol. II; M.W. Smith, Review of Hallowell, op. cit., American Anthropologist, Vol. 46, pp. 124-126.

[180] 2 Grateful acknowledgment is made to Dr. Alexander Lesser, leader of the party, and to William Bascom, Weston La Barre, Bernard Mishkin and Jane Richardson.

kill the offender, or at least throw dirt in his eyes. At other performances this precaution apparently was not necessary.

The shaman began by smoking and praying, sometimes [47] assisted by the singing of some old men. Presently a roaring was heard, the large tipi was shaken and filled with wind, then the small tipi vibrated. At this time drumming and singing were sometimes heard coming from the small tipi. The spirit of a dead person, often a renowned warrior or a shaman, came in the form of an owl. The flapping of wings was heard outside the smokehole; then the owl entered and fluttered outside the small tipi. From within the small tipi was heard the voice of the spirit asking why he had been summoned. At performances in which deer hooves and a whistle had been placed the firepit in advance, the spirit blew the whistle and rattled the hooves before speaking. The shaman asked who had come and the spirit replied with the name of some dead person. The shaman then smoked a pipe, offered the stem to the spirit to smoke, and put the question to him. The spirit might answer at once, or fly out of the tipi to return in half an hour or so with the answer. The spirit spoke in a high, muffled, nasal voice, and repeated everything twice.

At one seance, after the question had been answered, a woman spectator asked to speak to her dead brother. The owl, apparently acting as intermediary, consented and rushed from the tipi. Presently there was a surge of wind in the tipi and the spirit the woman's brother spoke. They carried on a brief conversation during which he mentioned that his world was a land of plenty and contentment. Then the spirit departed with the rush of wind.

Besides the Kiowa, the other western tribes reported to have practiced conjuring are the Cheyenne,[181] Gros Ventre,[182] Assiniboine,[183] Plains Cree,[184] Blackfoot,[185] Kutenai,[186] and Colville.[187] With respect to conjuring, the Kiowa affiliate most closely with the [48] northern Plains tribes, except the Cree, and the Kutenai. Thus the Kiowa share the importance of the owl in the rite with the Kutenai and Gros Ventre, the rattling of deer hooves spirits with the Kutenai, participation of ghosts in the séance with the Blackfoot and Gros Ventre,[188] and the use of a miniature tipi in place of the conjuring booth with the Blackfoot. These parallels offer some

---

[181] G.P. Grinnell, The Cheyenne Indians Vol. 2, pp. 112-117; Hallowell, *op. cit.*, p. 15, reports an unpublished account by E.A. Hoebel.

[182] A.L. Kroeber, Ethnology of the Gros Ventre, Anthrop. Paps. Am. Mus. Nat. Hist., Vol. 1, pp. 223, 276; J.M. Cooper, Field Notes (cited by Hallowell, *loc. cit.*).

[183] R.L. Lowie, The Assiniboine Anthrop. Paps. Am. Mus. Nat. Hist., Vol. 4, p. 49; E.T. Denig, Indian Tribes of the Upper Missouri, 46th An. Rep. Bur. Am. Ethnol., p. 492; D. Rodnick, The Fort Belknap Assiniboine, New Haven, 1938, pp. 54-55.

[184] D. Mandelbaum, The Plains Cree, Anthrop. Paps. Am. Mus. Vol. 37, pp. 261-262.

[185] J.M. Cooper, Field Notes (cited by Hallowell, *loc. cit.*); C. Denny, Blackfoot Magic, The Beaver, Sept. 1944, p. 15.

[186] V.F. Ray, *op. cit.*, pp. 207-208; H.H. Turney-High, Ethnography the Kutenai, Mems. Am. Anthrop. Ass., # 56, 1941, pp. 173-6.

[187] W. Cline, The Sinkaietk or Southern Okanagon of Washington, Series in Anthrop., # 6, pp. 152-153.

[188] Hallowell (The Spirits of the Dead in Saulteaux Life and Thought, J. Royal Anthrop. Inst., Vol. 70 pp. 42-44) has recorded the invocation of dead persons at conjuring performances among River Saulteaux.

confirmation of the Kiowa and Interior Salish tradition of the former northwestern habitat of the Kiowa. The Kiowa conjuring rite shows less specific resemblance to that of the Cheyenne, and even less to the Plains Cree seance.

Ray,[189] without being aware of the conjuring complex among the Kiowa and Blackfoot, postulated on the basis of trait distributions that the Plains Cree were the transmitters of the conjuring complex to the northwestern Plains and Plateau. It is evident that the materials on the conjuring complex in the Plains are still too fragmentary to permit a reliable historical reconstruction. But the accompanying table showing distribution of certain selected conjuring traits is suggestive. It seems to indicate that the diffusion of the complex in the Plains was no simple process, that there were crosslines of diffusion, and that probably some form of conjuring existed in the northern Plains before or at least independently of the advent of the [49] Plains Cree. It suggests also the probability that the Kutenai borrowed the complex from the Blackfoot[190] and/or the Kiowa rather than the Plains Cree. These suggestions will need to be tested by fuller data and against the broader historical problems of the northern Plains.

DISTRIBUTION OF SELECTED CONJURING TRAITS

	kt	bkf	kw	asb	gv	chy	pcr
Owl important	X		X		X		
Spirits of dead consulted		X	X		X		
Blanket curtain in place of conjuring booth	X	X			X		
Miniature tipi in place of conjuring booth		X	X				
Sweat lodge in place of conjuring booth				X*		X	
Conjuring booth							X
Shaking feature	X	X	X	?	X	X	X
Binding of medium	X	X		X	X	X	X
Bell rung by spirits		X		X			X
Deer hooves rattled by spirits	X		X				

kt = Kutenai, bkf = Blackfoot, kw = Kiowa, asb = Assiniboine, gv = Gros Ventre, chy = Cheyenne, pcr = Plains Cree

* According to Denig; Lowie's informant described it as a booth of buffalo hides draped around the branches of a tree trunk set into the ground in the center of the tipi (suggestive of the conjuring booth, but the shaman does not enter it).

---

[189] *Op. cit.*

[190] The present meager evidence hints at two forms of seance among the Blackfoot: (1) that recorded for the Piegan by Cooper, involving consultation of ghosts and use of a curtain in place of a booth (information on the binding feature is lacking); (2) that reported from the Canadian Blackfoot by Denny, involving binding of the shaman, use of miniature tipi, and bell ringing by the spirits. Both share the shaking feature. The bell feature is shared with the Plains Cree and Assiniboine.

THE SPIRIT WIGWAM AS DESCRIBED
BY TOMMIE MOAR, POINTE BLEUE
J. ALLAN BURGESSE
Arvida, P.Q.

TOMMIE MOAR who, at the time of writing (1943), is between sixty and seventy years of age, was born in the country to the north of lake Mistassini. His father was a half-breed employee of the Hudson's Bay Company. As a young man, Tommie moved to Mistassini where he entered the service of the great fur company as labourer and interpreter. He married Maggie Miller, half-breed daughter of the manager of the Mistassini Post.

About twenty-five or thirty years ago the Hudson's Bay Company transferred him to Pointe-Bleue and he was given charge of a small outpost from Pointe-Bleue, situated on lake Ashuapmouchuan. Tommie operated this post for a number of years as a Company servant but both he and his employers soon found that this arrangement was unsatisfactory. Accordingly, Moar took over the Ashuapmouchuan Post on his own account though the HBC gave him the necessary financial backing and purchased whatever furs he obtained. About eight years ago the post was abandoned and now Tommie is a pensioner of the Hudsons's Bay Company, resident at Pointe-Bleue. He speaks no French, the language of the region, and his English has a distinctly Scots flavour. He uses words and expressions which are rarely heard outside of the dales of Scotland and Northern England.

Tommie Moar described the spirit wigwam, which he claimed to have seen on several occasions, to the writer many times between 1932 and 1936. His story was also related, in the presence of the writer, to Dr. Julius E. Lips, then of Columbia University, who has used it in a number of published articles. [51]

While Moar had seen the rite several times among the Montagnais, the description given in the present paper appears to be chiefly of one which he saw as a boy in the region to the north of Mistassini.

According to Tommie, the spirit wigwam (Lac-St-Jean dialect: *GucaBitc^i G^{a}n*) is constructed of poles from three different varieties of tree. Some conjurers, indeed, use as many as five varieties but a really powerful shaman needs but three. These poles are thrust into the ground around the circumference of a circle, to a depth of from two to three feet. Their tips are then bent over towards the centre of the space thus enclosed and lashed together to form the framework of a very solid conical or hemispherical hut. Two hoops are affixed to the uprights, one just below the peak of the roof and the other at a height of three or four feet from the ground.

Formerly, the frame of the hut was covered with birchbark but Moar said that all those he had seen had been covered with ordinary Savannah or tent duck. An opening is left in the peak but the duck is well pegged down around the bottom.

The shaman takes no part whatsoever in the construction of the wigwam but he inspects it before entering. According to Tommie the conjurer enters the hut almost, if not entirely, naked, and this was confirmed by a number of Lac-St-Jean Montagnais who added that all religious objects – such as medals and scapulars – must be removed.

Once inside the wigwam, the shaman begins to chant and shake his rattle, the assembled tribesfolk joining in, accompanied by a drum. The chant begins slowly and softly, increasing in tempo and pitch to reach a climax when *MictaB^{i}o* manifests himself and the shaman is entranced. This phenomenon is accompanied by a number of peculiar noises which proceed from the interior of the wigwam. The sound of snowshoes in the snow; the thud of an axe biting into wood; the rasp and scraping of a paddle along the gunwales of a canoe, and the splash as it dips into the water; these and other familiar noises of the woods are heard to proceed from within the wigwam. After *MictaB^io* come the "little people" who are called *aBicilinutc* by [52] the Montagnais. Moar was not very clear as to the real purpose of these spirits but they would appear to furnish the comic relief. Their arrival is announced by fish, the paws of bear and other animals, the heads of beaver and smaller fur bearers which appear for an instant from beneath the canvas wall of the wigwam, only to disappear immediately. This part of the spectacle seems to have impressed Tommie Moar more than anything else. When he recounted it, he would shake his head and, pointing to his eyes, insist that he had seen it "with my own two eyes". He described how he had seen fish wriggling in the grass under the canvas wall of the wigwam. Their scales glistened in the sunlight, and this at a considerable distance from the water. The last of the spirits to arrive is the "flying man" (Lac-St-Jean dialect: *uBacDamaG^en*) and his coming is heralded by a swishing as of an arrow in flight.

The stage is now set. *MictaB^io* is the master of the wigwam and takes his place in the centre. The *aBicilinutc* play about on the ground at the canvas' edge and *uBacDamaG^en* is perched on the peak of the roof near the hole which has been left there to permit his ingress and exit. Questions are put to the unconscious shaman by the hunters clustered around the wigwam. As each request for information is expressed, *uBacDamaG^en* can be heard to shoot off from the top of the hut, returning a few instants later, presumably with the answer to the question. Replies to the hunters' questions are given in the voice of the shaman but Moar explained that it is really *MictaB^io* who speaks. Tommie could not furnish much information about the type of information furnished by *MictaB^io* on these occasions but he did remember that once he was present when a hunter asked for news of his family. He was informed that his wife had been seriously ill but had recovered. This news was proved to have been correct when the hunters returned to the post.

During the conjuring, the wigwam, so solidly constructed, can be seen to sway and shake as if moved by a giant hand. Tommie was quite emphatic that the shaman does not shake the wigwam himself, claiming that such a feat is quite beyond the capacity of an ordinary man. [53]

Sometimes, said Tommie, *MictaB^io*, *uBacDamaG^en* and the *aBicilinutc* are unruly and, when the time comes to finish the conjuring, the shaman has trouble in making them return to whence they come – though Tommie was far from clear as to where this place can be. However, he admitted that he had never heard of a conjurer who had failed to get rid of them. Nevertheless he insisted that the shaman is always greatly fatigued after an exhibition and must be assisted from the wigwam.

The last Spirit Wigwam to have been made at Pointe-Bleue – according to tradition – was made by one *Kakwa*, Mistassini hunter, who performed at the door of the church. The missionary, who is said by some to have been Fr. Georges Lemoine, O.M.I., and by others Fr. C.A. Arnaud, O.M.I, struck the wigwam with his pectoral crucifix and caused it to collapse about the ears of the shaman. *Kakwa*, so goes the tale, never again attempted to shake the wigwam.

Only one hunter now trading at Pointe-Bleue is said to be a shaman. He is *WesGijan*, the blue-jay, whose English name is Alex Blacksmith, and he is a member of the Mistassini band. None of the hunters of either the Mistassini or the Lac-St-Jean bands will admit to have seen him perform, and *WesGijan* will not talk.

Nowadays, the Lac-St-Jean Montagnais scoffs at the Spirit Wigwam but one cannot help but feel that he is not quite the sceptic he claims to be.

THE GROS VENTRE SHAKING TENT
REGINA FLANNERY
The Catholic University of America

ALTHOUGH the concept of the shaking tent is now known to be a widespread one, relatively few details are available on this rite as it was practiced in the Plains area. The following data, gathered among the Gros Ventres of Montana in 1940 from old and middle-aged informants who had often witnessed the performance, are offered in an attempt to fill in the picture as regards this one tribe.

When speaking English, the Gros Ventres refer to the rite as a "seance" and to the performer as a "spiritualist" inasmuch as it was carried out by a person who had access to the spirit of a deceased relative. The Gros Ventre word for spirit is *tsatsawâ•ᵃ*, which, incidentally, is the same word they now use for radio. The voice of the spirit can be heard, and, while the spirit cannot be seen, its presence is otherwise manifest by the noise of its activities. Among the latter we note especially the shaking of the tent as the spirit enters and leaves.

When information was desired regarding missing persons, the whereabouts of the enemy, etc., a spiritualist, who might be either a man or a woman, was asked to invoke the spirit over which he or she had control. The pertinent questions were asked and the spirit would supply the answers. There were two general methods of procedure. The so-called seance could be held either in the big dwelling lodge or in a small structure built for the occasion. Furthermore the performance was more or less elaborate, details differing according to circumstances, the individual spiritualist, and even the "personality" of the spirit invoked. But one invariable feature was the shaking of the tent.

The two accounts which follow will illustrate the general pattern as well as the differences in procedure. The first concerns a seance held in the winter at a time when this particular family [55] group was more or less permanently encamped. It was told by Mrs. Warrior, now a very old woman, as one of her childhood memories and was not elicited by questioning.

"Many, many years ago when I was a small girl, my father had gone on the warpath with several other men. When winter came, they hadn't returned. So my uncle (mother's brother) went to an old woman, Good Singer, who was known to be a spiritualist, although she was famous for other medicine powers as well. She consented and the seance was held in the lodge. My sister and I and our aunts and relatives were all there.

"A curtain was hung across the back part of the lodge and Good Singer was bound with ropes tightly knotted, then wrapped in a blanket so that only her head stuck out. She was behind the curtain and began to sing a certain song. She told us all to sing that song four times. I joined in the singing. When we finished we heard a humming sound and scraping and all kinds of noise through the opening at the top of the lodge. The top of the lodge began to shake and all at once we heard something slide from the top down behind the curtain where the old woman was, and land with a thump. That was her spirit, that is, the spirit of her son who had died long, long before.

"As soon as they heard the thump my uncle said: 'Here is the offering,' as he handed behind the curtain the pot containing a pup they had killed and cooked. We could hear the dishes rattling as the spirit ate. Soon all of the bones were picked clean and the spirit tossed them over the curtain so that they landed in our midst. The spirit then complained that they had tied his mother so tightly, and as he untied her we could hear the sound of the ropes as he worked at them. Then the ropes too came sailing over the top of the curtain. They were all knotted up in one bunch, and, try as they would, they couldn't unravel it.

"The spirit then complained again: 'Why did you tie my mother up so tightly?' and then asked: 'What did you call me for?' My uncle said: 'Well, I called you because these men went out on a war party and some, including Holy Weasel, didn't return. I want to know where they are and what became of them.' Then my uncle lighted a pipe and put it under the curtain. [56] When the spirit finished smoking he put the pipe outside the curtain and my uncle said: 'Well, I want you to hunt my brother-in-law to see where he is or what became of him.' Immediately the spirit made a noise and we could hear it going out of the top of the lodge which shook violently again. The people all sat quietly smoking and listening. Then old Good Singer called from behind the curtain: 'Sing again four times.' So they began to sing and I joined in. After the fourth repetition the spirit came back in the same way as it entered the first time, dropping down behind the curtain and landing with a thump. Every time the spirit goes in or out the top of the lodge shakes. Then the spirit made the exclamation which the Gros Ventres use to indicate that something terrible has happened, and continued: 'You should have told him [Holy Weasel] to stay at home. He and his party were killed. They were raiding the enemy and came across some Piegan. The latter made believe they were meeting the Gros Ventre in a friendly way, but when they got close they killed all the party except one who escaped.'

"Just before the spirit made this last speech, two little boys in the lodge had been playing during that ceremony and the spirit told them: 'Be quiet because I am going to tell you what happened.' And before they knew what happened to them these two little boys landed outside the lodge. The spirit must have pushed them out! And everybody was certainly quiet after that."

The second account will illustrate some differences in procedure when a spiritualist was consulted while a party was on the move and on the look-out for enemies. It was told to me by another old woman informant, Singer Sleeping Bear, incidentally to a long story of one of the journeys made by members of her father's group when she was a small girl.

"The party got as far as Canada and stayed all night. One of the men filled his pipe and took it over to another man, Rising Cross, and said: 'Now here. I am giving you the pipe. I want you to invite your spirit. I want you to ask your spirit if the road is clear (that is, if there is no enemy in sight).' Rising Cross took the pipe and prayed a few moments. The other men [57] made a small rounded lodge of willows, just like a sweat lodge. A few of them went in there with the spiritualist who just sat there with them as one of the group. He did, however, smoke the pipe and sing his song. Finally this little lodge shook so hard it almost fell over. It was like a terrible wind. Then a voice said: 'Yes, yes, what do you want?' Rising Cross said: 'Well, we want to know if the way is clear. We are looking for the enemy. How will the way be near where they are?' So the spirit said: 'Well, if you do as I say you are going to kill the chief (the father of a captive Piegan who had married among the Gros Ventres). Go up over the hill and you will see the plain just covered with lodges. If you don't turn back immediately after you kill that one man, you are going to have bad luck.'

"So the young fellows jumped on their fastest horses and went off. They found the situation as described by the spirit. The man whom the spirit mentioned was riding up the trail along the coulee accompanied only by a woman on horseback. When these two had gotten some distance from the lodges in the plain, the young Gros Ventre took after them and killed the man, but the woman wheeled her horse and sped back to the camp to give the alarm. The Gros Ventres said to one another: 'Now you know what the spirit told us. It told us to run just as soon as we killed him.' And the majority was in favor, but one man was obstinate. While they were arguing the enemies approached and were able to overtake most of them. Only a few escaped. It is always someone who doesn't believe the spirit who ruins the party."

That there might occasionally have been some room for doubting the validity of the information received through a particular spirit is suggested by a comment made by another informant, Al Chandler, a middle-aged man. He had mentioned an old woman spiritualist, David Man's grandmother, and said that she was honest about it and her spirit could be depended upon for the truth. He added, however: "But a man I knew used to hold seances and had his own brother as his spirit. This spirit always lied. When this brother was living he was a liar, so you couldn't expect his spirit to tell the truth!" [58]

As to the way in which the power was acquired, Al Chandler explained as follows: "It was customary to take some hair or a relic of a deceased relative after the body decays. (The Gros Ventres did not use to bury their dead like they do now.) Some would have a bone, others a whole lock of hair, and so on. Now if a person happens to take something the spirit likes, the spirit appears and asks: 'Why do you want that rib (or whatever part one takes)?' The man or woman might answer: 'I want you real near me and I want you to help me whenever I ask you.' That person gets in a kind of trance while the spirit takes to him that first time, and the spirit gives him a particular song which he must sing when he wants to invite the spirit. "

Apparently some leeway was allowed the individual in accepting the power, if the following can be taken as an indication.

"My adoptive father had the rib of an uncle of his who had been a medicine man of some kind. The spirit appeared to my father and asked: 'Why did you take that? What are you going to do with me?' My father replied: 'This is just for myself. I don't want to be the kind of person who owns spirits. If I need you myself I am going to call on you and I want you to help me, but I am not going to make you a public servant.' And that spirit did help him, personally, once or twice, but my father never got tied up in the ropes [as in the case reported by Mrs. Warrior]. By the way, the person who wants to find out something is the one that ties the spiritualist. He can tie the ropes as tight as he wants to and make as many knots as he pleases. The funny part of it is that it is just like the showmen with handcuffs, – the knots sometimes are still tied just like the person who wanted the information tied them originally, – although sometimes the spirit bunched the ropes all up in a mess. The whole tent shakes, too, and the skeptics look real hard, but the spirit will mock them by saying: 'Well, you need not look because you can't see anything anyway!'

"In conclusion I think we can say that the rite fits into the general ceremonial pattern of the Gros Ventres, but it was the only ceremony in which the shaking tent was involved. The [59] spiritualist, either man or woman, was approached in the same way as any other "medicine" or "holy" person when it was desired that they exercise their power. For this particular type of clairvoyance the power consisted in control over the spirit of a deceased relative, rather than some other kind of supernatural being. The spirit was invoked by a song learned from the spirit at the time the power was acquired, just as in other cases among the Gros Ventres the being bestowing power gave instructions as o procedure to the recipient. It is characteristic of the séance, however, that there was no set formula beyond the song and the questions could be framed by either the spiritualist or the seeker after information; while the answers were given by the spirit in ordinary language, understood by all, and the spirit made comments appropriate to the particular situation. Whether the regular lodge or a small separate structure were used, whether the Houdini trick was involved, and whether the spirit chose to eat or smoke, seem to be variable features which were employed according to instructions for carrying out the rite received by the individual spiritualist from the spirit along with the song.

THE SHAKNG TENT RITE AMONG PLAINS
AND FOREST ALGONQUIANS
Monsignor John M. Cooper
The Catholic University of America

THE purpose of the present paper is to bring together and make available some scattered field notes on the conjuring and " shaking tent " complex of northern North America, a subject that has recently evoked a good deal of discussion, particularly in the valuable interpretative monographs of Ray and Hallowell.[191]   The data to be presented are from the Algonquian-speaking Montagnais, Cree, Otcipwe, Blood-Blackfoot, and Gros Ventres (of Montana), and the Siouan-speaking Assiniboine. Only certain high-light features of the Montagnais, Cree, and Otcipwe rite will be mentioned; the complete field data gathered by the writer will be given in monographs to be published later. On the Blood-Blackfoot, Gros Ventres, and Assiniboine, my field data will be given here in full. Information obtained on the Blood-Blackfoot and Assiniboine shaking tent rite is very fragmentary. It was gotten under conditions that did not leave time or opportunity for detailed investigation. Leisurely field work on this item among these people would in all probability net a much ampler yield. Information on the Gros Ventre rite is much fuller, but, even so, is probably not exhaustive.

GROS VENTRE RITE

It was in 1931 during a very brief one-day reconnaissance visit to the Fort Belknap Reservation that the writer first heard of the shaking tent rite among the Gros Ventres, from a group [61] of men, including Stiff Arm, a noted Gros Ventre medicine man, who has since died. Only a few details were obtained: rite within a regular tepee with spectators present; the tying the performer with ropes, his escape therefrom, and after escape the ropes in a ball which could not be untied; the summoning of the spirit of the deceased relative by the performer; the shaking of the tent "as in a cyclone" when the spirit talking "from above " by the spirit; singing by the performer and by the others in the tepee. Later in August-September, 1939 and 1940, fuller information on the shaking tent rite was secured in connection with a general study of Gros Ventre society and religion, from The Boy and Thick, two of the older and best informed men among Gros Ventres. These fuller data here follow. Spiritual helpers among the Gros Ventres were of two kinds, ghosts of deceased persons and beings who had never been men. The latter, the ordinary guardian spirits, by far the more common, do not concern us here as they do not enter at all into the Gros Ventre shaking tent rite. Only ghosts so enter. A ghost helper, *tsatsawâ•'ᵃ* (-â- and superior a nasalized), was usually acquired in the following way. It was not sought by fasting and crying out on the hills, the customary procedure for acquiring non-ghostly guardian spirits and power. In fact there was either no quest of any kind or at most a somewhat indirect one. The usual sequence was as follows. A surviving relative would keep in his or her

---

[191]   V.F. Ray, Historic backgrounds of the conjuring complex in the Plateau and the Plains, in L. Spier et al., ed., Language, culture, and personality: Essays in memory of Edward Sapir, Menasha, Wis., 1941, 204-16, bibl. 215-16; A.L. Hallowell, The role of conjuring in Saulteaux society, Publ., Philadelphia anthropological society, v. 2, Phila., 1942, incl. bibl. pp. 89-96.

possession some memento or keepsake – something the deceased had prized greatly, some belonging such as a whip, or a tooth or bit of hair of the departed one. The keepsake was kept, not worn. It was kept not for the purpose of acquiring the ghost of the deceased relative (a father or other close relative), but solely or at least chiefly, so far as I could gather, out of regard for the departed. In most cases where such mementos were kept nothing happened. In some few cases, however, the keeping led to the acquisition of a ghost helper by the keeper. The first intimations the keeper had of the intentions of the deceased relative were knockings, or whistlings, or other kinds of disturbance around [62] where the memento was kept. After a while the ghost would come to the keeper, the surviving and talk to him (or her), telling his ghost helper, and finally putting him to sleep ("killing" him) and saying to him: "I shall be your *tsatsawâ•'a*.   In other words, it was the ghost, not the surviving relative, who regularly took the initiative and broke the ice. In face, the latter had little or no freedom to accept or refuse.

By the ghost the survivor in trance would be taught the procedure to use for summoning and dealing with the ghost, how to put incense in the smudge place in the person's own lodge, how to lay the pipe, the direction of stem and bowl, what kind of food to put out, and so forth. A key element in such teaching was a special song, given by the ghost to be sung in said rite. One such song, recorded by me in 1940 as sung by The Boy but not yet transcribed, a wordless song sung to the accompaniment of a drum, had belonged to a woman named "Woman." She had been taught it by the ghost of her deceased husband (or brother), *Wawathana'tca* * (*a*'s nasalized) "Bad-bad Bull." He had been a medicine man when still living, and this had been his "power" song. His ghost gave it to her both as the song to summon his ghost with and as a doctoring song. She had therefore both ghost-summoning and doctoring power.   While that old woman had both a ghost helper and doctoring power, the two things did not necessarily go together in the same person. One could have a ghost helper without having doctoring power, and vice versa. No one lacking a ghost helper could conduct the shaking tent rite, no matter how great power he had received by fasting and crying, and no matter what guardian spirit or spirits he had acquired. After her husband's death the above old woman had not married. People were a little afraid of her because she had this ghost helper. She was a capable old woman, with lots of horses; some of her breed of horses are still (1940) around. She died around 1907. [63]

Other songs, distinct from this summoning or shaking tent song, were also given and taught at times by ghost helpers. Two of them, both victory songs, were recorded as sung by The Boy in 1940. These two were given on occasions other than that which the surviving relative initially acquired his ghost helper.

After all the above teaching was concluded, the ghost of deceased relative belonged to the survivor and was supposed come whenever summoned by the latter in the manner the ghost told him while in trance to do. A great many Gros Ventre men and women had guardian spirits and "power" acquired by fasting and crying or otherwise. But fewer individuals, men and women, had ghost helpers. My informants in 1939 and 1940 could recall only four persons in the last two generations or last 70 years or so who had had ghost helpers.

In one case (see first of the two appended stories by Thick) two spirits tried to come to the shaking tent rite conducted by Woman, one bad and the other good, but whether the bad was one of her deceased relatives or not, she never knew. The people were under the impression that the bad one was an intruder who used to come first and try to "horn in" on the proceedings. No case of a given person clearly having more than ghost helper was recalled by my informants.

* Owing to delays and difficulties under present war conditions in obtaining symbols not in our

printer's stock *a* and *e* with a stroke above them are here printed in italic.

Ordinary "power" could be and often was transferred by the possessor to another person by donation or bequeathment. But a ghost helper never was so transferred and could not be.

It may be added that neither my informants, The Boy and Thick, nor my interpreter, Thomas Main, all highly intelligent and informed men, were at all sure of the etymology of the *tsatsawâ•'ᵃ*. The Boy thought it might connote the meaning "slave", "some one who is forced to do things." Thomas suggested a possible relationship to *tsatsa* -"coming, flight" plus -*wa*, an old Gros Ventre word, meaning unknown. The two words for ordinary ghosts as such are *tsa•kʳᵃ* (sing.; *tsa•k'an*: a's as u in English but), and *bie'teʳᵉ* (sing.; pl. *bi'eten*). *tsatsawâ•'ᵃ* is used exclusively for ghost helpers, not for an ordinary ghost, or ghosts in general. An ordinary medicine man called *nata'nhehi* (a's as u in but), but there was no special name [64] in use to designate those who had a ghost helper: of him or her it was merely said: "He (or she) has a *tsatsawâ•'ᵃ*.

Persons who had a ghost helper commanded great respect, and were bothered by no one. But capable medicine men on whom the people depended to doctor their sick were also greatly respected. My informants did not feel that either class of practioners as such had greater prestige than the other.

In the shaking tent rite, no other spirits than the given ghost had any part, and only the the one ghost ever had a part in a given performance. Neither guardian spirits, nor the Little Spirit, nor *Ba'a'*, nor the Supreme Being *iᶻtcibⁱnⁱa'tᵃ*; the *a* before *t* nasalized ã) enters into it in any manner. The summoned ghost came not from any of these or their abodes, but from *Basnaʳᵃbeʳᵉ*, the Big Sand, whither the souls of all Gros Ventre, except murderers of their own tribesmen, went after death and lived.

The function of the ghost helper was to give knowledge about past, present, future, or distant happenings, and counsel and direction in illness or danger. He imparted information. He did not as such grant power. Some of the many things he would be questioned about were: How a war expedition under way or an impending battle, or an illness, would come out? Where were the enemy located and what were their plans? Who had stolen a certain valuable article and where was it? He was not asked questions about trivial or silly matters, or about the fidelity or infidelity of a wife, although he sometimes volunteered information on such things. If some noted or loved person were critically ill, the ghost helper might be summoned and if it said: "His (the sick person's) soul is already over there," this meant he was going to die.

Where the services of one who had a ghost power were desired, the usual procedure was for the client or clients to go to him (or her) and offer him a pipe to smoke – this in accordance with general Gros Ventre practice in enlisting the aid of anyone with any kind of power. Those who had ghost helpers were commonly reluctant or even afraid to summon their helper; after the performance they felt tired and sore. If given a pipe to call the [65] ghost, they could not refuse, at least not easily. And if they accepted the pipe, they committed themselves definitely.

The summoning rite was performed only at night, with the fire out, regardless of the severity of the weather, and in darkness. In the two narratives by The Boy appended infra the helper spoke in the daytime, but had been summoned the preceding night. The rite was ordinarily performed in the performer's lodge, he being hidden out of sight of the clients or spectators behind a blanket-curtain hung up for this purpose to partition a segment of the lodge. Away from the camp, the rite was times performed in an emergency shelter or a sweat lodge. Before the rite, the clients got ready a pipe and tobacco, a puppy meat (an earlier Gros Ventre delicacy), and other food, and at the appointed time for the rite brought these to the lodge of the ghost-possessor.

The performer was then bound with thongs. The four fingers (thumb too?) of each hand were tied tightly together by interlacing them (somewhat after the technique of wrapped or twined basketry), the hands were tied behind the back, he was rolled in his blanket and tied around securely with thongs, with only his head protruding, and then was deposited behind the blanket partition out of sight of the spectators.

It appears to have been a common practice for the performer to challenge the most skeptical member of the party, and ask him to do the tying. Various stories of skeptics were narrated to me.

On one occasion when the main body of the Gros Ventres, at war with the Piegan (or Blackfoot), were camped on the east side of Judas River and a small band of them on the west side, the ghost helper of one of the Gros Ventres in the small band told them: "Tell the people to leave this small camp and go across the river to the big one, for the enemy is going to raid tonight." But many of the Gros Ventres of the small band said: "Ghosts are big liars. We are not cowards to run." Of the skeptics many remained, while about half crossed back to the big camp. About dawn, the enemy came as the ghost had predicted and nearly all who had remained at the small camp were massacred.

On another occasion when the Gros Ventres had (or were [66] about to have) a big battle with the Crows at Marias (at the junction of the Marias with the Missouri), a young man who was present at a ghost helper rite, with the fires out and pitch-darkness in the lodge, and who doubted that a ghost could come back, decided to experiment. When the ghost helper came and the noise was heard, the young man, who was sitting near the door in the darkness where no one else could see he was exposed, pushed his breechclout aside and exposed his genitals, saying to himself: "If this is really a ghost, he will see me and do something about it." All of a sudden the young man let out a yell as if hit by someone, and ran out of the lodge.   "You had better run. What is being done here is the real thing," said the ghost to the young fellow, and added to the crowd: "I hit that young fellow's genitals sharply with a stick; that is why he dashed out of the lodge." They then asked the young man: "Is that what happened?" And he replied: "Yes, He hit me good and hard there," and he became a believer.

This emphasis on skeptics in non-narrative and narrative accounts of the Gros Ventre shaking tent right would suggest that the rope-escaping feat, which we may call for short the "Houdini trick," had the purpose, overt and covert, of creating or confirming faith in the authenticity of the ghostly visitation.

The Houdini trick ordinarily formed part of the Gros Ventre shaking tent rite, but to judge from a couple of the stories appended to this paper, was not absolutely indispensable and could, in emergency, be omitted.

Right after being tied, the ghost-possessor to the accompaniment of his drum sang his summoning song which the ghost had given him. As the ghost helper approached the lodge, a whistling as of wind could be heard, and sometimes at least an owl call – owls and ghosts are closely associated in Gros Ventre thought, ghosts appearing or speaking as owls.   As the ghost came through the top of the lodge, the top would shake violently, and then the whole lodge would shake.

The ghost would then go to the performer and blow on him, and all the sinews and thongs would become untied, and they would be rolled in a ball so knotted and [67] tangled that it could not itself be easily unravelled and would so be thrown out at the spectators, or at the one who had done the tying, especially if he were a skeptic, with some such challenge to him from the ghost as: "You tied up this person. Now see if you can untangle this ball of thong."

Next the pipe would be lit and held up in the darkness in the direction where the ghost was supposed to be, for the ghost to smoke, and the spectators would see the pipe glow up rhythmically every time the ghost drew on it. The people in the lodge would finish smoking this pipe. After this the ghost would ask: "People, why did you send for me?" They would tell him what they wanted to know. If the ghost knew the answer offhand, he would answer at once. If he did not know, he would say "I don't know. I'll go and find out. You sing that song again [the one the ghost taught the performer when he first chose the latter; no other song was sung] and I'll come back and tell you."

As soon as the ghost went out, a little fire would be made, and the spectators had a smoke. Then they put out the fire and sang the ghost song. They would not have to wait long, "for a ghost travels just about as fast as a man thinks." On returning it would give the information that had been sought of it.

Most ghosts talked a whistling talk. But some – those possessed by Plenty-dry-meat-old-man and by Morning-star, two old men whose ghost helpers were among the greatest ones remembered and whose prophecies always came true – talked in a natural voice.

After the ghost helper had given the information desired (perhaps earlier, after his smoke at the beginning; I could clear up the point) he was offered the food that had been prepared. And the spectators, still in the dark, would hear the tapping of the ghost's fingernails on the plate or other sound of eating as the ghost partook of some of the food.

When he had finished eating, he would say something like: "If you are done with me, I shall go," and he would depart by way of the top of the tent, which would shake violently as it done when the ghost first arrived in it. After the ghost helper had taken his final departure, the performer would come out [68] from behind the blanketed enclosure, the fire would be re-lighted, performer would say the prayer customary among the Gros Ventres before all meals to the Supreme Spirit and other beings, then he or she and the others present would eat the food that had remained from the ghost's repast. Finally they would all sit around smoking and chatting a while before dispersing. I failed to gather any information on whether the performer receives any payment or not for his or her services in the rite.

Certain simplifications of the above procedure under emergency conditions as on war expeditions are noted or intimated in a couple of the following four narratives, the first two given by The Boy, the last two by Thick.

NARRATIVE 1

The following story was told by The Boy.

"A certain man had his deceased father as his ghost helper. The ghost helper used to speak Gros Ventre but in a bass voice. Everybody understood when they heard him.

"On one occasion the Gros Ventre tribe were camped near the forks of the Teton and Marias Rivers. While there a large group of the men decided to go on the warpath. So they left the main camp, went up the Missouri River and camped that first night at the mouth of Crow Creek where it empties into the Missouri River. When it was dark that night some of the men said: 'Let's offer the pipe to X [the one mentioned above who had the ghost helper; name not given] and ask him to find out whether our prospects on this war party are good or bad.' So they filled up a pipe and went to X, held out the pipe to him and asked him: 'Accept the pipe and call your spirit.'

"X accepted willingly and soon after they had smoked the pipe together they made a shelter where X was to do the spirit-rite. So they tied up X, filled the pipe again, put it there and sang a song four times. When they were singing it the fourth time they heard a voice in the air. The ghost helper arrived and the shelter shook as a lodge would have done in the same rite. When the spirit hit the ground, the ground shook too. The spirit [69] seemed excited and kept repeating: 'What do you want, my children?' and added: 'If you were in my place and were and feeble as I am, you wouldn't like to be disturbed. But here I am. What do you want?' They answered: 'We want to how this venture of ours is going to turn out, – well or badly.' Then they lit the pipe and offered it to the spirit and they could see from the rhythmic glaring of the pipe that the ghost helper was smoking. After he had smoked he replied: 'Well, know offhand. I'll have to look around and investigate. I am going away to look around. While I am gone you smoke and after a while sing again and I'll come back.' The ghost helper went away with a noise and commotion as always.

"They sat around and smoked and after a while sang again. The ghost helper came back blowing as if catching his breath, as an old man does, and said: 'My children, Crow Indians without number are invading the camp you just left. Knowing you are away they are so bold that they are peeping into the lodges at your women and watching them playing the hand game. Your women are in happy mood. These Crow Indians seem be preparing to take all the Gros Ventre horses. I shall go back and watch to see what they will do. Meanwhile you do as you did before: sit around and smoke and then sing. I'll come and make a final report.' And so they talked and smoked sang.

"Then the ghost helper came back bringing with him one hair from the head of a Crow. This was not a scalp but was only a hair representing a scalp and was wrapped around a piece of sagebrush. It was brought to convince the Gros Ventres there was no danger. Then the ghost helper reported: 'The Crows have taken practically all your horses and about sun-up will arrive where you now are. You need have no fear of the Crows provided you do just one thing. Be sure to kill the Crow with the blue blanket coat (with hood). He is the one brave man in the crowd. Kill him first and you will kill all the others. None of the Gros Ventres will be actually killed, but two of them will be wounded. In case you do not kill the Crow with the blue coat the outcome of the battle will be doubtful. But if you kill the [70] Crow with the blue coat you will kill all the Crows and get your horses back.' The Gros Ventres asked the ghost helper which two of their party would be wounded, but were not told by the ghost helper. If they had been told they would not have let these two go into battle.

"By the time they were through with the spirit it was near daylight. So they decided not to go to sleep but to wait up the rest of the night. [Here followed a long detailed description of the battle with the Crows beginning around daylight. The Crow with the blue coat escaped. Of the sixty Crows in all, forty were killed. No Gros Ventre were killed, but two were wounded – two members of my own [The Boy's] clan. While the party was still at the war main camp, some distance from the main camp, the ghost helper came and said: "I came to hear the news. Did you kill the man with the blue coat?' They answered: 'No.' The ghost helper said: 'It is your own fault. If you had, you would have killed all the Crows. But anyhow you did well and have done yourselves credit. I am going to teach you a victory song so you can sing it when you get back to camp'." So he taught them this victory song[192] and they learned it and he said to them:

---

[192] 2 This song as sung by The Boy was recorded in the field in 1940, together with about 120

'Well, my children, I am going home. When I get back to my place of abode I will celebrate that victory too. I will give you charcoal [it was the custom for returning victors to paint themselves black] and I'll bring charcoal to my own land and celebrate.'

"The foregoing incident happened in the time of my [The Boy's] grandfather, Crow Moccasin."

NARRATIVE 2

The story which here follows was also told by The Boy.

"The Gros Ventres were camped east of (the site of) Lewistown (south of the Missouri River). A party of Gros Ventre warriors left the camp to go on the warpath against the Sioux. One of this Gros Ventre party was known to have a ghost helper. [71] The party traveled north and when they arrived at the river they camped there. Some of the men said: 'Morning-star-appears (or Morning-star-is-up: the man with the ghost helper) should be approached to find out what our prospects are on this expedition.' It was agreed among themselves that they make a sweat lodge.

"Among those invited to sweat was Morning-star-appears. While they were sweating they offered the pipe to him to get him to call his helper. He agreed. Then they all smoked and got ready in the sweat lodge.

"The ghost helper came to the sweat lodge for the possessor right there. Just before the helper alighted he whistled violently and rapidly. Then the sweat lodge shook and they heard ghost helper say: 'What do you want? Why did you call me?' They said: 'We are going on the warpath after the Sioux. What success will we have? Is there any danger?' So they offered the lighted pipe to the ghost helper and saw it smoked by him. After smoking, the ghost helper said: 'I'll go and see first before I answer. You go ahead and smoke and after a while sing again.' This they did.

"The ghost helper came back in the usual way, and highly elated, and said: 'All right, I am ready to tell you. First here is a strand of hair of a man (a Sioux) whom you will kill tomorrow. This represents his scalp.' It was wrapped around sagebrush. He continued: 'I have found a big Sioux camp on Beaver Creek [east of the Little Rocky Mountains]. The Sioux are having a big Grass Dance. The one who is having the most fun is the one you are to kill tomorrow. He is a handsome man and has a sword. You will capture that sword when you kill him. Don't be afraid. No Gros Ventre will be killed but two of you Gros Ventres don't look good to me.' They said to the ghost helper: 'Name the two.' But he refused to do so, saying: 'Just don't be afraid. Go ahead to the place where the Sioux are and attack them. Choose now what kind of weather you wish after the fight tomorrow, and I will see that the weather will be that way.' They failed, however, to make a choice. The ghost helper also said: 'Every once in a while tomorrow take [72] a look at the sun. There will be all kinds of sun dogs tomorrow, changing every little while. When they appear you will know that I have told you the truth.'

"Then the ghost helper left and they Gros Ventre slept until early morning. [Here followed a long description by The Boy of the battle.] Just one Sioux was killed in the battle, a very handsome man with a sword, as the ghost helper had predicted. Likewise they saw the

---

other Gros Ventre songs, but I have not found it possible, as yet, to get any of the records transcribed for publication.

sundogs changing. The Gros Ventre, however, after this first skirmish realized that the Sioux would soon get reorganized and that their own situation was perilous. So they called on Morning-star-appears to cause such weather that the Sioux could not catch them. He sang his song, using his robe as a cover in which to enclose himself, and said: 'We wish rain.' At once a cloud appeared and in short time grew into a great black storm cloud; then came a perfect cloudburst, with thunder and lightning, in which you couldn't see any distance. Under this cover the Gros Ventre escaped from the pursuing Sioux and got back to safely with no loss of life, although two of their number had had narrow escapes, just as the ghost helper had said: 'Two of you do not look good to me.'

"The above occurred in Stiff Arm's time, when he was a young man. The man who killed the Sioux was Crazy Bull. I do not recall the name of the ghost helper, but this same ghost helper on this occasion taught the Gros Gros Ventre a song to use in their celebration after the victory."[193]

NARRATIVE 3

The following two stories were told me by Thick.

"A certain old woman (her great-great-grandchild is still living) had a ghost helper. Her name was 'Woman' but for various reasons she was nicknamed 'Bear Old Woman.' When I was about ten years old a party of Gros Ventres was camped at Lodge Pole, about two miles from the Little Rocky Mountains. One night Cree enemies came and stole all the Gros [73] Ventres' horses except those belonging to one man. This man loaned out his horses as far as they would go around to four of the Gros Ventres who went in pursuit of the Cree.

"Then that evening two of the other men, one of them my father, approached Bear Old Woman. They filled up a pipe just as you do when you go to someone to doctor you, offered it to the old woman, and asked her to find out from her ghost helper who stole the horses and where they were. Bear Old Woman, who had quite a temper, got angry right away as usual and pushed the pipe away as a sign of refusal. Finally one of the fellows there, a relative of hers, said: 'Well, let me smoke it' to force her to accept. She angrily grabbed the pipe and had through with the rite. When she took the pipe she rubbed hands on the ground and rubbed dust on the pipe and offered a prayer before smoking. The pipe was then smoked by her and by the two men who had approached her.

"Then they began to get things ready. They killed a puppy, singed its hair off at a fire, took its insides out without skinning, quartered it up and boiled it. They put the boiled meat on a plate and got ready some other kinds of food to give to the old woman. Then the two men filled up a pipe and they together with two other men and with a 'servant' went to Bear Old Woman's lodge. On arriving there they set down the plate of dog meat near the head of her bed, the pipe between the incense hearth and the lodge fire, and the other dishes between the lodge fire and the door.

---

[193] 3 This song as sung by The Boy was recorded in 1940.

"When everything was arranged and Bear Old Woman was still sitting on her bed, she said: 'Whoever is the greatest unbeliever among you, come and tie me up.' One of the four volunteered. Then the old woman got up and went to a place just south of the head of the bed, to a little enclosure made by hanging up a blanket. He hobbled her four fingers (thumb too?) with sinew, interlacing it in and out of the four fingers of each hand. Then he tied her hands together behind her back and also hobbled her feet. She was lying on a robe. He gathered the robe around her and tied her with rawhide thongs until only her head stuck out of the robe. And so he left her lying on her [74] back. He returned to his place woman and sat down.

"Then Bear Old Woman said: 'All right. Start to sing now.' They sang four times without stopping, the song belonging to the old woman's ghost helper. As they were singing the third time they heard an owl and the old woman said: 'Don't receive *that* spirit. He is bad. Continue singing.' So they continued and just as they finished the fourth time the old woman said: 'That is the one. Receive *that* spirit.' The people around heard these two owls.

"When the second owl lighted on top of the lodge, the top shook and the ghost helper spoke: 'What do you want me for?' They said: 'We want you to tell us where our horses are and who has them so we can find them.' The ghost helper answered: 'All right. I'll have to go look for them, but you go ahead and smoke this pipe [the one lying near the incense hearth]. When you have smoked up what is in the pipe, refill it and put it back in the same place and wait.'

"They had barely started smoking when the ghost helper was back again. So they just dumped out what was left in the pipe and refilled it. The helper said: 'Never mind. I am hungry and want to eat.' But they didn't mind him. The spirit then said: 'Your horses are not very far away from here. Your four friends have already recaptured your horses and are bringing them back.' He also said to my father: 'One of your horses has a thick broad rawhide rope around his neck and is dragging it, and that other man's mare's colt will play out on the trip back home.'

"After the helper had said all this, the four men judged that he was through, so they took the pipe and lit it and offered the helper a smoke. The inside of the old woman's lodge was dark as there was no fire. The helper took the pipe from their hands and then they saw it light up rhythmically as a pipe does when it is puffed, and after taking a few puffs the helper said to the men: 'You smoke the rest. I am hungry and want to eat.' They could hear him chewing on the dog meat inside where the woman was. After a while the helper said to the men: 'Here [75] You can eat the rest of this pup.' The meat had been eaten off of one hind leg of the pup so that just the bones were left. Then the ghost helper said: 'I see this foolish old woman here lying helpless.' Then they heard a noise as if the helper had struck the old woman with the flat of his hand and he was heard blowing. The next instant the ghost helper said: 'Here, try to untie this,' and the knotted sinew and rawhide thong hit the chest of the man who had tied her up.

"Then they heard the old woman give a long sigh. She had been in a trance all this time and was just coming out of it. Next the ghost helper said: 'Now I am going to leave you.' And they heard the same racket at the top of the lodge they had heard when he first came in and there was a violent shaking of the whole lodge, especially at the top of it.

"After the ghost helper was gone they kindled the fire again and there was light. Bear Old Woman came out of the enclosure and sat down on the bed and prayed with the bowls of food in her hand. Then she and the men ate and afterwards sat around and smoked and chatted. Then the men went home and told what the spirit had said.

"Next morning all the people in the camp, including the children, got up early and went up on the highest nearby ground to look for the four men coming back with the horses. Towards evening of the day the four Gros Ventres who had gone in pursuit of the thieves brought all the horses back, except the one which, as the spirit had said, had played out and could not stand the trip back. And one of my father's horses had a rope around its neck as the ghost helper had said it had. The pursuers had caught up with the Cree and surprised them asleep in a little swamp covered with grass and brush and so took the horses back home. On the return trip they got lost in a bad storm, went the wrong direction and not until daylight did they discover their mistake and so had to circle their way back. They had neither eaten nor slept during all the two days and night they had been gone.

"The above incident occurred just at about the time when the buffalo disappeared from this part of the country [1880's] [76]

NARRATIVE 4

Here is the second story told by Thick.

"There was a man by the name of Bird Child who had a ghost helper helper. Bird Child's wife had four brothers, one of them my father. One evening they filled a pipe and went to Bird Child's lodge to get him to find out from his ghost helper where there would be lots of buffalo and no danger, so they could go there and hunt. When they arrived at Bird Child's lodge they found him absent and only his wife in the lodge. Without invitation, they made themselves at home and asked their sister where Bird Child was. She answered: 'I don't know where he is nor when he will be back.'

"Being Bird Child's brothers-in-law they decided to take the liberty of using Bird Child's power and ghost helper, and of having a seance in his absence. They asked their sister where Bird Child's bundle was. She showed them. One of the four brothers took it down. They then agreed who was to be tied up and to represent Bird Child. The one of the four designated agreed. They had him lie down and two of them tied him up tight and laid him in an enclosure made along the side of the tent [as in preceding story]. They were half-fooling, not quite serious. Their sister couldn't say anything: they imposed on her. They even attached the man's hair to the ropes with which they bound him in the robe until only his mouth was visible.

"Then they started to sing and sang the same song four times without stopping. At the end they heard yelling in the air and said: 'There he is. He has come for us.' As the ghost helper arrived the tent shook and the helper said: 'Who's that lying back there?' and answered himself: 'Some crazy man or someone with no regard for anybody's rights.' Then they heard a commotion behind the enclosure. The bound brother started to hollow [holler] for mercy. Next one of the brothers who had done the tying got hit with all the ropes tangled in a knot.

"Then they heard the bound man being thrown towards the door, and saying: 'Hurry up and make a light before this ghost helper kills me.' The spirit had picked him up and was [77] trying to wedge him between the poles in the lodge. By this time, however, the other brothers had kindled a fire and of course as the flame flared up the spirit was gone. The ghost helper was good and mad, but anyhow had come."

BLACKFOOT-BLOOD RITE

On a casual visit to Browning, Montana, in August, 1931, writer was given some information by Mrs. Frances (Joseph) Brown of Browning on the Blackfoot shaking tent rite. The rite is performed by a woman who is a sort of "spiritualist" or medium," as Mrs. Brown put it. She summons the dead spirits [spirit?] and they come and answer questions. Only she can understand the language of the dead spirits and can converse with them. She tells their answers to the other people who are around. During the rite, people are all around in the tipi. A curtain is put over a part of the interior of the tipi, and the "medium" sits behind the curtain. The lights are extinguished. Food is put on a plate. During the rite noises are heard "inside" [apparently behind the curtain], and everything moves, including the tent itself. It was emphasized to me that this rite is an old Indian one, not a modern intrusion of white spiritualistic seances.

While talking with The Boy (Gros Ventre) in August 1940 about the Gros Ventre ghost helper complex, he told me the following story that his friend, Platted Hair, a Blood from Canada, had told him on a visit to him some time before:

A long time ago, before the Gros Ventres came and when the Snakes still occupied this part of the country, a large party of Bloods came over toward the Little Rockies and never returned to their home country. Their people at home did not know what to make of it. One of the Bloods in the home camp had a ghost helper. So they gave this Blood a pipe to summon his ghost helper. When the ghost arrived, he asked: "Why did you send for me?" They said: "Our young men went on a war party and did not return. What has happened to them?" The ghost said: "I'll go and see. You may sing the song. I'll come back and I may be able to tell you what has happened." So the [78] ghost went away. They waited and sang the song. When the ghost came back, they asked him: "What did you find out?" He replied: "I went clear to the Little Rockies and the Bear Paws. Between the two ranges, a creek makes a big bend, and in the middle of the big bend is a ridge. There your young men got killed."

When some years ago, The Boy told me, the road between Hays (at the foot of the Little Rockies) and Three Buttes was being built, on a ridge several holes were found in the rocks, and in one of the holes five skulls, as if a fight had occurred there. Platted Hair believed this to have been the scene of the above fight.

We may add that there has been a great deal of close association between the Gros Ventres and the Blackfoot-Blood-Piegan, especially in recent generations.

ASSINIBOINE RITE

The writer's first information on the shaking tent rite among the Assiniboine of Fort Belknap Reservation (which they have long shared with the Gros Ventres) came as a casual afterthought from a Gros Ventre {source} ~~informant~~ in 1931. After giving the summary account of the Gros Ventre rite recorded earlier in this article, he added that the same rite is also found among the Fort Belknap Assiniboine. In the summer of 1940, my chief Gros Ventre {source} ~~informant~~, The Boy, stated that the Fort Belknap Assiniboine also had the ghost helper concept. In the case of one ghost-possessor at least, there were bells on top [or at the top] of his lodge, and when the ghost helper came, the bells would shake and the whole top of the lodge would shake. This possessor's name was "Standing Dog," or "Dog Rises," or a similar name. One ghost is credited with having thrown a performer on top of the lodge frame. Further details were not known by The Boy, and I had no good opportunity to consult the Assiniboine themselves.

MONTAGNAIS-CREE-OTCIPWE RITE

The "shaking tent" rite is universal or practically so among [79] the Montagnais, Cree and Otcipwe. Most of the frequent records in the literature have been assembled by Ray and

Hallowell.[194] I have field records of its occurrence among the following:

(a) Montagnais: Whale River, Fort George, Eastmain, Nemiskaw, Neoskweskaw, Rupert House, Waswanipi, Mistassini; (b) Cree: (1) Eastern forest Cree: Têtes de Boule, Kesagami, Moose Factory, Albany, Cape Henrietta; (2) Western forest Cree: Ft. Chipewyan (Lake Athabaska), Ft. McMurray (Athabaska River); (3) Plains Cree: Rocky Boy (Montana); (c) Otcipwe(-Algonkin): Lake Abitibi, Wikwemikong (Manitoulin Island), Rainy Lake, Lake of the Woods, English River (affluent of Albany R.), Ft. Hope (upper Albany R.), Osnaburgh (ibid.).

In the 16 of the above 23 bands for which dependable data were secured regarding the type of tent used in the rite (relevant data on this point were not secured for Whale River, Eastmain, Mistassini, Wikwemikong, English River, Rainy Lake, McMurray), the tent was one specially constructed, not a regular dwelling lodge or a partitioned section thereof. In all 16 cases this tent was cylindrical or barrel-shaped or "vertical," – not bee-hive or low-domed shaped as sweat lodges usually are, nor strictly conical like tipis.

The chief spirit {source} ~~informant~~ or spokesman among the many spirits or beings who customarily come into the tent during the rite was:

(a) *Mista'beo* (*Micta'beo*), among the Montagnais of Eastmain, Rupert House, Waswanipi and Mistassini; (b) *Mi'kenak*, the turtle, among the Cree of Albany, Moose Factory, Kesagami, and Ft. Chipewyan (at this last place, *Mi'skenak*), and among the Otcipwe(-Algonkin) of English River, Lake of the Woods and Rainy Lake; *Oki'jiko*, among the Cree-speaking Têtes-de-Boule (also pl. *okijikouk*), and the Otcipwe(-Algonkin) Abitibi (as pl. *kijikuki*).[195] Mikenak was definitely denied among both [80] the Têtes-de-Boule and the Abitibi. *Mikenak*, an Otcipwe(-Algonkin) form, among the above listed Cree groups points to diffusion of the name, – not necessarily of this particular spokesman, as is evidenced by the Ft. Chipewyan *Miskenak*. *Mista'beo*, as spokesman among the above listed Montagnais band, is an independent non-human being or spirit, not a man's "other self" or kind of soul.

The "Houdini trick," in which the shaking tent performer escapes from the thongs with which he is tied, was found among the Cree of Ft. Chipewyan, McMurray, and Rocky Boy, the Otcipwe of Lake of the Woods, and the Otcipwe (-Algonkin) of Abitibi. This Abitibi occurrence marks the farthest eastern extension found by me of the trick in connection with the shaking tent.[196] I did not learn of its use among the Otcipwe of the upper Albany River at Ft. Hope and

---

[194] 4 Ray, 1941; Hallowell, 1942. See footnote 1.

[195] Cf. Paul Le Jeune, Relation of 1634 Thwaites JR, 6: 162, *khichikouai*, " genii of the air " or " genii of light, " who came into the Montagnais' shaking tent; ibid., 7: 100, *khichicouakhi*; same, Relation of 1637, JR, 11: 254, *ka-khichigou klietikhi*, "those who make the light," and *khichi-koueklihi*.

[196] Father R. Déléage, O.M.I., Letter of Nov. 1, 1863, in Rapport sur les missions du dicése de Quebec, Mar., 1864, # 16, pp. 74-75, reported the "Houdini trick" in connection with the shaking tent rite among, apparently, Grand Lake Victoria Otcipwe(-Algonkin)-speakers.

Osnaburgh, though fairly extensive information on the shaking tent rite was obtained at these two localities in 1927. The "Houdini trick" is definitely lacking among the James Bay Cree, the Têtes-de-Boule, and the Montagnais groups studied.[197]

Some further general and specific characteristics of the Montagnais-Cree-Otcipwe shaking tent rite will be given in the next section of the present paper.

GENERALIZATIONS

The following generalizations are based partly on the fore-going data, partly on the writer's still unpublished fuller field notes on the Montagnais, Cree, and Otcipwe(-Algonkin).

Certain characters are common to the rite as practised both among the forest Montagnais-Cree-Otcipwe and Plains Cree and among the Gros Ventres and – so far as our fragmentary [81] information goes – the Blackfoot-Blood and Ft. Belknap Assiniboine. These common features are: shaking of the top of the tent or lodge at entrance and departure of spirit; entrance and departure of spirit by way of top of lodge; departure, during rite, of spirit after being questioned, to find facts, and subsequent return to tent with desired answer; performer not possessed by spirit, but spirit(s) speak(s) to or in presence of performer; performer concealed from sight of spectators and clients during visitation by spirit(s); no trance or ecstasy by performer, and performers not of psychopathic personality as such; spirits summoned primarily to obtain through them knowledge, chiefly knowledge hidden by barriers of time (future) and space (distance), or counsel on practical problems; a smoke given the spirit(s), and spectators smoke; absence of direct participation of Supreme Being in rite (apart from a minor exception or two); rite as such concerned with personal beings, not with impersonal forces, and thus a religious, not a magical rite (as many define religion and magic).

In certain features, the rite among the forest Montagnais-Cree-Otcipwe and Plains Cree consistently differs from that among the Gros Ventre, Blackfoot-Blood and Ft. Belknap Assiniboine. In the rite as found among the former: while one the spirits is usually the chief informant or spokesman, other spirits and beings ordinarily come into the tent during the rite; all these spirits and beings are animistic, not manistic – never ghosts; humor, joking, trivial banter by the visiting spirit common; the "Houdini trick " absent from Montagnais and eastern Cree rite; food is not offered to the visiting beings.

On the other hand, in the rite as found among the Gros Ventres and, so far as our limited information goes, the Blackfoot-Blood and Ft. Belknap Assiniboine: one spirit only comes into the tent; the spirit that is summoned is exclusively a ghost, a deceased relative of the performer; humor, joking, trivial banter by ghost are lacking; the "Houdini trick" is customary, except in emergency; food, especially the delicacy, puppy meat, is offered to and partaken of by visiting ghost. So far as my information goes, among the above [82] Montagnais-Cree-Otcipwe, the power to summon the shaking tens spirit(s) is not thrust upon the person by any spirit, as it is among the Gros Ventres.

In general, the shaking tent appears to have much more relative importance and to play a much more preponderant role in the total magico-religious life than of the Montagnais-Cree-Otcipwe than of the Gros Ventres, Blackfoot, and Assiniboine.

That there is a historical relationship between the two above contrasted shaking tent complexes appears very probably from the many specific and distinctive elements they share in common and from the almost continuous geographical distribution of the complexes, a distribution moreover predominantly among the main body of Algonquian-speaking peoples of the taiga and adjacent open country and the aberrant-Algonquian-speaking groups of the Plains, the Gros Ventre , the Blackfoot, and the Cheyenne.

---

[197] It was earlier reported among the Cree of York Factory, by Thomas M'Keevor, A voyage to Hudson's Bay during the summer of 1812, London, 1819: 58.

ADDENDUM ON WIDER DISTRIBUTION

It has not been the purpose of the present paper to deal with the total distribution of the shaking tent rite and with the historical problems connected with such distribution. The following summary notes are added merely to contribute a mite toward filling out the picture of distribution as given in Ray's historical study and Hallowell's socio-psychological one.[198]

In the east, the shaking tent is not reported in our published sources, to my knowledge, south of the St. Lawrence. The record by Maurault for the Abnaki does not mention shaking of the conjurer's tent.[199] Inquiries by the writer in the field in 1931 among the Chipewyan and Dogrib of the Mackenzie-Slave watershed brought consistently negative results; in fact informants who knew well and gave many details of the rite as practised among the Cree of Ft. McMurray (Athabaska R.) and Ft. Chipewyan (L. Athabaska), on the Cree-Chipewyan borderline, and who were equally familiar with both Cree and Chipewyan [83] culture, emphasized that the shaking tent rite was practised the Cree only, and not by the Chipewyan, even in these areas when the two peoples were in very close contact and association.

To the far north, however, the "Houdini trick" and the shaking of the conjurer's hut on the arrival of his spiritual helper was earlier reported by Boas among the Central Eskimos.[200] Lowie has also recorded among the Crow a tent-shaking rite very like that of the Gros Ventres and Cheyenne.[201] The first report and discussion, by Donald Collier, of the Kiowa occurrence is published in the present issue of *Primitive Man*. Regina Flannery has called my attention to the occurrence of the shaking-of-the-tent motif among the early {Alabama} Creek.[202]

Still farther afield, I have come across no reference to a tent element in the many accounts of northern Asiatic {Saami} Lapp shamanism, but have made no thorough systematic search. In South America, I know of only one instance of a somewhat similar rite, that earlier reported among the Chiquitoan Manasi of eastern Bolivia. Part of the large public assembly hall was curtained off with mats, which part was reserved for the "high priest" alone and the visiting spirits. As the gods or spirits came down, a sound filled the air and shook the roof building and the mats. Chicha and food were offered the spirits. The people sang. The gods were consulted by the " high priest" about future events such as rains, harvests, fishing and hunting, whereabouts of game, outcome of prospective war raids, – the conversation

---

[198] Ray, 1941; Hallowell, 1942. See footnote 1.

[199] J.A. Maurault, Histoire des Abenakis depuis 1605 jusqu'à nos jours, Québec, 1866: 30.

[200] F. Boas, The central Eskimo, BAE-R 6 for 1884-85, Washington, 593-94.

[201] R.H. Lowie, The religion of the Crow Indians, AMNH-AP, v. 25, pt. 2 1922, 380-81; same, The Crow Indians, New York, 1935, 70-71.

[202] Captain Bossu, Travels through ... Louisiana, tr., London, 1771, 1: 264-65, among the Allibamon {Alabama}.

being audible to the crowd outside the curtained compartment.   The gods on departing shook the whole building as they ascended.[203] [84]

The more distant of the above instances, those from the Eskimo and Creek and from the Manasi of South America are merely set down here as of record. We are not justified – as yet – in assuming historical relationship. The distances seem too great, and the resemblances too vague and generic. What future more complete descriptive and distributional information may suggest remains to be seen.

---

[203] A. Metraux, The social organization and religion of the Mojo and Manasi, in *Primitive Man*, 1943, 16: 22-23.

To counter an *Allibamons* magician who threatened to "practice physic" to stop his boat from moving at all, Jean Bernard Bossu (1720-1792) [263] used fir resin to secure "enameled eyes" on the face of a 'tyger-cat' {panther ?} skin, and put a live squirrel inside it to rush toward these native skeptics.

"After this comic scene, I gave the skin to the Indian juggler, and desired him to make it revive as I had done. He owned, that my art was above the reach of his. I then bid him enchant my boat to prevent its going on; but he answered, that one physician against another could do nothing; that I was his master in the art and he an ignorant fellow*. All the savages who were out upon the winter hunt along the river, brought me provisions of roe-deer and turkies {turkeys}, that I might begin again to play off my trick; but for fear of being discovered, and to preserve my reputation, I said I could not do it over again, lest some one of them should be devoured by the revived creature ...

* The Indians repose a great confidence in their doctors; the juggler's hut is covered with furs, with which he covers and dresses himself. He goes in quite naked, and begins with pronouncing some words which no body understands; they are, as he says, to invoke the Spirit; after that he rises, cries, agitates himself, appears quite frantic, and gets into a profound sweat {fweat}.[†]

The hut shakes, and the spectators believe it is done through the presence of the Spirit; the language, which he speaks on this occasion, has nothing in common with the ordinary Indian language; it is nothing but the ravings of a [265] hot imagination, which these quacks have imposed upon their countrymen as a divine language; thus the most cunning people have always deceived the rest [reft].

† The heathen nations of the Russian empire have exactly such jugglers or conjurors as are here described. In the government of *Cazan* are the *Tcheremisses*, the *Tchuwashes*, and the *Wotiaks*, three nations; the first of which call their conjurors *Mushan*, the second *Yommas* or *Yymmas*, and the third *Tona* or *Tuno*; they are of both sexes, and make the same grimaces as these American Jugglers. In Siberia the *Tungusi*, the *Yakuli*, and *Byrati*, call their conjurors *Shamans*, and they perform the same tricks, and make many antic gestures at their pretended conjurations. Their dress is on these occasions likewise very remarkable, sometimes ornamented with the fangs and talons of beasts and birds of prey, sometimes hung with such a terrible quantity of several pieces of iron, as will both make the robe very heavy, and cause a great rattling noise at the least motion of the conjuror's body. The more we go east in *Siberia*, the more common is this kind of conjurors, and the more striking is the likeness between the savage inhabitants of *North America* and the savage Nomadic nations of the north-east parts of *Asia*. Some more hints of this similarity are pointed out in a note to *Kalm's Travels into North America*, Vol III p. 126. F.

Naval Captain Jean Bernard Bossu (1720-1792) Travels through that part of North America formerly called Louisiana, John Reinhold Forester, English translator, London M DCC LXXI ~ 1771

KOOTENAY "MEDICINE-MEN"

ABOUT the shamans of some of the less known tribes of American Indians very little is on record. Among the Kootenays of south-eastern British Columbia and northern Idaho the name of the "medicine-man," or shaman, is *nipik'ak•ādk•'ā*, a word derived from *nipí'k'a*, "spirit," because he has to do with "spirits," or the forms in which the dead may appear to the living. The "singing" of the shaman is termed *k•'ānūkunanūkanāmnäm*, which word is sometimes applied to the whole "medicine" procedure. The word *āwūmō*, "medicine," is also in use, but the expression *āwūmō* tít'kāt (literally "medicine-man") seems to be a neologism, suggested perhaps by corresponding expressions in the language of the whites; it is not quite "good Kootenay."

The actions of the Kootenay shaman have been described by Dr. Franz Boas, who visited these Indians in 1888, as follows:[204] "The shamans of the Kutonáqa are also initiated in the woods after long fasting. They cure sick people, and prophesy the result of hunting and war parties. If this is to be done, the shaman ties a rope about his waist, and goes into the medicine-lodge, where he is covered with an elk-skin. After a short while he appears, his thumbs firmly tied together by a knot, which is very difficult to open. He reënters the lodge, and, after a short time, reappears, his thumbs being untied. After he has been tied a second time, he is put into a blanket, which is firmly tied together like a bag. The line which is tied around his waist, and to which his thumbs are fastened, may be seen protruding from the place where the blanket is tied together. Before he is tied up, a piece of bone is placed between his toes. Then the men pull at the protruding end of the rope, which gives way; the blanket is removed, and the shaman is seen to lie under it. This performance is called *k•'eqnEmnām* (= somebody cut in two). The shaman remains silent, and reënters the lodge, in which rattles made of pieces of bone are heard. Suddenly something is heard falling down. Three times this noise is repeated, and then singing is heard in the lodge. It is supposed that the shaman has invoked souls of certain people whom he wished to see, and that their arrival produced the noise. From these he obtains the information and instructions which he later on communicates to the people."

When the present writer was among the Kootenays in 1891,[205] one member of the tribe gave the following free translation of a "medicine" song: "An Indian is crouching in the corner of his lodge beneath blankets, invoking the spirits. Soon the spirit enters [96] through the top of the lodge, passes beneath the blanket, and enters the Indian, who then flies away on high; by-and-by returns, and, sitting under the blanket, causes the spirit to depart again." This Indian applied the term *kEk•'áqámnam* to the whole procedure under the blanket. According to another informant, the "spirits" assume the form of some beast or bird, in which state the adept can summon them, and commune with them. The Kootenay "medium" gets behind a blanket in the tepee, as noted above, and summons the spirit to him, and, while under the blanket, imitates the voice, etc., of the beast or bird in whose form the spirit appears. The "spirit" is supposed to "fall down" through the smoke-hole of the lodge. The advent of the blanket (*sēet* or *tlāmātl*) has driven out the elk-skin (*āqk•ōktlā gitlk•'átlēs*) which was formerly the cover under which the shaman ensconced himself. With many Indian tribes the elk has always been great or good "medicine;" hence, perhaps the use of its skin here. In accordance with the general democratic

---

[204] Report Brit. Assoc. Adv. Science, 1889.
[205] Ibid., 1892.

character of Kootenay institutions, the coming and going of "spirits" is not bound up with intervention of the shaman, whose art has, nevertheless, been looked upon, in recent times, at least, as more efficacious. Probably, at an earlier stage in the history of these people, all persons of a seasonable age could "traffic with the spirits." It would not be surprising if not a little of the paraphernalia and *modi operandi* of the "medicine-man" among the Kootenays turns out to be borrowed from neighboring tribes.

A part of the business of the shaman was to predict the outcome of hunting and war expeditions, and in some of his efforts he had the assistance practically of the whole tribe, as, e.g. at the dance in the "great lodge" in winter, when good snow for game is "prayed for." The older midnight dance, occurring about Christmas time, is characterized as *mitǫātltítkētl*, evidently a derivative from *mitǫanē*, "he shoots," from the fact that guns were fired off, etc., during the celebration, in which much clapping of hands also took place. Among the Upper Kootenays the Roman Catholic missionaries have made a rather successful attempt to divert some of the energy formerly expended on the "great winter dance," to a recognition of the Christian holy day occurring at approximately the same time. But while they celebrate the Christmas of the whites, these Indians have not altogether forgotten the festival of their forefathers. Still less have the Lower Kootenays, who are much more "pagan" than their kindred farther "up country."

Concerning the "cure" of the shaman, Rev. W.F. Wilson[206] writes thus: "In cases of sickness these people have more faith in sorcery than in the use of medicines. They believe that some evil spirit has [97] caused the sickness, and that the evil spirit must be driven out. The patient usually is stretched on his back in the centre of a large lodge, and his friends sit round in a circle, beating drums. The sorcerer, grotesquely painted, enters the ring, chanting a song, and proceeds to force the evil spirit from the sick person by pressing both clenched fists with all his might in the pit of his stomach, kneading and pounding also other parts of the body, blowing occasionally through his fingers, and sucking blood from the part supposed to be affected."

The Kootenay shaman, as is the case with the "medicine-men" of many other tribes, seems to have been at one and the same time medium, doctor, and prophet.

That the doings of the Kootenay shamans made considerable impression upon the missionaries may readily be believed from the statement attributed to a Jesuit missionary in 1861:[207] "I have seen many exhibitions of power which my philosophy cannot explain. I have known predictions of events far in the future to be literally fulfilled, and have seen medicine-men tested in the most conclusive ways. I once saw a Kootenia Indian (known generally as *Skookum-tamahere-wos*,[208] from his extraordinary power) command a mountain sheep to fall dead, and the animal, then leaping among the rocks of the mountain-side, fell instantly lifeless. This I saw with my own eyes, and I ate of the animal afterwards. It was unwounded, healthy, and perfectly wild. Ah, Mary save us! the medicine-men have power from Sathanas."

During his stay among the Kootenays in the summer and autumn of 1891, the present writer obtained from various members of the tribe a considerable number of drawings of all kinds. Among these are two which the Indian who drew them said represented "medicine-men." The artist of these drawings was Bläswā, one of the oldest men of the Upper Kootenays,

---

206 *Our Forest Children*, vol. iii. (1889-1890), p. 165.

207 E.R. Emerson, *Indian Myths* (Boston, 1884), p. 404.

208 This is evidently a misprint for *Skookum tamahnewus* (*skūkEm tamā'nowas*), the term in the Chinook jargon for "strong sorcerer."

formerly a great warrior, and reputed as having been more skilful with the bow and arrow in the days of intertribal warfare than with the pencil to-day. The drawings were made with no interference or suggestion on the part of the writer, and may be taken as fair specimens of the Indian's artistic accomplishments. The first of the drawings occupied twenty, the second seventeen minutes in execution.

DRAWINGS OF "MEDICINE-MEN" BY THE INDIAN BLÄSWĀ.

FIG. I. This drawing represents the "Medicine-man" of the Kootenays, as he appears when taking part in the "great dance." He wears the special "shirt" of the shaman, and his head is adorned with the "horns" of weasel fur, characteristic of his office, and formerly [98] so much esteemed. It is not certain what he carries in his extended hand.

FIG. 2. This drawing was said by the Indian who made it to represent a "Medicine-man." If so, it must be what the Indians call the "Medicine-Man" of the whites that is pictured here. The beard, the expression on the face, the outstretched arms, and the general character of the drawing indicate that the idea of the figure on the crucifix (the Upper Kootenays are under Catholic influence) and of the priest presided over its execution.

This is a very curious picture. The artist who drew it said it was another "medicine-man" picture, and did not differentiate it particularly from the other drawing of a shaman. In the left hand is a small cup or basket (?) – the word *ātsūnánā* originally applied to a small (*nána*) bag or basket (*ātsū*) of birchbark, etc., has come to be used for cups and receptacles of a like sort – containing "medicine" (*āwūzō*). In the right hand is some other article. The expression on the face, the beard, the out-stretched arms, etc., suggest that the Indian has here given us a copy of the figure on the cross or crucifix seen at the Mission of St. Eugene, or in the possession of some of the Catholic missionaries. Perhaps the article in the left hand is the communion cup, and that in the right, the consecrated bread. In his second attempt to picture a shaman the old Indian had before his mind the Catholic priest and the figure of Christ upon the crucifix, the result being the very interesting picture here presented. This drawing, therefore, may belong to the class of art products which reflect the contact of pagan religious ideas with the new concepts introduced by missionaries of the Christian faith.

Some remarkable examples of such have been very recently discussed by Dr. Karl von den Steinen.[209] In the pipe-carvings of the Payaguás, which deal with the Garden of Eden and the Creation of Adam, it is the Deity who is represented by the unmistakable figure of a shaman in characteristic action and attitude. In connection with these phenomena, it is interesting to find Dr. Boas writing of the Nootka Indians of Vancouver Island:[210] "The name of the deity is kept a profound secret from the common people. Only chiefs are allowed to pray to him, and the dying chief tells the name, which is *Kātse* (i.e. the grandchild), to his heir, and teaches him how to pray

---

[209] *Der Paradiesgarten als Schnitzmotiv der Payaguá-Indianer.* Ethnol. Notizbl., Bd. ii (1901), pp. 60-65.

[210] Report Brit. Assoc. Adv. Science, 1890.

to the deity. No offerings are made to *Kātse*; he is only prayed to. In a tradition of the Nootka it is stated that a boy prayed to a being in heaven called *Ciciklē*, who is probably identical with *Kātse*. The boy is described as praying, his arms being thrown upward." Now *Ciciklē* is neither more nor less than *Jésus Christ*, and reveals the fact of French missionary influence; for in the Kootenay language, the speakers of which first came into contact with French missionaries of the Catholic faith, *Jésus Christ* is rendered by the Indians *Cīcēklē*.

There is need for a comparative study of the influence of [99] Christianity, as introduced from time to time among the Indians by missionaries of different faiths and languages, upon the religious concepts of the aborigines, and of the literary and artistic effects of this contact.

Alexander F. Chamberlain.

CLARK UNIVERSITY,
WORCESTER, MASS.

The Journal of American Folklore, Vol. 14, No. 53 (April - June, 1901), pp. 95-99.

A

aBicilinutc, 196

akamałnam = belt, 'corral', 117f, 125

akok!płułał = juniper, 121

akukłiłimi = holy ground, 112f, 122, 132

Allard, Charles, 139f

Andrew, Alexander, 93

Andrew, Pete, 87

Arbell, Chief Louis, 93

Arnaud, Fr. C.A, O.M.I, 196

atsika = braided thong, 115f

Atsina, 85, 116, 145, 151f

átsokan = mythics, 19

B

Bad-bad Bull, 201

Badger, 160f,

Badger blood, 8

Badges, 11, 160

Baptiste Pooyak, 7

Basna"ᵃbe"ᵉ = Big Sand, Atsina afterlife, 202

Bear Hat, Andrew, 93, 101

Bear Old Woman, 209f

Beaver, 22, 59,

Beaver ~ tribe, 26, 107

Beaver ~ spirit, 148, 196

Beaver Creek, 206

bebo'kowe, 5f

bells, 4f, 185, 210; sleigh bells, 4

Berens, 3, 14f, 20, 26, 30f, 42, 50f, 60f, 76, 124

berries, 10f, 146

Big Archer, 90

Bird Child, 209

bird-bone whistle, 123f

Bison, 85f, 124f, 151f, 166

bison robe, 90f, 124f

Bison ~ spirit, 103

Blacksmith, Alex ~ *WesGijan* ~ Bluejay, 196

Bluejay cult, 82

Blue-Robed-Cloud-Woman, 65, 78

bone tubes, 159f, 186

bone whistle, 82, 115f, 146

Bonners Ferry, 88, 92f, 100f, 110f, 124f, 131f, 141

booth, 7f, 93, 151, 164, 194f

Brinton, Daniel Garrison, 13, 64

Brown, Frances (Mrs Joseph), 211

Browning, MT, 211

buffalo pound, 9

buffalo-skin tipi, 190

Bull Thigh, 190

Bull Woman = *niłsik pałki*, 115f

Bullhead ~ Sculpin ~ *q!iq!um*, 97f*, 113f, 121f, 130f, 148

Bullrobe, Abraham, 88, 100f, 110, 113, 124, 134f, 147f

Bullrobe, Susanne, 88f, 99f, 115, 136

bundle, 7f, 81, 158*; Bird Child's, 211; Ghost, 154; Skull, 154

Butler, John, 3

Butler, Laurence, 3

C

cábandawan = multi-family dwelling, 38

castoreum, 148

Caterpillar, 90

Catholicism, 76, 94f, 133, 148

Cattle Owner, 8

Caye, Peter, 93

Chamberlain, Alexander, 87

Chandler, Al, 201

Charley Littlepipe, 4

Chief Dance, 5f

Chief Drum, 4f

Chief Fiddler ~ Sandy Lake Saulteaux, 37

Chief Kustata ~ Gustave, 113

Chief Mountain, 112

Chiefs-son = bear, 10

Christians, 7, 34, 64f, 72f, 89f, 95, 142, 172f, 185

clients, 81f, 123, 138f, 194, 204 214

cloudburst, 207

coagulated blood, 8

Colvilles, 95f, 153f, 162f, 195

Coming-day, 8f

Please report any & all Typo-Gnomes so they can be Zapped away!

ACCULTURATING AMELIA ~ Round Valley 1937 California
AIDING EYAK ~ Alaska's Orphan
ALASKA EDGE ISLAND ~ Siberian Yupiks of St Lawrence Island
ALL SOULS ~ Conjuring, Divining, Redeeming, Reviving Native Vitalities
ALLIED MOUNDS ~ Touching the Earth, Modeling the World, Reaching the Sky
ANIMAL PEOPLE ADVENTURES ~ Native North American Tribal Stories
AT BAY ~ Cultures Converging through Southwest Washington
BALLARD BULWARK ~
CHACO ECHOES ~ Pervasive Keresan Priesthoods
CHACOKIA ~ Chaco, Cahokia, Cities & Ceremonies ~ Bundles & Blood Lines Centuries Ago   > 10
CHEHALIS CHANGER ~ I, II, bilingual
CHINOOK CONCERNS ~ Emma Millett Luscier, Isabella Bertrand, Verne Ray
CIRCLING FOUR CORNERS ~ Re-Viewing Native American Indiens
COAST SALISH SCULPTURES ~ Updating Wingert's Classic Study
CREEK MVSKOKI TALWA TOWNS ~ Speck, Swanton, Hewitt, Opler, Howard
CROSSING ~ LINES: An Educational Memoir of Native North America
DEL-AWARE ~ Lenape Legacies
DELAWARE INTEGRITY ~ Rituals, Removals, Reforms by Lenape Indiens
DISCLAIMING TREATIES I ~ Puget Tribes 1927 Testimonies
DISCLAIMING TREATIES II ~ Puget Tribes 1927 Testimonies   > 20
ELDERS' DIALOG ~ Ed Davis & Vi Hilbert Discuss Native Puget Sound Language, Culture, & Heritage
EVERGREEN ETHNOGRAPHIES ~ Hoh, Chehalis, Suquamish, and Snoqualmi of Western Washington
FEDERAL FISH FILES ~ Swindell 1942 Treaty Rights Report
GEORGE GIBBS NORTHWEST ARRAY ~ Full Reports, Place Names, Word List, Artifact Names, and Guide
GRASSROOTS JANET ~ Advancing Salish and Traditional Cultures
HERMAN HAEBERLIN REGAINED ~ Anthropology and Artifacts of Puget Sound 1916-17
HERSTORY NW ~ Women Upholding Native Traditions
INDIEN ~ ETHNOGRAPHY: Cultural Traditions of Native North America
INDIEN ~ ETHNOLOGY: Grounded, Gendered, Meaningful Cultural Traditions
LESCHI IN LOVE ~ A Novel of Native Puget Sound > x2   > 30
MARCO MUCK MASKS ~ Frank Cushing on Marshes and Mounds
MINTER BAY ~ Land, Lore, Loss, and Lucre in the South Salish Sea
NATIVE MET HOW ~ Improving Posterity
NATIVE PROPHECY NW ~ Dancing Hope
OLD LUKH ~ Native Puget Sound in Daily Life, Places, and Stories
OVER THE FALLS ~ Sdoqwalbixw Survivance Surrounding Seattle
PACIFIC PLATEAU PORTRAYALS ~ People Places Ponderings
RAY'S ARRAY ~ Raymond D Fogelson's Works
RIGHTING NATIVE PLACES ~ Adventures in Northwest Geography
SAHAPTINS STUDIES ~ Columbia River Plateau, Cora Du Bois, Homer Garner Barnett, Gerald Raymond Desmond > 40
SALISH SOLUTIONS ~ Uniquely Northwest Diversity
SALISH SYSTEMS ~ Kinship Networks of the Northwest
SDOQWALBIXW
SDOQWALBIXW SURVIVANCE
SEANCING SHAKING SPIRITS ~ Embodying Spirit Powers in Conjuring Abodes
SM TSM'SYEEN ~ Real Tsimshians; Coast, Sgüüks, Gitxsan, Nisga'a
SOUND SALISH STRAITS ~ Central Salish Sea Cultures
UNSETTLING SEATTLE ~ Arresting Local Talent and Academic Illiteracy
WICHITA KINSHIP & CULTURE ~
WRITING WORDS IN WARY WORLDS ~ World Wide Improved Spellings of Native America Languages   > 50

RESCUES, RANTS, & RESEARCHES ~ Re-View of Jay Miller's Writings on Northwest Indien Cultures ~ JONA Memoirs #9
TRIBAL TRIO of the Northwest Coast by Kenneth D Tollefson ~ JONA Memoirs #10
INTERWEAVING COAST SALISH CULTURAL SYSTEMS ~ Collected Works of Pamela Thorsen Amoss ~ JONA Memoirs #14